VIRGINIA MILITARY INSTITUTE, LEXINGTON, VA.

NICHOLS ENGINEERING HALL

THE NEW MARKET BATTLE MONUMENT

JACKSON MEMORIAL HALL
SMITH STATUE

THE BARRACK

The Corps Forward

The Biographical Sketches
of the VMI Cadets
who fought in the
Battle of New Market

Edited by Colonel William Couper
Foreword by Colonel Keith E. Gibson

Buena Vista & Charlottesville, Virginia

Library of Congress Control Number : 2005926608

Couper, William (1884—1964)
ISBN 0-9768238-2-9   (softcover : alk. paper)

1. Virginia Military Institute, 1839-2005. 2. Battle of New
Market, May 15, 1864. 3. American Civil War 1861-1865

1 3 5 7 9 10 8 6 4 2

All images in this book courtesy of the VMI Musuem
and the VMI Archives.

Published by
Mariner Publishing,
A Division of
Mariner Companies, Inc.
212 East 21st Street
Buena Vista, Virginia 24416-2716

This book is printed on acid-free paper
Manufactured in the United States of America

Foreword

*"It was an ordinary rail fence, probably about four
feet high, but as I surmounted the topmost rail I felt
at least ten feet up in the air and the special object
of hostile aim. But in clearing this obstruction I
was leaving all thought of individuality behind."*

Cadet John Howard's experience is a telling
recollection of passage. The order had been given for the
VMI Cadet Corps to move forward, out of Jacob Bushong's
orchard and into the wheat field beyond. The four-foot-
high rail fence that separated them gave some vestige of
protection to the untried cadets. Howard recalled his sense of
vulnerability as he crossed the top rail—he was the individual
interest of enemy fire. Quickly moving into the wheat field a
transformation took place—Cadet Howard left "all thought
of individuality behind," and became part of something
greater. It was the 'Corps Forward,' moving as a single body,
confidence and courage drawn from shared experience.

The passage across the split rail fence led to victory
for the Confederate forces that rainy Sunday afternoon of 15
May 1864. It was a unique moment in American collegiate
history—never before or since has a college student body
been called into pitched battle and led a victorious charge
against the enemy. The price of heroism was great: 57 cadets

were wounded, ten died. But for the members of the VMI Cadet Corps, the passage was one of moving from boyhood to manhood—a moment that would define their subsequent lives.

The life stories of those 257 cadets who crossed over the fence that day, provides a fascinating glimpse into the post-war years. Many of the young men who fought at New Market led lives of personal and professional achievement: 57 became lawyers, 17 doctors, 19 engineers, 5 clergy, 15 legislators—state and national, 23 public officials, 17 educators, and 9 pursued the arts. At least two became inventors.

Included here, in these brief biographical sketches, is the story of Otis Glazebrook, who shepherded Woodrow Wilson's war proclamation against Germany through Congress, as well as the heroic story of John Bransford. During the Spanish American War he became a US Navy Surgeon and manned a gun at the Battle of Santiago Bay (for which Congress awarded him a specially struck medal). The James brothers became educators after the war, went to Texas, and helped to create Texas A&M University. William Beattie became the sheriff of Crittenden, Arkansas and was gunned down while attempting to make an arrest in 1881.

Surgeon Blair Taylor was the replacement physician for the 7th Cavalry after General George Custer's ill-fated 1876 expedition. Charles Turner became the Adjutant General of Montana. As US senator from West Virginia, Charles Faulkner became the close confidant of President Calvin Coolidge. Moses Ezekiel became a world renowned sculptor. In 1904 he created the beautiful heroic bronze statue "Virginia

Mourning Her Dead"—a tribute to the cadets who fell at New Market.

This site of valor is preserved as New Market Battlefield State Historical Park. Each fall the new entering class of VMI freshmen—"Rats" as they are called at VMI—visit the battlefield and learn the story of their predecessors. The new cadets hear the story of Cadet Howard standing at the split rail fence—unsure of his next move. They learn of his resolve to move forward, finding strength in the unity of the Corps numbers. And they begin to understand their own untapped potential as they stand at this point of passage in their own lives.

It is not just cadets who visit the battlefield in New Market; over 50,000 visitors each year come to learn about Cadet Howard and the VMI Cadets. The Bushong Family orchard is still there. The home in which the family found shelter is preserved for us to experience. The split rail fence still divides the orchard from the wheat field. It remains a place for us to reflect on the passage.

Keith E. Gibson
VMI
Lexington, Virginia
May 2005

WILLIAM NELSON
Class of 1865

Cadet Sergeant William Nelson, great-grandson of Thomas
Nelson, signer of the Declaration of Independence, is shown
here dressed in the typical cadet field uniform. Nelson
graduated second in his class.

After the war he became a lawyer and practiced in New
York City and Austin, Texas. Note the waterproof oilcloth
cover on his kepi. This photograph was taken in Richmond,
circa Spring 1865.

Contents

Eleven member of the Class of 1867, all veterans of the Battle of New Market. From left to right—Front: Thomas G. Hayes, Hardaway H. Dinwiddie, Edward M. Tutwiler, Robert Cousins, Hugh W. Fry. Back: Patrick Henry, unidentified, Nicholas J. Bayard, John L. Tunstall and John S. Webb.

Illustrations

V. M. I. Museum. There are four other somewhat similar contemporary photographs in the museum. In this photograph, the Washington monument, which was re-inaugurated on Sept. 10, 1866, shows. A row of temporary cabins, one of which shows at the right, was built in 1865 and served as quarters for the cadets until the barrack was restored. The restoration extended over the years 1866 to 1869, and the sections were utilized as completed.

After the destruction of the buildings in Lexington the corps of cadets secured a building in Richmond, Va., which was at the time being used as a hospital. It was assigned to the Cadets by the Secretary of War when the Surgeon-General graciously consented to transfer his activities to other quarters. This building was built for use as the Alms House and looks today about as it looked when it was built. This photograph was taken in 1933, no photograph taken in the sixties having been located. In the cemetery directly opposite this building is the grave of Colonel Claude Crozet, the president of the first board of visitors of the Virginia Military Institute.

Chronological Table

Interruptions caused by war conditions make the following chronological table of value in following the period of cadetship of the men listed in this book. All of them served in the various campaigns which took place during their particular period of cadetship, but to avoid repetition, the military service with the corps of cadets, other than that in the New Market campaign, has been omitted save in a few cases where some interesting or informative point is brought out.

Prior to 1861 classes were graduated on July 4th, or the nearest week day thereto.

April 21, 1861: Corps under command of Major (later "Stonewall") Jackson left for Richmond to drill Confederate troops. The cadets soon joined the various organizations and the corps, as such, was disbanded.

July 4, 1861: Class of 1861 was graduated *as of* this date.

December 6, 1861: Class of 1862 was graduated *as of* this date.

January 1, 1862: Institute reopened. The men who would have been first classmen, class of 1862, having entered the military service, were declared graduates as of December 6, 1861.

May 1-20, 1862: Corps away with "Stonewall" Jackson on the McDowell campaign.

May 15, 1863: Corps escorted body of General "Stonewall" Jackson to the grave.

July 3, 1863: Class of 1863 was graduated in Lexington.

August 25, 1863: Corps marched to Goshen; Averill's first raid.

November 6-11, 1863: Corps marched to Covington; Averill's second raid.

December 15-19, 1863: Corps marched to Rockbridge Baths and then to Buchanan; Averill's third raid.

May 11, 1864: Corps left Lexington at 7:00 A. M. and marched eighteen miles; camped near Midway.

May 12, 1864: Arrived in Staunton, eighteen miles, and camped south of the town. (Col. Shipp's report.)

May 12, 1864: Later on twenty-four members of the class of 1865, all veterans of New Market, were declared graduates *as of* this date, apparently selected so as to include the New Market cadets, one of whom was killed in the battle. Several members of this class, however, continued at V. M. I. as cadets until April 2, 1865. (This date, assigned in contemporary records for the graduation of this class, is about six weeks *prior* to the date of graduation of the *following* class—the class of 1864.)

May 13, 1864: Corps marched about nineteen miles to and camped that night at Mt. Crawford, near Harrisonburg.

May 14, 1864: Corps marched fifteen miles and camped at Mt. Tabor, seven miles south of New Market.

May 15, 1864: Corps took part in the battle of New Market.

May 16-17, 1864: Caring for wounded.

May 20, 1864: Corps arrived in Harrisonburg.

May 21, 1864: Corps arrived in Staunton.

May 22-23, 1864: Corps en route to and arrived in Richmond.

May 24, 1864: Corps reviewed and addressed by the President.

May 28, 1864: Corps addressed by Mr. Speaker Bocock, of the Confederate House of Representatives, who publicly communicated to the corps the resolution* of the House.

May 28, 1864: Corps transferred from Fair Grounds (Camp Lee) to Carter's Farm. Assigned to duty under Gen. G. W. C. Lee, commanding the Local Defense Troops.

June 7, 1864: Corps left Richmond in the morning.

June 7, 1864: Corps arrived in Lynchburg at 11:00 P. M.

June 9, 1864: Corps arrived in Lexington by canal-boat at 3:00 P. M.

June 11, 1864: Corps in Lexington during bombardment of Lexington. Cadets retreated and camped near Balcony Falls.

June 12, 1864: V. M. I. burned by command of General Hunter.

June 15, 1864: Corps left for Lynchburg.

June 16, 1864: Corps arrived in Lynchburg 8:00 A. M. In trenches but not in action during Hunter's repulse, by Confederate forces under General Early, and retreat westward.

June 24, 1864: Corps left Lynchburg.

June 25, 1864: Corps arrived in Lexington by canal-boat.

June 27, 1864: *Fourteen* members of the *class of 1864,* all veterans of the battle of New Market, were graduated and the corps was furloughed.

October 1, 1864: Corps assembled at Camp Lee, near Richmond, Va., as temporary buildings at V. M. I. had not at the time been completed. Engaged in military duties in trenches around Richmond but no academic work.

October 27, 1864: Corps under Lt. Gen. Pemberton (then Lieut. Colonel); encamped at Poe's Farm as infantry support for nearby battery; under Lt. Gen. Ewell and comprised a part of the Confederate forces of the Dept. of Richmond.

---

*Extract from the Journal of the Confederate House of Representatives, First Session, Second Congress, May 23, 1864:

"Mr. Miles, under a suspension of the rules, submitted the following resolution:

"Resolved, That the thanks of the House of Representatives of the Confederate States, are hereby unanimously tendered to the Cadets of the Virginia Military Institute and the Officers who commanded them for their gallant conduct in the battle of the 15th instant, near New Market, in the Shenandoah Valley of Virginia.

"Resolved further, That the Speaker of the House communicate this resolution to the Cadets, in such form and at such time as may seem to him proper.

"Mr. Swann called the question, which was ordered.

"And the resolution was adopted."

December 12, 1864:   Moved from Poe's Farm to Alms House, Richmond; some of the cadets granted 10 day furlough to procure clothing, etc.

December 28, 1864:   Academic work resumed and corps quartered in the Alms House, in Richmond, a building which had been completed about 1861 and utilized as a hospital.

March 11, 1865:   Corps ordered to the line of battle between the canal and the Westham road, several miles west of Richmond; expected attack by Federal cavalry under General Fitzhugh dispatched by Sheridan from Columbia. Withdrawn two days later.

April 1, 1865:   Corps occupied Fields' abandoned works on the Charles City road at night and just before sunrise (April 2nd) they relieved the last of the Confederate infantry and assumed command of this section of the line. Evacuation orders issued and cadets relieved late that (April 2nd) afternoon by a squadron of cavalry.

April 2, 1865:   Corps disbanded at the Alms House on eve of evacuation of Richmond by the Confederate forces, each cadet finding his way home or elsewhere as best he could. A considerable number of them followed the canal to Columbia, Fluvanna County, and dispersed there.

October 17, 1865: Academic work resumed at V. M. I. in Lexington.

July 4, 1866:   *Ten* cadets, *class of 1866*, all members of the New Market corps, were graduated. Thereafter the sessions opened and closed on regular schedule.

July 4, 1867:   *Class of 1867, eleven* cadets, all veterans of the battle of New Market, were graduated.

July 3, 1868:   *Class of 1868*, eleven cadets, *four* of them veterans of the battle of New Market, were graduated.

July 2, 1869:   *Class of 1869*, twenty-three cadets, *four* of them veterans of the battle of New Market, were graduated.

July 4, 1870:   *Class of 1870*, fifty-two cadets, *three* of them veterans of the battle of New Market, were graduated.

January 16, 1875:   Two hundred fourteen (214) cadets, all veterans of the battle of New Market, were granted diplomas (honoris causa) under the following order:

"The Board of Visitors unanimously orders that, the Academic Board concurring, diplomas be awarded to all cadets participating in the battle of New Market to whom diplomas have not been awarded in the regular course."

The Battle of New Market

Prefatory Note

This brief sketch,* of the part taken by the V. M. I. Cadets in the battle of New Market, has been prepared for the benefit of the Corps of Cadets on the celebration of the 50th anniversary of the battle *on the battle-field;* or, at least, for the benefit of those members of the Corps, who may desire to obtain a reasonably accurate knowledge of what the New Market Corps actually did on that occasion; but who have neither the time nor the inclination to read a detailed history of the battle. It is believed that the accompanying map of the battle-field (prepared by Capt. B. A. Colonna, V. M. I. 1864, and Maj. B. B. Morgan, V. M. I. 1893), supplemented by these facts, will accomplish the object in view.

This sketch is based on Prof. E. R. Turner's book, *The New Market Campaign;* on original data used by him; on original data in the writer's possession; on what the writer actually saw during the battle; on a careful examination of the battle-field in 1911; and on a careful study of the Colonna-Morgan map.

All of the *quotations,* with the exception of one from Col. Shipp's Official Report of the battle, are from a letter, written from New Market four days after the battle, by Frank Preston, (Captain B Co., and Assistant Prof. V. M. I.), describing the march and the battle. This is considered much more reliable authority for what the cadets actually did, than the "recollections" of participants on either side, written many years after the event.

The writer has studiously avoided expressing any opinions as to the effect of the cadets' participation in the battle, because he wishes each reader of this statement to draw his own conclusions from the facts alone.

PRESTON COCKE,

V. M. I. (N. M.) 1867

Richmond, Virginia,
May, 1914

---

*Selected for use in this volume, because of its brevity and authenticity. The story of this battle has been told by many participants, historians, and other writers. The most exhaustive study is "The New Market Campaign" (203 pages), by Edward Raymond Turner, Professor of European History, University of Michigan (Whittet & Shepperson, Richmond, Va., 1912); the most readable accounts are those by John S. Wise, V. M. I., '66, in his "The End of an Era" (Houghton Mifflin Co., 1899), and "The West Point of the Confederacy" (Century, XXXVII, 461-471, Jan. 1889); a combination of the two styles appears in "The Military History of the Virginia Military Institute," by Col. J. C. Wise, V. M. I., '02 (J. P. Bell & Co., Lynchburg, 1915). Turner, in his book, devotes fifteen pages to a bibliography and he there acknowledges the tremendous labor of Captain Henry A. Wise (see Sketch No. 281 herein) in accumulating data from participants and other sources.

Salient Features of the Battle in Connection with the Part Taken by the V. M. I. Cadets

CONDITIONS WHICH CAUSED THE BATTLE.

General Franz Sigel's march up the Shenandoah Valley from Winchester to New Market, Va., in May, 1864, had, as its objective point, the town of Staunton, where he could cut the Virginia Central Railroad (Now the C. & O. Ry.), and thus deprive General Lee's army and Richmond of one of their chief sources of supply; and whence he might, eventually, force his way to the rear of General Lee's army, then south of the Rappahannock River.

The only Confederate States force in the Valley, in May, 1864, was that of Gen. J. D. Imboden, consisting of cavalry, mounted infantry, and a battery of six guns, aggregating about 1,500 men. When Imboden heard of Sigel's advance, about May 2nd, he notified the Superintendent of the V. M. I. to hold the Corps of Cadets in readiness to reinforce his little army. As the Valley of Virginia was, in May, 1864, in the military department of Gen. John C. Breckinridge, C. S. A., who was then in Southwest Virginia, he at once assumed active command of the Confederate States forces for the defence of the Valley. And owing to the small number of Breckinridge's available forces, the Corps of Cadets was ordered, on May 10th, to join Breckinridge's Southwest Virginia forces at Staunton; from which point, the whole force could march down the Valley to join Imboden; or to which point, Imboden could fall back to join Breckinridge; either of which movements would necessitate a battle in the upper half of the Shenandoah Valley.

THE MARCH TO NEW MARKET.

The cadets were awakened by the long-roll on the night of May 10th, and ordered to march early the next morning on the road to Staunton.

On Wednesday morning, May 11th the corps left barracks and marched all day over the old Staunton road, (always in bad condition, especially in the rainy season), to the town of Midway, about 18 miles north of Lexington, and went into camp, sleeping in the rain that night.

On May 12th, the corps marched "in a drenching rain, through mud and water, to Staunton," about 18 miles.

On May 13th, the corps, having joined Breckinridge's veterans in Staunton, marched some 18 or 20 miles down the Valley Pike to a point south of Harrisonburg.

On May 14th, the corps continued down the pike, through Harrisonburg, to within about 7 miles of New Market, a march of about 15 miles, and went into camp in a body of woods on the east side of the pike.

On the 14th, there was some skirmishing and an artillery duel between Sigel's advance column and Imboden north of New Market. (See small scale map.)

On Sunday, May 15th, about 1 a. m., a pitch-dark and rainy night, the cadets were quietly aroused, and after a prayer by Capt. Frank Preston, B Co., the corps commenced its march to the battle-field; but it did not reach the vicinity of New Market until some time after sun-rise, because of one or more protracted stops.

THE CADETS IN ACTION.

The corps, after marching and waiting on the pike for probably 10 hours, (the battle proper having commenced about 11 a. m.), was marched by column by the left flank from the pike to a point south of "Shirley's Hill," about one mile south of New Market, and was there, for the first time, formed into line of battle behind a fence at right angles to the pike. (See map, south-west corner.)

The corps then advanced north, in line of battle in the third and last echelon, over the crest of Shirley's Hill. (See map, position 1-b.) As the United States batteries did not get the range of the corps, until it reached the north slope of Shirley's Hill on its descent to the "River Road," there were no casualties up to that point. But on the descent, (probably somewhere near the present barn), CAPT. HILL, of C Co., and CORPORAL J. S. WISE, of D Co., and several others were wounded by the explosion of one or more United States shells. This was the corps baptism of blood.

In the ravine north of Shirley's Hill, (near "River Road"), the cadets were halted and made to discard their blankets, etc. And here they saw, for the first time, a sight which amazed them more than the carnage of battle: The officers of the veteran command, composing the second echelon, almost in front of the corps, when their regiment was ordered to advance, had to force the skulkers into ranks at the points of their pistols. The delay in the ravine, while seemingly quite long, is said to have been only a half hour. This was the lull before the storm, for the second or hottest part of the battle commenced between 1 and 2 p. m. It was probably during this interval, or a little earlier, that Imboden crossed over to the east side of Smith's Creek, with the intention of re-crossing it to the pike side, in order to turn Sigel's left flank; but the high water in the creek prevented him from consummating this movement. (See map, position 26.)

After ascending the south end of the "Bushong" plateau, (which extends about one mile north to the Bushong House, see map), a march in line of battle of one-quarter to one-half mile over this open and comparatively level ground, brought the corps within easy range of the three United States six gun batteries on the top of the "Bushong Hill." A glance at the map will show that Sigel's last position (map positions Nos. 20 to 25), was the very strongest he could have taken, as it filled the narrow neck between the Shenandoah River and Smith's Creek, both of which were practically unfordable from the recent rains. This line, of almost one mile in length, with 18 guns on its right flank and four on its left, had to be charged and driven from its position, in order to win the battle.

When the corps reached the point several hundred yards south of the Bushong House, it was subjected to "a terrible fire of artillery." Here, CABELL, first Sergeant D Co., and JONES and CROCKETT, privates D Co., "fell dead from the explosion of one shell." Here also, but possibly a little farther back, the corps came within range of the United States musketry fire. Almost immediately after the explosion of the shell in D Co., McDOWELL, private B Co., "fell, pierced through the heart with a bullet."

The corps marched steadily and continuously over this open plateau up to the south front of the Bushong House through "mud, in many places over the ankles," a portion of the time being under both artillery and musketry fire; the alignment of the battalion was like that on parade; the gaps in the ranks, caused by the killed and wounded men, were filled automatically, as if nothing unusual had happened; and at no time did the corps' battle line even waver.

When the corps reached the Bushong House, which was near the center of its line of march, it divided in half; A and B Companies passing it on the east side, and C and D Companies on the west. This necessarily broke the previous alignment, which was never fully restored. This movement brought the whole corps into the Bushong orchard (say from 50 to 100 yards in width), where it came within from 200 to 300 yards of the three United States batteries on the top of the Bushong Hill, which "poured incessant volleys of canister and grape into us;" to this incessant fire of artillery, must be added the musketry fire of the 34th Mass. Infantry, immediately in front of the corps. (See map, position 23a.) "In this fatal orchard," STANARD and JEFFERSON, privates B Co., fell mortally wounded; "and, in fact, almost all our loss was here," including Col. Scott Shipp, in command of the corps, who was wounded. Capt. Henry A. Wise, of A Co., then took command, and retained it until the end of the battle.

The deadly fire of shells, grape, canister and bullets, to which the corps was subjected in the Bushong Orchard, did not cause it to retreat, or even to fall back temporarily; but the cadets "ran forward" to the remains of a demolished rail fence on the north edge of the orchard, "laid down behind the fence, and began, for the *first* time, to fire upon the enemy," the corps, by its rapid advance, having just gotten into the *first* line of battle and filled a gap, caused by the change of position of one or more other commands. (The location of this old fence is believed to correspond to that of the present wire fence on the north side of Bushong's present orchard.) Unfortunately, this position of the corps is not given by Prof. Turner on the Colonna-Morgan Map; though it is, by far, the most important one held by the corps during the entire battle, since it filled a wide gap at a critical moment.

Beyond question, this was the crisis of the battle. The 51st Virginia Regiment on the left flank of the corps gave way, and had to be rallied. And about this time (say 3 p. m.), possibly a quarter of an hour earlier, the 62nd Va. Reg., on the right flank of the corps, while advancing in the rocky field just northeast of the Bushong House, had to fall back to prevent annihilation. (map Confederate States positions 18 and 19.) Position 19 was evidently the most fatal spot on the battle-field; for Capt. Woodson's Missouri Co. (attached temporarily to the 62nd Va.), lost 60 out of 70 men, or 85 per cent., in killed and wounded. (See monument to Woodson's Co., just northeast of Bushong Yard.)

The stop of the corps at the orchard fence could not have been over 15 or 20 minutes. But whether long or short, it was the period of the greatest anxiety, during the day, to both officers and men; because it seemed that the next move, on either side would probably determine the result of the battle; and this proved to be correct. For Col. Edgar (an old V. M. I. graduate, commanding the 26th Va. Battalion), had succeeded in turning the United States right flank on the top of Bushong's Hill. (map, Confederate States position 16, and United States positions 20 and 21.) The success of this movement stopped the artillery fire and lessened the musketry fire against the corps, and probably against the 51st and 62nd Va., and speedily caused the United States line in front and to the left of the corps to break and retreat.

When the heavy artillery fire ceased, the command was given to the corps to charge. This order was obeyed, not only with alacrity, but with enthusiasm; "and though the company organizations were gone, yet they rallied round the colors and formed some sort of a line as we advanced." So eager were the cadets to charge the enemy, 100 or 150 yards off, that it was difficult for them to find time to load and shoot their old-fashioned muzzle loading muskets. This, the final charge, commenced in the wheat field, then a field of mud, just north of the Bushong Orchard, and continued for some distance north towards the Pike bridge over the Shenandoah. (See small scale map.)

The pursuit of the retreating army by the cadets continued until the corps "was halted by order of General Breckinridge." The company organizations and the parade alignment of the corps were never completely restored after the pursuit commenced.

The battle proper ended about 4 p. m., though there was some cannonading later in the day on Rude's Hill, about three miles north of the town. (See small scale map.)

It is a question of some doubt, whether any of the nine cadets, who were killed or mortally wounded, fell in this final charge; though a few of the cadets are said to have been wounded after the corps left the Bushong fence. The writer regrets that he cannot

locate, with any degree of accuracy, the points where Corporal Atwill, A Co., private Haynes, B Co., and private Wheelwright,
C Co., fell; but he presumes that all three were killed or mortally
wounded in "the fatal orchard."

As it is the desire of the writer, that this brief statement shall contain nothing but the *undisputed facts* of the cadets' connection with
the battle, no effort will be made to fix the location, number, or condition of the United States guns captured by the cadets, since these
questions have given rise to much controversy, and no definitive
conclusion has yet been reached.

The cadets were credited with the capture of from 60 to 100 prisoners.

As the V. M. I. section of artillery under Capt. Minge (Cadet
Capt. A Co.), could not follow the corps across Shirley's Hill, Colonel Shipp ordered Captain Minge to join the "general artillery column in the main road (Pike), and report to Major McLaughlin."
(See map, artillery positions 4 and 13.)

The prompt execution of this order by Captain Minge (witnessed
by the cadets from Shirley's Hill), as he took the cadet battery down
the Pike towards the enemy at a sweeping gallop, was one of the
most inspiring sights of the day, and it possibly bore fruit in the
conduct of the corps at a later hour.

OPPOSING FORCES.

Prof. E. R. Turner's estimate of the opposing forces, probably
the most careful one ever made, is as follows:

	INFANTRY	CAVALRY	ARTILLERY	TOTAL	GUNS
United States....	4,700	1,000	300	6,000	28
Confederate States.	3,400	900	200	4,500	18

But probably not over 4,000 United States troops and 2,000 Confederate States troops took an active and continuous part in the battle.

CASUALTIES.*

CORPS OF CADETS.

	ENGAGED IN THE BATTLE	DIED ON THE FIELD	DIED FROM WOUNDS OR EFFECTS	WOUNDED	TOTAL	PER CENT
Officers	6	..	..	2	2	33.3
Cadets	257	5	5	45	55	21.4
Total	263	5	5	47	57	21.7

*For details see Appendix, page 254.

"Died on the Field of Honor"

For several generations a beautiful and impressive custom has been followed at the Virginia Military Institute on the fifteenth day of May. Cadets in the several companies are assigned to represent those who were killed or mortally wounded in the battle of New Market. The names of the dead are called with the current rolls and as the name of each New Market hero is called, his representative steps two paces to the front, salutes, and reports, "Died on the field of honor."

A similar practice is followed at some of the alumni association meetings held on New Market Day. There, after extinguishing the lights, alumni in different parts of the room respond as the roll of the cadets who lost their lives in the battle is called.

This custom is based upon an incident of history graphically described by Col. J. C. Wise in his Military History of the V. M. I. (p. 337):

"Latour D'Auvergne entered the military service of France in 1767 and fought with distinction throughout the early years of the Revolution in the armies of the Alps and the Pyrenees. Time and again he distinguished himself in battle, and was offered promotion, but each time he refused it. As a simple captain, he led 8,000 grenadiers, known on account of their murderous bayonet charges as the Infernal Column. He left the army in 1795, but re-enlisted as a substitute for the only son of an old friend in 1799, and fought with Massena in Switzerland. Again he declined promotion, but Napoleon, in 1800, caused him to be officially borne on the rolls as the 'First Grenadier of France.' He was killed on the 22d of June of that year in Bavaria, whereupon the whole French army mourned for him three days. His heart was embalmed, placed in a silver vase carried by his company, and his saber was placed in the Church of the Invalides. Every morning until the close of the empire, at the roll call of his regiment, his name was called and the eldest sergeant replied: 'Mort sur le champ de l'honneur.'"

SERGEANT CABELL

CORPORAL ATWILL

PRIVATES

CROCKETT	JONES
HARTSFIELD	McDOWELL
HAYNES	STANARD
JEFFERSON	WHEELWRIGHT

MOSES J. EZEKIEL
Class of 1866

"The V.M.I., where every stone and every blade of grass is
dear to me; and the name of
Cadet of the V.M.I.,
the proudest and most honored title I can ever possess."

Key to Map

Cross-hatched colored lines indicate artillery. The cadet artillery served with the other Confederate artillery.

1 Third echelon on Shirley's Hill; *a*, 26th Battalion; *b*, Corps of Cadets.

2 Second echelon on Shirley's Hill; *a*, 22d Regiment; *b*, 23d Battalion.

3 First echelon on Shirley's Hill; *a*, 51st Regiment; *b*, 62d Regiment.

4 Confederate artillery on Shirley's Hill, under McLaughlin.

5 Cadet Battalion in reserve, marching down Shirley's Hill.

6 Second echelon sheltered by hill, just before advance upon second Federal position; *a*, 22d Regiment; *b*, 23d Battalion.

6¹ 26th Battalion attached to the left of second echelon, before moving forward to the left of first echelon (7¹).

7 First echelon sheltered by hill, just before advance upon second Federal position; *a*, 51st Regiment; *b*, 62d Regiment.

7¹ 26th Battalion forming left of first echelon.

8 Two sections of Snow's Battery in New Market.

9 Federal troops in New Market; first Federal position.

10 Imboden's cavalry, Confederate right, to south of woods, before moving to cross Smith's Creek.

11 30th Battalion, Confederate skirmish line.

12 First (Moor's) line in second Federal position; *a*, 18th Connecticut Regiment; *b*, 123d Ohio Regiment; *c*, Von Kleiser's Battery.

13 Confederate artillery under McLaughlin in advanced position, firing upon second Federal line upon Bushong's Hill.

14 Second Confederate line defending Confederate right; *a*, 22d Regiment; *b*, 23d (Derrick's) Battalion extended in skirmish line.

15 Cadets in reserve behind Wharton's line, just before reaching the Bushong House.

16 26th (Edgar's) Battalion marching behind 51st Regiment, because of bend in river.

17 51st Regiment marching on both sides of ridge near river.

18 62d Regiment in hollow after retreat from advanced position at 19.

19 62d Regiment in advanced position on Bushong's Hill.

20 Company of 34th Massachusetts Regiment supporting Federal artillery on Sigel's right.

21 Federal artillery on extreme Federal right, near river-bluffs; *a*, Carlin's Battery; *b*, Snow's Battery.

22 Von Kleiser's Battery on summit of Bushong's Hill, after retreat from Federal first line (12*c*).

23 Thoburn's Brigade, Federal second line, on Bushong's Hill; *a*, 34th Massachusetts Regiment; *b*, 1st West Virginia Regiment; *c*, 54th Pennsylvania Regiment.

24 Ewing's Battery.

25 Federal cavalry under Stahel.

26 Imboden's artillery and cavalry across Smith's Creek, on Federal left flank.

27 Du Pont's Battery in most advanced position, covering Federal retreat.

28 12th West Virginia Regiment in reserve.

In addition to the corps of cadets, both Confederate infantry brigades, two regiments, and a battalion were commanded by V. M. I. graduates, viz.: Brig. Gen. Gabriel C. Wharton, '47; Brig. Gen. John Echols, '43; Col. George H. Smith, '53 (62nd Va. Regiment); Col. George S. Patton, '52 (22nd Va. Regiment); Lieut. Col. George M. Edgar, '56 (26th Va. Battalion).

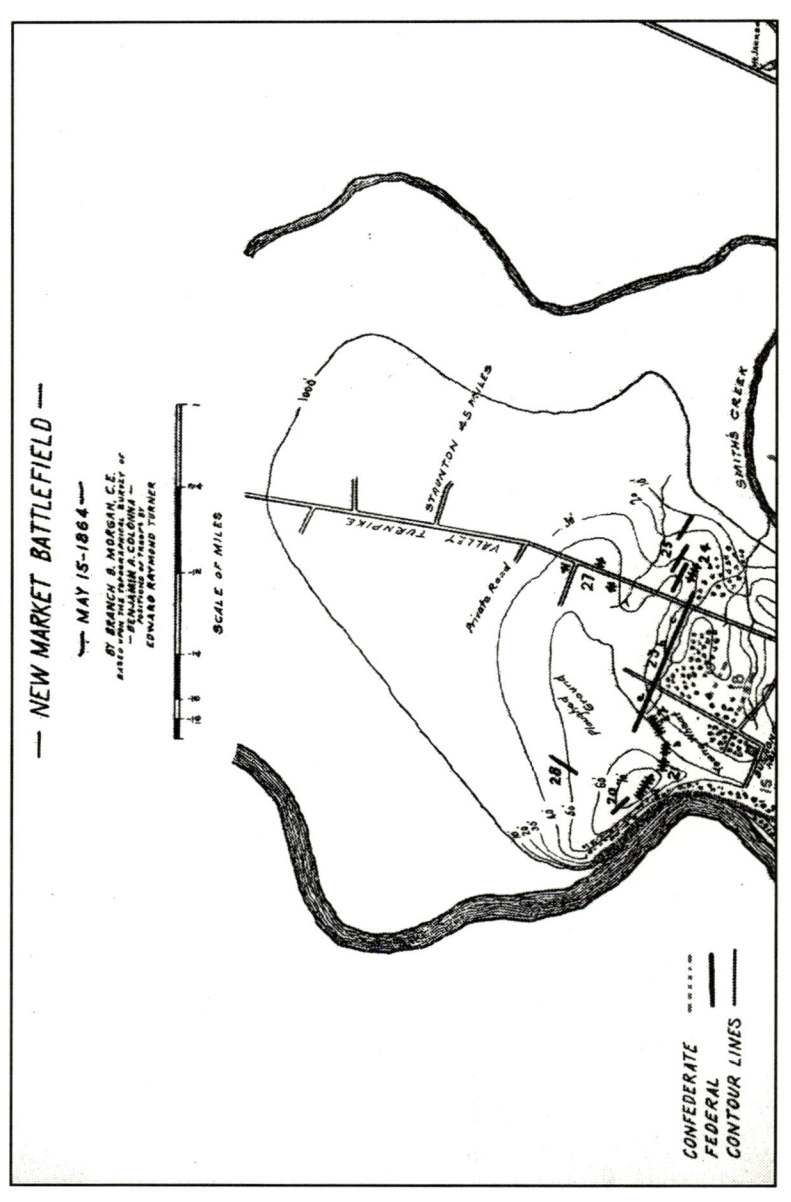

Two sections of the Branch B. Morgan New Market Battlefield map.

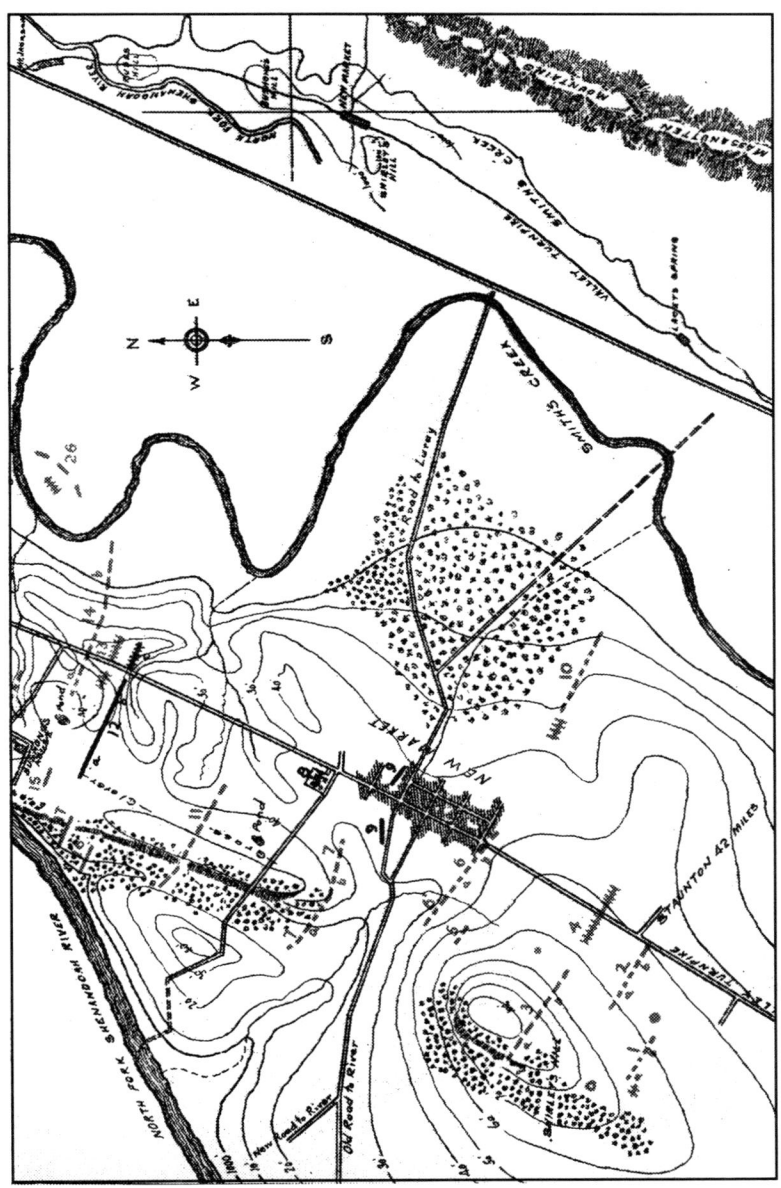

Note: sections overlap 1/4 inch at center.

EDWARD M. TUTWILER
Class of 1867

"The command was given to rise and charge. We rushed
for the battery . . . we shot down the horses. The Federals
served the guns until we got right on them."

—Richmond *Times-Dispatch*, June 23, 1912

Cadets at New Market

1. Roger Atkinson Adams—1866.

Merchant

Born in Dinwiddie Co., Va., in 1847 (he was 16 when he matriculated). He was named for his uncle-in-law, Roger Atkinson, a brother of Bishop Atkinson, who married Mary Withers, his aunt.

Parents: Thomas Adams, Methodist minister, and Elizabeth Withers, an aunt of Thomas Withers, V. M. I., '69.

Maternal Grandparents: Thomas Withers, and Elizabeth Grammer.

On Sept. 6, 1862 he was entered at V. M. I. by his uncle and guardian, Dr. Thomas Withers, from Petersburg, Va. In the battle of New Market he was a cadet private in Co. A and he remained in the corps until it was disbanded at the Alms House in Richmond on April 2, 1865—at that time he was a second classman and he had been appointed a cadet sergeant January 24th of that year.

He entered the hardware business in Baltimore with the firm of Hopkins, Harden, & Kemp. While there he was, about 1871, superintendent of St. Peters Sunday School. In an effort to regain failing health he took a trip to South America and while there he died, unmarried, "about 1872."

2. Samuel Burton Adams—1867.

Insurance—Miner

Born January 17, 1849.

Parents: John Dunning Adams, of Little Rock, Ark., and Catherine Yeiser, of Danville, Ky.

Grandparents: Samuel Adams, formerly Governor and Treasurer of Arkansas, and Rebecca May.
Daniel Yeiser and Catherine Fauntleroy Samuels.

He matriculated at V. M. I. Nov. 17, 1863, from Little Rock, and remained until the end of the session. In the battle of New Market he was a cadet private in Co. "C." Only two other cadets in the battle were younger than Adams; they were L. S. Davis, and Roane.
On January 17, 1919 he wrote:

"After the battle of New Market we went to Richmond and made camp out in the edge of the town. An order came to pass in review before President Davis and the Governor of Virginia, and I got into a panic on account of the dilapidated condition of my clothes. I took into my confidence Sergeant Ezekiel with an effort to get excused, but he said it would be impossible because he could not spare me, and he said, 'Go ahead and they will give you a new suit.' So after the parade, next morning sure enough they issued me a new suit which had just been brought in by a blockade runner. The suit was made in Austria and was a beautiful gray, but it was intended to be worn by a man who weighed about two hundred pounds and stood about six feet tall. The coat had wooden buttons on it. So as I was only a small youngster I took it in to a tailor in Richmond and had him to make me a suit, which I suppose took about ten days. When I got it, it was the prettiest suit I ever saw; and the next morning after I put it on, my guardian, Colonel Robert W. Johnson, Confederate States Senator from Arkansas, appeared on the scene and took his son and Chester G. Ashley and myself and sent us to the University of North Carolina. That would make me leaving Richmond along about the first part of June (1864).

"I remained at the University of North Carolina until December when I went to spend the holidays with one of my chums down in Halifax County, I went back to the University and got my traps and returned to Halifax, North Carolina, breaking away from my guardian with a view of getting back home. I stayed there some time waiting to get funds and to arrange my matters so I could leave. The first of April I received a remittance and also a notification that I had been made a First Lieutenant on the staff of Major General James F. Fagan in the Trans-Mississippi Department. I got me a horse and was all ready to go, went to the station to see if there was any further mail for me, and found that General Lee had surrendered."

After the war, being in bad health, he took a trip to Europe and then went to work. He was ticket agent for a railroad; long in the insurance business (Adams & Boyle) in Little Rock, Ark.; and was president of the Mescal Mining Co., operating properties in the Verde Mining District of Arizona. Later in his busy life he retired and visited with his daughters.

He was married three times:

1st, Mary Boyd, of Halifax Co., N. C.

2nd, Sallie Haney, of Youngstown, Ohio.

Children: Katharine, m. Farrar L. McCain, Judge of the Superior Court, Muskogee, Okla.
Irene, m. Julius L. Witz, a manufacturer of Staunton, Va.
Ella, m. Felix Tachoir, of Houston, Texas, a dealer in cattle and packing products.

3rd, Margaret Dennison, of Little Rock.

His brother, Dean Adams, married Amelia M. Wright, dtr. of Morehead Wright, who was formerly governor of Arkansas.

In 1921 he was sergeant at arms, Arkansas Senate.

He died in Little Rock, December 25, 1928.

3. Reuben Cornelius Akers—1867.

Merchant

Born January 13, 1845, in Appomattox Co., Va. Gen. Lee surrendered on adjoining farm in 1865.

Parents: Bryan Akers, born in Campbell Co., Va. (1802-1880), youngest child; farmer in Appomattox until 1849 when he moved to Lynchburg, and Martha Moten Moon.

Grandparents: —— Akers, born in Ireland and came to America in 17—; lived in Campbell Co., Va., and Agnes Bryan, of Botetourt Co., Va.

J. P. Moon, born in Charlotte Co., Va., officer war of 1812; lived near Campbell C. H.; died 1833, and Elizabeth McKinney, born in Charlotte Co., Va., a sister of Gov. McKinney of Virginia.

Married: 1870, Clara Rumbough.

He matriculated at V. M. I. July 25, 1863, from Lynchburg. He was dropped from the rolls on January 29, 1865 when he failed to return on furlough. He was a cadet private in Co. D and was slightly wounded in the right arm at the Battle of New Market. After the war he entered his father's business in Lynchburg.

Died in April, 1894.

4. William Kirkwood Alexander—1867.

Merchant

Born at Campbell C. H., Va., April 16, 1846.

Parents: John Dabney Alexander and Mary Pannill, both of Campbell Co., Va.

Grandparents: John Alexander, of Scotland, and Sarah Lewis, of Rockingham Co., Va.

Samuel Pannill, of Green Hill, Campbell Co., and Judith ——, of Orange Co., Va.

After attending school at Greenwood, he matriculated at V. M. I. July 25, 1863, from Campbell C. H., and left at the end of the session.

At the battle of New Market he was a private in Co. "D" of the Cadet Corps. Later he was a lieutenant on the staff of Gen. Longstreet, C. S. A.

He was a bachelor.

After the war he engaged in the building materials supply business (lumber, cement, lime, etc.), and during the Spanish-American War he served as Captain and Quartermaster.

Letters were received by his family from him shortly after he was mustered out of the army but he then dropped from sight and has not been heard from since about 1900.

5. Donald Allen—1867.

Civil Engineer

Born January 18, 1848, at "Mt. Prospect," Bedford Co., Va.

Parents: Robert Allen (b. 1794) and Frances R. Harvey, lived in Shenandoah Co., Va., moved from there to Bedford County in 1839. He represented the former district in Congress three terms.

Grandparents: James Allen and Jean Steele, they lived in Shenandoah Co., Va., and he was one of the judges of the old General Court of Virginia.

Matthew Harvey and Magdalene ——, who lived at Mt. Joy, near Buchanan in Botetourt Co., Va.

On January 7, 1864, he matriculated from Liberty, now Bedford City, and was a cadet until January 18, 1865 when he resigned to enter the army.

In the battle of New Market he was a cadet private in Co. A. After two years spent on his mother's farm he entered Washington College and was graduated there in 1869 in civil and mining engineering.

Married: Nov. 11, 1879, Mary D. Haile, dtr. of Columbus Haile, of South Carolina, but later of Staunton, Va.
Children: ——, m. B. O. Blackford.
Donald Allen, Jr.
Mary (d. 1912), m. Roy Patterson.
Harvey Allen.

After a brief service under Major Jed Hotchkiss, topographical engineer, in Staunton he was an assistant engineer on the Alabama and Chattanooga railroad and from there went to Costa Rica, where he continued his railroad engineering until 1877 when he returned to this country. He was associated with numerous railroads and was for two years engaged in government construction work at Galveston. He was superintendent of the Houston & Texas Central Rwy., at Waco, Texas; supt. of the L. & N. Rwy., at Evansville, Ind.; and agent of the M. K. & T. Rwy., at Kansas City.

Early in his career (1876) he was the city engineer of Staunton, Va., his most notable work being the construction of the city water works.

Two of his brothers, graduates of V. M. I., were killed in battle: James W. Allen, '49, Col., 2d Va. Inf., killed at Gaines Mill, June 27, 1862; and Robert C. Allen, Col., 28th Va. Inf., killed at Gettysburg, July 3, 1863.

Because of failing health (rheumatism) he resigned from his position in Kansas City in 1906 and lived in Staunton, Va., until his death on April 14, 1908.

6. Charles Jefferies Anderson—1869.

Merchant—Soldier—Legislator—Banker

Born August 12, 1848, in Richmond, Va.

Parents: George W. Anderson (b. 1823 in Anne Arundel Co., Md., and long a merchant in Richmond), and Margaret Lydia Horne, of Lancaster, Pa.

Grandparents: John Anderson, and Eleanor ——
John Horne, and Eleanor, daughter of Col. Joseph and Lydia Jordon Jeffries, of Lancaster, Pa.

He matriculated at V. M. I. March 29, 1864, from Richmond, and was a cadet until the corps was disbanded on the evacuation of Richmond. In February 1866 he returned and continued his studies until his graduation July 2, 1869, standing 18 in a class of 23. During the last session he was fourth cadet captain. He was a cadet private in Co. A in the battle of New Market.

On leaving V. M. I. he became a member of the firm of Geo. W.

Anderson & Sons, of Richmond. In later years he was vice-president of the Richmond Trust Company.

Always keenly interested in military affairs, he joined the Virginia volunteers in 1871 and after serving through the various grades he succeeded Fitzhugh Lee as brigadier-general in 1885 and continued as such until 1893. He then became Adjutant-General of the State of Virginia and served until 1898; he again served the state in this capacity 1906-1910. His portrait, in uniform, hangs in the Jackson Memorial Hall at V. M. I.

He took an active part in political affairs, having been elected to the Council of the City of Richmond in 1902; served in the Virginia House of Delegates in 1903-04, and in 1906 was elected to the Virginia State Senate.

His entire life was one of service and for many years he was president of the Richmond Male Orphan Asylum, succeeding his father in that position. For seventeen years he was a member and for two years president of the Board of Visitors of V. M. I. He was a member of the board of the Soldiers' Home; a prominent Mason; a charter member of the German Club and a member of other local clubs.

As a hobby he kept a scrap-book, which in the fulness of time formed seventeen large volumes. These books, mines of historical and general information, are now in the Virginia State Library.

An editorial written in his native city after his death best mirrors this useful citizen and loyal alumnus. It reads:

"When he came to write his will General Charles J. Anderson put upon paper an indelible likeness of himself. Here one sees in all his charm the kindly old gentleman whom Richmond knew and loved. The hand that formed the words disposing of the property accumulated during the course of a long and useful life was guided by the broad sympathy and the sweet charitableness which characterized the General in his every earthly contact.

It was not a great estate, as estates go these days. But it was considerable, representing the fruits of honest business dealings and wise investments. It might have been larger if General Anderson had cared more for himself and less for his fellowman. But that would have been unlike him

....

Those institutions and those undertakings that had been nearest to him during his life he wished to be remembered after death. To two churches, in one of which he had been a beloved vestryman, he gave a total of $55,000. The Virginia Military Institute, object of his regard for more than half a century, could not be forgot. And so he created a fund, to be administered for the benefit of deserving boys who in the future will wish to be educated at the great Lexington school, but who will lack funds of their own to gratify that desire. From his modest fortune there were many other notable bequests, running a wide range of charities and institutions. There was no discrimination of color or creed. Protestant and Catholic were remembered alike. The Y. M. C. A.'s for white and colored shared equally in the generosity of the testator. In the broad sympathies of General Anderson there was no room for narrow prejudice of any sort..................."

Since his death six worthy young men have annually been the beneficiaries under one of the scholarships which were founded on his bequest of $25,000 to the Virginia Military Institute—truly a great and enduring monument.

General Anderson died on August 8, 1925, at the home of his sister-in-law, Mrs. James H. Anderson, 1508 Grove Ave., Richmond, Va. Following services at St. James Episcopal Church, of which he had been a vestryman for thirteen years, he was buried in Hollywood Cemetery.

Never married, he was survived by two nieces, Mrs. Mary Anderson Howison, of Ashland, and Mrs. Peyton Fleming, of Richmond; one nephew, George R. Anderson, of Santa Rosa, Calif.; one great-niece, Miss Margaret Howison, of Ashland; and two first cousins, William Dennis, of Washington, and Albert Percy Dennis, of Richmond.

"He has put off his uniform, but as he marches on he wears on his heart a little bronze cross of a New Market man and the unshaken Cross of a proud but humble follower of an undying faith."

7. Andrew Alexander Arbuckle—1867.

Farmer

Born in Greenbrier Co., now West Va., June 16, 1847.

Parents: James Harvey Arbuckle (b. Jan. 1, 1818, Greenbrier Co.) and Mahala Frances McPherson.

Paternal Grandparents: James Arbuckle (b. Nov. 17, 1776, at Ft. Union, Va., now Lewisburg, West Va.) and Catharine Alexander (b. Aug. 20, 1781, in Augusta Co., Va.)

His great-grandfather, "Capt. Matthew Arbuckle (d. 1781) with his company of mountaineers piloted Gen. Andrew Lewis with his army from Ft. Union, now Lewisburg, W. Va., to Point Pleasant, and there commanded his company which fought through the battle. He was sent back to command at that place in 1776 and remained until the close of 1777. He was present when Cornstalk was killed. Tried to prevent the killing but was unable to do so."

Matriculated Oct. 30, 1863 from Lewisburg, (West) Va., and was a cadet one year. In the battle of New Market he was a Cadet Private in Co. "D." After Hunter's raid at Lexington he went to Lynchburg with the cadet corps and when the corps disbanded a few days later he was with Capt. Anrick's command in Western Virginia.

Married: in March, 1870, Rightie Estill (d. 1915), of Richmond, Ky. They had eight daughters (Estelle, Sarah, Mary, Ann, Elizabeth, Virginia, Myrtle, and Rightie) and one son, who died in infancy.

After the war he was a clerk in the shoe store of D. M. Bright, Richmond, Ky., 1866 to 1871. He then moved to Missouri and has engaged in farming near Estill. He lives now at Fayette, Howard Co., Mo.

8. Chester Grafton Ashley—1867.

Railroad Service

Born August 13, 1847, in Little Rock, Ark.

Parents: Gen. William E. Ashley, a widely known citizen of Arkansas who gave up his career at the bar to manage the large estate of his father—an estate much reduced by the war, and Fanny Grafton.

Paternal Grandparents: Chester Ashley, a lawyer who represented Arkansas in the U. S. Senate from 1844 to 1848, and Mary Watkins Worthington Elliot.

After attending school in Catonsville, Md., he matriculated at V. M. I. on November 17, 1863 from Little Rock, and remained throughout the session. In the battle of New Market he was a Cadet Private in Co. A. He then entered the University of North Carolina and remained there until hostilities began between Johnston's and Sherman's forces, when he left the University and joined a North Carolina regiment with which he remained and fought until the end of the war.

After a short period at home in Little Rock he went abroad and studied for two years in Geneva and Paris. Following the death of his father, in 1868, he returned home.

After a short time he entered the railroad service, and after rapid advancement, while connected with the Houston and Texas Central R. R., he died in Houston, Texas, on September 30, 1876.

"He was a bright, handsome young man, of polished manners, always perfect in dress, and very attractive to all the ladies in his social life, as well as being admired and loved by all his associates." He was survived by a widowed mother and an only sister, Mrs. Frances Ashley Johnson, wife of Col. Benjamin S. Johnson, 27th Regt. Arkansas Volunteers, C. S. A.

9. Samuel Francis Atwill—1866.

"Died on the Field of Honor"

Born at Atwillton, near Montrose, Westmoreland Co., Va., on Jan. 31, 1846.

Parents: Samuel Bailey Atwill (b. Sept. 18, 1802), of Westmoreland Co., Va., and Jane Ann Broun (b. Nov. 25, 1814), of Northumberland Co., Va.

Grandparents: Francis Atwill, of Westmoreland Co., and Nancy Lyell, of Richmond Co., Va.

Thomas Broun (b. June 11, 1777), in Lancaster Co., Va., who m. Oct. 29, 1807, Elizabeth G. Lee, dtr. of Charles and Sarah Lee, of Cobbs Hall, Northumberland Co., Va.

He matriculated at V. M. I. May 20, 1862, from Montrose, about six weeks before the close of the session. The following year, 1862-63, he was a fourth classman. During his third class year he was appointed a Corporal on Feb. 11, 1864 and during the battle of New Market, in which he was wounded, he served as fourth Cadet Corporal in Co. "A."

On June 27, 1864 he, having been advanced to the second class, was promoted to be a Cadet Sergeant.

"Struck in the calf of the leg, his wound was considered severe, though not dangerous. Being removed to Staunton, he had almost gotten well, when he was attacked with lockjaw, and died in the most excruciating agony. His pain was so intense that he could not touch the bed without a groan of agony, and death came to him as a blessed relief."

He died July 20, 1864, at the home of Dr. F. T. Stribling, in Staunton.

By Special Order No. 10, issued on May 5, 1866 Cadets Glazebrook, Overton, Dinwiddie, and Anderson all of whom were in the battle of New Market were detailed to proceed on May 7th "to New Market and remove the bodies of the cadets there interred, and also at, or near, Harrisonburg and Staunton, and convey them to the Institute." This was done "in order to comply with the desires of the parents, instructors, classmates, and comrades, of the gallant and lamented dead, who fell at the battle of New Market, May 15, 1864, that their honored remains should rest together on the grounds of the institution where they were trained to arms and which they illustrated by their courage."

Pursuant to this order the bodies of Cadets Atwell, Jefferson, Jones, McDowell, and Wheelwright were brought to Lexington and on May 15, 1866 services were conducted. The remains of these five cadets are now buried beneath the New Market Battle Monument.

10. John Seldon Bagnall—1865.

Cotton Broker

Born February 7, 1844, at Norfolk, Va.

Parents: William Douglass Bagnall (b. Norfolk) and Elizabeth Daingerfield Stark (b. Rolleston, Princess Anne Co., Va.)

Grandparents: Richard Bagnall (b. Bristol, England) and Sarah Hancock Seldon, dtr. of Rev. William Boswell Seldon, Rector of St. Johns Church, Hampton, Va.
Daingerfield Stark, of Princess Anne Co. and Elizabeth Westwood Moseley, dtr. of Edward Hack Moseley, of Rolleston, Princess Anne Co.

Matriculated at V. M. I. on January 6, 1862, from Norfolk, just after it re-opened following the suspension caused by the corps marching to Richmond, April 21, 1861, to help train the troops there assembled. His cadetship was concurrent with the troublous war years and he remained a cadet until April 2, 1865, at which time he was a first classman. At graduation, which was by decree of the board of visitors as of May 12, 1864, he stood 15 in a class of 24. He was a cadet private Co. A in the battle of New Market.

He was for many years, until he retired, with the firm of C. W. Grandy and Sons, cotton factors, in Norfolk.

He never married and was the last surviving member of a family, which for generations had been closely identified with the history of Norfolk. His closest surviving relative was Mrs. Mary Bassett Watkins, of Hampton, a first cousin.

He died May 14, 1922 and the services were held at Christ (Episcopal) Church, Norfolk, of which he was a communicant.

The following paragraph from his will bespeaks the heart of this fine alumnus:

"I give and bequeath to Educational and Charitable Institutions the sum of Twenty-four Thousand Dollars, as follows: Christ Episcopal Church, Protestant Hospital, and Virginia Military Institute the sum of Five Thousand Dollars each. The Covington Home for Boys the sum of Three Thousand Dollars, The Seamen's Bethel the sum of Two Thousand Dollars. The Episcopal Church Home, the Jackson Orphan Asylum, Infant Sanatarium, Boys Home and Kings Daughters the sum of One Thousand Dollars each."

The Bagnall Scholarship at V. M. I. is founded upon his bequest.

11. William Henry Barney—1866.

Merchant

Born August 24, 1844, near Shrewsbury, New Jersey.

Parents: William Henry Barney, who was born on Nantucket Island, Mass., and moved to Mobile, Ala., in 1838 or 1839, and Mary Corlies, born in New Jersey.

Maternal Grandparents: Benjamin Corlies and Phoebe ——, of New Jersey.

He was a student at Haverford College when the war broke out. He transferred to V. M. I.; matriculated from Mobile, January 1, 1862; and was advanced to the third class in Sept. 1862; he repeated the third class in 1863-64 and during this session was a cadet private in Co. D in the battle of New Market. He returned as a second classman but dropped out on January 5, 1865 and served as a private in the Otey Battery, C. S. A.

Married: Sallie Roane Norvell, dtr. of Fayette Henry Norvell, a professor of languages and mathematics, Marshall County, Miss.
They had a son, Oscar Norvell Barney.

After the war he was engaged in the hardware business.

On New Market day in 1890 he presented Gen. Scott Shipp, who commanded the cadets in the battle, with "a copy of the History of the 34th Mass. Infantry which was commanded by Col. W. S. Lincoln and captured by our own boys, in which you will notice many complimentary remarks as to your gallant command on that date."

He died in Mobile, Oct. 12, 1892 and is survived by his widow, 155 South Conception St., Mobile, Ala., and by his son.

12. Daniel Cary Barraud—1867.

[Name changed. Formerly D. C. B. Wilson]

Lawyer

Born about 1847 (he was 16 years and 8 months of age when he matriculated).

Parents: Samuel Mazyck Wilson, of Portsmouth, and Myra Barraud (a daughter of Dr. Daniel Cary Barraud) of Norfolk.

After attending Horner's (?) School in North Carolina, he matriculated at V. M. I. from Norfolk on Sept. 3, 1863. He left at the end of the session.

—2

In the battle of New Market he was a cadet private in Co. "C." He served with the Norfolk Light Artillery Blues and was, at one time a courier in Gen. Rossers command. He was wounded at the battle of the Crater, near Petersburg.

Married: in Sept., 1869, Courtney B. Cocke, a daughter of Gen. Philip St. Geo. Cocke, of Belmead, Powhatan Co. and who was a member of the V. M. I. Board of Visitors from 1846 until 1852 and from 1858 until 1861 (for five years its president).

He practiced law in Norfolk and later moved to Richmond, where he engaged in the real estate business.

His sister, Mary Catherine Wilson, married Capt. Richard Coke Marshall, they have had four sons graduated at V. M. I. (Samuel Wilson Marshall, '91; Gen. Richard Coke Marshall, Jr., '98; St. Julien Ravenel Marshall, '01; and Myron Barraud Marshall, '02.)

He died at his home in Richmond on June 28, 1908 and was survived by his widow, two sons (D. Cary Barraud, who was killed in a railroad accident at Flomaton, Ala., April 9, 1911; and Philip Barraud, and two daughters (Myra and Mary).

13. Bolling Walker Barton—1866.

Physician—Teacher—Lecturer

Born at "Springdale," the historic family estate near Winchester, Va., November 24, 1846.

Parents: David Walker Barton and Frances L. M. Jones.

Grandparents: Richard Peters Barton and Martha Walker.
William Strother Jones and Ann Maria Marshall.

Matriculated at V. M. I. Sept. 25, 1862, from Winchester. He stood 30 among 125 in the fourth class and was on July 4, 1863 promoted to 4th Corporal in Co. B, in which capacity he served in the battle of New Market. Later he reported "Jefferson wounded, I spent the night on the battle field with him, he died the next day.. Cocke, private, I recall from his having had his gun shot to pieces immediately in my front, I being a file closer." In the third class he stood 13 among 54. He later was appointed First Lieutenant, in the First Foreign (the Irish) Battalion of the second corps, army of Northern Virginia.

Five of his brothers also served in the Armies of the Confederacy: Lieut. Charles Marshall Barton, V. M. I., '56, was killed in the battle of Winchester, May 25, 1862, in sight of his father's home; Lieut. David R. Barton, was killed in the battle of Fredericksburg, December 13, 1862, and his body, buried on the battlefield, was not recovered; Lieut W. Strother Barton, who lost a leg at Mine Run in 1863, died from the effects of the wound; Robert T. Barton, a distinguished lawyer, served with the Winchester Rifles and the Rockbridge Artillery; and Capt. Randolph Barton, V. M. I., '64, of the 33rd Va. Infantry, who was wounded seven times and had five horses killed under him.

Besides his six sons David W. Barton had two sons-in-law in the Confederate Army—Dr. John Baldwin and Colonel Thomas Marshall.

After the war he studied abroad receiving a certificate of attendance at Beaujean Hospital, Paris, and was later graduated in medicine at the University of Maryland. He practiced his profession in Baltimore, Md., and later on taught botany and physics in Mme. Le Fevre's Miss. Hall's, and The Arundell School. He was also Lecturer in Botany at Johns Hopkins University.

In 1872 he married Ella Jane Gibson. No children living.

He retired about twenty years before his death and made his home with his cousin and adopted brother, Bolling W. Haxall, of "Exning", near Middleburg, Va. After Mr. Haxall's death he continued to live at "Exning" with Mr. and Mrs. Thomas Underwood Dudley, she being his niece.

Dr. Barton died of pneumonia on February 18, 1924 while on a visit to "Vauclause", the home of his sister, Mrs. Randolph Barton, near Baltimore, and was buried from Emmanuel Church, Middleburg, Va.

14. Nicholas James Bayard—1867.

Druggist—Orange Grower

Born in Roswell, Ga., March 26, 1848.

Parents: Nicholas J. Bayard, of New York, moved to Savannah, Ga. in 1830, and Eliza Barrington Hand, a widow when she married Bayard.

Grandparent (Maternal): Roswell King of Roswell, Ga.

He matriculated at V. M. I. August 17, 1863, from Rome, Ga., and while a fourth classman he was a cadet private in Co. B in the battle of New Market. He continued on at the institute until July 4, 1867 when he was graduated, standing eighth in his class.

Married: Grace, the daughter of Dr. Robert Battey, of Rome, Ga.
Children: Julia Barrington (Holland).
Nicholas Ralph Bayard.

Later he took a course and was graduated in Civil Engineering at Lafayette College, Easton, Penn.; he also took a course at the Pharmaceutical College in Philadelphia. Was a druggist in Rome, Ga., but owing to ill health, moved to Florida and engaged in the cultivation of oranges.

On Nov. 20, 1883 he died of a congestive chill, in Jacksonville, Fla. His wife and children survived him.

15. James Bowen Baylor—1867.

'Civil Engineer

Born May 30, 1848, at "Mirador," near Greenwood, in Albemarle Co., Va.

Parents: Dr. John Roy Baylor, of "New Market," Caroline Co., Va., and Anne Bowen, of Albemarle Co., Va.

Grandparents: John Baylor and Maria Roy.
James M. Bowen, of "Mirador," and Frances Stark.

After attending the Dinwiddie School, he matriculated at V. M. I.

on February 17, 1864 from Milford Depot, Va., and was a cadet until April 2, 1865. He wrote "I distinctly remember the burning of Richmond and leaving it as the Union troops entered from the south and my reaching our plantation, near Milford, 40 miles north of Richmond, hatless, having lost my hat in swimming one of the rivers, to find my mother all alone with our old slaves, and their troubled expression when she told them of the fall of Richmond and that they were now all free."

In the battle of New Market he was a cadet private in Co. D. He attended the University of Virginia from 1868 to 1873, took both academic and scientific courses. He has the degrees of B.S., C.E., and LL.D.

Married: Ellen Bruce, of "Staunton Hill," a sister of U. S. Senator Bruce,
   of Maryland, and three children survived them:
   Sarah Evelyn, m. Pelham Blackford, of Richmond.
   Anne Courtenay, m. Wm. Alexander Fisher, Jr., of Ruxton, Md.
   John Baylor, of Washington, D. C.

He entered the temporary service of the U. S. Coast and Geodetic Survey in 1873 and the following year was appointed "Permanent Aid" after an examination in which he stood second among thirty-five competitors—the first stand was won by Henry W. Blair, V. M. I., '70. Then followed thirty-one years of service as a field officer of this important governmental agency, his work taking him to every section of the country. He eventually settled in Richmond, Va.

He was the author of numerous papers on scientific subjects and took a prominent part in the preparation of the survey of the natural oyster beds, rocks, and shoals of Virginia, followed by an active interest in oyster legislation based on the survey. Similar surveys were made in Louisiana.

In 1902 he was one of three commissioners appointed by the U. S. Supreme Court to restore and establish the boundary line between Virginia and Tennessee. This line extends through rugged mountains and had been in dispute about a hundred years. The line established by the commission was confirmed by the Court.

In 1903 he represented the Baylor family at the dedication of the new "Carroll buildings" of Baylor University, Waco, Texas. These buildings had been erected at a cost of 160 thousand dollars, and at that time the degree of LL.D. was conferred by this, the oldest, university in Texas.

"Mirador", his birthplace was disposed of by the Baylors and was the childhood home of Col. William H. Langhorne, V. M. I., '04, and of the famous Langhorne sisters, among them Lady Astor and Mrs. Charles Dana Gibson. His boyhood home, "New Market", is also one of the famous Virginia homes and he was the sixth Baylor in line to own it.

He died May 23, 1924 at the home of his daughter, at Ruxton, Md., and was buried in Hollywood Cemetery, Richmond, Va.

16. William Fountain Beattie—1867.

Cotton Planter—Sheriff

Born February 16, 1846, near Glade Spring, Va.

Parents: Madison Beattie and Martha Cunningham.

Grandparents: William Beattie and Mary ——.
George Cunningham and Mary ——.

Matriculating from Glade Spring he was a cadet at V. M. I from March 3, 1864 until January 28, 1865 when he resigned to enter the Confederate army. He fought as a cadet private, Co. D in the battle of New Market and later resigned to join the First Virginia Cavalry. He entered Emory and Henry College in Aug. 1865 and graduated in June 1869, taking the full college course. Afterward engaged in cotton planting in Crittenden Co., Arkansas, and in the Spring of 1878 was appointed by the Governor of Arkansas to fill a vacancy in the sheriff's office. In the Fall of 1878, he was elected to fill the same office and continued to discharge its duties to the time of his death. He was killed near Marion, Crittenden Co., Arkansas, while attempting to make an arrest on April 21st, 1881.

(This information from his brother, George A. C. Beattie, of Glade Spring, Va.)

17. William George Bennett—1866.

Lawyer—Jurist

Born January 5, 1847, at Weston, West Va.

Parents: Jonathan M. Bennett, War Auditor of Va., and Margaret Jackson, of the "Stonewall" Jackson family.

Grandparents: William Bennett who settled in Lewis Co., Va., in 1797, and ——.
Capt. George W. Jackson (a regular army officer whose father, Col. George Jackson, had been a Revolutionary soldier and a member of the convention of Virginia which adopted the federal constitution, and for many years a member of Congress from Virginia) and ——.
George W. Jackson was a first cousin of "Stonewall" Jackson's father, and two of his brothers (John George Jackson and Edward Broke Jackson) were members of Congress.
John George Jackson was the first man to be married in the White House, marrying a sister of Mrs. Madison. He was also the first U. S. District Judge for the western district of Virginia.

He was an eye witness of the battle of Seven Pines and later matriculated at V. M. I. on July 9, 1862, from Richmond.

As a third classman he was a cadet private in Co. B, and in the battle of New Market he served with the artillery section.

On July 4, 1866 was graduated with eighth stand in a class of ten —all of them veterans of New Market.

He participated in the various campaigns in which the corps took part during his cadetship and was in the breast works with the cadet battalion in front of Richmond the day of the night upon which that city was evacuated.

For several months in 1864, after the battle of New Market, he drilled a battery of artillery stationed at Charlottesville, Va.

Before surrendering he hid away his sword—and so well was it hidden that it was not found for over forty-five years afterwards, when it was unearthed and returned to him as untarnished as when last worn. It rested on his funeral casket.

He was one of the first members of the A. T. O fraternity and presided at the first congress of the fraternity.

Married: On the the 28th of March, 1872, Allie Brannon, oldest daughter of Judge John Brannon of the Supreme Court of Appeals and member of the Board of Visitors, V. M. I., 1863-64.
Children: John Brannon (lawyer, of Weston).
Margaret, wife of Robert Crain, of Baltimore.
Hunter McCauley (lawyer, of Weston).
Bertha, wife of T. T. Vandergrift, of Carlyle, Pa.
William Bland Bennett, V. M. I., '05.

He graduated in law at the University of Va. and was a pioneer in the building of the Clarksburg and Weston narrow gauge road; also the Weston Buchannan railroad. ·

For six years he was a member of the board of directors of the West Va. Hospital for the Insane.

In 1888 he was elected Judge of the eleventh circuit of West Va., an office he held for 16 years in a district normally republican.

He was a staunch democrat. As a judge his opinions commanded the utmost respect.

He was a prominent Mason and filled the offices of Grand Master of the Grand Lodge of West Va., Grand High Priest of the Grand Royal Arch chapter, and Grand Commander of the Grand Commandery. "All of these honors seldom fall to the lot of one Mason."

Probably the largest owner of farm land in Lewis County, he was a great lover of horses, an extensive breeder of blooded cattle and thoroughbred horses, and had one of the best stock farms in the state.

He died Nov. 8th, 1916 at his home in Weston, West Va., and was survived by his widow and five children.

18. Edmund Berkeley, Jr.—1867.

Railroad Executive

Born April 17, 1847, Aldie, Loudoun Co., Va.

Parents: Edmund Berkeley and Mary Lawson Williams, of Prince William Co., Va.

Grandparents: Lewis Berkeley and Frances Callender Noland, of Aldie, Va.
Judge Thomas Lanier Williams and Mary McClung, of Knoxville, Tenn.

Married: Julia Lou Ramsey, of Jackson, Tenn., on Oct. 6, 1879.
Children: Rev. Alfred Rives Berkeley, an Episcopal Minister.
Dr. Green Ramsey Berkeley, of Norfolk, Va.
Mary Lou Berkeley, who married Rev. Jennings Wise Hobson, V. M. I., '09, an Episcopal minister.

He prepared for college in Hanover County, Va., where the members of the family were refugees. Matriculated at V. M. I., October 7, 1863, from Aldie, and was a cadet until the corps disbanded at the Alms House in Richmond. In the battle of New Market he was a cadet private in Co. D and was there wounded by being struck in the head by a piece of shell. Writing to Preston Cocke in 1903 he said:

"J. S. Wise was mistaken as to Color Sergeant Evans being the only man who was standing when the corps laid down. You were immediately on my left, Crockett was on my right and George Ward was immediately behind me, and I remember distinctly that we did not hear the order to lie down, and we advanced some few yards beyond the fence to a very large tree, I think it was a poplar, and that you and I were both wounded while we were standing. Colonna, our Captain, was very near us and my recollection is that he was standing at the time we were wounded, as was also Captain Robinson. I also recollect distinctly the 62nd Va. Regiment breaking and running by us and a large number of them were rallied and went back into the fight with us. You remember I found Stannard badly wounded, lying just behind the fence where the corps laid down. I went up to Hanna, our 1st Lieutenant, and showed him that I was wounded and he told me to go to the rear, but I found Stannard, whose leg was broken by a grape shot, and I tried to make a turnaquet of an old towel and stop the bleeding, and he died a few minutes afterwards, while I was with him. I then found that the corps had charged on and I tried to overtake it, but got so weak that as I passed General Breckenridge and his staff, he had me put on a horse in charge of a courier and sent back to the field hospital"..............................

In the spring of 1865 he joined Mosby's Battalion and on one occasion was captured but managed to escape.

In Sept. 1865 he entered Washington College and was graduated there with the degree of B.S. in 1868; the following year he received degrees in both civil and mining engineering; and in 1869-70 he served as Asst. Prof. of Applied Mathematics and Chemistry.

The next five years were spent in the southwest—two years on the Texas frontier surveying the Houston, International & Great Northern R. R.; 1875 to 1880 with the Mobile & Ohio R.R. as assistant engineer and in 1880 he became chief engineer of the Cairo & Columbus R.R., which position he held until 1884, when he became Division Superintendent of the Richmond and Danville, now a part of the Southern Railway.

With the Southern Railway he remained eleven years during which time he had charge successively of divisions with headquarters at Atlanta, Ga.; Richmond, Va.; Greensboro, N. C.; and Columbia, S. C.

In the spring of 1896 he became Division Superintendent of the Seaboard Air Line Railway, with headquarters at Atlanta, Ga., and so continued until the summer of 1906 when he was promoted to the position of General Agent of the same railroad.

He died November 29, 1906 at the German Hospital, in Philadelphia, Pa.; was buried in St. Paul's Churchyard, Haymarket, Va.; and was survived by his widow and three children.

19. Reuben Joseph Binford—1867.

Merchant

Born in Richmond, Va., Sept. 4, 1847.

Parents: John James Binford and Pamelia Bunch Locket.

Grandparents: John Binford and Susanna Lyon, they resided in Chas. City County, Va.

He lived and was educated in Richmond until he matriculated at V. M. I. on January 21, 1864, and remained until the end of the session. During this period he took part as a cadet private Co. A, in the battle of New Market. After war went to New Orleans to live with his uncle, Ed. T. Locket, of the firm Locket and Locket. This firm soon went out of business and his uncle moved to Arkansas. He (Binford) remained in New Orleans and went in business with Briggs, Payne and Co., a wholesale grocery and commission house. Seven years of this time he traveled extensively for his company through the Gulf States. It was during this period that he met Miss Harriet C. Munnerlyn, daughter of Col. Chas. J. Munnerlyn, a member from Georgia of the first Confederate Congress. Binford and Miss Munnerlyn were married in 1873.

In 1875 he located in Columbus, Ga; organized the firm of Pearce, Binford and Co., wholesale grocers; and was highly esteemed in business circles.

At one time he was Captain of the City Light Guards, of Columbus, Ga.

He died while on a visit to the home of his father-in-law, Col. Munnerlyn, nine miles from Bainbridge, Decatur County, Ga., Tuesday the 17th of January, 1882, in the 35th year of his age. Three children, a daughter; two sons (one of them R. Joseph Binford, an electrical engineer); and his wife survived him. He was buried in Columbus, Ga.

20. John Sergeant Blankman—1867.

Lawyer—Inventor

Born about September, 1848, in Fredericksburg, Va.

Parents: Dr. Mitchell Arnold Blankman, a dental surgeon of French parents, who later practiced in Richmond, and Jane B. ——, a granddaughter of Capt. Louis Mason, a soldier in the Revolutionary War.

Grandfather: Captain —— Blankman, who was a soldier under Napoleon in the battle of Wagram.

He matriculated at V. M. I. from Richmond on January 22, 1864, when he was 15 years and 3 months old, and was a member of the corps until the end of the session. When the corps went on the New Market Campaign he was, with thirteen others, left at the institute to guard the property—at that time he was a cadet private in Co. C. Someone reported to his mother that he had been wounded and she endeavored to reach him, after passing through much mental agony.

Because of poor health he could not report in the fall but a letter from his father indicates that he did report for a short time about Christmas 1864.

He then entered Georgetown University and after two years study there went to New York and was graduated in law. He practiced his profession in Washington, D. C., where he was also engaged in the real estate business. During his life he engaged in various other occupations—at one time following civil engineering; at another he was a stock broker; and from time to time he worked on devices on which patents were granted. Among his patents were: Sight for Fire-Arms (Patent No. 395,944); Adjustable Tubular Gun-Sight (No. 420,261); and Distance-Measuring Machine (No. 435,201). His sister, Mrs. Lydia J. Combs, of Washington, D. C., wrote: "His rifle-range and gun-sight patents were taken out in the United States, France, England, and Germany. Foreign letters of congratulation poured in on him. French scientists wrote him a splendid testimonial. It reached him as he lay dead, and I asked them to lay it on his coffin."

He died, unmarried, in Washington, D. C., March 10, 1900, from the effect of injuries received in the West about a year before while on a trip over the mountains.

21. Robert Montague Blundon—1867.

Merchant

Born October 28, 1845, in Northumberland Co., Va.

Parents: William Blundon and Sarah Jane Wildey.

After attending Northumberland Academy and Farnham Institute he matriculated at V. M. I. on July 31, 1863, from Burgess Store in his native county. At the time mail service to the county was cut off by war conditions and he had to be notified through Robt. L. Montague, via Jamaica, Middlesex County. In the battle of New Market he was a cadet private in Co. C. He returned the following session and remained until Richmond was evacuated; meantime, on January 24, 1865, he was made a corporal in his old company. While a cadet he roomed with Sir Moses Ezekiel, an intimate friendship which existed ever after.

Married: April 22, 1868, Sallie Anne Downing, of Northumberland Co., Va.
Children: Sarah Caroline.
Robert Jackson (V. M. I., '94).
Lula Katharine.
Laura Gertrude.
Montague (V. M. I., '02).

After the war he entered the mercantile business near his home in Virginia, and in 1871 became a partner in the wholesale grocery firm of J. A. Edmundson & Son., (established 1848), Baltimore, Md., and continued an active member until his death.

On his return home following the Semi-Centennial Celebration he wrote

"To the Institute, which I believe is destined to be the leading school in the South. The alumni wherever scattered have always come to the front in the various avocations they have entered, and no better test of the worth and merit of any institution can be had than this. Accompanying me to the Semi-Centennial were the following Alumni: Rev. Walter W. Williams, '53, rector of Christ Church; Prof. (Capt.) Henry A. Wise, '62, Supt. of Schools; Thomas G. Hayes, '67, U. S. District Attorney; T. Herbert Shriver, '67, Deputy Collector of the Port; besides several others who are occupying high and honorable positions in this city (Baltimore)."

He died June 24, 1902, and his youngest son was graduated from his Alma Mater the following day.

22. Albert Boggess—1864.

Professor

Born April 23, 1839, at Ten Mile Creek, now Lumberport, Harrison Co., West Va.

Parents: Albertus Boggess and Anne Wood.

Grandparents: Samuel Boggess and Elizabeth Dorsey (D'Arcy), Maryland. Benjamin Wood (son of John Wood and nephew of Governor Wood, of Va.), and ——.

He matriculated at V. M. I. July 30, 1860, from Lumberport, and after a period of cadetship of four years he was graduated on June 27, 1864, standing 10 in a class of 14. When the corps was ordered to Richmond April 21, 1861 it was his misfortune to be left at V. M. I. with the guard detail but he saw service later on the various campaigns in which the corps took part. In the battle of New Market he was 2nd Lieutenant of Co. C. A few weeks later on he was graduated and went into the Confederate Army as a drill master and continued in the service in Col. Preston's command until the end of the war. After Lee's surrender he returned to his home in Harrison county, but because of the devastation wrought by the war he determined to seek new fields and went to Texas. There in January, 1866, he became professor of mathematics at Waco University, afterwards Baylor University, Waco, Texas.

Married: On July 11, 1877, Nannie Elizabeth Shivers, in Falls Co., Texas. They had five children.

Professor Boggess died Dec. 13, 1891 "loved and honored by all who knew him for his faithful work as teacher, and for his life of purity and unpretending heroism. The Virginia Military Institute was ever his ideal in all things scholastic."

His son, Robert Woodfin Boggess, was a V. M. I. cadet, class of 1913; also his grandson, Albert Boggess, III, class of 1927.

23. Samuel William Booth—1867.

Merchant

Born about 1844, at matriculation he gave his age as 18 years.

Parents: Patrick Henry Booth and Ann Maria Maynard, of Surry County, Va. (She died Feb. 25, 1911, aged 98.)

Grandparents: Col. Samuel Booth, and ———.
Capt. Wm. Maynard, and Virginia Laughton.

He matriculated at V. M. I. Nov. 8, 1862, from Petersburg, Va., and was a member of the corps until the evacuation of Richmond. He repeated the work of the fourth class in 1863-64 and during that session he was a cadet private in Co. C in the battle of New Market.

A brother Benjamin D. Booth, attended V. M. I. and was a member of the class of 1868.

Married: Ella Kate Somers, a dtr. of Jerome Somers, of Petersburg, Va.

After the war he was a merchant in Petersburg, Va., where he died July 26, 1925.

24. Henry Clay Bowen—1867.

Farmer—Lumber Dealer

Born April 3, 1846, in Fauquier Co., Va.

Parents: William A. Bowen, of Fauquier Co., Va., and Ellen Dade Fitzhugh, of Culpeper Co., Va.

His brother having served in the army and been sent home wounded, he was sent as a refugee to Brookland School, Greenwood, Va., where he was in attendance when he matriculated at V. M. I. on February 17, 1864. In the battle of New Market* he was a cadet private in Co. A, and continued in the corps until February 6, 1865 when he resigned to enter the military service. He was then a member of Mosby's Battalion, as was his brother.

Married: In December, 1869, Georgia Carmichael Rothrock, a dtr. of Col. William I. Rothrock.

After the war he returned to his home, Remington, Va., and was engaged in farming and the lumber business. In later years the firm style was H. C. Bowen & Son, dealers in lumber, ties, and piling.

He died in the University Hospital, at Charlottesville, Va., on March 5, 1928 and was buried at his home. His wife and two children, Mamie and Champ Taliaferro, pre-deceased him.

He was survived by the following children: Ellen Fitzhugh, wife of S. C. Brittle, of Warrenton; Ella C., wife of M. L. Mickley, of Charlotte, N. C.; William T. Bowen, of Fayetteville, N. C.; Henry M. Bowen, of Greenwood, Va.; and three residents of Remington, Va., Georgia C., wife of L. M. Brittle, Charles H. Bowen, and John McGill Bowen.

---

*In writing about the battle to Capt. Henry A. Wise on May 5, 1909, he said among other things: "I remember when we were at the orchard, 'Skin' Ross, Pendleton of Co. A, and myself were shooting through the fence and a ball struck Pendleton in the forehead. He jumped up and ran to Ross and exclaimed, 'Skin, I'm dead'..................... I remember well when you lost your coat-tail and the seat of your trousers and Lewis Wimbish gave you a pair of Yankee trousers."

25. William Brownley Bowen—1867.

Physician

Born June 21, 1846, at "Clover Hill," Warren Co., Va.

Parents: Edwin Bowen (b. Warren Co.) and Eliza Frances Johnston (b. Clarke Co.)

Grandparents: James Bowen and Amelia Brown, both born in Culpeper Co. John L. Johnston (b. Warren Co.) and Emma Brownley (b. Clarke Co.)

At the beginning of the war he and his brother, James Pollard Bowen, V. M. I.; '66, joined the Warren County Cavalry, commanded by their uncle, Walter Bowen, V. M. I. '43 and served with Ashby's Cavalry. Later, on August 13, 1862, he matriculated at V. M. I., from Ninevah, Va., and was a cadet for two years, repeating the fourth class. In the battle of New Market he was a cadet private in Co. B and a few months later he joined Mosby's Rangers and served with them until the end of the war.

He studied medicine at the University of Virginia in 1869-70 and then transferred to the University of Maryland where he was graduated in 1872.

Married: On Sept. 13, 1881, Emma Louisa Sommerville, a dtr. of Dr. Wm. Sommerville, of White Post, Clarke Co., Va.
Children living in 1912: Frances, wife of —— Cunningham; Brownley Baker; Edith Cary; Ada Clarke; Amy Stanley; Helen Aby; and Edwin Bowen.

He practiced his profession in Washington, D. C., at Stephens City, Va., and after about 1885 at Moorefield, West Va.

On Sept. 2, 1908, Dr. Bowen died of apoplexy. His wife survived him.

26. John Francis Bransford—1867.

Surgeon, U. S. Navy

Born July 3, 1846, in Chesterfield County, Va.

Parents: Benjamin Hatcher Bransford, and Hannah Elizabeth Walke.

Grandparents: Francis Bransford, and Sarah Hatcher.
John R. Walke, and Martha Patteson Branch.

Great-grandparents: John Bransford, who came over from England with his father, John, about 1730, and Judith Ammonette, a Huguenot.
John Walke, and Hannah Watkins.

He matriculated at V. M. I. from Winterpock, Va., August 1, 1863, and was a cadet private Co. B at the battle of New Market,*

---

*Extracts from his accounts of the battle: "I was in B Company, Woodlief was my front-rank man until he was wounded and I took his place. I was near Capt. Preston and Capt. H. A. Wise was on our right.................I heard Capt. Preston say 'They are going to run. They are trying to limber up!' and Capt. Wise gave the order to rise and charge............ Atwill was at my side, and seeing me look down, asked if I was shot, and said, 'I'm hit in the foot too. Come on, let's keep it up...................'
..............."Hanna cut one with his sword, Garrett used his bayonet, and Jim Harvie the butt of his gun.".......................

where he was wounded by a stray bullet that struck him in the foot after the Federal ranks broke. The following session, February 15, 1865, he resigned and joined the First company, Richmond Howitzers and fought until the surrender at Appomattox.

Married: February 14, 1888, Elizabeth, daughter of Alfred Baker, of Augusta, Ga., banker and financier, and Sarah Elizabeth Thayer, of Massachusetts.

After the war he was agent for the Clover Hill Mine Co., at Osborne, Va., but soon took up the study of medicine at the Medical College of Virginia, graduated in 1867, and in 1872 was appointed assistant surgeon in the U. S. Navy, being the first ex-Confederate soldier so recognized. After a service of eighteen years (Past Asst. Surgeon, 1875; Surgeon, 1885) he resigned in 1890 and purchased the Stony Point property in his native county, near Richmond, Va.

He returned to the naval service in the Spanish-American War and served as surgeon aboard the Gloucester, the converted yacht Corsair, formerly owned by J. Pierpont Morgan. In the battle of Santiago, being an experienced marksman, he was at his request placed in command of a gun and served it during the remarkable fight with the Spanish torpedo boat destroyers, Pluton and Furor. The action of the Gloucester was one of the noteworthy episodes of that brief engagement.

It fell to his lot to dress the wounds of the Spanish admiral, Cervera, and many other officers who were brought aboard the Gloucester—a service performed immediately after the fatigue of battle. He was one of twenty-eight promoted for conspicuous gallantry in the battle of Santiago, and by special act of Congress he was retired, March 12, 1901, with the rank of past assistant surgeon and awarded a medal.

He had two children, Alfred Baker (b. Nov. 21, 1892), and Henry Walke Bransford (b. April 7, 1894), both of whom met a tragic death when a row boat capsized in James River on August 24, 1911.

The shock of this tragedy prostrated him and death followed in a short time. Dr. Bransford died November 11, 1911 at Stony Point, near Bon Air, Va.

Member of the Board of Visitors, V. M. I.; R. E. Lee Camp No. 1, Confederate Veterans; and at the time of his death was Commander of the R. A. Woldridge Camp, Confederate Veterans of Chesterfield, and a member of the Richmond Howitzer Association.

His portrait hangs in the V. M. I. Library.

27. Robert Lewis Brockenbrough—1866.

Lawyer—Teacher

Born October 13, 1846, at Lexington, Va., the fifth child of his parents.

Parents: Judge John White Brockenbrough, long associated in various capacities with Washington College, and Mary C. Bowyer, of Lexington, Va.

He matriculated at V. M. I. from Lexington, August 28, 1862, and was a cadet for two years. In the battle of New Market he was 3rd Corporal of Co. A. When Dr. Upshur delivered the address at the unveiling of the New Market Monument in 1903 he said: "In the battalion where all did well Evans, our color bearer, and the color guard, Wood, Atwill, Royster, and Brockenbrough are worthy of special commendations for their splendid valor." After the session he entered the military service and was assigned to Gen. Jos. E. Johnston's army, at that time in South Carolina. He was soon promoted to the grade of First Lieutenant and so served until the cessation of hostilities.

He then entered Washington College and was graduated in 1868, being the valedictorian of his class. While a professor at the Texas Military Institute he studied law and in after years practiced that profession in St. Louis, Mo.

Married: While in Austin, Texas, Mary Grasty, dtr. of a Presbyterian minister, and she with one son survived him.

In his later years he was principal of the public schools in Brunswick, Mo.

After a short illness he died April 26, 1886 and was buried in Mexico, Mo., beside two of his children. A handsome monument was erected to his memory by the school children of Brunswick.

28. James Andrew Brown—1867.

Physician

Born 1847, at Powhatan C. H., Va., at the home of his uncle, Col. Wm. C. Scott, 44th Va. Reg't, C. S. A.

Parents: James Andrew Brown (born, lived and died near Buckingham C. H., Va., was a successful merchant, who died shortly after his son's birth, leaving his wife, three daughters, and his son well provided for) and Mary Campbell Scott.

After attending various private schools he matriculated at V. M. I. from Powhatan C. H., on April 11, 1864, giving his age as 17 years. He fought as a cadet private in Co. D in the battle of New Market. After the war he went to California for a short while and then to Kentucky. Later he came back to Virginia and studied medicine at the Medical College of Virginia, from which he was graduated with the degree of M. D. in 1871. Dr. Brown died of consumption about 1880.

29. Edward (Carter) Stanard Buffington—1867.

Physician

Born August 11, 1847, in Cabell County (West) Va.

Parents: Peter Cline Buffington, of Cabell Co., the first mayor of Huntington, and Eliza Jane Stanard, of Richmond, Va.

Grandparents: Col. William Buffington, and Nancy Scales, both born in Cabell Co. (West) Va., on the Ohio River.
Edward Stanard, born at Roxbury, Spotsylvania Co., Va., and Rebecca Carter, born at Blenheim, Albemarle Co., Va.

He matriculated at V. M. I. on August 22, 1863, from Giles C. H., Va., where the family refugeed, and was a cadet for one year during which he was a cadet private in Co. C in the battle of New Market. Later he served as a midshipman in the Confederate navy. He entered V. M. I. on the same day L. C. Rickets entered and the letter recommending them both was written by Maj. Gen. A. J. Jenkins, a gallant soldier who never attended V. M. I. although numerous biographical sketches have stated that he did.

From 1866 to 1868 he attended Wesleyan College, at Millersburg, Ky.; and then went to Jefferson College, in Philadelphia, where he was graduated in medicine in 1872.

Married: In 1873, Anna, daughter of Richard Henry Lyell, of Richmond, Va., and their son, Richard Lyell Buffington, was born December 4, 1875.

A few years before his death on February 24, 1929, of heart failure, Dr. Buffington lost his sister, Mrs. David Brydon Tennant (née Willie Ann Buffington), of Petersburg, Va. and the mother of W. Brydon Tennant, Mrs. Henry Fairfax, Mrs. John Stewart Bryan, all of Richmond; David B. Tennant, of Oatlands, Loudoun Co., Va., and Dr. Charles C. Tennant, of Charlottesville.

A loyal and enthusiastic alumnus to the end, his career is best summarized by the following editorial from the Huntington Herald Dispatch:

"Dr. E. S. Buffington who died Sunday evening at the age of 81 years, was a man of many distinctions. Eldest son of a family in which the actual beginnings of Cabell county was enwrapped, he was young 'Marse' Stanard to his father's slaves long before the city of Huntington was conceived. Advent of the Civil War brought to his then boyish shoulders heavy responsibilities. To him fell the duty of conveying family property to safety and of seeing to the well being of the household.

"These duties performed, he was sent by his father to Virginia Military Institute. But when the northern forces threatened Richmond he went with his fellow cadets to the defense and became one of the famous war graduates of the old school. When the war ended he was a midshipman in the Confederate navy.

"Of the riches that had been his father's and his when the war began, there were left when it ended only the broad fields and the stately home. Liquid assets had gone. Stanard Buffington worked with his own hands in the fields for sustenance for himself and his own. After a few years fortune smiled again on the Buffingtons. The still youthful Stanard studied medicine. It was strange twist of fate which sent him back from Baton Rouge where he had gone to participate with his uncle. Yellow fever was raging in the south and his uncle forbade him to stay. So he came home again to find a new and promising city awaiting him. Here he remained.

"His father, Peter Cline Buffington, I, was the first mayor of Huntington and the son was one of his early successors. He spent some years, too, as chief deputy sheriff of the county and participated as such in events which must have been reminiscent of his war days. In these aspects his career was filled with thrilling episode and romantic adventure. He never lost touch with them nor interest in them. His devotion to his comrades of the Confederacy never ceased while he lived and as long as his health permitted he took active part in the affairs of the community.

"But he was best known and best remembered as a doctor of medicine. He was an outstanding exemplification of the family doctor type. He, like many of his fellows, went about doing good. He practiced for the love of humanity, going when and where he was called and trusting to the honor, generosity and ability of his patients for his pay. For those who could not pay he had the same interest and feeling as for those who could and did.

"His was a heroic life and his physical figure was heroic, too. Who, who knew him in his prime can forget that stately manhood? Who, of those who knew him at all can forget his gentle kindness, his warm friendship, his alluring comradery? Those who knew him not, but read his story will feel themselves enthrilled by the richness of his life. But his friends, knowing all these things, will remember most of all that they loved him, not because of what he achieved, but because of what he was."

30. William Dennis Buster—1866.

Died While a Cadet

Born in Charlotte Co., Va., about 1845 (he gave his age as 17 years when he matriculated).

Parents: James S. Buster, of Coles Ferry, Charlotte Co., Va., and Martha Rice.

Grandparents: James Buster, and —— Dr. Wm. Rice, of Charlotte, Va., Patrick Henry's family physician at the time of his death, and ——

He matriculated at V. M. I. from Coles Ferry, Va., October 2, 1862 and stood 70 in the fourth class; 36 in the third class; and a fatal illness and the disbandment of the corps occurred during his second class year.

In the battle of New Market he was a cadet private in Co. A; he was wounded in the battle but returned the following session. Following service in the trenches around Richmond, he was stricken with typhoid fever.

On January 13, 1903, C. B. Tate wrote of him as follows:

"He was ill in the barrack's hospital, Almshouse, Richmond, on the night of the evacuation of the city. At the request of a roommate of his, with the aid of myself and two others, he was carried to some Confederate Hospital, I do not recall which one, within the city, and turned over to the authorities. Within the last few years I learned through a reliable relative of his that he died in that hospital."

W. I. Jordan, of South Boston, Va., who married his sister, Elizabeth Buster, wrote in 1904: "W. D. Buster, my brother-in-law died in Richmond about the time of the evacuation 1865, either in hospital or at the home of a comrade, and was buried in his section of Hollywood (cemetery). I have forgotten the name of his cadet friend and father whose section he was buried in......He was in the New Market fight......and afterwards came home on furlough and brought with him two cadet friends, Van and Winder Garrett of Williamsburg. He then went back and joined the cadets in Richmond and was taken with typhoid fever and died." Died about April 1865.

31. William Hazlewood Butler—1868.

'Cotton Broker

Born March 5, 1846, in Caroline Co., Va.

Parents: Dr. John D. Butler, and Lucy Ellen Gatewood, both of Caroline Co., Va.

Grandparents: Isaac Butler, and Nancy Cobb, of Hanover County.
George Washington Gatewood, and Lucy Temple, of King and Queen Co., Va.

He was a student at Fleetwood Academy, King and Queen County, before he matriculated at V. M. I. on August 15, 1863, from Sparta, Va. In the battle of New Market he was a cadet private in Co. A. Six weeks after the battle he dropped out but returned to the institute in the fall of 1866 and was graduated in 1868, standing fourth in his class and having the rank of cadet Captain. He was the nineteenth initiate in the A. T. O. fraternity after its foundation.

From 1868 to July 1870 he was commissioned Captain and assistant professor of Mineralogy, Latin, and Tactics at V. M. I.

Married: In 1878, Jennie, daughter of Thomas Smith, of Hope. Ark.

After leaving V. M. I. he went to Arkansas and engaged in farming for two years and then he moved to Texarkana, Texas, and entered the cotton brokerage business.

He died September 10, 1896, in Caroline County, Va., where he had returned from Texarkana a very short time before.

He was survived by his widow and four children: Bryan Butler, of New Mexico; Mrs. Mollie Sugg; Mrs. Lucy Phillips, and Miss Charleigh Butler, of Denver, Colo.

32. Robert Gamble Cabell—1867.

Physician

Born July 16, 1847, in Richmond. One of nine children. Brother of William H. Cabell (Sketch 33), who was killed in the battle of New Market.

Parents: Dr. Robert Gamble Cabell and Margaret Caskie, both of Richmond. They were also the parents of James Caskie Cabell (d. 1924) and Henry Landon Cabell, of Richmond; Mrs. Albert C. Richie, mother of the Governor of Maryland; Mrs. John D. Lottier, of Richmond, and Mrs. Boykin Wright, of Augusta, Ga.

Grandparents: Judge Wm. H. Cabell (b. Dec. 16, 1772; d. Jan. 17, 1853), formerly Governor of Virginia and later President of the Court of Appeals. He spent fifty years of his life in public service. On his maternal side he was descended from James Caskie, of Richmond, President of the Bank of Virginia.

Married: Anna Harris Branch (d. 1915), Nov. 14, 1877.
Children: James Branch Cabell, the distinguished novelist; Robert Cabell; and John Lottier Cabell, V. M. I., '01, of Savannah, Ga.

He matriculated at V. M. I. July 25, 1863, from Richmond. Fought as a cadet private Co. B in the battle of New Market, with his brother, Wm. H. Cabell, who was killed in that battle. After the

—3

war he entered the Medical College of Virginia, where he took his degree. Later he became Supt. of Central Lunatic Asylum, at Petersburg. On retiring from that post he entered the drug business and established the firm of Cabell & Chelf, in Richmond. In Sept., 1908, Dr. Cabell was elected Superintendent of the City Home of Richmond and continued to hold that position until his death, May 7, 1922, at Stuart Circle Hospital, in Richmond, after a brief illness.

33. William Henry Cabell—1865.

"Died on the Field of Honor"

Born November 13, 1845, in Richmond. He was an older brother of Robert Gamble Cabell, see sketch No. 32 for parents, grandparents, and kin.

After passing through the usual scholastic preparation he entered Richmond College and while there expressed a desire to enlist as a private in a volunteer company, of which his brother, James Caskie Cabell, was lieutenant. Because of his youth his father persuaded him to defer his active military career, but as a preparation for it he matriculated at V. M. I. on December 31, 1861. He was admitted to the third class but on January 13, 1862 he was placed in the fourth class and completed the work with distinction. In the third class he stood 3 in a class of 41, and in the second class he stood first among 24.

He was promoted to First Sergeant Co. "D" and served in that capacity in the battle of New Market.

At the time the cadets marched away to this battle he was under medical treatment; for some months his health had been impaired and he had been granted a furlough to visit his father, a physician, to obtain his professional advice.

The following is quoted from Walker's V. M. I. Memorial published in 1875:

"The cadets were now in battle array. Cadet W. H. Cabell and Cadet Robert G. Cabell, Jr., two brothers, were stationed in the same battalion. One portion of our line wavered under a fierce fire of canister and musketry, and to sustain it the cadets were ordered to advance. They rushed with all the enthusiasm and valor of youth impetuously to the charge, and every obstacle yielded to their unfaltering and unflinching courage. The flag of the cadets waved in triumph over the artillery of the North, and victory perched on the banners of the South. Cadet R. G. Cabell, Jr., passed bravely and uninjured, and reached the enemy's cannon without a wound, while his noble, learned, accomplished, beloved, and unfortunate brother, struck by a cannon-ball in the chest, was left mortally wounded on the field of battle. The casualties and havoc of war, in the moment of triumph, are lost in the exultation of the victors, and the welkin rung with the shouts of the cadets, forgetting for a time the great price with which the battle had been been won. R. G. Cabell, Jr., participated in the triumph, but he soon saw that his brother was missing, and with sad, foreboding heart, he retraced his steps to ascertain his fate. He found him dead in the path of the charge, his head pierced and torn by the fragment of a shell. Truthful as he was brave, sincere and ingenuous as he was accomplished, affectionate and gentle, with every attribute which dignifies humanity, his 'noble spirit sought the grave to rest forever there.'

"In his annual report to the parents of the cadets, General F. H. Smith, Superintendent of the Institute, wrote to Dr. R. G. Cabell, the bereaved father of W. H. Cabell, saying, 'Cadet William H. Cabell fell in the gallant discharge of his duty in the sanguinary battle of New Market, 15th May, 1864.'

"His remains, temporarily interred at New Market, were afterwards removed to Hollywood Cemetery, near the city of Richmond, and by his side repose the ashes of his mother."

34. John Carmichael—1870.

Civil Engineer

Born Dec. 22, 1847, at Augusta, Ga.

Parents: Robert Dunlap Carmichael, Augusta, Ga., and Louisa Watkins Smith, Abingdon, Va.

Grandparents: John Carmichael, and Mary Eliza Eve.
William Smith, and Harriet Craig. His great-grandfather, Robert Craig, was captain in Revolutionary War and laid out the town of Abingdon, Va., after the war.

He matriculated at V. M. I. on April 23, 1864 from Augusta, Ga., and was a cadet private Co. A in the New Market Corps, but having been detailed on guard duty at V. M. I. was not in the battle. At the end of the session he was appointed adjutant and first lieutenant of one of the organizations of Georgia troops and soon afterward was commissioned captain.

He returned to V. M. I. in the fall of 1865, entered the fourth class; dropped out in 1866-67; and then continued his cadetship until July 4, 1870 when he was graduated, standing 34 in a class of 52. He was fourth cadet captain. The following year he was assistant professor of drawing at V. M. I.

Married: February 13, 1872, Virginia Brooke Tucker (d. 1928), third daughter of Hon. John Randolph Tucker, Professor of Law at Washington College, and Laura Powell.
Children: John Randolph Tucker Carmichael (d. 1910).
Harry St. Geo. Tucker Carmichael, Kyrock, Ky.
Laura Powell, wife of Oliver P. Alford, Chicago, Ill.
John Carmichael, Hagerstown, Md.

He was in command of squad which fired the minute gun at Gen. Lee's funeral and was escort to Mrs. "Stonewall" Jackson at the unveiling of the Jackson monument.

A brother (See Sketch No. 35) was in the battle of New Market and two grandsons have been graduated at V. M. I. (Harry St. Geo. Tucker Carmichael, '27, and John Randolph Tucker Carmichael, '31).

A'fter teaching one year at V. M. I. he engaged in farming and then followed the general practice of civil engineering until he was appointed an engineer in the U. S. Land Office during Cleveland's first administration. Later, he was Inspector of Surveyor-Generals, U. S. Land Office, in Mr. Cleveland's second term, and in 1897 he was an engineer on the Nicaraguan Canal.

On May 18, 1898, during the Spanish-American War he was commissioned a Captain in the United States Volunteers.

Captain Carmichael died at Lakeland, Florida, August 17, 1898 and was buried at Lexington, Va.

35. William Smith Carmichael—1867.

Locomotive Engineer

Born March 25, 1846, at Augusta, Ga.
  See sketch (No. 34) of his brother, John Carmichael.

He matriculated at V. M. I. from Augusta, Ga., July 30, 1863 and was a cadet for one session, during which time he served as a cadet private in Co. B in the battle of New Market. On leaving the institute he became a brigade drill master in the Confederate army. He received his appointment in December 1864 and served until the end of the war.

He then followed the trade of a locomotive engineer and was one of the first members of the Brotherhood of Locomotive Engineers.

A prominent Mason, he spent the later years of his life as Tiler of the Masonic Lodge in Augusta, Ga., at which post he served until the dread disease, locomotor ataxia, rendered him helpless. He died in the City Hospital, Augusta, Ga., on May 24, 1914, after an illness of fourteen months.

In 1876 he wrote specific instructions concerning his funeral arrangements and these were faithfully carried out. He was buried in the old Carmichael Cemetery, about four miles South of Augusta, in his New Market cadet uniform and in the coffin was placed a small sealed tin box, presumably the repository of mementos of an old sentiment, and other keepsakes. He never married and requested that the inscription "Dreams Unrealized" be engraved on his monument.

36. William Murray Chalmers—1867.

Teacher

Born   October 4, 1845, at "Springfield," Halifax Co., Va., the home of his father and grandfather.

Parents: David Chalmers, and Sarah Embry Coleman. He was president of the Secession Convention and three of his sons were V. M. I. cadets (Wm. M., '67; Joseph W., '63; Algernon C., '68).

Grandparents: James Chalmers, who came from Scotland, and Sarah Watkins (née Williams), widow of Micajah Watkins and a grand-daughter of Nathaniel Williams, of the Yadkin Valley, N. C.
  Henry E. Coleman, and Ann Gordon.

Married: 1868, Emma Norvell Radford, daughter of Capt. Winston Radford of Bedford Co. Six children were born to them, four of whom lived to be grown: Mrs. W. G. Wills, of Lynchburg; Mrs. Waller Jameson, of Roanoke; David Chalmers, of Kansas City; and W. M. Chalmers, of Toledo, Ohio.

A grandson, Walker G. Wills, Jr., was graduated at V. M. I. in 1919.

He matriculated at V. M. I. July 30, 1863, from News Ferry, Halifax Co., Va., having previously attended Randolph Macon College in 1861 and the University of North Carolina in 1862. He fought with the corps of cadets in the battle of New Market as a private in Co. C.

After the war he was graduated at the University of Virginia and later had charge of schools in Tennessee, Kentucky, and Mississippi.

The last eleven years of his life were spent as principal of the Danville (Va.) High School.

He died June 21, 1895, after a short illness of five days, in Danville.

37. Edward Dunscomb Christian—1867.

Tobacconist

Born May 15, 1848, Richmond, Va.

Parents: Dr. Andrew Henry Christian (born 1811, graduated in medicine at U. of Va. 1831. Lived and died, 1890, in Richmond, Va.), and Mary Anne Whitfield.

Grandparents: Henry Asbury Christian, and Lucy Wood Dunscomb. Richard Whitfield, and Ann Booker Jeffries.

His ancestors were among the English settlers in the colonial period, some of whom received patents in Charles City County, Va., as early as 1694. He matriculated at V. M. I. January 2, 1864 and was a cadet private in Co. B in the battle of New Market and was wounded in that battle. He returned the following session but resigned on February 28, 1865 to enter the Confederate army.

Married: Nov. 1872, Helen Campbell Palmer, daughter of George Sidney Palmer, Richmond, Va. They had four sons and two daughters:
Edward Dunscomb, Jr., V. M. I. '93, died in 1926;
Richard Henry Christian;
Seddon Christian;
Helen Dunscomb Christian (died 10-19-29);
Dorothy Ann, wife of Frederick Scott Campbell; and
Rev. George Palmer Christian.

The "Confederate Veteran" of December 1909, recorded this:

"Wartime Romance.—The Pennsylvania Regiment held their Reunion in Richmond, Va., and incidentally a wartime romance was discovered. In a lobby of a hotel one of the veteran Pennsylvania officers, Captain Roach, met Capt. E. D. Christian, of Richmond. The two men had last met where in the heat of battle at Cold Harbor they fought a desperate hand-to-hand duel with swords, only being separated by the rush of the charging columns of Federals. The recognition was mutual, and the one time enemies, now friends, clasped hands and went off together to tell each other the history of their lives since this momentous meeting."

A resident of one of the greatest tobacco centers in the world he became a successful and prominent tobacco merchant and business man; vice-president of the New York and Southern Construction Company; and president of the Richmond Paper Manufacturing Company.

He died on January 12, 1899.

38. Gaylord Blair Clark—1867.

Lawyer

Born April 16, 1846, in Mobile, Ala.

Parents: Francis Barnard Clark, railroad builder of Mobile, and Helen Mary Shepherd, of Orange Co., Va.

Grandparents: Willis Fish Clark, physician and native of Connecticut, and Charity Barnard, of Massachusetts.
James Shepherd, and —— Verdier, a daughter of Paul Verdier. She died and he married secondly Lucinda Taylor who raised Helen Mary Shepherd.

His preparatory work was done under the tutelage of Dr. (later Gen.) Wm. N. Pendleton at Lexington, Va., in whose home he resided. He matriculated at V. M. I. from Mobile on August 26, 1863 and later in the session fought as a cadet private in Co. D at the battle of New Market. He returned the following session and stayed until the corps disbanded, April 2, 1865, and in the few remaining days before Lee's surrender he endeavored to raise a company in North Carolina. Returning to the institute he was graduated on July 4, 1867, standing third in a class of eleven.

In the offices of Ames R. Manning and Percy Walker, prominent members of the Mobile bar, he read law and was admitted to the bar in 1870 but continued his studies for two more years before practicing his profession.

In 1879 he was elected to the state legislature and was active in civic and social affairs throughout his busy life. As attorney for the Western Union Telegraph Company, the Louisville and Nashville R. R., the Grand Trunk Railroad, the Quarantine Board, the River Commission and similar widely varied activities and corporations his labors carried him before the U. S. Supreme Court, for which he qualified in 1881, and the Supreme Courts of Alabama, Mississippi, Florida, and Louisiana.

Married: April 15, 1881, Lettice Lee Smith, daughter of Col. Robert White Smith, a prominent cotton merchant of Mobile. Their children:
Gaylord Blair Clark, Jr.;
Gaylord Lee Clark; and
Lettice Lee, wife of Franklin Heard Lyon.

After a lingering illness of three weeks, Gaylord B. Clark died on June 14, 1893, and was buried in Magnolia Cemetery, Mobile.

A marble bust of him, by Daniel C. French, was placed in the State Capitol, Department of Archives and History, in 1911.

A brother, Francis Barnard Clark, Jr., was graduated at V. M. I. in 1870.

39. John Henshaw Clarkson—1867.

Merchant—Manufacturer—Orange Grower

Born in Essex Co., Va., August 23, 1846.

Parents: William J. Clarkson, and Lucy Ann Cox.

Grandparents: John Clarkson, and Mary Gatewood.
James Livingston Cox, and Judith Brockenbrough.

Married: January 27, 1869, Martha Harrison Turner, in Richmond, Va.
They had six children: James E., John Henshaw, Jr., Louise, William
T., T. Harrison, and C. Chancellor Clarkson, V. M. I. '15.

A grandson, Holland Wright Clarkson, was graduated at V. M. I. in 1921.

Before entering V. M. I. on August 12, 1863, he had attended, and
he matriculated from, Fleetwood Academy in King and Queen Co.,
Va., one mile from Maple Valley, his father's plantation. His cadetship continued until the evacuation of Richmond. He was a cadet
private Co. B in the battle of New Market and was detailed from
his company to look after the dead and wounded.

Some time after the war he moved to St. Louis, Mo., where he ran
a fashionable clothing establishment. In the nineties he formed in
St. Louis (changing headquarters to Chicago some years later) the
Clarkson Glue Co., manufacturers, importers and dealers in all
grades of glues and gelatines, with branch offices in St. Louis, New
York, Philadelphia, Buffalo, and Cincinnati. He was president of
this company for many years.

Mr. Clarkson moved to Winter Haven, Fla., about fifteen years
ago and bought the River Lake Park Orange Grove, engaging in a
"mail order" business to dispose of his home-grown oranges and
grapefruit. He is still living at Winter Haven, Fla.

40. Frederick William Claybrook—1864.

Lawyer—Clergyman

Born Aug. 3, 1844, Heathsville, Northumberland County, Va.

Parents: Colonel Richard A. Claybrook, C. S. A. member of legislature
from Northumberland Co., and Charlotte T. Brown, of Windsor.

Grandparents: Rev. Richard Claybrook, of Middlesex Co., Va., and ——.
Richard T. Brown, merchant, of Westmoreland Co., Va., and ——.

He prepared at the Northumberland Academy, and at Hanover
Academy, taught by Hilary P. Jones, which latter school was suspended during the war.

He entered the third class at V. M. I. from Lottsburg, Va., on
Jan. 31, 1862. During his cadetship he took part in Jackson's Mc-
Dowell Campaign and was one of the sergeants detailed to keep watch
over the remains of "Stonewall" Jackson when he lay in state in his
V. M. I. section-room. Later he took part in repelling Averill's raiders as a sergeant in Co. B. During the battle of New Market he was
Second Lieutenant in Co. D, but was detailed to and served with the
cadet artillery section in the battle, being in charge of one of the two
3-inch rifled guns. He was graduated June 27, 1864, standing 8 in
a class of 14. After graduation he served from July 1864 until February 1865 as a lieutenant in the Confederate Army.

From 1866 until 1873 he practiced law and then he entered the
Baptist ministry.

Married: June, 1884, (first) Mary Franklin Dew, of King and Queen

County, daughter of Benjamin F. Dew and Mary Susan Garnett. They
had five children:
Frederick William Claybrook, b. April 29, 1885;
Mary Susan Claybrook, born Aug. 31, 1886;
Charlotte T. Claybrook, born Aug. 18, 1888;
Elizabeth Garnett Claybrook, born Nov. 25, 1889;
Benjamin F. Claybrook, born May 7, 1893, who was one year old when his
mother died.

Married: July 1895, (secondly) Anna Maria Garnett (a cousin of his first
wife), daughter of Reuben M. Garnett, of King and Queen Co., and
Elizabeth Williams, of Fredericksburg. There were three children by
this marriage:
Reuben Garnett Claybrook, born Aug. 27, 1896;
Lelia Fauntleroy, born June 29, 1898, wife of Robert Opie Norris, of
Northern Neck, Va.; and
Richard A. Claybrook, born Aug. 3, 1900 and died Oct. 30, 1901.

"In Oct., '66, I was licensed to practice law and followed my profession until Feb., 1873, when I was converted, joined the Baptist church and entered
the ministry which under God's blessing has been in a measure a success."

Rev. Claybrook died at his home in Kilmarnock on Friday evening,
August 14, 1914. Interment was in the burying ground at Old
Moratico Baptist Church, near Kilmarnock. The Freemasons of
Lancaster Union Lodge, of which he had long been the secretary,
conducted the services at the grave.

41. Thomas Rufus Clendinen—1867.

Lawyer

Born March 31, 1847, in Baltimore, Md.

Parents: Dr. Alexander Clendinen, Baltimore, Md., and Marie Louise Belt,
a daughter of Capt. Walter Belt, of the U. S. Navy.

Married: Twice. His first wife was Alice (the daughter of Mrs. J. Alexander Shriver), who died on Thanksgiving Day, 1896. Two daughters,
Alice and Rose. In 1908 he married Mrs. Mary H. English, at her
home in Charles Town, W. Va.

When the Civil War broke out young Clendinen left Baltimore and
enlisted with the Alabama forces. He was captured in 1862 and
was placed in a Union prison. After his release he entered the
V. M. I. on May 6, 1864 from Saltville, Va., and a few days
later he took part as a cadet private in Co. D in the battle of New
Market.

He returned to Baltimore in 1865 and studied law, being admitted to the bar in October, 1866, at the age of 19. He owed
a great deal of his prominence to his connection with two famous
will cases in the Baltimore courts—the Hardesty will case and
the Berry will case. At one time he was counsel for the Baltimore and Philadelphia Steamboat Company, and had the reputation of never losing a case for them. In due course he was appointed president of the Park Board by his old friend, Thomas
G. Hayes, V. M. I. '67 (See Sketch No. 107), after the latter became
Mayor of Baltimore in 1899. A great lover of horses, he lived for

many years at Mount Vernon Place where he kept a stable of thoroughbreds. After leaving the Park Board he made his home at Riverdale, Prince George County, Md., where he died on March 25, 1910.

42. John L. Cocke—1867.

Cotton Factor

Born April 18, 1848, at Melrose, Sequatchie Co., Tenn.

Parents: Daniel Flowerree Cocke (born in Fauquier Co. Moved to Sequatchie Co., Tenn., and lived there from 1834 to 1858; then to Hamilton Co., Tenn. and lived near Chattanooga until the Civil War. After the war he lived near Franklin, Tenn. He was the general purchasing agent of the Army of Tennessee, with the rank of Major), and Margaret A. Roberson.

Grandparents: Washington Cocke and ——
James Roberson and ——

He matriculated at V. M. I. August 18, 1863 from Chattanooga, Tenn., and left at the end of the session.

"Before I entered V. M. I. I saw some service under my cousin, Col. Henry M. Ashby, who commanded the 2nd Tennessee Regiment, and afterwards I accompanied Gen. John H. Morgan on his celebrated raid through Kentucky, Ohio, and Indiana, and was among the number who escaped by swimming the Ohio River near Buffington's Island and made our way from there through West Virginia to Dublin, where we took the cars for East Tennessee and from there to the V. M. I."

In the battle of New Market he was a Cadet private in "Co. 'B' and was in the front rank next to the color bearer, Evans." He was a cadet until the corps was disbanded, April 2, 1865 and attended the University of Virginia the following session.

Married: Adelaid S. Sledge, dtr. of Col. Norfleet R. Sledge, of Como, Miss. They had no children.

In 1868 he went to Memphis, Tenn., and worked for Newton Ford & Co. In 1884 went in business for himself. In 1904 the style of the firm was J. L. Cocke & Co., Cotton Factors and Commission Merchants, 349 Front Street, Memphis.

Failing health then caused him to retire and he moved to Como, Miss., where he resided until his death on July 24, 1913.

He is buried at Como and was survived by his wife; two sisters, residing in Franklin, Tenn., and a brother Samuel W. Cocke, V. M. I., 1875, of Memphis.

"No one who knew John Cocke in the morning time of his life will fail to call to mind his splendid courage, his great cheeriness, his glorious sense of humor, and his loving charity of judgment toward his fellowman. He had no personal difficulties with all his splendid courage, he had no enemies with all his dauntless energy, and he passed into that dreamless silence which must come to all, beloved by those who knew him, esteemed and respected in this community in which he died."

43. (John) Preston Cocke—1867.

Lawyer

Born at "Oakland," in Cumberland Co., Va., November 8, 1845. He dropped
his first name early in life.

Parents: William Armistead Cocke, the fourth owner of "Oakland," and
Elizabeth Randolph Preston, of Lexington. They had four sons: Wil-
liam Fauntleroy Cocke, killed at Gettysburg; Thomas Lewis Preston
Cocke; Capt. Edmond Randolph Cocke; and (John) Preston Cocke.
It was at "Derwent," the home of Thomas Cocke, about two miles from
"Oakland," that the family of Gen. Robt. E. Lee lived in the interim between
the surrender at Appomattox and the time he became President of Washing-
ton College.

Grandparents: William Cocke, the third owner of "Oakland," and Jane Armistead, of Hesse, Gloucester Co., a great grand-daughter of Col. Wm. Byrd,
the founder of Richmond.
Thomas Lewis Preston, of Rockbridge Co., and Edmonia Madison Randolph.

His interest in V. M. I. never waned and it was largely through
his wise counsel and enthusiastic interest that the labors of Capt.
Henry A. Wise, who spent so many years in accumulating historical
matter concerning the battle of New Market, were finally incorporated in Dr. Turner's book—The New Market Campaign. His account of the part taken by the corps of cadets in the battle appears
in this volume.

He matriculated at V. M. I., August 8, 1863, from Cartersville,
N. C.; left at the end of the session; and in the battle of New
Market he was a cadet private in Co. "D." From Sept. 18, 1864
until the surrender at Appamattox, April 9, 1865 he was a private
in Co. G, Cumberland Troop, of the 3rd Virginia Cavalry, 1st Brigade. He was wounded twice, slightly: first, at New Market; and
second, in a skirmish near Brock's Gap, Shenandoah Co., in November 1864.

Married: Nov. 15, 1870, Eliza Bernard Meredith, dtr. of John Alexander
and Sarah Ann (Bernard) Meredith, who was reared and educated in
Richmond. She died Nov. 2, 1922, having been run down by an auto-
mobile on Oct. 3rd.
Children: Ella Meredith Cocke.
Edmonia Madison Cocke.
Sarah Bernard Cocke, m. Oct. 18, 1910; Joseph Pope Nash, of Richmond
(children: Preston; Joseph Pope, Jr.; Bernard Meredith).
Elizabeth Preston Cocke, a graduate of Sweet Briar College.

After the war he attended Washington College (Spring, 1865 to
June 1867) and three years at the University of Virginia, studying
law in 1869-70. He obtained his license in 1870 and moved to Richmond Jan. 1, 1871, forming a partnership with Judge John A. Meredith and later (1875) became associated as a partner with Charles
V. Meredith under the firm name of Meredith & Cocke. This firm
was in existence for forty-seven years and Preston Cocke was because of his learning, resourcefulness, and dignity revered as a distinguished member of the Virginia bar.

He claimed bass fishing, whist, and pedestrianism as his hobbies.

When the Howitzer Monument in Richmond was erected he posed for Sheppard's design.

He died January 15, 1917 at his home, 206 West Franklin St., Richmond, after an illness of several days and services were conducted at St. James Episcopal Church, of which he had been a vestryman for many years.

"The Cocke family has been so closely connected with V. M. I. and other educational institutions in Virginia that the following brief outline seems pertinent. There were four cadets named Cocke in the New Market battalion. At least three of them belonged to the same family but descended from different branches. The ancestral line of J. Preston Cocke is here given. Richard Cocke, first of the name came from England prior to 1632, and settled twelve miles below Richmond. In 1632 he was a member of the House of Burgesses from Weyanoke, and in 1654 he represented Henrico Co. The line continued through his son Richard Cocke, II, and Richard Cocke, III. Then came Bowler Cocke, I, who was in the House of Burgesses from 1756 to 1761 and who secured land patents on a tract of 2,400 acres on the south side of the James River on Muddy Creek, comprising the plantation long known as the Oakland estate. This plantation was inherited by Bowler Cocke, II, who served in the House of Burgesses from 1767 to 1769, and was in turn inherited by his son, William Cocke, the third owner referred to above. (Extracted Hist. of Va., 1929, Vol. 4, p. 230.)

44. Philip St. George Cocke—1866.

Farmer

Born about 1844 at his parent's home, "Belmead," Powhatan Co. He was one of four sons and seven daughters. A younger brother was in the battle of New Market also. (See Sketch No. 45.) An older brother, John B. Cocke, V. M. I., '56.

Parents: Philip St. George Cocke [b. April 17, 1809, at "Bremo," Fluvanna Co.; d. Dec. 26, 1861. Member of the board of visitors V. M. I. from 1846 until 1852; from 1858 until 1861; and for five years its president. Brigadier-General, C. S. Army, commanded the first brigade at the battle of Bull Run (First Manassas)] and Sally Elizabeth Courtney Bowdoin (d. 1872), of Four Mile Tree, Surry Co.

Grandparents: Gen. John Hartwell Cocke (1780-1866. A soldier of the War of 1812, he was one of the founders and a member of the first board of visitors of the University of Virginia. For details of his useful life and that of his son, Gen. Philip St. Geo. Cocke, see Dict. of American Biography, Vol. 4. Va. Mag. Hist. & Biog., Vols. 3, 4, and 5 gives genealogical data of this and various branches of the Cocke family) and Ann Blaus Barraud (d. 1816), dtr. of Dr. Philip Barraud, of Norfolk. John Tucker Bowdoin and Sarah Edwards Brown (1794-1815).

He matriculated at V. M. I. Aug. 15. 1862, from Belmead Mills, when 18 years of age; entered the third class; and repeated that class the following session, standing 20 in a class of 54. In the battle of New Market he was a cadet private in Co. A. He resigned, while a second classman, on March 6, 1865 to enter the Confederate Army, joined the Norfolk Light Artillery Blues and served until the end of the war.

On June 12, 1909, he wrote from Lower Bremo, Va.:

"I went to Mississippi to a cotton plantation directly after the war and staid out there 8 or 9 years and returned to Virginia and owned a farm in Powhatan County. About 15 years ago I sold it and decided to return and live on interest of proceeds of money safely invested. I found the older I got that it was out of my sphere to deal with free negroes, so I've been spending my time during spring, summer, and fall here on my brother's place, with his widow and her children up to this time."

He died unmarried, in Charlottesville, December 31, 1913. Interment at Grace Church, Fluvanna County, Va.

45. William Ruffin Coleman Cocke—1867.

Lawyer

Born August 7, 1846, at "Belmead," Powhatan Co., the third son of his parents.

Parents, grandparents, etc. See Sketch (No. 44) of his brother, Philip St. George Cocke.

He matriculated at V. M. I. Sept. 3, 1863 from Bremo Bluff and remained until June 27, 1864, the end of the session. He stood first in a class of 187. In the battle of New Market he was a cadet private in Co. "B." He joined the Norfolk Light Artillery Blues and remained with that organization until April 2, 1865, when he was captured and was imprisoned at Point Lookout until June.

In Oct. 1865 he entered the University of Virginia; took the academic course two years, law one year. Admitted to the Virginia bar in 1868 and that same year took charge of the Malvern Plantation, near Columbus, Miss.

Married: April 26, 1871, Clara Vernon Pollard, dtr. of Col. Charles Leed and Virginia Scott Pollard, of Montgomery, Ala. Her brother, Robt. L. Pollard, V. M. I., '74.
   Children: Charles Pollard Cocke (lawyer), d. in New Orleans, 1908.
       Philip St. George Cocke, V. M. I., '94, Cotton Broker, Dallas, Texas.
       Paul Lee Cocke.
       Cary Hartwell Cocke.
       Virginia Scott Cocke, m. David Russell Lyman.
       Clara Vernon Cocke, m. Forney Johnston.
       Wm. R. C. Cocke, II, V. M. I., '06, General Counsel, Seabord Air Line Rwy., Norfolk, Va.

He practiced law at Montgomery, Ala., from 1871 to 1875, when he returned to Virginia and established himself at Lower Bremo, Fluvanna Co. This estate has descended in direct line in the Cocke family since taken up under crown grant of George II.

He died July 31, 1883.

46. John James Coleman—1867.

Farmer

Born May 21, 1844, at Jerdone Castle, Louisa County, Va.

Parents: Clayton Glanville Coleman, born in Spotsylvania Co., Va., and Sarah Jerdone Coleman, born in Louisa Co., Va.

Grandparents: William Burwell Coleman, and Maria Baptist, of Spotsylvania Co., Va.
   Francis Jerdone, of Louisa Co., Va., and Mary Byars, of Hanover Co., Va.

Matriculated at V. M. I. August 25, 1862, from Bumpus, Va.,

and was a cadet private in Co. D in the battle of New Market. He entered the fifth class and was with the corps until it was quartered in Richmond. On January 21, 1865 he resigned to enter the Confederate Army and was a first lieutenant in the Virginia State Guard. He was a farmer and county magistrate in Louisa County, Va., for many years; never married; and died at Williamsburg, Va., Aug. 11, 1914. (Two of his brothers were V. M. I. cadets: Clayton Glanville Coleman, Jr., '59, and Clarence Coleman, '66.)

47. Benjamin Azariah Colonna—1864.

Geodetician—Civil Engineer

Born October 17, 1843, in Accomac Co., Va.

Parents: John Wilkins Colonna (1805-1871), a Confederate soldier, born in Accomac Co., Va., and Margaret Jones, of New York City.

Grandparents: Benjamin Colonna (1763-1851), a soldier of the Revolution and of the War of 1812, and Elizabeth Beech, both of Accomac Co., Va. Azariah Jones, of Brooklyn, N. Y., and Cornelia Westervelt Cheney, of New York City.

In preparatory school he was taught by James V. Hall, V. M. I. '52, after which he matriculated at V. M. I. August 3, 1860 from Pungoteague, Accomac Co., Va., and was a cadet for four years, being graduated June 27, 1864 with 13 stand in a class of 14. Near the end of his first year he was a member of the corps which marched away to war* under "Stonewall" Jackson. With the other cadets he acted as drill master of the troops which were assembled at Camp Lee, at the Fair Grounds in Richmond. He was then in the 21st Virginia Regiment, in which Scott Shipp was a Major; then for ten days in the 36th Va. Reg't. In the battle of New Market he was Cadet Captain of Co. D. "The rains, which had fallen more or less about every day since we left Lexington, gave us a thorough drenching on the 14th, and did not hold up for us on the 15th. The roads and fields were very wet, the ploughed fields almost miry, so that to march across the fields even at slow time was hard work, and at double quick, exhausting. The sky was overcast all day, and there were several hard showers, and a heavy, damp atmosphere all day." After his cadetship he served in various capacities, usually as Captain, in several commands, viz.: Marquis Augusta Co., Va. Bat.; Byrds Battalion Junior Reserves; First Foreign Battalion, he was given a company of Frenchmen who served under him with devotion until the surrender of Johnston's army at Greensboro, N. C., April 26, 1865.

Married: Nov. 3, 1890, Fannie Bindon Bailey, daughter of Wm. Henry Harrison, of Ithaca, N. Y., and Eileen Alton, of Limerick and Dublin, Ireland. They had six children, one of whom died before 1911:
Eileen Alton, wife of Thomas B. Mitchell, Detroit, Mich.

---

*As this is written, Feb. 27, 1933, there are but two survivors of that corps, Capt. John M. Cunningham, '62, Brandy, Va., and Dr. T. Vaden Brooke, '64, Sutherlin, Va. (Dr. Brooke died March 12, 1933.)

Benjamin Allison (V. M. I., '14), a lawyer in New York City.
Fannie Bindon, wife of William P. Tate, of Fries, Grayson Co., Va.
John Owen (V. M. I., 22).
Flora.

The war over he returned home to find his father's possessions swept away and so he engaged in teaching, surveying and farming until July, 1870, when he entered the service of the U. S. Coast and Geodetic Survey. He passed through all the grades of this service in fourteen years of constant activity from coast to coast and throughout the interior of the country. In August, 1884, while doing astronomical and trigonometrical work on the Strait of Fuca, Washington, he was caught in an avalanche of stone and ashes causing spinal paralysis, from which he never completely recovered. In this condition, with mind active and alert, he was assigned to duty in charge of the Washington office. There the duty of reorganizing the Survey fell on his shoulders. It was a painful task but one necessary to be performed in order to save the Survey and it was successfully performed.

He resigned from this service in March 1895 and began at once, with his brother, Charles J. Colonna, the construction of a large marine railway at Norfolk, Va. This led to a study of steel floating dry docks which resulted in his being invited by Senator Chandler, chairman of the U. S. Senate Committee or Naval Affairs, to appear before that committee and the Assistant Secretary of the Navy, Theodore Roosevelt, and give them the benefit of his expert knowledge on this subject. As a result he had the satisfaction of seeing an appropriation made in 1899 for the steel floating dry dock at New Orleans.

In 1900 he returned to Washington, where the remainder of his life was passed in retirement, attending to the management of his own properties there.

In the Jackson Memorial Hall there is a large portrait of the typical New Market Cadet, for which Colonna was selected as the model.

He died March 11, 1924 at his home in Washington, D. C.

To him more than any other man is due the complete mapping of the battle field at New Market. His expert knowledge of the subject, coupled with his intense interest and love of accuracy, has preserved for all time a true picture of that much discussed battle ground.

To him is due the clear cut account of the episode when Col. Colston (old "Polly") rode up to the marching cadets on his beautiful charger, "Pompey" and quietly turned them back to the barrack in the troublous pre-war days — an incident which has been frequently and inaccurately reported. To him is due the best description of the flag carried by the cadets at New Market—a flag neither state nor national but peculiar to the V. M. I. Corps of Cadets.

48. James Parke Corbin, Jr.—1867.

Farmer—Clerk of the Court

Born Sept. 27, 1847, at Moss Neck, Caroline County, Va.

Parents: James Parke Corbin, Laneville, King and Queen County, Va., and Jane Catharine Wellford, Fredericksburg, Va.

Grandparents: Richard Corbin, and Rebecca Parke Farley, King and Queen County, Va.
John Spotswood Wellford, of Fredericksburg, Va., and Frances Page Nelson, of Hanover Co., Va.

Married: February 6, 1877, Edmonia Fitzhugh Ficklen, daughter of Joseph Burwell Ficklen, and Anne Elizabeth Fitzhugh, Stafford County, Va. They had no children.

He was entered at V. M. I. from Caroline Co., April 9, 1864 by Dr. Wm. N. Wellford of Danville and stayed until the close of the session, during which he was a cadet private in Co. D at the battle of New Market. He then transferred to Washington College.

Following his marriage in 1876, he resided at "Moss Neck," the place of his nativity. In 1894 he moved to Fredericksburg and was appointed Clerk of the Courts of that city on the 8th day of July, 1895, and performed the intricate duties of the office with such success and satisfaction that at the following election in 1901 he was elected by the people without opposition, a tribute that his merit and elegance of manners had won for him in the hearts of all classes of his community.

In early life he was confirmed as a member of the Protestant Episcopal Church, and for many years was an active and useful member of the vestry of St. George's church in Fredericksburg, Va. He was a member and Past Master of Masonic Lodge No. 4, and was at the time of his death District Deputy Grand Master of his Masonic District. He was also Past Grand Commander of the Knights Templar of the State.

In declining health for some months, his death occurred suddenly on May 28, 1904. He is buried in the family lot in the City Cemetery, Fredericksburg, Va.

49. Charles Thompson Corling—1867.

Merchant

Born Nov. 1, 1842, in Petersburg, Va.

Parents: Charles Corling, and Minerva Spencer Thompson.

He matriculated at V. M. I. February 15, 1864 from Petersburg and was a cadet until January 16, 1865, when he resigned to enter the Confederate Army. During his cadetship he was a cadet private in Co. A in the battle of New Market, in which he was wounded. Later he was aide-de-camp on the staff of Gen. Bushrod Johnson and was promoted to the grade of Captain. He was a member of R. E. Lee Camp of Confederate Veterans and of the Masonic fraternity.

After the war he was financially unable to return and complete his studies at V. M. I. and was for some time engaged in the dry goods business in Petersburg, the style of his firm being White, Carling & Co. For twelve years he was chief clerk of Miller & Rhoads, the large department store of Richmond, Va.

Married: In 1868, Nannie, the daughter of Capt. Samuel MacCorkle, of Lynchburg, Va. They had seven children:
Mary Evelyn, Sallie Perry, Anna Blanche, Emily Adele, Susie Tazewell, Callie Warwick, and Charles MacCorkle.

Capt. Carling died November 20, 1911 and in accordance with his wish was buried in his Confederate uniform.

50. Robert Henry Cousins—1867.

Civil Engineer

Born November 24, 1847.

Parents: Alexander Winfield Cousins, Amelia County, Va., and Martha F. Newbill, Spotsylvania County, Va.

Grandparents: Henry Newbill, Essex County, Va., and Jane Crenshaw Moore.

Married: Julia Weber Wooldridge, of New Orleans, La., and they had three children:
Robert Winfield, Julia Stone, and Albert Sidney Cousins.

He entered V. M. I. from Crimea, Va., on February 16, 1864. Private Co. "A," at battle of New Market. Returned to the Institute and was graduated on July 4, 1867, standing 4 in a class of 11 members who were graduated on that day. Retired civil engineer and living at Austin, Texas, as late as 1925.

The following statement is one among many similar ones which have been made:

"In executing this advance the right of the Cadets marched directly towards Kleiser's Battery, and from the beginning of the advance to the time we passed this battery there were no Confederate troops in front of us, and Kleiser's Battery did not cease firing and abandon their guns until we were within a few yards of them. In passing the battery I went between the guns." (R. H. Cousins, letter, May 12, 1909.)

We do not have a complete sketch of Mr. Cousins's career. On December 8, 1886, Donald Allen, V. M. I., '67, wrote from Waco, Texas, that Cousins was with the Houston and Texas Central Railway Company as superintendent of masonry. In 1925 he had retired from active duty and was living at 2004 Whitis Avenue, Austin, Texas. A card sent to him in October 1926 was returned marked "addressee not found."

51. John Thomas Crank—1867.

Railroad Service

Born June —, 1847, near Charlottesville, Va., one of twelve children. Family home bought 1824, sold in 1920.

Parents: George H. Crank, and Miss E. Branham, both of Louisa Co., Va.

Married: In November, 1883, Miss V. Hume, of Sherman, Texas, daughter of Alfred Hume, of Greene County, Va.
Children: Douglas Crank (died in infancy).
George H. Crank.
Thomas Vernon Crank (drowned at Newport, R. I., in Aug. 1909).
Thelma Corneille Crank.

He matriculated at V. M. I. Dec. 31, 1863, from Charlottesville, Va., and was a cadet for the remainder of the session, during which he served as a cadet private in Co. B at the battle of New Market.

After the war he went to Dallas, Texas, where he was in the service of the Houston & Denison R. R. until 1890, when serving as conductor he was severely injured in a rear end collision, near Waxahachie, which left him an invalid. He was a member of the Masonic Lodge for over 50 years. The last public affair he attended was the V. M. I. banquet on March 31, 1923, when General E. W. Nichols, then Superintendent of V. M. I., visited and addressed the Dallas Alumni.

In his last years he lived in Dallas and there he died on August 29, 1923. Interment was at Denison, Texas, where he had made his home from 1883 to 1916.

52. William Beamish Crawford—1867.

Merchant—Farmer

Born March 31, 1845, in Staunton, Va.

Parents: Hugh J. Crawford, Jr., of Staunton, Va., and Caroline Sowers.

Grandparents: Hugh J. Crawford, Sr., and Frances ——, of Richmond, Va. John C. Sowers, and Mary ——, of Staunton, Va.

He matriculated at V. M. I. on August 4, 1863, from Staunton, and was a cadet until the end of the session, during which he was a cadet private in Co. C, in the battle of New Market.

With the close of the Civil War, he moved to Quincy, Ill., where he married Miss Clara Smith of that city. When the mercantile business in which he engaged proved too confining, he moved to Nelson, Nebraska, where he engaged in farming. There he died on July 26, 1892. He had lost his only son by death some time before and one daughter, Mary S. Follmer, of Nelson, Nebraska, survived him.

53. Samuel David Crenshaw—1867.

Invalid

Born about February 1, 1845, about eight miles south of Liberty (now Bedford), Va.

Parents: Col. Richard Crenshaw, a farmer, and Martha Ann McDaniel.

Grandparents: David Crenshaw, and Elizabeth Hobson. Balda McDaniel, and Nancy Hobson.

He matriculated at V. M. I. August 21, 1863, from Liberty and

—4

was a cadet for one year, during which he was a cadet private in Co. D and as such served in the battle of New Market.

He was a fine specimen of a man physically, being about six feet tall, well proportioned, fond of athletic exercise and popular with his comrades. The cannons' roar and the din of battle affected the drums of his ears and he never recovered from the effects of the engagement. On his return home his deafness gradually increased, disease set in, and his brain was so seriously affected that his relatives, after judicial and medical examination, sorrowingly consented to his becoming a patient at the Western State Hospital, at Staunton, Va. He was admitted May 3, 1866. Although he was never violent he was hopelessly demented and so remained until his death on May 16, 1908.

54. Beverly Sydnor Crews—1867.

Tobacconist

Born December 17, 1846, in Belmont, Halifax Co., Va.

Parents: John B. Crews, and Fannie Sydnor, both of Halifax Co., Va.

Grandparents: John B. Crews, and Ann Bullock.
William Sydnor, and Susan Barksdale, of Halifax Co., Va.

After attending the Danville Military Academy he matriculated at V. M. I. from Meadsville, on January 16, 1864 and was a cadet until January 18, 1865 when he resigned to enlist in Mosby's Rangers. He was a cadet private in Co. D in the battle of New Market.

In 1865-66 he attended the University of Virginia and then was with a large book establishment. Later in life he was a tobacconist in Danville, Va., where he was president of the Chamber of Commerce.

Married: First, Georgian Cowen Woolfolk in October, 1871. They had four children:
John Allen Crews, Hosiery Manufacturer, of Chatham, Va.
Mamie Woolfolk, first wife of Dr. David B. Drewry, V. M. I., '93.
Bessie Gordon, second wife of Dr. Drewry.
Carry Leigh Crews.

Married: Secondly, Anna Flemming Cornick.

He died July 1, 1896.

55. John Ashton Crichton—1866.

Teacher—Civil Engineer

Born July 21, 1845.

Parents: Winfield Crichton, and Harriet Hicks.

Grandparents: James Crichton, of Scotland, and —— Winfield.
Thomas Hicks, and Sallie Lewis, dtr. of Ben Lewis.

He matriculated from Diamond Grove, Va., January 1, 1862, the day on which the V. M. I. was re-opened; was a cadet when the corps was disbanded April 2, 1865; and was graduated July 4, 1866, standing 6 in a class of 10. He repeated the fourth class. In the battle of New Market he was a cadet private in Co. C but served with the artillery section during the engagement.

He always lived in Brunswick County, Va., and his career, as summarized by his mother on January 25, 1904 was as follows:

"After he graduated he taught school in Capt. W. Gordon McCabe's School in Petersburg, Va. He was employed on the Norfolk & Western Railroad drawing a map of the road for Gen. Wm. Mahone (V. M. I., '47). Mr. Hoffman and Mr. Hunter (two railroad men), I think Mr. Hoffman was president of the road, were with John on the road from Glade Springs to Saltville, Va., when the hand car jumped the track, threw John in the middle of the track, ran over him and he was paralyzed from his hips down. He was taken to Petersburg to Mr. McCabe's and was there several months. When he could be moved I took him to Blue Ridge Springs. In the fall I carried him to New York to Dr. Neftele; he used electricity. John was very much benefited, returned to Petersburg, and resumed his drawing the map for Gen. Mahone. It was too confining for him, his health gave way and I took him to the mountains again, to Glade Springs, where he died. Rather a singular thing: When he was first hurt he was carried to Glade Springs; was on a hand car with Messrs. Hoffman, Hunter and Fuque. He rode out one day, the last time he was up there, with the same gentlemen. The sun was so hot it was thought he had a sunstroke; was carried to the same hotel and died there."

"Jane" Creighton, as he was affectionately known by all his cadet comrades, died June 26, 1880, and was buried in Petersburg, Va.

56. James Henry Crocken.

Musician—Fifer (not a cadet)

Born Feb. 10, 1821, in Georgetown, D. C.

Early in life he enlisted as a musician in the Marine Corps at Washington and served in that capacity through the war with Mexico, taking part in numerous engagements along the coast of California and Mexico. About 1854 he entered the service of the V. M. I. and was one of its three musicians on the New Market Campaign. While the corps was quartered in the Alms House, in Richmond, he had charge of the ordnance stores and was granted the Sutler's Shop concession. He continued at V. M. I. in these capacities until 1885 when, with his family, he removed to Lincoln, Nebraska, to join his son, William Jacob Crocken, who was graduated at V. M. I. in 1877 and who was at the time connected with the Burlington railroad at that place.

Married: March 26, 1844, Julia Anne Lidia Marks and ten children were born to them:
Francis James, George Washington, Sallie Virginia, William Jacob (V. M. I., '77), Henry Marks (V. M. I., '79), Edward Marshall, Julia Bertha, Herbert Lee, Mary Lucretia, and Martha Rodgers.

He died at Lincoln, Neb., August 5, 1889. His wife died May 9, 1903, at Oakland, Calif.

57. Charles Gay Crockett—1867.

"Died on the Field of Honor"

Born December 3, 1846, at the family residence, "Glenbrook," near Wytheville, Va., the sixth child and fifth son of his parents.

Parents: Gustavus A. Crockett (b. Wythe Co., Va.), and Elizabeth E. Erskine, b. at Union, Monroe Co. (West) Va.

Grandparents: Robert Crockett (b. Wythe Co., Va.), and Agnes Stuart, b. Greenbrier Co. (West) Va.
Henry Erskine, and Agatha Estill, b. Monroe Co. (West) Va.

He matriculated at V. M. I. on February 1, 1864, from Wytheville, and about fifteen weeks later while a cadet private in Co. D he was killed in the battle of New Market.

Capt. Frank Preston wrote four days after the battle:

"In the advance on this third position, we were subjected to a terrible fire of artillery. When within four hundred yards of their (the Federal) line three of our boys fell dead from the explosion of one shell, Cabell, Jones, and Crockett; and fifty yards further on McDowell, from my company, fell pierced through the heart with a bullet."

58. Henry Stuart Crockett—1867.

Physician

Born in Wythe Co., Va., September 22, 1846.

Parents: John Stuart Crockett (his mother was a Miss White, of Greenbrier Co., West Va.), and Margaret Buchanan Taylor, Wytheville, Va.

He matriculated at V. M. I. September 3, 1863 and the following spring was a cadet private in Co. D in the battle of New Market.

Resigned as a cadet in Richmond on January 29, 1865 to enter the Confederate army.

Returned home and joined a cavalry company which was organized in Logan Co., (W.) Va., with the intention of joining the command of Col. V. A. Witcher, but the news of Gen. Lee's surrender changed the plan.

From Jan. 1866 to June 1870 he was employed in a general mercantile store in Columbus, Miss. Studied medicine at night "through the kind assistance of Dr. T. H. Mayo, of Columbus, who loaned me his books."

In October 1870 he entered the medical department of Washington University, Baltimore, Md., and was graduated in February, 1872.

Married: On May 28, 1873, Minnie Hour. They had four sons and one daughter.

Owing to ill health he decided to move with his family to Georgia but before doing so his wife died in May, 1907.

In July, 1908, he married his cousin, Mattie Fulton Preston, widow of the late Col. Frank Preston, of Washington Co., Va.

Mrs. Preston was a sister of C. M. Fulton who was also a New Market Cadet. (See Sketch No. 81.)

After practicing in Wytheville three years he returned to Rural

Retreat, Wythe County, and practiced there. In March, 1882, he was appointed first assistant physician at the Insane Asylum, Staunton, Va. He returned to Wythe County in 1884 and remained until 1892, when he located first in Shelby County and later at Wilmore, Ky.

He was never very strong physically and in order to escape the colder winters of Kentucky he spent the early part of 1906 in Georgia; liked the climate, and bought a plantation near Americus, and there he lived with three of his sons.

Dr. Crockett died September 8, 1908 of malaria in Americus, Georgia, and was buried there.

59. Simon Cullen—1867.

Warehouseman and Merchant

Born April 22, 1846.

Parents: Simon Cullen, and Eliza Trent Roche.

Grandparents (Maternal): Charles Roche, and Mary Archer (a daughter of John Archer and Elizabeth Randolph).

The Richmond Whig, of Feb. 16, 1864, printed an interesting article concerning two Federal officers who escaped from Libby Prison. They were re-captured about twelve miles from Richmond and returned by two lads—"Simon Cullen, employed at Gray's Drug Store in this city, and Walter Sydnor."

He was entered at V. M. I. by Dr. Patrick Cullen, on April 5, 1864 from Richmond, Va. Six weeks later he was a cadet private in Co. B when the corps of cadets fought at New Market, but he was not in the battle as it fell to his lot to be left in Lexington with the guard detail at V. M. I. He continued in the following session until February 13, 1865 when he resigned to enter the Confederate army, thereupon he joined Chew's Battery.

Married: In February, 1874, Miss Jeannette Skillman, and they had six children. Of these, he was survived by: Mrs. Annie Cullen Palfrey; Mrs. Graham Stafford; and Edward Conway Cullen.

"Simon Cullen came from Texas to Louisiana in the year 1869 with several large herds of cattle for New Orleans markets. He settled in Rapides Parish the same year and engaged in planting and farming, especially in the cultivation of Bermuda hay, and in fact, was the first in Rapides Parish, if not in Louisiana, to demonstrate its utility and bring into use this great and indigenous forage crop, which in a few years attained large proportions and was one of the necessary products for forage for large planters and liverymen, almost equalling corn and oats as food for all kinds of stock. In 1872 or '73 he engaged in the warehouse and commission business, erecting a large and commodious warehouse on the banks of Red River at Alexandria, La., which was then the shipping and receiving point for a large portion of middle Louisiana and eastern Texas. He was agent for the large line of steamboats that plied between New Orleans and St. Louis, up the Red River and its tributaries, receiving and shipping thousands of bales of cotton, sugar, molasses and all other produce raised in the rich valley of the Red River. He was elected treasurer of Rapides Parish and school board for several years."

He died December 12, 1891.

60. James David Darden—1867.

Merchant

Born April 10, 1845, near Courtland, in Southampton Co.

Parents: Richard J. Darden, and Caroline F. Pope, both of Southampton Co.

Married: In 1875, Mary Jane Harris, daughter of Newel Harris and Mary Jane Thomas. They had three children:
Newel Richard Darden.
Mary Carolyn Darden.
Minnie Newman Darden, who in 1909 married Joseph Brown Prince, Jr., son of her father's old V. M. I. comrade, J. B. Prince, '63.

He matriculated at V. M. I. from Jerusalem, Va., August 1, 1863, and was a cadet for one session, during which he fought with the corps in the battle of New Market as a private in Co. B.

"In that battle he was shot through the left thigh, falling from the shock, but immediately arose and though bleeding profusely, followed his gallant comrades, when he was again wounded in the left arm, the ball severing the arteries, causing such exhaustion from loss of blood that he was unable to proceed. Cadet Jefferson who was afterwards killed in the battle improvised a bandage from his canteen strap and bound it securely around the arm, which undoubtedly saved his life.

"He was found after the battle in an unconscious condition by Dr. Newman of Harrisonburg, Va., who conveyed him to his own residence, where he was wooed back to life by the skill of the Doctor, and the gentle ministrations of his wife and daughter.

"A few weeks after, his father, also a Confederate soldier, had him transported on a couch, by devious and tortious ways, to his home in Southampton."

He returned to the institute the following session but resigned on February 27, 1865 and

"Even before his wounds were healed, he joined the Army under Johnston in North Carolina, and was assigned to the Commissary service under Major Tannehill. He continued patiently and with broken strength in that service until the surrender of General Johnston with whose army he was paroled."

The war over, he attended Randolph Macon College for one session and then returned to Courtland, Southampton Co., in 1867, and entered the mercantile business.

He died in his home "Lyn Caroll" at Newsom, Southampton Co., on Oct. 31, 1899, and was survived by his wife and his three children.

61. Gideon Allen Davenport—1865.

Insurance—Banker—Capitalist

Born August 20, 1845, in Richmond, Va.

Parents: Isaac Davenport, Jr. (b. 1815, in Hallowell, Me., d. 1896, in Richmond) founder of Davenport & Co., insurance brokers, of Richmond, and Eliza Nye Allen (1819-1889).

Grandparents: Benjamin Davenport, and Sarah Turner.
Gideon Allen and Betsy Nye.

He matriculated at V. M. I. January 1, 1862, from Richmond, and was a cadet until the evacuation of Richmond in April 1865, at which time he was the cadet battalion quartermaster, with rank of first lieutenant. He was graduated with fifth stand in a class of twenty-four. In the battle of New Market, he was the battalion quartermaster-sergeant and served with one of the cadet companies. He left Richmond at the time of the evacuation and was paroled at Danville.

Married: First, Eliza Wilkins (1852-1875), daughter of Thomas C. Bruce, of Halifax Co., Va.

Married: Secondly, Ann Clark, daughter of Alexander H. Rutherfoord.

After the war he finished his education abroad, traveling extensively, and to the day of his death was a student, being particularly interested in matters historical. On his return from abroad he entered the office of Davenport & Co., brokers and insurance agents, but soon took a railroad contract for grading and bridge building. Returning to Richmond he again entered the office of Davenport & Co., and in 1878 was admitted to partnership in the firm. He retired from the firm, established by his father just before the Civil War, in 1898 and although a director in the First National Bank, of which his father was president when it was re-organized in 1865, he engaged no more in active business.

He died at his home, 203 West Franklin St., Richmond, after a short illness on August 5, 1918.

He was survived by his widow; three daughters, Mrs. Harry B. Wayland, and Misses Elizabeth and Mary H. Davenport; one son, Alexander Rutherfoord Davenport, V. M. I. '07; and a brother, Charles Davenport, whose son Isaac Davenport, (d. 1916) was graduated at V. M. I. in 1901.

62. Andrew Jackson Davis—1866.

Farmer

Born in Mecklenburg Co., Va., about 1844 (he was 19 years of age at matriculation).

Parents: John Davis and Mrs. Mary A. Pennington Davis, of Palmer Springs, Va.

At sixteen he ran off from Randolph Macon College and joined the 56th regiment. Because of his youth his father persuaded him to continue his education. He matriculated at V. M. I. on February 16, 1863 from Palmer Springs and was a cadet for two years during which he served in the battle of New Market in the cadet artillery section, at the time he was a cadet private in Co. C. On February 25, 1865 he resigned in order to enter the Confederate army. After examination before a military board he was commissioned a first lieutenant and assigned to duty in Gen. Jos. E. Johnston's command, which was then retreating before Sherman's army. He was assigned to a regiment of mercenaries who had been captured by the Confederates but who preferred to fight in the forces of their captors rather than be confined in prison.

"My regiment was considered by Sherman to be deserters and several of them when caught, were shot. Our commander retaliated, and it was my painful duty on one occasion to have seven Yankee prisoners shot. I was on duty until we reached Greensboro, N. C., where Johnston surrendered."

Married: Miss Annie Lieu Scott, of Prince Edward Co., Va., and they had
    five children:
    Miss Mary P. Davis.
    Mrs. E. L. Faulkner, of Henderson, N. C.
    Andrew Jackson Davis.
    John Archer Davis, and
    George W. Davis.

After the war and until his death he engaged in farming. Died October 5, 1915 at Oakland, Mecklenburg Co., Va.

63. John Alexander Davis—1867.

Farmer—Bookkeeper—Invalid

Born in Bedford Co., August 15, 1846.

Parents: Dr. William Davis and Mary G. Alexander, both of Bedford Co.

Matriculated at V. M. I. April 4, 1864 from Lynchburg. At the time the family was temporarily living in Florida, one of his sisters having married Governor Bloxam, of that state. He was a cadet private in "A" Co. at the battle of New Market and left at the end of the session. Later he was with Capt. Dyke's (Tallahassee, Fla.) battery.

He never married and in politics he was a Democrat.

After the war he was a farmer and then a bookkeeper. While living in Lynchburg he was Captain of the Lynchburg Artillery Blues.

Later in life he was afflicted with a form of epilepsy which affected his mind and he became an inmate of the Western State Hospital, the Superintendent of which wrote in 1904. "The captain is much loved and honored by us all." Some years later he was transferred to the Epileptic Colony, at Madison Heights, where he died July 17, 1912.

64. Lewis Stuart Davis—1867.

Grazier

Born April 17, 1849, at Greenup, Kentucky.

Parents: Colonel James Ward Davis (b. Jan. 17, 1819; d. 1903) and Margaret Stuart.

Grandparents: George Naylor Davis, and Harriet Bragg.
    Lewis Stuart, and Sarah ——.

He matriculated at V. M. I. on August 5, 1863, from Lewisburg, Va. (now W. Va.) and was a cadet for one year during which he was a cadet private in Co. C. In the battle of New Market he served with the cadet artillery section and he was the youngest cadet in the battle, having passed his fifteenth birthday just twenty-eight days before. Later he was attached to a cavalry regiment. His brother,

Geo. N. Davis, V. M. I. '78, thinks it was Col. Cochran's 14th Va. Cavalry.

Married: Helen, daughter of Honorable John F. Lewis, of Rockingham County, Va. They had no children.

After the war he was a grazier and so continued until his death on June 14, 1901.

65. Thomas Dixon Davis—1864.

Merchant—Court Clerk

Born April 16, 1843, at Lynchburg.
Brother of Samuel R. Davis, '74, Micajah Preston Davis, '75, and Creed Wills Davis, '79.

Parents: George Dixon Davis, and Ann Mary Wills, daughter of Hon. John Wills, who represented Lynchburg in the legislature.

Married: Sept. 10, 1877, Lulie Brown, of Alabama.

He matriculated at V. M. I. from Lynchburg on January 13, 1862 and was a cadet until June 27, 1864, when he was graduated—standing at the head of a class of twenty-four. While a first classman he resigned on Jan. 25, 1864, at his father's request, but shortly thereafter he entered again and was the cadet First Lieutenant of Co. C. On May 10, 1864, one day before the corps left on the New Market Campaign, he left V. M. I. on a fourteen-day furlough made necessary because of family afflictions and was, therefore, not in the battle. Immediately after graduation he joined the Confederate army and was attached to the secret service. He was commissioned lieutenant and later was promoted to the grade of captain.

After the war he studied in Germany. When he returned to Lynchburg he entered his father's hardware business; subsequently was assistant postmaster; and later became cashier of the Kris Banking Company. On February 22, 1901, he was elected Clerk of the Corporation Court of Lynchburg, which office he held at the time of his death, June 24, 1925.

66. Jesse Irvine Dickinson—1867.

Farmer

Born April 25, 1848 in Prince Edward Co., Va.

Parents: Asa D. Dickinson, born Nottoway Co., Va., and Sallie Cabell Irvine, born Bedford Co., Va.

Grandparents: Robert Dickinson, of Nottoway Co., and Mary Purnell Dupuy.
Jesse Irvine, of Campbell Co., Va., and Clementina Cabell, of Nelson Co., Va.

He was a student at Hampden Sidney College before he matriculated at V. M. I. on January 22, 1864 from Prince Edward C. H. He completed the session as a cadet and during that time served as a cadet private in Co. D in the battle of New Market, in which battle he was wounded in the leg.

In the following spring he was commissioned a lieutenant in the Confederate Army and actually started from his home but because of Lee's surrender he never reached his command.

After the war he moved to Texas and was a farmer all his life until his later years when he lived with his brother, Asa Dupuy Dickinson, V. M. I. '78, at 3316 Avenue G, Fort Worth, Texas. He died, unmarried, October 12, 1929.

67. John Lea Dillard—1867.

Lawyer—County Judge

Born December 22, 1847, at Martinsville, Henry Co., Va.

Parents: Col. Hughes Dillard, born in Patrick County, Va., March 17, 1817, and Martha Ann Dillard, born in Rockingham County, N. C., a descendent of Major John Redd, a revolutionary soldier.

Grandparents: General John Dillard, and Matilda Hughes. Col. Peter Dillard and Betsy Redd.

The paternal great-grandfather of the subject of this sketch was Colonel John Dillard, of Revolutionary fame, who was wounded at the battle of Guilford Courthouse. The Dillard family came from England to the Colony of Virginia at an early date; settled first in the Tidewater country; and later moved to Nelson, Albemarle, and Amherst counties under grants from George III.

Before matriculating at V. M. I. from Franklin C. H., on May 3, 1864, he attended Bingham School. Twelve days later as a private in Co. B, he fought in the battle of New Market. He returned the following session but resigned March 6, 1865 to enter the Confederate Army. After the war he attended the law school of the University of Virginia, 1866 and 1867.

On July 2, 1872, he married Lucy Dillard Spencer. His only child, Harrison Spencer Dillard, died while attending a medical school in Baltimore.

He was the first Judge of Henry County, at the age of 22 years. Resigned Judgeship and was elected commonwealth's attorney in 1874.

Judge Dillard died March 16, 1875, aged 27 years, at Orlando, Florida, and was buried in the family burying ground at Marrowbone, Va.

His nephew and namesake was graduated at V. M. I. in 1896.

68. William Dillard, Jr.—1867.

Lawyer—County Judge

Born at "Edgewood," Amherst Co., Va., August 23, 1846.

Parents: General Terisha Washington Dillard, born at Buffalo Island estate in Amherst County, Va., Sept. 1817 (Died May 1863) who married, Dec. 5, 1844, Mary Elizabeth Dillard, born at "Edgewood," Amherst County, May 31, 1826 (Died March 1886).

Grandparents: Col. James Spottswood Dillard, and Narcissa Elizabeth
Turner.
Col. William Dillard, and Sallie Stovall Christian.

Married: March 15, 1892, Mary Evans of Amherst, Va. They had one
son, William Evans Dillard (V. M. I. 1913).

He matriculated at V. M. I. from Allens Creek, Va., August 21, 1863 and was a cadet for one session. While a cadet private in Co. D he was wounded in the head and in the right leg at the battle of New Market. He returned home after the battle but later joined his company and at Camp Lee drilled raw recruits until a severe attack of pneumonia contracted at Camp Lee invalided him home for a year.

After the war he attended and was graduated from the Law School at the University of Virginia. "He became Judge of the County Court of Amherst, Dec. 17, 1879, which position he filled for eighteen years, winning the reputation of being one of the most able jurists in the State. He represented the typical Virginia gentleman of the 'old school'—cultured, witty, and with a brilliant memory." After a lingering illness of several months, Judge Dillard died Oct. 4, 1898, at Amherst Court House, Va.

69. Hardaway Hunt Dinwiddie—1867.

Educator

Born Oct 25, 1844, at Lynchburg, Va.

Parents: James Dinwiddie, and Mary Turner, of Lynchburg.

Educated at Lynchburg High School before entering V. M. I. on Sept. 4, 1862. First corporal company "C," corps of cadets, and "on the colors" at the battle of New Market. He remained with the corps while it was stationed in Richmond and after the war returned to Lexington and was graduated on July 4, 1867, standing first in a class of eleven. He was adjutant and valedictorian of his class. After serving as post adjutant for some time, he resigned and went to Texas where he helped to establish the Texas Military Institute near Austin. There he held the chair of chemistry and physics until the school was closed in 1878. He was then elected to the same position at the Texas Agricultural and Mechanical College, located near Bryan, Texas, and later he was elected chairman of the faculty of that college and so continued until his death on Dec. 11, 1887. He was a member of the Alpha Tau Omega, fraternity.

On June 17, 1874, he married Miss Frances Jeannette Evans, (died April 23, 1924) daughter of Mr. and Mrs. C. Evans, who were among the first ten white families to move to San Antonio in 1838. They had one child—Dr. Robert L. Dinwiddie, a physician in San Antonio, Texas.

70. James Travilla Douglass—1865.

Lawyer—Professor

Born Sept. 9, 1844, at Mordington, near Charles Town, (West) Va.

Parents: Judge Isaac Richardson Douglass and his wife, Margaret Gertrude Stephenson, of Charles Town, W. Va.

Grandparents: William Douglass, and Hannah Travilla.
William Stephenson, and ——

During the year 1861, he was a private in Co. "G," 2nd Virginia Infantry Stonewall Brigade, from which he was honorably discharged to enter the V. M. I. on January 9, 1862. He was fourth Cadet Sergeant Co. A, in the battle of New Market and in July 1864 after the corps had been furloughed to go home he saw service with General Early's Army around Washington, D. C. Afterwards he joined a troop of cavalry and while scouting and fighting in the rear of Sheridan's Army, he was captured and taken as a prisoner to Camp Chase, in Ohio, and held for about nine months. He, with a party of some 500 Confederate prisoners of war, was paroled on May 31, 1865, at Vicksburg, Miss.

From September 1865, to July, 1866, he was assistant professor of military science and commandant of cadets at the Maryland Military Institute. Then followed two years of teaching in a private family in Tennessee, near Memphis. In August, 1868, he opened a private school at Liberty, Bedford County, Va., studied law, and was admitted to practice law in July, 1870. Removed to San Francisco, Calif., in August 1874, where he engaged in teaching in Cooper Medical College. Injured by falling bricks during the earthquake on April 18, 1906.

Married: The widow of Dr. Samuel Meredith, who was formerly Sarah Lewis, daughter of Henry M. Bowyer, of Greenfield, Botetourt County, Va., and they had one son, James Hubard Douglass.

The New Market cross belonging to "J. Douglass" was found in July 1915 by Robert M. Green, on a mountain near Oroville, California, and it was restored through General Charles J. Anderson, of Richmond, Va., who had served in Company "A" of the New Market corps with Douglass.

He died in San Francisco, April 21, 1910, from pleurisy.

71. William Tandy Duncan—1865.

Merchant

Born Jan. 31, 1844, near Sheppards, Buckingham County, Virginia.

Parents: George M. B. Duncan, of Tennessee, and Mary Jane Gills, of Virginia.

Grandparents: William S. and Nannie W. Duncan, of Tennessee.
Archer and Lucy Gills, of Virginia.

On February 25, 1869, he married Miss Louisa A. Johnson, daughter of Alexander Johnson, of Cumberland County, Va., and they had six children, of whom one daughter was living in 1910.

He matriculated at V. M. I. on Feb. 15, 1862, from Buckingham Mine (now Dillwyn) Va., and while a second classman he was third cadet sergeant in Co. A in the battle of New Market. He was graduated with the class of 1865, standing 8 in a class of 24. Immediately after graduation he received an appointment in the Engineering Corps of the Confederate War Department with the rank of Captain; served until the close of the war; and surrendered with General Joseph E. Johnston at Greensboro, N. C.

Soon after his marriage he moved to Huntsville, Ala., where he engaged in the mercantile business until his death on Aug. 27, 1895.

72. John Robert Dunn—1867.

Farmer—Merchant

Born Nov. 4, 1846, in Greenbrier Co. (West) Va.

Parents: John W. Dunn and Maria (Taylor) Dunn, of Greenbrier County, Va. (now W. Va.).

Married: Sept. 1875, Miss Mary Henning, of Ronceverte, W. Va.
 Children: Mrs. Juliet T. Kauffelt.
 Virginia A. Dunn.
 Mrs. Maria McCartney.
 Mrs. Mary P. Johnson.
 John W. Dunn.
 Dora Arnold Dunn.
 Gertrude K. Dunn.

Matriculated at V. M. I. Sept. 1, 1863, from Lewisburg, and was a cadet for two sessions during which he was a cadet private in Co. C in the battle of New Market. He was with the corps until it was furloughed at Richmond in 1865.

After the war he engaged in farming and in mercantile pursuits at his father's old home near Ronceverte, West Va., and continued to be so engaged until his death on November 8, 1906.

73. John Cabell Early—1867.

Farmer—Merchant

Born February 29, 1848, at Charleston, W. Va.

Parents: Capt. Samuel H. Early, and Henrian Cabell, Lynchburg, Va.

Grandparents: Col. Joab Early, and Ruth Hairston.
 Dr. John Jordan Cabell, and Henrian Davies.

After attending Dr. Gessner Harrison's Academy and Prof. Holcombes' Belle Vue Academy he matriculated at V. M. I. from Lynchburg on January 14, 1864. Three months later (April 9) he was granted a 14 day furlough because of his health and hardly had he returned to the institute when the corps left on the New Market Campaign. He was left with the guard detail at the institute—a bitter disappointment. He remained a cadet until the evacuation of Richmond and while in the corps Moses Ezekiel was one of his roommates. Cadet private Co. C.

His first military service, at thirteen years of age, was when he carried provisions and supplies to soldiers. He arrived on the field of the first battle of Manassas just as the fighting stopped. At fifteen years of age, or on the first of May, 1863, he went with Lee's Army through the Maryland and Pennsylvania Campaign and served at the Battle of Gettysburg as a courier. He was sent back by his uncle, Gen. Jubal Early, to carry home Capt. Samuel H. Early who had been badly wounded. Then he joined Kenmore's battery and stayed with it until he was appointed a cadet at V. M. I. After the war he engaged for the rest of his life in farming, lumbering, and merchandising.

Married: Sept. 21, 1876 Miss Mary W. Cabell, of Buckingham Co., Va., and they had five children. Their youngest son, Jubal Anderson Early, V. M. I., '07, later entered the U. S. Naval Academy.

He was a member of the Swedenborgian Church, and a man of great public spirit.

He died at his home in Campbell Co., Va., June 25, 1909.

His portrait hangs in the V. M. I. Library.

74. Joseph Rowland Echols—1865.

Merchant—Railroad Contractor

Born August 27, 1843, at Balcony Falls, Rockbridge County, Va.

Parents: Capt. Edward Echols (born Sept. 30, 1817, in Campbell County, Va., and died Oct. 3, 1874), and Elizabeth Patton Rowland (born in Botetourt County, Va., Oct. 23, 1818).

Paternal grandparents: Joseph Echols (born in Campbell County, Va., March 23, 1789), and Eliza Frances Lambert (born Jan. 14, 1795, and died March 1875). She was the daughter of Meredith Lambert and Elizabeth Price, of Campbell County.

Married: Oct. 2, 1873, Bessie V. (died April 13, 1900) daughter of Roderick Douglass McCulloch and Elizabeth McClanahan Nash, of Missouri.

Children: Mary Cabell, wife of Daniel A. Overby.
Harriett Miller, wife of Howard S. Lanier.
Joseph Rowland Echols, Jr., m. Lillian A. Echols, of Texas, he died June 4, 1908, leaving no children.
Robert McCulloch Echols, m. Rosa Van Horn, of New Orleans, La., he died Oct. 7, 1904, leaving no children.

His boyhood days were spent in Rockbridge County, Va., where he attended General Pendleton's school and later Washington College. On January 15, 1862, he entered the V. M. I. and was admitted to the third class. The following year, as third cadet Sergeant in Co. D, he was in the battle of New Market. Hunter having destroyed the buildings in Lexington about a month later, he went with the cadets to Richmond, Va., and remained with them until the corps was disbanded just before the evacuation of that city.

After the war he was a commission merchant and ran a line of boats on the James River. About 1868 he went into railroad construction work with C. R. Mason and with Mason Hoge & Co. and continued in the contracting business to the time of his death on September 9, 1889.

Six of his nephews, sons of Ernest Echols of Glasgow, Va., attended V. M. I. viz. Charles Little, '17; Ernest Carter, '14; Frank, '15; Joseph, '18; Percy, '25; and Ralph Echols, '21.

75. Christopher Melville Etheredge—1865.

Merchant—Insurance—City Treasurer

Born Oct. 16, 1844, Princess Anne County, Va.

Parents: Christopher Etheredge, of Princess Anne County, Va., and Frances Latimer Hunter (both died before he matriculated at V. M. I.).

Grandparents: Christopher Etheredge, and Mary ——. Jacob Hunter, and Polly ——.

Married: Mary Washington, daughter of Washington Lafayette Riddick, of Nansemond County, Va. Their children:
Melville Riddick Etheredge.
Frank Hunter Etheredge.
Mary Rose, wife of Nathaniel Riddick Withers, V. M. I. '92.
Frances Marion Etheredge.
Leoline Catherine Etheredge, and
Laura Frazier, wife of John Franklin Pinner, of Suffolk, Va.

On January 6, 1862 he matriculated at V. M. I., from Kempsville, Va. As a second classman he took part as fourth cadet sergeant Co. D in the battle of New Market and remained with the corps of cadets until it disbanded in Richmond in 1865.

After the war he taught for a short time; was then in the mercantile and insurance business; and later was made City Treasurer of Charlotte, N. C., which position he filled for many years.

He died in Charlotte, December 29, 1916.

76. Willis Melton Eubank—1867.

Physician

Born Dec. 13, 1847, Nelson County, Va.

Parents: Royall H. Eubank, of Hanover County, Va., and Caroline Elizabeth Melton, of Nelson County, Va.

Matriculated at V. M. I. from Nelson Station, Va., on February 22, 1864 and about three months later he served as a cadet private Co. D in the battle of New Market. He continued as a cadet until April 2, 1865. After the war he studied medicine at the Medical College of Virginia and was there graduated with the M.D. degree. Returning in 1870 to Nelson, his native county, he spent the remainder of his life. He lived at Arrington and was a fine man, a high type of the old school country physician, whose life was a benefaction to his community.

Dr. Eubank died, unmarried, in 1918.

77. Oliver Perry Evans—1865.

Lawyer—Professor—District Judge

Born June 2, 1842, near Jackson Court House, W. Va.

Parents: Ephraim Sayre Evans, Justice of the Peace of Jackson County, Va. (now W. Va.), and Ruamy Wright, daughter of Joseph Wright.
His grandfather, Jonathan Evans, was the son of Edward Evans, one of three brothers who came to America from Wales.
In 1876 he married Nora M., daughter of Senator James Talbot Ryan, a prominent pioneer of California. Their children: Perry, Beatrice, Julia, and Nora Evans.

On January 15, 1862 he matriculated at V. M. I. from Jackson Court House. As a second classman he was the second cadet sergeant of Co. B and in the battle of New Market he was the color bearer for the corps of cadets. The regular color bearer, W. B. Shaw, was on furlough at the time. Evans' conduct in this battle was most conspicuous. A few quotations from the End of an Era will illustrate:

"'At-ten-tion-n-n! Battalion forward! Guide Center-r-r,' shouted Shipp, and up the slope we started. From the left of the line, Sergeant-Major Woodbridge ran out and posted himself forty paces in advance of the colors, as directing guide, as if we had been upon the drill-ground. That boy would have remained there, had not Shipp ordered him back to his post; for this was no dress parade. Brave Evans, standing six feet two, shook out the colors that for days had hung limp and bedraggled about the staff, and every cadet leaped forward, dressing to the ensign and thrilling with the consciousness that this was war." . . . . .
"The men were falling right and left. The veterans on the right of the cadets seemed to waver. Colonel Shipp went down. For the first time the cadets appeared irresolute. Some one cried out, 'Lie down!' and all obeyed, firing from the knee,—all but Evans, the ensign, who was standing bolt upright, shouting and waving the flag." . . . . .
"Manifestly, they, the cadets, must charge or fall back. And charge it was; for, at that moment, Henry Wise ('Old Chinook', beloved of every boy in the command) sprang to his feet, shouted out the command to rise up and charge, and, moving in advance of the line, led the Cadet Corps forward to the guns. The battery was being served superbly. The musketry fairly rolled, but the cadets never faltered. They reached the firm greensward of the farmyard in which the guns were planted. The Federal infantry began to break and run behind the buildings. Before the order to limber up could be obeyed by the artillerymen, the cadets disabled the teams, and were close upon the guns. The gunners dropped their sponges, and sought safety in flight. Lieutenant Hanna hammered a gunner over the head with his cadet sword. Winder Garrett outran another and lunged his bayonet in him. The boys leaped upon the guns, and the battery was theirs. Evans, the color-sergeant, stood wildly waving the cadet colors from the top of a caisson."

After the war he studied law at Washington College, now Washington and Lee University, and in 1868 went to San Francisco, Calif., to practice his profession. He soon had an extensive practice and among his clients was Judge S. C. Hastings who employed him to prepare the act of legislature under which was organized the Hastings School of Law, which the founder endowed with one hundred thousand dollars. Evans was one of the first directors and also a professor in the school.

He was appointed by the governor of California Judge of the Fourth District Court for San Francisco, a court corresponding with that of the Circuit Court of Virginia. Under the state's new constitution he was one of the first Superior Court judges elected for San Francisco, he took his seat in 1880. This office he resigned in 1883 in order to resume his practice.

Judge Evans died at his home in Berkeley, Calif., May 15, 1911, the forty-seventh anniversary of the Battle of New Market. Having been stricken with paralysis eight years before, he had been in a feeble condition since his affliction. His son, Perry Evans, a graduate of the Univ. of Calif., and of the Hastings College of Law, succeeded his father in his profession.

78. Moses Jacob Ezekiel—1866.

Sculptor

Born October 28, 1844, on East Main St., Richmond, Va.

Parents: Jacob Ezekiel, and Catherine de Castro, of Richmond, Va.

Grandparents: Ezekiel Jacob Ezekiel, who with his wife, Rebecca Israel, came from Amsterdam, Holland and settled at Philadelphia, Pa., in 1808 and are buried there.
Jacob de Castro, and Hannah Pepper both of Richmond.

He had stopped school and started on a mercantile career when he decided to attend college. He matriculated at V. M. I. September 17, 1862 and continued as a cadet until July 4, 1866, when he was graduated at the foot of a class of ten. While a third classman he was in the battle of New Market as a cadet private in Co. C. (See sketches Nos. 123 and 197 for his remarks on some incidents.) In the following session he was a sergeant in Co. C and in that capacity he served with the corps of cadets in the trenches around Richmond—he considered this one of the great services of his life and it is so recorded on his tomb.

In the year following his graduation the financial reverses met with by his family because of the war induced him to revert to his mercantile profession but from early boyhood he had been interested in art and he soon (1867) began a course in anatomy at the Medical College of Virginia and then did some work in painting and modeling. At this time he made a portrait bust of his father, and an ideal bust of "Cain, or the Offering Rejected." Early in 1868 he went to Cincinnati and while there studied in the Art School of J. Insco Williams, and the studio of the sculptor T. D. Jones, where he executed his statuette of "Industry." On May 18, 1869 he sailed for Europe and entered the Royal Art Academy of Berlin, gaining the Michelbeer Prize of Rome, for his basso relievo of "Israel" in 1873. After that his fame was made and he was awarded many medals and distinctions, particularly the "Crosses for Merit and Art" from the Emperor of Germany, and another from the Grand Duke of Saxe-Meiningen; was created "Chevalier" and afterwards "Officer of the

—5

Crown of Italy" by the King; received the Gold Medal of the Royal
Society of Palermo, Italy; Silver Medal from the Esposizione Na-
tionale de Belle Arti, Rome (1893); Silver Medal at the St. Louis
Universal Exposition (1904); Raphael Medal from the Art Society
of Urbino, Italy; elected member of the Society of Artists, Berlin;
and of the Academy of Urbino, Italy; and made an Honorary Member of The Cincinnati Art Society; besides many others.*

The V. M. I. is fortunate in having two portraits of this distinguished alumnus, one in the Jackson Hall and one in the Memorial
Rooms. Two heroic statues and a statuette also adorns the grounds
and halls—"Stonewall Jackson", "Virginia Mourning Her Dead",
and "Thomas Jefferson."

He died in Rome, March 27, 1917, of pneumonia. Within two
weeks his country entered the world war but long before that when
Italy entered the war he had been instrumental, to a great extent, in
organizing the American-Italian Red Cross Relief Committee and he
had labored day and night in helping Americans in distress. He was
survived by three brothers, Henry C., Louis P., and Walter A. Ezekiel, all of Cincinnati; and by six sisters, Mrs. William H. Brauer,
of Richmond; Mrs. L. J. Workum, Mrs. Bernheim, Mrs. Seymour

---

*"Ezekiel executed in marble and bronze nearly two hundred monuments,
statues, busts and relievos, the principal ones being as follows: Basso Relievo of 'Israel,' Royal Art Academy Berlin (1873); marble relievos of
'Welcome' and 'Farewell' for the Leo Villa, Berlin (1873); marble group
of 'Religious Liberty' for Fairmont Park, Philadelphia (1876); twelve heroic Marble Statues of the 'Great Artists of the World,' for the niches
around the Corcoran Art Gallery, Washington, D. C. (1880-1884); bronze
monument of 'Thomas Jefferson' at Louisville, Ky.; and a replica at the
University of Virginia in Charlottesville, Va.; bronze statue of 'Christopher
Columbus' for the Columbus Memorial Building, Chicago (1892); marble
bust and memorial tablet of 'Lord Sherbrooke' in the Margaret Porch of
Wesminster Abbey, London, England; Fountain of 'Neptune' at Netturno,
Italy; marble torso of 'The Martyr', and marble bust of 'The Infant Mer-
cury' in the Peabody Museum, Baltimore; marble torso of 'Judith'; colossal
bust of 'Washington'; bronze bust of 'Christ'; marble bust of 'Longfellow';
and, bronze statue of 'Eve Hearing the Voice', in the Cincinnati Art Museum; Confederate Soldiers Monument in the National Cemetery, Arlington,
Virginia; bronze group of 'Homer and Guide', at the University of Virginia,
Charlottesville, Va.; bronze statue of 'Stonewall Jackson' in the Capitol
grounds, Charleston, W. Va.; and, replica on the Campus of the Virginia
Military Institute at Lexington, Va.; marble recumbent statue of 'Christ in
the Tomb' and memorial tablets in the Chapel of the Consolation, Rue de
Goujon, Paris, France; bronze statue of 'Virginia Mourning Her Dead' at
the Virginia Military Institute, Lexington, Va.; Statue of 'Napoleon at St.
Helena,' Rome, Italy; bronze seated statues of 'Edgar Allan Poe' in Wyant
Park, Baltimore, Md.; 'Senator Daniel' in Public Park, Lynchburg, Va.;
and 'Anthony J. Drexel' in Fairmount Park, Philadelphia; marble bust of
Thomas Jefferson over the speaker's chair in the United States Senate
Chamber, Washington, D. C.; Confederate Soldiers' Monument on John-
son's Island, Lake Erie; Confederate Memorial Gateway at Hickman, Ky.;
Portrait marble and bronze busts of Franz Liszt; Cardinal Gustav von
Hohenlohe; Benjamin Berkely Hotchkiss; Abraham Lincoln, Bellamy Storer;
Rufus King; and many other statues, statuettes, busts and relievos of dis-
tinguished citizens, and private individuals, in Europe and America."

Samuels, Miss Sally Ezekiel, all of Cincinnati, and Mrs. Rebecca J. Collier, of Brooklyn.

The distinguished sculptor Henry K. Bush-Brown, speaking at the Memorial Services on March 30, 1921, in the Scottish Rite Temple, Washington, D. C., said:

"He established his studio in the ruins of the Baths of Diocletian. . . . Every Friday afternoon Ezekiel kept open house for his friends and here one heard the finest music by the greatest talent and met not only the best people of Rome, but also eminent strangers who might be visiting the city from all parts of the world. Therefore, an invitation from him was one of the prized artistic opportunities of Rome. Here the Queen Mother and other members of the Royal Household were frequent visitors . . . Early in this Roman life he made the acquaintance of Franz Liszt, the eminent musical composer, and Cardinal Gustave von Hohenlohe, the Papal representative of Austria. An intimate friendship grew up between these three which lasted throughout their lives. They formed in themselves a lovely trinity of art, music, and religion . . . After a residence of over thirty years in the Baths of Diocletian it nearly broke his heart to have the government demand the possession of this part of the ruins as an adjunct to the National Museum. On leaving these he was given by the Municipal authorities the tower of Belisarius on the Pincian Hill overlooking the Borghese Gardens, which furnished him a home for the rest of his years, while he took a studio and work rooms in the Via Fausta just off the Piazza del Populo."

On March 30, 1921, following memorial services which were conducted by the great of a land, and escorted by a guard of honor of eight V. M. I. cadets, the creator of the magnificent and impressive Confederate Monument in the Arlington National Cemetery, Virginia, was there buried in accordance with his will among his old comrades. On the top of his footstone is a bronze plate bearing this legend:

MOSES J. EZEKIEL

SERGEANT OF COMPANY C, BATTALION OF CADETS

OF THE

VIRGINIA MILITARY INSTITUTE

Thus, in characteristic modesty lies sleeping Sir Moses Ezekiel, eminent artist and devoted alumnus, who wrote:

"The V. M. I., where every stone and every blade of grass is dear to me; and the name of Cadet of the V. M. I., the proudest and most honored title I can ever possess."

79. Charles James Faulkner—1867.

Lawyer—Jurist—U. S. Senator

Born September 21, 1847, at (Boydville) Martinsburg, Va. (now West Va.).

Parents: Charles James Faulkner (1806-1884), a distinguished lawyer, statesman, and soldier, who among other things was a member of the V. M. I. board of visitors (1848-52); member of Congress; minister to France; and on Gen. "Stonewall" Jackson's staff; and Mary Wagner Boyd.

Grandparents: Major James Faulkner, a native of Ireland, who commanded the American forces at Craney Island, Va., in 1813, and Ann Mackey, a daughter of Capt. Andrew Mackey, a member of the Society of the Cincinnati.

Gen. Elisha Boyd, a soldier in the war of 1812 afterward prominent in state militia affairs and the builder of the family homestead "Boydville," near Martinsburg, and Anne Holmes.

His preparatory education was received in private schools in Ellicott City, Md., in Paris (France) ; and Geneva (Switzerland) while his father was U. S. Minister to France. He matriculated at V. M. I. September 1, 1862, from Martinsburg, and was admitted to the fifth class and was a cadet until January 10, 1865, when the corps was quartered in Richmond. In the battle of New Market he was a cadet private in Co. B. Many letters in the official files tell of his conduct in handling prisoners taken on the battlefield. Capt. Frank Preston wrote four days later:

"Then everything was forgotten but the excitement of pursuit. We ran after them in not much better order, but in far better spirits, and firing as we ran. The Cadets captured from 60 to 100 prisoners. One of my company, Faulkner, took 23 to the rear. We pursued the enemy about half a mile . . . until we were halted by order of General Breckinridge."

Married: Nov. 6, 1869, Sallie, daughter of John and Elizabeth Winn, of Charlottesville. They had five children:
Charles Pierce Faulkner (1870-1908), V. M. I. '93.
Jane Winn, wife of Dr. Wm. White, Nashville, Tenn.
Mary Boyd, wife of Edgar N. Carter, of Vermont.
Charles James Faulkner, attorney, Chicago, and
Sallie Winn, wife of Stephen R. Snodgrass, of Martinsburg, W. Va.
He married secondly on January 3, 1894, Virginia Fairfax Whiting and they had one child, Whiting Carlyle Faulkner, of Richmond.

The varied and useful career of this worthy citizen compels staccato treatment in this booklet. Immediately after the cessation of his cadetship he served as aide to General J. C. Breckinridge, and afterwards to General Henry A. Wise, surrendering with that officer at Appomattox.

On his return home he studied under the direction of his father until October, 1866, when he entered the University of Virginia; graduating (LL.B.) in June, 1868; was admitted to the bar in September, 1868; was elected Grand Master of the Masonic Grand Lodge of West Virginia in 1879; in October, 1880, was elected Judge of the Thirteenth Judicial Circuit of West Virginia, composed of the Counties of Jefferson, Morgan, and Berkeley; was elected to the United States Senate as a Democrat, to succeed Johnson N. Camden, March 4, 1887; was re-elected in 1893; when the Democratic Party controlled the United States Senate was Chairman of the Committee on Territories of that body; on constitutional grounds he organized and led the contest in the Senate against the passage of the Blair Educational Bill when it was defeated; with Senator Gorman, of Maryland, was one of the most active leaders in the defeat of the Force Bill, speaking at one period of the contest, at the request of his party, from 10 P. M. until 10 A. M. the next day, this being necessary to meet a move of the Republicans, which would have forced a vote on the main question which if it had succeeded at the time would have carried the bill; served on the Judiciary, Appropriations, District of Columbia, Pacific Railroads, Territories, Indian Depredations, Claims, and other important Committees of the Senate.

He was a member of the bar of the Supreme Court of the United States; member of the American Society of International Law, National Geographic Society, Committee of One Hundred of the American Association for the Advancement of Science; a Trustee of the Alumni Endowment Fund of the University of Virginia; was a permanent chairman of the Democratic State Convention of West Virginia in 1888, and was both temporary and permanent chairman of the Democratic State convention in 1892; was chairman of the Democratic Congressional Campaign Committee in 1894 and 1896; appointed a member of the joint commission of the two Houses of Congress to investigate the question of the price of railway mail transportation and postal-car service, and all sources of revenues and expenditures of the Post Office Department, under Act of Congress approved June 13, 1898; appointed a member of the International Joint High Commission of the United States and Great Britain for the adjustment of differences in respect to the Dominion of Canada, on September 19, 1898.

After retiring from public life he devoted his time to the practice of his profession and to the management of his large agricultural interests in West Virginia.

In the late eighties he was treasurer of the committee which eventually erected the New Market battle monument at V. M. I. and to the time of his death he was present at the alumni meetings—ever courteous, eloquent, ardent, and constructive.

Known in his state as "The Grand Old Man of Berkeley County," Senator Faulkner died January 13, 1929 at "Boydville", the place of his birth.

(His great-nephew, Harry Flood Byrd, has recently been appointed U. S. Senator from Virginia and at one time one of his fellow members in the senate was his old New Market corps comrade, Thomas S. Martin.)

80. Hugh Walker Fry—1867.

Farmer—Accountant—Real Estate

Born November 14, 1846, at Charlottesville, Va.

Parents: Lt. Col. William H. Fry (1st Va. Reg't, C. S. A.) of Fredericksburg, Va. and Jane M. Watson, of Albemarle Co., Va.

Grandparents: Hugh Walker Fry (d. 1872), and Maria White, both born in Fredericksburg, Va.
Richard Watson, and Anne Clarke, both born in Albemarle County, Va.
On June 8, 1876, he married Fannie B., daughter of William Allen Langhorne, of Lynchburg, Va. They had no children.

When he was a few months old his father moved from Charlottesville to Richmond, where he entered the firm of Hugh W. Fry & Sons, commission merchants, one of the largest in the south. In

April, 1861, he enlisted, at the age of fifteen, in his father's command, the First Virginia, and saw actual military service until May, 1862. On July 25, 1862 he matriculated at V. M. I. from Richmond and the following session while repeating the fourth class he was a cadet private in Co. C in the battle of New Market. At his graduation on July 4, 1867 he stood tenth in his class.

He always took much pride in having, with Sam Taylor, started the game of baseball at V. M. I. The following has been extracted from a letter from him in the 1914 Bomb:

"By the latter part of October, school again was commenced with about 200 cadets. Early in November we were ordered to the outer line of fortifications below the city of Richmond, two miles north of the James River. We were well drilled, and were being continually trained and taught to handle heavy ordnance, until the 23rd of December, when we were relieved by a company of wounded and convalescent soldiers. We were then quartered in the Alms House. . . . On the evening of the evacuation of Richmond we were told to disperse ourselves among Lee's army, and were given the privilege of joining whatever command we saw fit. . . .

"In October, 1865, I was one of four cadets that returned to the Institute. The other three were Marshall, Glazebrook, and Bennett. For two weeks we made up the entire corps of cadets. But in time old cadets returned and new cadets matriculated until we had a normal attendance again.

"In the fall of 1866 I was a First Classman, and lieutenant of B Company. I recall with great pleasure and pride that it was this year that the first game of baseball was played on the V. M. I. parade grounds and the first nine organized. Samuel Taylor,* '70, of Richmond, was my roommate. I have not heard of Sam for many years, and do not know where he is. He was a good friend and a fine fellow. I remember that fall that Sam had returned to the Institute from Richmond, where he had been spending his vacation. The day after his arrival he asked me to accompany him to the parade ground. Once there he instructed me to stand off from him about fifty feet. I did so. Sam twirled his arm around two or three times and let fly an object at me. Instinctively I was in the act of dodging, but Sam cried, 'Catch it, you clodhopper!' So I caught it. Not knowing what the missile was, I asked Sam, 'What in tarnation is this thing?' Sam replied, 'You stupe, it's a baseball.' By that time a crowd of cadets gathered around, and we formed a circle. For some time we were carried away with the sport of passing the ball from one to the other.

"Sam Taylor had gotten a book of Spalding's Rules, and he had been playing ball in Richmond that summer. Garland Longstreet, another cadet from New Orleans, had played ball that summer too. It was not long before we organized the first baseball team at the Virginia Military Institute. That year we played twenty-three match games; won twenty, lost one, and tied two. The bats we used were like those in use now, but the ball had a rubber center, and although it was the same size as the one now in use, it could be knocked further, which accounted for the many home runs and big scores in those days. We used no gloves, chest protectors, or masks. In recording the game we merely accounted for the runs, outs, flies caught, and flies missed. The pitcher threw a hard, straight ball, and in that day the curve was not known. The batsman had the privilege of calling for the kind of ball he preferred, either high or low. Strikes were counted when the batter struck at the ball and missed.

"I recall every man who composed the first nine we had. They were: Ely Burwell, Baltimore, pitch; Hugh Fry, Richmond, catch; Samuel Taylor,

---

*He died June 3, 1914, in St. Louis, Mo., after the writing and before the publication of this letter.

Richmond, short stop; C. W. Davis, Rockbridge County, first base; Mike Riley, St. Louis, second base; Garland Longstreet, New Orleans, son of General Longstreet, third base; Thomas H. Wilkinson, Bedford County, Va., left field; John B. Purcell, Richmond, center field, and Patrick Henry, Clarkesville, Tennessee, right field. Mike Riley was captain. In those days our military and academic duties could not be interfered with for baseball, and we had little practice. Most of our match games were played with Washington College. . . ."

Following his graduation he farmed for seven years, and then worked as an accountant for about thirty years, during which he lived in Kansas City, New York, Savannah, and Charleston, S. C. In his later years he settled in Roanoke, Va., and about 1913 he was an incorporator and secretary of the Dixie Specialty Company manufacturers of boiler compounds and washing powders; and for several years was active in the real estate field.

Declining health compelled him to retire from business altogether, and he died on July 9, 1919, after an illness of four months, in the 72nd year of his age.

He was survived by his widow; two brothers, B. D. Fry, of Roanoke, and E. S. Fry, of Ivanhoe, Va.; and four sisters, Mrs. Jere Bunting (whose son Jere Bunting was graduated at V. M. I. in 1920) and Mrs. Mary Pretzman, of Bristol; Mrs. John Plaine, of Salem, and Mrs. H. L. Burwell, of Chase City, Va.

81. Charles Montraville Fulton—1867.

Died While a Student

Born Aug. 18, 1847, at Rich Valley, Smyth Co., Va.

Parents: Creed Fulton, and Mary Smith Taylor.

Grandparents: Samuel Fulton, and Martha Powell.
Major James Taylor, and Sally Smith.

He matriculated at V. M. I on Sept. 22, 1863, from Saltville, Va., and before the end of the session served as a cadet private in Co. C in the battle of New Market. The following session he remained with the corps until December, 1864, when it was quartered in the Alms House in Richmond, Va., at which time his resignation was accepted. Then he, together with Henry S. Crockett (his roommate at V. M. I.), went to Logan County, W. Va., and organized a company of cavalry but before they received their commissions General Lee surrendered and the troop disbanded at Tazewell Court House and returned home.

That fall, 1865, he matriculated at Emory and Henry College and was graduated in 1869, taking second honor in his class and receiving the debaters medal in the Calliopian Society. In October, of the same year, he went to the University of Virginia, but his health failed after a few months and he was forced to return home. He stood high in his classes at the University, was an active debater in the Washington Literary Society, and could he have remained he probably "would have won the debaters medal in that society. But on the very night that the medal was awarded to Linden Kent—June 27, 1870—his spirit returned to the God who gave it."

His sister married secondly Henry S. Crockett, his classmate (See sketch No. 58).

82. Griffin Taylor Garnett—1867.

Lawyer—Com'w'th Attorney—Circuit Judge

Born Oct. 2, 1846, at "Kalamazoo," Essex County, Va.

Parents: Thomas Burke Garnett, and Virginia Marcella Spindle, both of Essex County, Va.

Matriculated on January 13, 1864, from Montague P. O., Va., and four months later while a cadet private in Co. D at the battle of New Market, he fell wounded upon the field, from which he was borne by his comrades. Before recovering from the effects of his wound, Richmond fell and the confederacy was but a memory.

After the war he entered the law office of Judge Robert Lynch Montague, of Middlesex County, Va., under whom he prepared himself for the practice of his chosen profession.

Married: Nov. 29, 1871, Ellen Douglas, the only surviving daughter of Christopher T. and Juliet Browne, and lived for the remainder of his days at "Poplar Grove," Mathews County, Va.

Children: Marcellus Burke Garnett.
Christopher Browne Garnett.
Leslie Combs Garnett.
Ellen Douglas Garnett.
Taylor Garnett, and
Jenifer Garnett (b. Dec. 12, 1889; d. Jan. 1, 1919, in Brest, France).

He was appointed by Judge Kemp as the Commonwealth's Attorney of Mathews County which position he held for sixteen years, making an able, fearless and aggressive prosecuting officer. During his incumbency of the office of Commonwealth's Attorney, he was appointed Superintendent of Schools of Mathews County, giving up this position later on because of the demands of his profession. He resigned the office of Commonwealth's Attorney to accept the Judgeship of the county courts of Mathews and Middlesex, to which position he was elected by the Legislature of Virginia in 1886. In 1900 he was elected a member of the constitutional convention, representing the counties of Mathews and Gloucester in that body. When the county court system was abolished, Judge Garnett was elected to the Judgeship of the 13th Judicial Circuit. For many years before his elevation to the bench, he was chairman of the Democratic party of his county.

Judge Garnett died on February 3, 1910, closing a distinguished career extending over a period of more than thirty-five years, during which time no son of Mathews County ever enjoyed more fully the confidence, affection, loyalty and love of the people of that county.

A brother, Jenifer Garnett, was a cadet at V. M. I. in the class of 1863.

83. Henry Winder Garrett—1867.

Lawyer—Farmer

Born December 23, 1844, at Williamsburg, Va. Descended in direct line from Sir George Yardley, Colonial governor of Virginia, during whose administration representative government was first introduced in America, when the first representative legislative body met at Jamestown in 1619.

Parents: Robert Major Garrett, of Williamsburg, Va., and Susan Comfort Winder, of Northampton Co., Va.

Grandparents: Richard Garrett, of Yorktown, Va., and Anne Major, of Williamsburg, Va.

John Harmonson Winder, of Northampton Co., Va., and Comfort Quenton Gore, of Worcester Co., N. J.

He matriculated at V. M. I. April 22, 1863 and in the following session, while repeating the fourth class, he served as a cadet private in Co. A in the battle of New Market, where the following incident occurred:

"Colonel Shipp was slightly wounded . . . In the meantime we were commanded by Assistant Professor Henry A. Wise. One cadet, Gibson, received at this point some five or six wounds. Soon after getting up from behind the fence, and advancing upon the charge, to my unspeakable joy I beheld the boys in blue running for dear life; and here I will say was the only time that I remember when complete discipline was not maintained. Every fellow, both among the Yankees and ourselves, went pretty much 'on his own hook,' the enemy routed, retreating in disorder, and we shooting and taking prisoners as occasion offered. About this time I looked off to my right and saw an officer that I afterwards heard was a Colonel, or Lieutenant Colonel (and it may be the same that you mention in your letter to me as having the conversation with Dr. McGuire). I think he had been trying to rally his men; at any rate, a cadet, John F. Hanna (late of the firm of Hanna & Johnson, lawyers of Washington, D. C., and who was killed in 1885 by a fall from his horse), ran up to capture him, but the officer was a gallant fellow and would not surrender. He drew his sabre and he and Hanna had a hand to hand fight with swords, both holding on to the bridle of the officer's horse. The officer would no doubt soon have killed Hanna, but I saw Winder Garrett, son of Dr. Garrett of Williamsburg, Va., run up to Hanna's assistance. The officer seeing Garrett coming, let go the horse and turned to run, when Garrett struck him in the back with one of those villainous bayonets I have mentioned, and he fell to the ground. I have often hoped he was not much hurt, for he was certainly a brave fellow." (Wyndham Kemp, letter to General James M. Goggin, March 25, 1888. Several other cadets also described this hand to hand encounter in letters now in the official files.)

The following session he returned to the institute, with his brother (See sketch No. 84), but resigned on January 19, 1865 in order to join the Confederate forces. He served with Mosby's Rangers until the cessation of hostilities.

After leaving V. M. I. he attended William and Mary College, later studying law at the University of Virginia. After he was admitted to the bar, he practiced his profession and engaged in farming at and near Williamsburg, Va., where he died, unmarried, on May 6, 1879.

84. Van Franklin Garrett—1867.

Physician—Professor

Born July 31, 1846, at Williamsburg, Va.
(See sketch of his brother, Henry Winder Garrett, No. 83, for kin, etc.)

He matriculated at V. M. I. April 22, 1863 and in the following session, while repeating the fourth class, fought as a cadet private in Co. B in the battle of New Market. The following session he joined the cadet corps in Richmond but resigned on January 25, 1865 to join the Confederate forces.

"After General Lee's surrender, I was going South, in the effort to join my brother, Robertson, then with Forrest's command. And when I passed through Greensboro, N. C., I heard that President Davis and General Breckinridge had their headquarters there. And I called on General Breckinridge to ask his advice and assistance as to what I should do. When I told him that I was a cadet and had been under his command at New Market, he was very kind and fatherly to me, and in parting with me said, 'give my thanks to your fellow-cadets wherever you meet them, and tell them from me that they won the day for us at New Market.'" (Letter, April 26, 1909.)

"After the war my education was continued at William and Mary College. I then took the medical course at the University of Virginia. From the University I went to Bellevue Medical College, New York, where I graduated and remained several months longer, dissecting and pursuing my studies.

"After leaving New York, I was offered a position to teach Natural Science in Giles College, Tennessee. I accepted this offer and remained at the College teaching for three years. During this time I acquired a fondness for the profession of teaching and an amount of proficiency and experience in teaching the branches of Natural Science. While a teacher in Giles College, William and Mary conferred upon me the honorary degree of Master of Arts. I resigned my position at Giles College to engage in the practice of my profession in Baltimore.

"While in Baltimore I reviewed my professional studies by a full course at the University of Maryland. I continued my practice in Baltimore up to the time of my brother Winder's death, at home, when it became imperative for me to return home, as my father's age and infirmities were advancing upon him."

On April 29, 1896, he married Harriet Guion, daughter of Francis Tillou Nicholls (General, C. S. A.; twice governor of Louisiana; Chief Justice of the Supreme Court of Louisiana; crushed the "Louisiana Lottery" by veto).

Children: Caroline Winder, wife of George P. Dillard, of Charlottesville, Va.
Van Francis Garrett, of Flint, Mich.
Mrs. Sclater Montague, of Hampton.
Harriet Nicholls Garrett, of Williamsburg, Va.

From 1888 to 1924 Dr. Garrett was professor of chemistry at William and Mary College, and professor-emeritus until his death on November 19, 1932. He was buried at Old Bruton Parish Church of which he had been senior warden for many years.

He was a member of Delta Psi, Phi Beta Kappa and the Magruder-Ewell Camp of Confederate Veterans.

85. Harris Walker Garrow—1865.

Cotton Merchant

Born November 16, 1846, in Mobile, Alabama.

Parents: Judge William Mallory Garrow, of Mobile, and Virginia Louisa Cunningham Walker (b. March 27, 1820). They were married May 14, 1838.

Grandparents: Samuel H. Garrow, and Mary Brown.
Judge Robert Walker (b. in Charles City County, Va., June 10, 1774), and Ann Martha Cooper (b. in New York, Aug. 11, 1782). They were married Jan. 3, 1799.

He matriculated at V. M. I. from Mobile on January 4, 1862, and as a second classman was third cadet sergeant in Co. B in the battle of New Market and was wounded. The following session he returned and was a cadet until the corps was disbanded. One of the last orders published at the Alms House, March 31, 1865, promoted him to be First Lieutenant in Co. D.

Married: In 1875, Lina, daughter of Dr. Robison Miller, of Mobile, Ala. They had two sons:
Harris Walker Garrow, Jr., V. M. I., '96.
J. von Wanroy Garrow (named for an ancestor of his mother).

He moved to Texas in 1877 and engaged in the cotton business; helped to organize the Houston Cotton Exchange, and was its vice-president from 1882 to 1886, and president of the exchange for ten years beginning in 1892. He was one of the best known cotton men in Texas and his advice and counsel was sought and given in the affairs of the Houston Cotton Exchange for thirty-five years.

He died at his home, 415 West Alabama Street, Houston, Texas, at 1 o'clock Wednesday morning, December 13, 1916, aged 71. He was stricken with pneumonia a few days before and his death came as a great surprise and shock to his friends.

His wife, two sons, and a sister, Mrs. J. M. Bullock, of Alexandria, Va., survived him.

His grandson, Harris Walker Garrow, III, was graduated at V. M. I. on June 22, 1921.

86. Franklin Graham Gibson—1868.

Teacher—Lawyer

Born November 24, 1844, in Lewis County (West) Va.

Parents: William Gibson, and Isabella Graham, both of Augusta County, Va. His mother died when he was a small boy.

Grandparents: John Gibson, son of David Gibson, born in Kilrain, Ireland.
Thomas Graham and ——

The Gibsons and Grahams were Scotch-Irish who early populated the Shenandoah Valley counties. The father and mother of cadet Gibson moved from the Valley to Pocahontas County and later to Lewis County, W. Va., where they owned a large cattle growing estate.

Franklin Graham Gibson, the youngest of twelve children, matriculated at V. M. I. from Big Skin Creek, Lewis Co., on Sept. 1, 1863. Later in the session while a cadet private in Co. B at the battle of New Market he was painfully wounded. One leg was shattered below the knee; another ball passed through his thigh; one through a hand, causing the loss of two fingers; another in the cheek. He was removed to Staunton and in June following the war he returned to Lexington where he resumed his studies and was graduated on July 3, 1868. His wounds, seven in all, crippled him for life.

Following his graduation, he taught school for one term near Chillicothe, Mo., and was then elected professor of French and mathematics of Richmond College, Ray County, Mo. In the meantime he read law and was admitted to the bar on March 6, 1873. He was appointed prosecuting attorney of Ray County in 1876 and had a successful career.

He never married and his death occurred on November 3, 1903, at Iatan, Platte Co., Mo.

87. Otis Allan Glazebrook—1866.

Episcopal Minister—Diplomat

Born October 13, 1845, at 114 East Clay St., Richmond, Va.

Parents: Larkin White Glazebrook, the youngest of twelve children, and America Henley Bullington, of Henrico Co., Va.

Paternal Grandparents: John Glazebrook, of Hanover Co., Va., and Judith Blackwell (b. 1779), eleventh child of John and Mary Richardson Blackwell, of Fauquier Co.

At an early age he entered Randolph-Macon College but he seemed to have a decided urge for things military and so he transferred to V. M. I. As a mere lad he had been a marker for the First Regiment of Virginia and somewhat later he was an orderly attached to the Commonwealth Guard, a crack military organization of Richmond.

He matriculated at V. M. I. on December 31, 1861 and was a cadet until July 4, 1866, when he was graduated—standing first in a class of ten and with the rank of cadet adjutant.

In the battle of New Market he was the First Corporal in Co. D and during the battle was the gunner on one of the two three-inch rifles in the Cadet Artillery section.

While still a cadet he founded with two other New Market V. M. I. Cadets (Alfred Marshall, see sketch No. 152, and Erskine M. Ross, see sketch No. 211) the Alpha Tau Omega Fraternity. The first meeting was held at his home in Richmond on September 11, 1865, and the first chapter was established at the Virginia Military Institute.*

---

*Several founders of the Pi Kappa Alpha Fraternity were V. M. I. cadets; one of these cadets, J. E. Wood, was in the battle of New Market. (See Sketch No. 287.) The Sigma Nu Fraternity was also founded at V. M. I. and numerous chapters of other fraternities were established but all were abolished by action of the board of visitors on June 29, 1885. Realizing the advantages of fraternities under certain forms of student life, the board was faced with the disadvantages under a military system where men all live together in the same manner and where one cadet may rank with another in military matters.

Married: October 17, 1866, Virginia Calvert Key (d. 1906), daughter of General Francis H. and Sara Henderson Smith. Her father was for fifty years the superintendent of V. M. I. They had twelve children, of whom five were living in 1911:
Dr. Larkin White Glazebrook.
Virginia Calvert Key (d. 1924), wife of Henry Grant Morse.
Frank Henney Glazebrook.
Haslett McKim Glazebrook.
Otis Allan Glazebrook, Jr.

He married secondly on September 5, 1914, Emmaline A., a daughter of Francis E. and Josephine A. Rumford, of Wilmington, Del. The ceremony was performed in St. George's English Cathedral, Jerusalem, to which city Miss Rumford had gone on a visit to Dr. Glazebrook's daughter, Virginia.

His marriage occurred, shortly after graduation, at a time when he was studying law in the offices of Judge Crump, of Richmond, but his taste was for the ministry rather than the forum and he entered the Protestant Episcopal Theological Seminary, at Alexandria, from which he was graduated in 1869.

The first seven years of his ministry were served in the missionary fields of Virginia; then followed four years as a rector in Baltimore; and three years at Christ Church, Macon, Ga. While living in Macon he was seriously injured in a railroad wreck and used crutches a long time—while convalescent he spent six months in Europe with his brother, Waverly Mayo Glazebrook. On his return he became the chaplain, in 1883, of the University of Virginia and remained there until Nov. 1, 1885 when he accepted a call to St. John's Church, Elizabeth, N. J., a ministry which lasted twenty-eight years.

His interests, however, were varied. Expressed briefly he was Chaplain of the 3rd N. J. Regiment in the Spanish-American War and at other times was chaplain of the Grand Lodge of Masons of New Jersey; of the New Jersey Commandery of the Military Order of Foreign Wars; of the Fifth Regiment, of Baltimore; and of the Southern Society of New York, among others.

In civic affairs he took an active interest; was long the friend of Woodrow Wilson, and publicly suggested Princeton's president as a candidate for governor long before Colonel Harvey became "the original Wilson man." This friendship, coupled with his forty-five years of service in the Christian ministry, prompted his acceptance of the duties as U. S. Consul at Jerusalem. Almost immediately the World War began and, as he expressed it, "the most important and absorbing work of my life was awaiting me." As the various nations were caught in the maelstrom their affairs were turned over to the United States Consulate. Soon he was intrusted with the interests of Russia, England, France, Italy, Serbia, Montenegro, and Japan. All sides proclaimed his praiseworthy administration of this trying task. Said Walter Hines Page, he "founded a new diplomacy in the East and raised a consulate to the dignity of an embassy." Or as seen from the other side by Zeki Bay, the Turkish Military Commander of Jerusalem. "He is not only a consul by man's appointment, but of God's, a perfect gentleman and the ideal diplomat."

After six years labor at Jerusalem he was rewarded by a transfer to Nice, France, the choicest post in the consular service, and there he remained until his retirement in March 1929.

Dr. Glazebrook died at sea on April 26, 1931, two days before the Red Star liner Belgenland completed a cruise around the world.

(A brother, Thomas Ritchie Glazebrook, '70; a grandson, Larkin White Glazebrook, Jr., '18; and a nephew, Marshall Ambler Glazebrook, '25, were V. M. I. cadets.)

88. Hilary Langston Goode—1867.

Accountant

Born June 6, 1846, at Mossingford, Charlotte County, Va.

Parents: Hilary Mackiness Langston Goode (b. Sept. 15, 1815), of Charlotte County, and Sallie Anderson Boyd (b. 1822), of Mecklinburg County. They were married in 1838.

Grandparents: Hilary Goode, and Sallie Bacon, both of Charlotte County. Richard Boyd, and Lucy ——, of Mecklinburg County.

He matriculated at V. M. I. on August 28, 1863, from Mossingford, Va., and later in the session fought as a cadet private in Co. C in the battle of New Market. Following the battle he went with the corps of cadets to Richmond but resigned on March 22, 1865, to enter the Confederate States Army.

After the war he went to Texas and made his home at Beaumont, where he was employed as an accountant with the Wells Fargo Express Co.

He married Miss Helen Owen, of Texas, and to them were born two sons, Benjamin and Elgin.

On May 8, 1921, he entered the Texas Confederate Home at Austin, from Calvert, Texas, and died there on December 23, 1925. Interment was in the State Cemetery at Austin.

He was one of a large family, his brothers and sisters being: Martha A., wife of E. A. Roberts; Wm. E. Goode, who married Amanda Taylor, of Texas; Richard B. Goode, who married Martha B. Goode, of Charlotte Co., Va.; Sallie J. Goode; and Lucy B. Goode.

89. James Hugh Goodwin—1867.

Farmer

Born May 16, 1845, in Louisa County, Va.

Parents: James Robert Goodwin, and Elizabeth Boxley, of Louisa County, Va.

Grandparents: John Spiller Goodwin, and Annie Thompson. Benjamin Chapman Boxley, and —— Hawes, all natives of Louisa County.

At the time of his matriculation at V. M. I. July 29, 1863 his family resided at Fredericks Hall. On the day before his nineteenth birthday he took part as a private in Co. C corps of cadets, in the battle of New Market, where he was slightly wounded. He remained with the corps until the fall of Richmond, but did not return to Lexington the following fall.

In 1870 he married Miss Nora Garnett and they had three children: James Robert, Elizabeth, and Grace. In 1885 he married secondly, Ellie Hutt and of this union there were three children: Hugh, George, and Jack.

He engaged in farming all his life with the exception of a few years immediately preceding his first marriage. His postoffice was Rapidan, Va., and he died at his home on February 9, 1906, in the sixty-first year of his age.

90. Alfred Eli Goodykoontz—1867.

Farmer

Born July 30, 1844, at Floyd Courthouse, Va.

Parents: David Goodykoontz, born in Pennsylvania, and Ruth Harter, born in Virginia.

Paternal Grandparents: George Goodykoontz and his wife, Mary Beaver, both natives of Pennsylvania.

He matriculated at V. M. I. on Sept. 12, 1862, from Floyd C. H., Va., and was admitted to the fifth class. The following session he participated in the battle of New Market as a private in Co. A.* He resigned his cadetship in the summer of 1864 and joined Jenkins' Cavalry which was organized at Christiansburg, Va.

He engaged in farming following the war and on April 17, 1870, he married Ellen E., daughter of John Grayson Cecil, of Pulaski County, Va. They had two children.

He died in Floyd County, Va., on Nov. 16, 1874, aged 30 years.

91. William Clark Grasty—1867.

Merchant—Insurance

Born June 26, 1847, at Danville, Va.

Parents: Thomas Grasty, born in Orange Co., Va., Feb. 17, 1810, and Mary Garland Stone, born in Danville.

Grandparents: Goodrich Grasty, of Orange Co., and Elizabeth Morton, née Coleman, of Orange Co.

Capt. Samuel Stone, and Phoebe Housen Clark (a lineal descendant of Lord Housen), born in Pittsylvania Co., Va.

He attended Danville Military College before entering V. M. I. on September 3, 1863. Toward the close of the session he fought with the corps of cadets in the battle of New Market as a private in Co. B. Later he was sent to Richmond to drill recruits for the Confederate army. After a short time he went into active service and was captain of a company of Virginians when the war closed.

---

*In "The Military History of the Virginia Military Institute" by Col. J. C. Wise, the following appears on page 335:

"Goodykoontz had been detailed by the Commandant to remain with the equipment, etc., and stayed with it until the morning of the 16th, until which time the fact that he had not been relieved was forgotten."

After the war he went into the mercantile business and established the wholesale boot and shoe firm of Bramlett & Grasty, of Boston, Mass. He was later one of the incorporators, with Gen. John B. Gordon and Alfred Colquitt, U. S. Senator, of the Furman Farm Improvement Co., of Atlanta, Ga., one of the largest fertilizer establishments in the south. Then he went in the insurance business and was state manager of the Policy Holders Union.

"Major" Grasty, as he was affectionately known by all his friends, (his rank was that of Captain) died, unmarried, on June 21, 1913 at Atlanta.

A brother Samuel G. Grasty, was a cadet at V. M. I. in the class of 1864.

92. John Bowie Gray—1867.

Farmer—Stock Raiser

Born May 30, 1846, at "Travellers' Rest," Stafford County, Va.

Parents: John Bowie Gray, of "Travellers' Rest," and Jane Moore Cave, of Fredericksburg, Va.

Paternal Grandparents: John Gray, of "Travellers' Rest," and Lucy Robb, of Port Royal, Va.

"Travellers' Rest" was the home of the Gray family for many generations and its name echoed the sentiment of its owners, "Enter ye weary, no matter whence you came and whither you go, and have rest." It was from here that the subject of this sketch matriculated at V. M. I. on Sept. 29, 1863 and during his first session he served as a private in Co. D at the battle of New Market. He remained with the corps during those turbulent days in the trenches around Richmond, and later at the Alms House. After the war he returned to the institute and was graduated on July 4, 1867, standing 9 in a class of 11.

Married: On Nov. 10, 1870, Mary, fourth daughter of Major Bushrod Washington Hunter, C. S. A., formerly Lieutenant, U. S. N., of Alexandria, Va., and his wife, Mary Frances, daughter of Colonel George Blow and Eliza Waller, of Sussex Co., Va. (Mrs. Gray died on Aug. 31, 1920.) They had three children:
Mary Hunter Gray, b. Sept. 24, 1871; m. Sept. 29, 1897, Ernest Deans, of Wilson, N. C. (Children: Mary Hunter Deans, b. Sept. 22, 1898; Aylmer Gray Deans, b. Sept. 1, 1902; and Margaret Roundtree Deans, b. Dec. 12, 1906.)
Janie Moore Gray, b. July 5, 1874; m. Oct. 18, 1905, John Lyle Hagan, of Danville, Va.
Aylmer Bowie Gray, Jr., b. Feb. 1, 1879; m. Oct. 11, 1905, Nannie Bynun Warren, of Wilson, N. C. (One child: John Bowie Gray, III., b. Dec. 29, 1906.)

After the war he returned to his home "Travellers' Rest" and lived there the remainder of his life, engaged in farming and breeding registered live stock.

He died at his home, near Fredericksburg, Va. on October 8, 1930.

The Charge of the V. M. I. Cadets at New Market

The V. M. I. Cadets at the Battle of New Market

93. George Washington Gretter—1864.

Teacher

Born June 9, 1845, in Richmond, Va.

Parents: David B. Gretter, of Richmond, Va., and Martha Winn, of Charlottesville, Va.

Paternal Grandparents: M. Gretter, of Alexandria, Va., and Joanna ——, of Richmond, Va.

Prior to entering V. M. I. from Richmond on Dec. 31, 1861, he attended the private school of William Dabney Stuart, V. M. I., '50. In his senior year he was cadet first lieutenant in Co. B in the battle of New Market and after he was graduated served as a Lieutenant in the Confederate States Army. He was graduated on June 27, 1864, standing 11 in a class of 14.

Married: In 1868, Belle P., daughter of Col. Robert Smith, of Tazewell County, Va. Their children were:

D. Sterling Gretter (dead).
William Cecil Gretter.
Dora A. Gretter (dead).
Mattie Gretter (dead).
Robert S. Gretter (dead).
George K. Gretter.

After the war he taught school in southwest Virginia a few years and in September 1870 moved to Stockton, California where he farmed until 1875. He then taught school until 1898. For twelve years he was a member of the Monterey County (Calif.) Board of Education, and was president of the board for one year. He later removed to Watsonville where he was secretary of the Pajaro Valley Board of Trade. When this organization merged with the Chamber of Commerce and took the name of "The Commercial League," Mr. Gretter went to Pacific Grove (Calif.) where he was teacher and principal of public schools 15 years, and made his home with his son, W. C. Gretter, a druggist in that town, where he died. His son sent notice of his recent death on January 25, 1919 but efforts to get exact date have been unsuccessful.

94. Edward Lumpkin Hamlin—1867.

Lawyer

Born at Athenia, Marshall Co., Miss., January 24, 1845.

Parents: William B. Hamlin, of Virginia, and Lizzie Lumpkin, Athens, Ga.

He matriculated at V. M. I. on July 25, 1863, from Memphis, Tenn., and later in that session he served as a cadet private in Co. D in the battle of New Market. The following year he returned, when the corps were stationed at the Alms House in Richmond but he left on January 9, 1865. He was then assigned to the staff of Gen. Wright and served until the end of the war.

After the war he returned to Memphis and studied law under the

—6

tutelage of Judge Henry G. Smith, after which he was graduated at Harvard·University in 1867.

Being admitted to the bar he was associated with his distinguished preceptor, Judge Smith, and began life with prospects as brilliant as his attainments were great and personal character admirable, when his career was terminated by his death in De Soto Co., Miss., Aug. 26, 1870. He was challenged to a duel by Edward T. Freeman, V. M. I., 1862, and died at his hands. He accepted Freeman's challenge with his father's consent. This was the last fatal "affair of honor" to occur between Tennesseans.

His last words were, "Tell mother I died as I have lived — a gentleman," and to his opponent, "I hold no ill feeling towards you."

His New Market cross of Honor was sent to the nearest of kin who could be located, namely Miss Anna Lumpkin Force, 4343 Morgan St., St. Louis, Mo., the daughter of his cousin and adopted sister, Mrs. Houston T. Force.

95. Mark O. Hankins—1867.

Civil Engineer

Born at Bacon's Castle, Surry Co., Va., September 11, 1846.

Parents: John H. Hankins, and Louisiana Wilson, both born at Cherry Hall, James City Co., Va.

Grandparents: John Hankins, and Elizabeth Winfrey (?), born in James City Co., Va.
James Wilson, born in Surry Co., and Margaret Ricks, born in Southampton Co.

He matriculated at V. M. I., March 12, 1864, from Bacon's Castle, Va., and two months later when the corps left on the New Market Campaign he was a cadet private in Co. B. As he was one of those detailed to guard the institute he was not in the battle. He staid until Hunter burned the barracks and then went with his cadet company to Lynchburg where he saw the artillery duel.

At the end of the session he was placed on furlough with the rest of the corps but he did not return, he remained instead with his oldest brother, Capt. James De Witt Hankins, commander of a battery of Light Artillery near Richmond, until the war was ended.

In a letter to Col. Joseph R. Anderson, in 1909, he expresses his appreciation of the New Market Medal which he had just received saying:

"It brings with it an inspiration for good deeds and noble thoughts. And though I may not have won it at New Market, I assure you I hope to deserve it in the class of Life's Battle, and feel a comfort in its possession."

After the war he attended school for four years under James W. Keeble, V. M. I. '57, who afterwards became a minister in the Episcopal church. His first engineering experience was with Maj. Randolph during the late sixties when he assisted in the location and construction of what is now a part of the Chesapeake & Ohio Railway along New River in West Virginia.

Later, he was employed by the Southern Railway, on numerous branches, as locating and constructing engineer. During this time he was in charge of the original shops at Knoxville, Tenn., and located and constructed the road from Winston-Salem to Wilksboro, North Carolina; the Greenbrier Railway, in West Virginia; and the extension of the Big Sandy Railway, in Kentucky, from Whitehouse to Elkhorn City.

In 1911 he was appointed second assistant city engineer of Richmond, Virginia, and in August, 1915, was advanced to chief engineer, head of the city bureau of sewers and bridges, which office he held until his death.

Married: First, in 1877, Miss Annie Birchett, of Vicksburg, Mississippi, who died in 1899. They had no children.

Married: Secondly, in 1901, Miss Mabel Ligon, of Pocahontas Co., West Va.

He died November 11, 1929, at the age of eighty-three at his home, 500 North Meadow St., Richmond, Va., being at the time one of the oldest members of the Robert E. Lee Camp of Confederate Veterans.

Besides his widow, he was survived by one brother, Louis Hankins; three daughters Elizabeth, Dorothy, and Louise; and three sons James De Witt (V. M. I. '23); Mark Ligon (V. M. I. '25); and John Warwick Hankins.

96. John Francis Hanna—1864.

Lawyer

Born in Philadelphia at the home of his grandparents, Aug. 20, 1843.

Parents: Francis Hanna and Eliza F. Keefe, of Philadelphia.

Grandparents: James Hanna, and Elizabeth ——. Devout Catholics.
John Keefe (son of Joseph Keefe and Mary Leonard), and Elizabeth Whitney Gill, of New York.

Attended Gonzaga College, conducted by Fathers of the Society of Jesus (Jesuits), where he was the recipient of premiums for success in studies and good conduct. Subsequently he entered Georgetown University from which he received the degree of B.A., the diploma was given after the war.

From Georgetown University he entered V. M. I. He matriculated on Jan. 22, 1862, from Manassas, Va., and was admitted to the third class. He was a cadet First Lieutenant, Co. D, in the battle of New Market and later performed further military service as is hereinafter mentioned.

He was graduated with the class of 1864 standing fourteenth in his class.

Many cadets have told of his hand to hand encounter with a federal officer in the battle of New Market, one of these accounts has been incorporated in Sketch No. 83. The jacket worn by him is preserved in the V. M. I. Museum with this inscription:

"This jacket was worn by Cadet First Lt. John Francis Hanna of D Co.

Bat'n of Cadets, Virginia Military Institute, in the Battle of New Market, Va., May 15, 1864. It is presented to the V. M. I. by his sisters, Miss Cecelia Hanna and Mrs. Anna Hanna Forney, of Washington, D. C., this seventh day of Feb. 1916, through B. A. Colonna, Capt. Co. D, May 15, '64."

Returning home after the war, he studied the languages and read philosophy with a German professor. Spent one year abroad in company with Mr. James M. Johnston who was later his law partner. They both entered the office of Judge Walter Cox, of Washington, D. C.

He attended the Columbian, now Geo. Washington Univ., Law School in 1867-68. Received his degree in 1869, practiced in the Court of Claims and the U. S. Supreme Court.

His portrait hangs in the Jackson Memorial Hall at V. M. I.

He was injured by the falling of his saddle horse, Oct. 25, 1885 and died at his home Mt. Vernon, Va., Oct. 31, 1885.

His Cross of Honor was sent to his sister, Miss Cecelia Hanna, 1435 Fairmont St., Washington, D. C.

His classmate, Captain B. A. Colonna, wrote a tribute to his memory from which the following brief abstract is quoted:

". . . Mr. Francis Hanna and his son John Francis Hanna, were my companions for the first time early in January, 1862, on a night stage ride from Goshen to Lexington, Va., and on that stage coach were laid the foundation of friendships that lasted during our lives. . . . We were second classmen and cadet sergeants when Stonewall Jackson's remains were brought to V. M. I. and laid in State in his old class room. Hanna was sergeant of the guard and without precedent or advice he conceived his duty readily and clearly and saw that the cadets on duty at the bier, one at the head, another at the foot, stood at parade rest continually day and night so long as 'Old Jack' was with us for this purpose. They were relieved hourly. . . . After graduating in June following the Battle of New Market, Va., he was along with others of the class of 1864 appointed second lieutenant in the provisional army of the Confederate States and served with distinction on the staff, first with General Imboden and next with General Echols. He also during a critical period of some weeks served as captain of infantry in the trenches in front of Fort Harrison and for his proficiency and bravery received the thanks of his commanding officer. . . .

"The Washington Law Reporter, Vol. XIII, p. 695, Nov. 7th, 1885, in an editorial too long to be reproduced here in full, says:

" 'Perhaps the most positive and conspicuous trait of Mr. Hanna's character was his absolute fidelity in the discharge of the duties of life. His unusual physical and moral courage never allowed him to temporize for an instant. His duty once determined he reckoned not the risk in performing it. Neither times nor places nor the fear of bodily harm nor the taunts of men could swerve him from the line he had laid down.' . . ."

97. John Spraggins Hannah—1866.

Grain Merchant

Born November 21, 1845, at Cedar Hill, Charlotte Co., Va., the home of his grandfather.

Parents: George Cunningham Hannah, and Ann Eliza Spraggins.

Grandparents: George Hannah, who was a Captain in the War of 1812, and was a near neighbor and friend of John Randolph of Roanoke, and Lucy Morton.

Dr. John D. Spraggins, and Almira ——.

His people on both sides were descended from pre-Revolutionary settlers in Virginia; one of his ancestors figuring as a sea captain who carried the non-combatants, women and children, from York-town during its siege by General Washington.

Another commanded a company made up of students of Hampden-Sydney College at the Battle of Guilford Court House.

On January 1, 1863 he matriculated at V. M. I., from Coles Ferry, Va., and in the following session served as a cadet private in Co. D in the battle of New Market. After the battle he entered the Confederate Army, and was made 2nd Lieutenant in Captain Summers' Company, then in east Tennessee, under the command of Gen. Hood. Soon afterwards his regiment was sent to Salisbury, North Carolina, to guard the Federal prisoners there. When Gen. Stoneman's raid released these prisoners, he was captured and carried off to Tennessee to prison. While a Federal prisoner he was mistaken by the notorious guerilla commander, Kirk, for Captain Isaac Avery, to whom he bore a close resemblance, and at whose hands Kirk had suffered serious discomfiture. Hannah narrowly escaped being shot.

After his release from prison he went into business with Daniel and Marshall, of Smithville, Va., then to Hull, Atkinson & Co., a dry goods house of Baltimore, for which firm he was a traveling salesman. After two years he entered the firm of W. P. Harvey & Co., wholesale grocers. He soon gained control of the southern trade of this firm which he built up and placed upon such a solid basis that he was intrusted with the management of their branch house in Chicago, and was finally made a partner. He was a member of the Board of Trade, Chicago.

Married: Miss Annie Carrington in 1884, and had two children, Elizabeth and Miles Carrington Hannah.

He died July 5, 1901.

He had three brothers who were cadets: Samuel Baldwin Hannah, '63; George Baxter Hannah, '65; and Joel Morton Hannah, '68.

98. Richard Walton Baugh Happer—1867.

Auctioneer

Born February 14, 1847, in Norfolk County, Va.

Parents: George Douglas Happer, and Eliza Ann White, both born in Norfolk County, Va.

Grandparents: William Happer, born in Norfolk County, and Mary E. S. Wise, born in Accomac County.
John Robbins White, and Lydia ——, both born in Norfolk County.
He was the great-great-grandson of Col. George Douglas, a member of the Virginia House of Burgesses.

Young Happer ran away from Horner's Military Academy, Oxford, N. C., and enlisted September 1, 1861, at Craney Island, Va., giving his age as 16 (actual age slightly over 14), as a drummer boy in company G, 9th Regiment of Virginia Infantry, C. S. A. He was discharged Aug. 11, 1862 by order of General Lee, on account of being under age. On Feb. 24, 1864, he was entered at V. M. I. by Geo. D. Happer, of Weldon, N. C., and was a private in Co. B at the battle of New Market. He returned the following session but left on January 10, 1865 and entered Southgate Institute, Norfolk, Va.

Married: In October, 1873, Miss Mary Thomas, daughter of Mills Ely Marshall, of Isle of Wight County, Va. There were eleven children of this union, the following being alive in September, 1919:
M. M. Happer, in lumber business, Kinston, N. C.
Minnie, wife of A. A. Pruden, Chaplain and Major, Coast Artillery Corps.
Richard Walton Baugh Happer, Jr., Major, Ordnance Dept., U. S. A., Gievres, France.
H. A. W. Happer, in fire insurance business, Harrisonburg, Va.
W. W. Happer, in tobacco business, Durham, N. C.
C. T. Happer, with So. Bell Tel. & Tel. Co., Decatur, Ala.
George D. Happer, tobacco buyer, New York City.

Mr. Happer was associated with James Y. Leigh Co., auctioneers, Norfolk, Va., until about 1885, when he moved to North Carolina and engaged in the tobacco business in Winston for two years and then in Durham until his death which occurred on November 1, 1892, at Durham, N. C.

99. William Charles Hardy—1864.

Merchant

Born about 1842 or 1843 (he was 19 years of age at matriculation) in Norfolk, Va.

Parents: Thomas Asbury Hardy (b. in North Carolina, March 8, 1800, and d. July 27, 1876), a prominent merchant, and Elizabeth M. Pierce (b. in North Carolina Dec. 15, 1812, d. March 16, 1881). Both parents are buried in Norfolk, Va.

Paternal Grandparents: Rev. Edward Hardy and Lydia Jarvis, both of North Carolina.

He entered the Virginia Military Institute on Jan. 6, 1862, and was assigned to the 3rd class. He was the 1st Lieutenant in "A" company, battle of New Market. Later he was appointed a lieutenant and drillmaster in the Confederate Army and served until the end of the war. At graduation he stood 5 in a class of 14.

Mr. Hardy never married. For many years he was a member of the old firm, Hardy Brothers, merchants, of Norfolk, Va. His death occurred on December 12, 1900.

A sister married General Arthur McArthur, of the United States Army, and two brothers attended V. M. I:

Edward Mahone Hardy, '60 and Thomas Asbury Hardy, Jr., '60.

100. Willis Overton Harris—1867.

Lawyer—Educator—Circuit Judge

Born February 5, 1847, at Mill Quarter, Powhatan County, Va.

Parents: Hilary Harris, and Phoebe Ann Hobson, both of Powhatan County.

Grandparents: Nelson Harris, and Mary Pryor, of Buck Hill, Louisa County, Va.
Joseph Hobson, and Mary ——, of Blenheim, Powhatan County.

He was educated at home and in the schools of the neighborhood until Aug. 29, 1863, when he entered V. M. I. He took part as member of the corps of cadets, private in Co. B, in the battle of New Market where he received a slight wound. He returned the following session and remained with the corps until it was disbanded on April 2, 1865, when he returned home and worked on his father's farm.

From 1866 to 1868 he attended the University of Virginia where he received his LL.B. degree. After his graduation he went to Kentucky and opened a law office in Louisville. In 1886 Mr. Harris entered the faculty of the law department of the Univ. of Louisville as lecturer on real property, and from 1890 until his death he was dean of that institution.

Judge Harris's wife was Caroline, daughter of Benjamin J. Adams, of Louisville, Ky. They had two children:
Caroline Throckmorton, wife of Wilson Cochran.
William Overton Harris.

In 1887 and 1888 he served as chancellor of the Jefferson Circuit Court under appointment from Gov. Proctor Knott. For eight years he served as major of the First Battalion of the First Regiment of the Kentucky State Guards. He was director and counsel of the Citizens National Bank, Louisville Public Warehouse Company, and the Kentucky Branch of the Guarantee Company of North America.

Judge Harris died July 6, 1911.

An older brother, Joseph Hobson Harris, '54, attended the V. M. I.

101. Carter Henry Harrison—1867.

Civil Engineer

Born Sept. 17, 1845, near Staunton, Va. (Nephew of Maj. Carter Henry Harrison, V. M. I., '50, who died from wounds received in the Battle of Bull Run, July 13, 1861; and brother of Judge Geo. M. Harrison, former chief justice of the Virginia Supreme Court of Appeals, died Nov. 22, 1923.)

Parents: Henry Harrison (1823-1912), of "West Hill" near Staunton, and Jane St. Clair Cochran (d. 1870).

Grandparents: Carter Henry Harrison, of Clifton, Cumberland Co., Va., and Janetta Ravenscroft Fisher.
George Moffatt Cochran, of "Elk Meadows" near Staunton, and ——

On August 4, 1863 he matriculated at V. M. I. from Staunton and later in that session he served as a cadet private in Co. A and was wounded by a piece of flying shell at the battle of New Market. He was carried wounded from the field and did not return to the institute the following session.

For several years immediately following the war Carter Harrison remained at home and together with his brother aided in restoring the waste places about his father's farm.

Married: June 22, 1896, Catherine Cook, daughter of Robert Randolph Duval. They had no children.

He then turned his attention to the profession of a Civil Engineer. From 1868 until his death he engaged, with marked success, in his engineering work. The first part of his professional career was spent in railroad engineering and later he became city engineer of Staunton, an office he held until 1908, after which he practiced his profession in that city.

He died in Staunton May 16, 1917 survived by his wife; a sister, Rosa St. Clair, wife of Major Carter P. Johnson, U. S. A.; and several brothers, Judge George M. Harrison, former chief justice of the Virginia Supreme Court of Appeals; Randolph Harrison, of Lynchburg; William B. Harrison, of Denver; Edward C. Harrison, of Augusta Co. and Beverly R. Harrison of Spotsylvania Co., Va.

102. William Lambert Harrison—1867.

Farmer

Born about 1846 (he was 18 years of age at matriculation).

Parents: William Mortimer Harrison, and Caroline Rivers Lambert.

Grandparents: Thomas Randolph Harrison (b. at "Clifton," Cumberland Co., Va.) and Eliza Maria Cunningham (b. at "Burleigh Hall," Cumberland Co., Va.)
General William Lambert, at one time mayor of Richmond, Va., and ——— ———.

He matriculated at V. M. I. January 23, 1864, from Richmond and about four months later fought with the corps of cadets in the Battle of New Market as a private in Co. C. He resigned his cadetship January 1, 1865, about the time the corps went into quarters at the Alms House, in Richmond, and enlisted in the First Company of the Richmond Howitzers with which he served until the surrender at Appomattox, April 9, 1865.

He never married and after the war he engaged in farming on the magnificent Harrison estate, "Westover," on the James River, for the remainder of his life.

He died February 16, 1919.

103. Alva Curtis Hartsfield—1866.

"Died on the Field of Honor"

Born June 5, 1844, in Wake Co., N. C.

Parents: Wesley Hartsfield (b. Wake Co., N. C., April 30, 1810), and Candace Smith (b. Wake Co., N. C., April 1, 1810).

Grandparents: Andrew Hartsfield (1766-1864), of Franklin Co., N. C., and Siddie Pitt, born in Chatham Co., N. C., February 11, 1779.
John Smith, and Lucy Barham, both born in Wake Co., N. C.

He prepared for college at Lewisburg, N. C., and in 1862 entered the University of North Carolina, at Chapel Hill, and stood well in his academic work. On April 8, 1863 he transferred to the V. M. I. and in the following year, as a third classman, he took part as a cadet private Co. B in the battle of New Market. In this battle he was wounded, but with the rest of the corps he went on to Richmond where he was placed in a hospital, primarily because of an attack of measles. His brother, J. A. Hartsfield, of Wyatt, N. C., wrote on October 27, 1909:

"We had a letter from him after the battle of New Market giving a description of the fight. Spoke of putting the Yankees to flight and of pursuing them. Also spoke of meeting me in a few days. He was taken sick with measles in camp and sent to the hospital at Richmond. After he was convalescent a relative succeeded in getting a furlough for him to come home and as the Yankees had cut the R. R. between Petersburg and Richmond, he attempted to walk the distance. The exertion caused a collapse and he was found unconscious in the streets of Petersburg and sent to hospital there where he died June 26, 1864. I went to Petersburg after the war in order to bring his remains home but failed, as I found the graves so badly mixed I had to give up the attempt."

The brief account printed in Walker's Memorial in 1875 agrees with this and it would appear that he should be listed among those who died from the effects of the battle of New Market. A similar case was that of Haynes (See Sketch No. 109) and both of these men died weeks before Atwill (Sketch No. 9) whose death, however, was reported in time to be included in the original lists of cadets killed or mortally wounded at New Market.

104. James Blair Harvie—1867.

Farmer—Real Estate

Born February 24, 1847, at "Fighting Creek," in Powhatan Co., Va.

Parents: Dr. John Brockenbrough Harvie, and Mary Elizabeth Blair, both born in Richmond, Va.

Grandparents: Edwin James Harvie (b. Albemarle Co., Va.), and Martha Jane Hardaway (b. Nottoway Co., Va.).
John G. Blair, and Sarah Anne Eyre Herron, both of Richmond.
He was a double first cousin of J. Seddon Harvie (Sketch No. 105).

He matriculated at V. M. I. on August 29, 1863 from Powhatan Co., Va. In the battle of New Market he was a cadet private in Co. D. The following session he returned; on January 24, 1865 was made Corporal, Co. D; resigned on February 23, 1865; enlisted as a private in Thompson's Horse Artillery, formerly Col. Chew's battery; and served until the surrender of Johnston's army at Greensboro, N. C.

Married: April 22, 1875, Mary Lucy, daughter of William Walthall and Virginia Bernard Michaux, of Powhatan Co., Va. They had seven children:
Virginia Bernard, wife of James E. Cannon.
James Beverley Harvie, m. Margaret Chamberlayne.
Mary Blair, wife of Charles M. Graves.
Sara Herron (dec.), who married H. R. Wayt.
John Brockenbrough Harvie, m. Audrey Gerard.
Jacob Michaux Harvie.
Emilie Glasgow Harvie.

After the war he engaged in farming and later was president of R. B. Chaffin & Co., Real Estate Agents, Brokers, and Auctioneers, of Richmond, Va.

At present he resides at No. 1620 Park Avenue, Richmond, Va.

A brother, Dr. Lewis Edwin Harvie, was in the class of 1863 at V. M. I.

105. James Seddon Harvie—1867.

Merchant—U. S. Deputy Marshal

Born October 4, 1846, and named for the Hon. James A. Seddon, Secretary of War, C. S. A.

Parents: Lewis E. Harvie, and Sarah Herron Blair, both of Amelia Co., Va.

Grandparents: Edwin James Harvie, of Richmond, Va., and Martha (Patty) Jane Hardaway.
John G. Blair (son of Parson Blair, the well known Presbyterian minister), and Sarah Anne Eyre Herron, both of Richmond, Va.
He was a double first cousin of James B. Harvie (Sketch No. 104).

On August 1, 1863 he matriculated at V. M. I. from Chula Depot, Va., and was a cadet for one session during which in the battle of New Market he was a cadet private in Co. D. He returned the following session but resigned on February 23, 1865, to enter the Confederate States Army.

When the State agricultural and mechanical college was opened at Blacksburg, Va., in 1872 he became the farm manager and so continued until he was appointed United States Deputy Marshal. Later he was a U. S. Commissioner; in the tobacco business in Richmond, Va.; and then engaged in mercantile life in Christiansburg, Va. Altogether he lived in Montgomery County about thirty years and the last five years of his life were passed at "Dykeland", the home of the Harvies near Mattoax, Amelia Co., Va. There he died, unmarried, November 1, 1917. He was buried in Hollywood Cemetery, Richmond.

Two of his brothers were cadets: Col. Edwin James Harvie, '55; and Seddon Harvie, '71.

106. Arthur Wells Hawks—1867.

Lecturer—Evangelist

Born December 12, 1847, at Hadley, Mass.

Parents: Major Wells J. Hawks (d. 1873, C. S. A., Commissary General of "Stonewall" Jackson) and Sarah Smith.

His childhood and youth were spent at Charles Town, (W.) Va. While preparing at the academy there, he attended the trial of John Brown; saw him hung; and later acted as courier for his father before entering V. M. I. where he matriculated April 14, 1864, and was assigned to Co. B as a cadet private. Being one of the cadets left on guard duty at V. M. I., he did not take part in the battle of New Market, but he went with the corps on the Lynchburg Campaign.

While there he received an indefinite furlough and went to serve with his father. He was captured near Berryville, Va., and was in prison at Harper's Ferry one month before being exchanged.

His father served on "Stonewall" Jackson's staff as Commissary General; enjoyed his highest esteem and confidence; and his was the last name on General Jackson's lips:

"A few moments before he (Jackson) died, he cried out in his delirium, 'Order A. P. Hill to prepare for action! Pass the infantry to the front rapidly! Tell Major Hawks . . .' then stopped, leaving the sentence unfinished." (Dr. Hunter McGuire's report.)

Starting in 1876 he was continually on the lecture platform. At the height of his career he averaged a thousand miles a week on the road, lecturing to millions of persons and visiting nearly all the large cities of the country except those on the Pacific coast. He was superintendent of the Patapsco Mission, Baltimore, and an elder in Franklin Street Presbyterian church, of which he was one of the oldest members.

Major Hawks married Jessie Leache, of Warrenton, Va., daughter of Dr. Willett Leache and —— Hunton. They had two sons and a daughter: Arthur W., Jr., Ruxton, Md.
Wells J. Hawks, of New York City.
Jessie Leache, wife of H. F. Myers, Ruxton, Md.

While on a lecture tour at Plymouth, N. Y., he was taken to see a little sick girl. He was introduced as Mr. Hawks, but the child meeting him a second time greeted him with, "Hello, Sunshine!" The appellation clung to him and he was thereafter universally known as "Sunshine Hawks, the Laughing Philosopher." Fond of a good story, even if on himself, he once told of a negro in Mississippi who said, "Boss, they calls you Sunshine, but you looks like moonshine."

His platform literature described him as preacher, lecturer, author, soldier, traveler, and poet.

Having been a courier around the camp with his father in the Civil War, he spent much of his time entertaining soldiers in the camps during the Spanish-American and World Wars, lecturing and talking to the soldiers. In the latter he gave two years' voluntary service in the Army and Navy Y. M. C. A. organizations without salary.

After giving his lecture on Sunshine and Shadow over 6,000 times he retired from the lecture platform, in 1925, at the age of 78, and made his home with his son, Arthur W. Hawks, Jr., at Ruxton, near Baltimore, Md., where he died on January 5, 1933, aged eighty-five.

107. Thomas Gordon Hayes—1867.

Lawyer—Legislator—U. S. Dist. Att'y—Mayor of Baltimore

Born January 5, 1844, at Tracy's Landing, on Herring Bay, in Anne Arundel Co., Md. (Brother of William C. Hayes, see sketch No. 108).

Parents: Rev. Thomas Chilton Hayes, and Juliana Gordon, who was a niece of Commodore Thomas ap Jones, U. S. N., and of Gen. Roger Jones, U. S. Army.

Maternal Grandparents: William Gordon, and Martha Corbin.

He was at school in Alexandria when the war broke out but enlisted in the Alexandria Riflemen, which company subsequently became famous as a component part of the Seventeenth Virginia Regiment. He was later transferred to the tenth Virginia Cavalry, commanded by Col. J. Lucius Davis. He then served with the "Wise Legion" until it returned to the east, when he left the army and on January 1, 1862 matriculated at V. M. I. from Alexandria, Va. The following session he repeated the work of the fourth class. As a third classman he served as first cadet corporal in Co. B in the battle of New Market and then continued his cadetship until July 4, 1867 when he was graduated with fifth stand in his class. He was cadet captain of one of the two companies which at that time comprised the battalion.

After graduation he was elected to the chair of natural sciences in the Kentucky Military Institute where he remained for four years. While there he studied law under Attorney-General Rodman, of Kentucky, and was admitted to the bar in Frankfort. In 1872 he returned to Baltimore and began the practice of his profession.

He was elected to the Maryland Legislature in 1879 and was recognized as one of the ablest debaters in that body. Then he went to the State Senate; was city counselor under the old charter; in 1886, during President Cleveland's first term, he was United States District Attorney; and in 1891 was elected to the State Senate for the third time.

Many of the vital features of the organic law of the city of Baltimore were prepared by him and he was called "The Father of the City Charter" when he was elected mayor in 1899. In the four years of his administration Baltimore became known as "the City without Graft".

An old bachelor of the most pronounced type, he was modest and unpretentious though in public life he was fearless, independent, and unyielding. He figured in some of the stormiest political debates that took place in Baltimore in his generation.

The contentment of his home life he attributed to good health—the result of regular habits; the care of his sister Julia, to whom he was deeply devoted; and his profession. The Baraca class of the Central Methodist Episcopal Church, South, Sunday School, which he taught, was probably the dearest thing to his heart. It started in 1909 with forty members and soon grew to more than a hundred. He wrote his own lessons which were published in The Baltimore Sun.

While in apparently perfect health, he died suddenly from apoplexy, at Oakland, Garrett Co., Md., Aug. 27, 1915.

Three days later The Sun in an editorial said:

"One thing which made the late Mayor Hayes a commanding figure not only during his term of office as head of our municipal government, but which gave his an almost unique position to the end was his intellectual and moral courage. . . . The gods distribute physical courage very generously and fairly evenly, but moral or intellectual courage is a far rarer endowment, and is conspicuous by its absence in many public men. Mr. Hayes proved not only that he was not afraid of his enemies, which is a state of mind not at all difficult to cultivate, but that he was not afraid of his friends. . . . Maryland has not many politicians of the straightforward, uncompromising type of Tom Hayes, who say exactly what they mean and mean exactly what they say. May his political tribe increase."

108. William Chilton Hayes—1867.

Merchant

Born April 29, 1845, in Alexandria, Va. (Brother of Thomas G. Hayes, see sketch No. 107 for parents, etc.).

At the beginning of the war he enlisted as a private in Co. B, 15th Regiment of Va. Volunteers and served until September 26, 1862 when he was discharged because of his youth. At that time his father was dead and his mother who was refugeeing in Richmond, entered him, on October 22, 1863, at V. M. I. from her old home in Alexandria. Later in the session he took part with his older brother in the battle of New Market. In this battle he was assigned to the Cadet Artillery section, he having been detailed to this duty from Co. A, in which he was a cadet private. The following session he returned and remained until Richmond was evacuated.

Efforts to trace his career have been unsuccessful. In 1915 his sister wrote:

"He was a merchant. My brother Willie went from home some years after the war and did not let us know where he was. About twenty years ago we heard of his death, but could trace no details in regard to where or when he died. He never married."

109. Luther Cary Haynes—1867.

"Died on the Field of Honor"

Born February 11, 1845.

Parents: William C. Haynes and Maria ——.

On Nov. 10, 1863 he matriculated at V. M. I. from Centre Cross, Essex Co., and in less than a month (Dec. 6th) was granted a thirty day furlough because of a severe family affliction. The furlough was, on Jan'y 7th, extended until further orders. Reporting back in time to take part in the battle of New Market as a cadet private in Co. "B", he was mortally wounded in that battle "and died a month later" (probably on June 15, 1864), at the old Powhatan Hotel Hospital in Richmond. Interment was at his home—"Sunny Side", Essex Co.

Although always carried on the rolls and on the bronze tablet on the New Market Battle Monument as wounded, it was not until his sister, Mrs. D. L. Richardson, of 824 West North Ave., Baltimore, Md., furnished the information in 1904 that it was known that his wound was fatal. On Nov. 11, 1910, the facts were presented by Col. Jos. R. Anderson, '70, in an address before the Richmond Alumni and since that time his name has been included in the roll-call of the cadets who lost their lives in the battle of New Market.

110. Patrick Henry—1867.

Planter—Levee Commission Representative

Born August 31, 1846.

Parents: Gustavus Adolphus Henry (1804-1880; born in Kentucky; moved to Clarksville, Tenn.; known as the eagle orator of the south; member of the Confederate senate) and Marion McClure (1813-1882).

Grandparents: General William Henry (1761-1824; born in Charlotte Co., Va.; lived in Kentucky; in wars of Revolution and 1812) and Elizabeth, daughter of Matthew Flournoy.
Hugh McClure (born in Ireland in 1769; settled at Clarksville, Tenn.) and Susan Gibson (born in Albemarle Co., Va., in 1783).

On January 10, 1863 he matriculated at V. M. I. from Montgomery Co., Tenn., and the following session was promoted (Sept. 28, 1863) to be a corporal. At the time of the battle of New Market he was third cadet corporal Co. B, but during the battle he was attached to the artillery section—being one of the two gunners. He returned the following session when he was cadet sergeant-major and remained until the corps was disbanded at the evacuation of Richmond. For the brief period until the end of the war he was a captain on the staff of General John Adams. In the fall of 1866 he returned to V. M. I., entered the first class and was graduated on July 4, 1867, as second cadet captain and standing second in his class. The following year he was assistant professor of languages at V. M. I. until failing eyesight compelled him to resign.

Married: 1871, Ellen M. Barker, of Montgomery Co., Tenn., daughter of John W. Barker and Ellen Morris (formerly of Louisa Co., Va.). She was a sister of the wife of his brother, Major Thomas Frazier Henry. They had no children and she died in 1890 in Colorado where she had gone for her health and was buried in Clarksville, Tenn.

He engaged in cotton planting in Arkansas and was very successful. This work interested him in the levee problem and after serving in various capacities he became the Washington representative of the Interstate Mississippi River Improvement and Levee Association. For twenty years he followed this work; was widely known and respected throughout the Mississippi valley; and it was stated publicly by those interested in the project that Capt. Henry did more toward reclaiming riparian and swamp lands than any other person, or as Judge Robt. L. Taylor of the Commission said: "This man has obtained more money from the United States treasury for the levees of the Mississippi valley than any other man in or out of Congress."

Always interested in politics he maintained his citizenship at Henrico, Arkansas, where nearby at Laconia Circle he owned a large estate and operated a cotton plantation. He also operated a stock farm and owned a summer home at Clarksville, Tennessee, where he died on November 23, 1908.

111. Philip Barbour Hiden—1865.

Lawyer—Teacher—Clerk

Born May 22, 1842 in Orange, Va.

Parents: Joseph Hiden (son of Joseph, and member of Va. Legislature) and Cornelia Upshur Terrill (née Nalle), both of Orange, Va. Her father was Martin Nalle (See Sketch No. 174).

He served as a private in the 13th Virginia Infantry from April 1861 until Christmas. Entered V. M. I. January 9, 1862 from Orange and was admitted to the third class, but on January 27th was transferred to the fourth class. He continued his cadetship until he was a first classman and the corps was disbanded on April 2, 1865. At graduation he stood 23 in his class. As a second classman he was a private in Co. A in the battle of New Market. His studies were continued at the University of Virginia and at Washington College; the degree B.L. was awarded at the latter in 1867.

Married: Bettie Hawes, daughter of James R. Goodwin, of Louisa Co., Va. She died May 3, 1914 in Washington, D. C.

He was the first mayor of Orange, Va., after its re-incorporation in 1871 and he practiced law there for many years; engaged in farming for a time and then entered the employ of the U. S. Indian service and taught in the Indian Schools in Arizona. For the last ten years of his life he was employed in the General Land Office, in Washington, D. C.

He died while on a visit to the home of his son, P. W. Hiden, Newport News, Va., January 7, 1915 and was buried in Rock Creek Cemetery, Washington, D. C., by the side of his wife; survived by six children, two daughters and four sons:

Lizzie C., wife of W. S. Hoge, Jr., of Washington, D. C.
Nannie M. Hiden, of Conway, Arkansas.
Dr. Martin B. Hiden, of the United States Navy.
J. George Hiden, attorney of Culpeper, Va.
Wm. C. Hiden, of Silver Springs, Md.
Phillip W. Hiden, of Newport News, Va.

His brother Rev. Dr. James Conway Hiden, was graduated at V. M. I. in 1857.

112. A(rchibald) Govan Hill—1859.

Teacher—Accountant

Born February 10, 1839, in King William Co., Va.

Parents: Edward Hill, and Elizabeth T. Govan, both of King William Co., Va.

Grandparents: John Hill, and Fannie ——, both born in King William Co. James Govan, who emigrated from Scotland, and Betsy Garlick. They lived in King William Co.

After attending Rumford Academy, in King William Co., presided over by John H. Pitts, V. M. I., '44, for about three years, he matriculated at V. M. I. on July 30, 1856 and was admitted to the third class. He was graduated on July 4, 1859, standing 18 in a class of 29, of these 23 were graduated. Twenty-eight of his twenty-nine classmates held commissions in the Confederate Army and one became a Colonel in the Federal Army.

He taught a year in Powhatan County and then entered the University of Virginia where he studied until "towards the close of the session (1860-61) we formed a company called 'The Sons of Liberty' for drilling and were afterwards ordered to Harper's Ferry, where we remained about a week. We returned to the University, stood a few examinations, and afterwards I was chosen 1st Lieutenant Co. H, 53rd Va. Reg't and served on the Peninsular under Gen. Magruder." In the fall of 1862 he was appointed Lieutenant and assistant instructor in French and Tactics; in the following session, 1863-64, his teaching duties were the same but he was promoted to be a captain and as such was the tactical officer in charge of Co. C, corps of cadets, in the battle of New Market, where he was seriously wounded early in the battle by a shell which fractured his skull. He was away on furlough for six months but returned and continued teaching at V. M. I. until the evacuation of Richmond.

Married: Bettie A. Vest, of Louisa Co., and they had three children:
A(rchibald) Govan Hill, Jr.; J(ames) Murry Hill; and Blanche Vest Hill who married Edward N. Vest, of Charlottesville, in November 1920, at the home of her uncle C. B. Vest, in Louisa County.

After the war he continued teaching (Goshen, Va.; and the following in Tennessee: Paris Male Academy; Masonic High School, Gallatin; Columbia High School) for about five years and then went to Florida with the intent of raising oranges but the Agricultural College was then being constructed and he was offered the position of custodian before its completion. He remained in Florida about five years and then moved to Portsmouth, Va., where he engaged in merchandizing for about eight years. He then went to Central America as Professor of English in the government College, El Liceo de Costa Rica. On his return he was an instructor in modern languages at the Louisa high school and then was a bank accountant in Louisa until he suffered a paralytic stroke.

"One incident I mention. Capt. Von Kleiser, who was a Yankee Captain of a battery* at New Market after the war boarded at the same hotel as myself. We became quite well acquainted and he afterwards taught me the German language. The cadets captured one of his guns at New Market. Capt. Von Kleiser was an ex-officer in the Austrian army."

He died at his home in Green Spring, Louisa Co., Va., on October 20, 1914 and was buried with Masonic honors at "Corduroy," the residence of Capt. C. B. Vest in Louisa County.

---

*"Four hundred yards to the front of his main position, Sigel placed the 123d Ohio and 18th Connecticut, of Moor's Brigade, the left of the former resting on the pike and the latter prolonging the line to its right; Von Kleiser's 30th New York Battery, with six 12-pounder Napoleons, took position across the pike, and abreast of Moor's right." (Wise's Mil. Hist. of V. M. I., p. 309.)

Two of his brothers and a grandson attended V. M. I.: Edward Carmichael Hill, '59; William Moorman Hill, '68; and A. Govan Hill, '33.

113. James Maurice Hill—1867.

Farmer—Canner

Born January 21, 1846, at Rural Retreat, Hanover Co., Va. The acceptance of his appointment in 1863 is signed J. Morris Hill.

Parents: Walker R. Hill, and Susan N. Tiernan.

Grandparents: James Hill, and Mary Walker, of Charles City, Va.
Dr. James Tiernan, and Elizabeth Lewis, of Powhatan Co., Va.

After studying at Powhatan Academy and at Washington and Henry Academy (Hanover Co.) he matriculated at V. M. I., February 27, 1864 and remained until the close of the war. In the battle of New Market he was a cadet private in Co. A.

Married: March 6, 1877, Lucy, daughter of Capt. William Royall, of Powhatan Co., Va., and to them were born seven children: Royall, Maurice, Claiborne, Mortimer, Willie, Mabel, and Ella.

After the war he engaged in farming and conducted a large cannery until 1892 when he moved to Los Angeles. He was a trustee of Washington and Henry Academy and Secretary of the board of trustees; took an active part in church affairs; and was superintendent of the Methodist Sunday School at Shady Grove Church in Hanover Co., Va.

In 1909 his address was 1309 Southerland St., Los Angeles, California, but efforts to get in touch with him in recent years have been unsuccessful.

114. John Horsley—1866.

Farmer

Born February 21, 1845, at "Mountain Retreat," near Lovingston, Nelson County, Va.

Parents: John Horsley, merchant and farmer, and Mary Mildred Cabell.

Grandparents: William Horsley, a lieutenant in the United States Army, and Martha Megginson.
Frederick Cabell and Alice Winston.

In the Spring of 1861, he enlisted in company H, 49th Virginia regiment, Early's brigade, Jackson's corps, and was honorably discharged immediately after the first battle of Fredericksburg (December 1862). He had enlisted without his mother's consent and she secured his discharge on the plea of his being under age and in order to have him attend the Virginia Military Institute. He matriculated on February 23, 1863, from Lovingston, Nelson county, Va., and was a private in Co. "D" at the battle of New Market. In the fall of 1864 he joined Colonel John S. Mosby's brigade and remained with him until the close of the war. About April 12, 1865, he took

—7

part in a skirmish between Mosby's men and a body of Federals who were on a gunboat at the Rappahannock river.

As soon as the war was over he returned home and commenced to farm. This, combined with the cattle and apple business, he followed until his death.

On October 14, 1868, he married Rose, daughter of Dr. John Shelton and
his wife, —— Diggs. There were born to them three sons:
Dr. J. Shelton Horsley of Richmond, Va.
Dr. Frederick Cabell Horsley of Lovingston.
Guy W. Horsley, who died when young in New Mexico.
Mrs. Rose Shelton Horsley died on December 11, 1911.

Mr. Horsley held many places of honor and trust in the county government, having been at different times one of the commissioners of revenue, a member of the board of supervisors, a land assessor, a school trustee, member of the school electoral board, and a member of the board of review.

On Sunday, July 2, 1922, while talking with his son, Dr. J. Shelton Horsley, who had come from Richmond to see him, he was paralyzed, and without regaining consciousness, died at his home, "Mountain Retreat," the following Thursday, (July 6th).

A grandson, Caperton Braxton Horsley, was in the class of 1923 at V. M. I.

115. John Clarke Howard—1866.

Civil Engineer—Railroad Service

Born February 27, 1846, at Richmond, Va.

Parents: Thomas C. Howard (b. in Richmond in January, 1816), and Rosabelle Elizabeth Burfoot.

Grandparents: Thomas Chester Howard, of York County, Va., and Eliza
Washington Pope.
Matthew Burfoot, and the widow of —— Wooldridge, née Julia Lavinia Clarke.

He entered V. M. I. on September 1, 1862, from Scottsville, Va., but resigned his cadetship on October 11th. On July 30, 1863, he re-entered and served as a cadet private in Co. A at the battle of New Market,* receiving a slight wound in one hand.

"With the rest of the corps in 1864 I was furloughed, and proceeded to my home. I did not return to the Institute, resigning and entering the Confederate Army—the Powhatan Artillery, with which I remained until the close of the war. I studied law at the University of Virginia during the session of 1867-68, but practiced a very short time, circumstances seeming to point me toward civil engineering."

Mr. Howard followed transportation and the civil engineering profession all his life, being employed by many different companies. In 1903 he was with the Seaboard Air Line Railway. His last position

*"Recollections of the Battle of New Market" by him were printed in the Confederate Veteran vol. 34, pp. 57-59 (1926). One of the best written accounts of the battle and of the feelings and thoughts of a participant. It should be read as a whole and its length precludes inclusion here.

was record clerk in the traffic department of the Richmond, Fredericksburg and Potomac Railroad.

On November 25, 1874, he married Mary, his first cousin, daughter of Edward Calthorpe Howard, of Richmond, Va. In 1884 a son was born to them but he lived only a year. This loss was replaced in 1887 by the birth of twins, Edward Thomas and Ethel, wife of Dr. W. A. R. Goodwin, of Williamsburg, Va. Mrs. Howard died at her home in Ashland on January 14, 1918.

He died at the home of his daughter in Williamsburg on December 6, 1925. The funeral took place from Bruton Parish Church and interment was in Hollywood Cemetery at Richmond.

116. William James Hubard—1865.

Teacher—Civil Engineer—Lecturer

Born February 8, 1845 in Philadelphia, Pa.

Parents: William James Hubard (of England, a distinguished sculptor who cast in bronze the Houdon Washington Statue,* and who was killed by an explosion while working with Commander John M. Brooke on shells for use in guns of the iron-clad "Merrimac") and Maria Mason Tabb, of Gloucester Co., Va.

Grandparents: William James Hubard, of England, and Mary —— Thomas Tabb, of Gloucester Co., Va., and Lucy ——

He matriculated at V. M. I., March 11, 1862 from Richmond and was a cadet save for a short period until April 2, 1865 when the corps was disbanded; at graduation he stood 17 in his class. As a second classman he was a cadet private in Co. A in the battle of New Market. The following autumn he was commissioned a lieutenant in the First Confederate Foreign Battalion and so served from November 1864 until he re-entered the institute on February 23, 1865 and for the remainder of the session was private secretary to the commandant, Scott Shipp.

Married: Mary Booth (d. May 8, 1924), daughter of Nathaniel W. Troutman, of Long Branch, N. J.

After the war he taught school for several years and then was engaged in civil engineering and in business until 1896 when he was employed as Assistant Lecturer and then, in 1898, as Grand Lecturer of the Grand Royal Arch Chapter of Masons of Virginia and in this work he continued until his death.

He was a prominent member of many Masonic orders and in 1901 was Grand High Priest of the Grand Chapter of the Royal Arch Masons of Virginia, which in 1924 established as a memorial to him "The W. J. Hubard Scholarship." The proceeds of a five thousand dollar fund are annually used for the assistance of a worthy cadet

---

*This statue, unveiled at V. M. I. July 4, 1856, was the first bronze statue to be cast whole in the United States—two failures preceded the successful casting. The statue was carried off by Hunter's raiders in 1864 but was restored in 1866.

at the Virginia Military Institute, the beneficiary being selected by the Grand Chapter.

He died at his home, 103 East Grace St., Richmond, Va., April 20, 1917, and was buried in Hollywood Cemetery.

He was survived by his widow and one son, N. Walter Hubard, V. M. I., '98, of Richmond.

117. Charles Buckler Hundley—1867.

Farmer—Merchant

Born November 15, 1846, at Montague, Essex Co., Va.

Parents: Dr. Thomas James Hundley, b. Rose Hill, Essex Co., and Maria Emily Layton, of Essex Co.

Grandparents: Capt. Larkin Hundley, b. Rose Hill, Essex Co., Va., and Victoria Montague.
Capt. Charles Grymes Layton, of Essex Co., and ——

He matriculated at V. M. I. on March 3, 1864 from Montague, Va., and a few months later was a cadet private in Co. B in the battle of New Market. Between the end of the session and the end of the furlough, when the cadets reported for duty in the trenches around Richmond on October first, he served with Mosby's Battalion. His cadetship terminated with the evacuation of Richmond.

After the war he worked for a railroad, engaged in farming, and then operated a general merchandise store at Lakeview, Va.

He died, unmarried, at the home of his brother, Alwyn Hundley, in Fredericksburg, Va., after a lingering illness of Bright's disease, on October 6, 1908. Interment was in the family burying ground at his former home in Essex County. Survived by his brother and a sister.

118. Robert Craig Hupp—1867.

Railroad Service

Born April 13, 1846, at Salem, Va.

Parents: Abraham P. Hupp, Captain of the Hupp-Griffin Battery or Salem Flying Artillery until killed in battle in 1862, and Columbia Ann Huff.

He matriculated at V. M. I. May 30, 1863; was admitted to the fifth class; and was a cadet until January 27, 1865, when he resigned to enter the army. He was a cadet private in Co. B in May 1864 but was not in the battle of New Market.

"I was at my home in Salem on a short sick leave of absence and in the meantime the Cadet Corps was ordered out and so quickly that the battle was fought and ended before I had heard of it. . . . I was with the corps on all the other marches to points on the C. & O. Rwy., Millboro, Goshen, etc., to repel the expected raiders and down the canal tow path from the Institute to Lynchburg when driven out by Hunter from Lexington. . . . We were under fire in front of the Institute, while Gen. McCausland's batteries were firing from an elevated point on our parade ground and Gen. Hunter was bombarding us from the hill across the river. We moved to the churchyard, a little nearer town; soon we were ordered to march in the direction of Lynchburg."

On leaving the institute he

"went immediately to the lines in front of Richmond and joined Capt. 'Griffin's Battery of Artillery' (formerly 'Hupp's Battery') and was with them over two months, until we surrendered at Appomattox C. H. It was a very brief service but it was full of excitement all the while, especially during the evacuation of Richmond and the hasty, rapid march to Appomattox."

The war ended he spent the remainder of his life in the railroad business in the auditing and traffic departments. For many years he was with the freight traffic department of the Michigan Central Railroad, in Detroit, but because of his health he spent the winters in the South in his later years.

He died, unmarried, in Cumberland, Md., on May 24, 1918 of pneumonia and is buried in Woodlawn Cemetery, Detroit, Mich., beside his brother, Charles J. Hupp, with whom he had long been associated in the railroad business.

119. Jacob Peck Imboden—1867.

Mining Engineer

Born September 15, 1846, at Christian's Creek farm, Augusta Co., Va.

Parents: George Imboden, and Isabella Wünderlich.

Grandparents: John Imboden and ——, of Christian's Creek, Augusta Co., Va.
Daniel Wünderlich and Susana Saunders.

He was one of five brothers who gained distinction for bravery in the Confederate Army, and all continued in service until the surrender of General Lee. The others were Gen. John D.; Col. George W.; Major James A.; and Capt. Francis M. Imboden. The last named, V. M. I., '64, and Gen. Imboden were with the regular troops at New Market when their younger brother fought there as a cadet.

Matriculated at V. M. I. from Waynesboro, Va., on March 31, 1864 and a few weeks later took part in the battle of New Market as a cadet private in Co. D and was there slightly wounded by a fragment of shell. He did not return to the Institute after the session ended but joined Capt. Frank's Company of Mosby's Battalion and remained with it until the end of the war.

Married: Johnnie Meems, of Kentucky, who died in Richmond, Va. Later he married, secondly, Anna Stuart Dickenson, of West Virginia.

After the war he engaged in mining in Missouri and West Virginia, later going to Georgia as superintendent for a mining company there.

From 1884 until his death managed mines which he owned in Central America.

On December 3, 1899 he was murderously wounded at San Pedro Sula, Honduras, by a native, Joaquin Hernandes, with whom he had had no difficulty but who was endeavoring to murder one of Imboden's friends. The friend recovered from the three bullets which struck him but Imboden, who was shot in the body, died two days later, December 5, 1899.

He was survived by his widow and three children: Frank Bliss Imboden; George Howard Imboden; and Gertrude Imboden.

120. Fleming Wills James—1868.

Educator—Soldier—Jurist—Financier

Born April 11, 1847 in Richmond, Va. Brother of John Garland James (See sketch No. 121).

Parents: Henry James, a merchant of Richmond, born in Hanover Co., Va., and Eliza Maria Wills, of Fluvanna Co., Va.

Grandparents: Rev. Garland James, of Hanover Co., Va., and Sallie Peatross, of Caroline Co., Va.
Dr. John Wills, of Fluvanna Co., and Mary Maria Quarles, of Louisa Co., Va.

Matriculated at V. M. I. from Richmond on August 11, 1862 and as a third classman was cadet private in Co. A at the battle of New Market. The following session he was a member of the corps in the second class until it was disbanded on April 2, 1865 after which he served as a lieutenant of infantry in Hardee's Corps on its retreat from South Carolina and was then transferred to A. P. Stewart's Corps with which he remained until Gen. Johnston's Army was surrendered at Greensboro, N. C., where he was paroled.

His father's business having been destroyed in the conflagration when Richmond was evacuated he had to go to work. His older brother, however, had been able to return to the V. M. I. by being allowed easy tuition terms and after he was graduated the subject of this sketch returned to V. M. I. on Sept. 8, 1866, repeated the work of the second class, and was graduated July 3, 1868 with first stand in his class, and was fourth cadet captain. The first three years of his cadetship he was in the class of 1866. In the class with which he is identified, and was graduated, there were three other Richmond boys who had distinguished careers: Dr. Charles A. Ellett, Col. John B. Purcell, and Hon. Melville I. Branch, later of Georgia.

Married: June 27, 1870, Isobel May Porter (d. 1922), of Austin, Texas.
Their children living in 1905 were:
Henry James, of Abilene, Texas.
Mrs. Isobel J. Hodsen, of Mickleson, England.
Mrs. Edith M. Hardin, of Big Springs, Texas (died later).
Winfield Scott James, of Roscoe, Texas.

After graduation he went to Texas and, with his two brothers (See Sketch No. 121), organized the Texas Military Institute. There he was professor of Engineering and Tactics and was commandant until 1879. During the reconstruction era he organized the volunteer militia of Texas, being commissioned as Colonel and as the force increased in size he was promoted until he became Major General in charge of the organization.

Meantime he studied law and practiced his profession in Austin, in Weatherford, Colo., and Blair, Texas; served as county judge and twice as judge of the 32nd District of Texas. In 1884 he organized and was president of the First National Bank, at Baird, Texas. In 1889 he organized the Farmers' and Merchants' National Bank, of Abilene, Texas, of which he became the managing vice-president; he also organized and built the Roscoe, Snyder, & Pacific Rwy.; organized the Abilene Trust Co., of which he was president and general counsel for many years, and many other financial institutions. He brought millions of dollars of eastern capital to West Texas.

In matters political he was always active but held no office. Member, Board of Managers of the Texas Epileptic Colony.

General James died in Abilene, Texas, September 21, 1918, following an illness of ten days. He was survived by his wife, two sons, and a daughter.

"General James was a lion-hearted soldier, a gifted orator, an astute lawyer, and a successful banker and financier. His personality had all the power of a born leader of men and all the charm of the old-school Southern gentleman."—Abilene Reporter.

121. John Garland James—1866.

Educator—Financier

Born December 1, 1844, at Chatham, Fluvanna Co., Va. Brother of Fleming Wills James (See Sketch No. 120 for parents, etc.).

Matriculated at V. M. I. from Richmond, Va., on August 11, 1862 and continued a cadet until July 4, 1866, when he was graduated, standing second in his class. In the battle of New Market he was third cadet corporal in Co. C, acting at the time as one of the color guard. The following session was much interrupted; as he wrote "I was in the intermediate lines with the corps of cadets when Richmond was evacuated in 1865. The corps was disbanded that night by General Ewell, post commander of Richmond, and with others I left the city, going up the canal to Fluvanna County." Shortly after this the Alpha Tau Omega Fraternity was founded (See Sketch No. 87) and the founders felt that it was essential to the success of the new organization that he become a member for, as Glazebrook later said, "James was the profoundest scholar I ever knew." When the corps returned to Lexington in the fall of 1865 the cadets boarded for a time at various houses in the town. As it worked out Glazebrook and James were assigned to the home of Mrs. Compton and it easily followed that James, in October 1865, became the first initiate of the Alpha Tau Omega Fraternity.

After graduation he became a professor at the Kentucky Military Institute (1866-67) where he was succeeded by Tom Hayes (Sketch No. 107). In 1868 he went to Bastrop, Texas, and organized a private school but the following year he went to Austin and there founded, with his two brothers F. W. James, (See Sketch No. 120) and Charles A. James the Texas Military Institute of which he was superintendent until 1879. At the T. M. I., the first military school established in the state, many prominent Texans were educated. The Texas Agricultural and Mechanical College was founded in 1876; there were some difficulties with its successful operation and so in 1879 James was called as its second president; the T. M. I. was suspended; and he continued in his new work until 1883 when he resigned to engage in banking.

Married: February 6, 1883 Mrs. Clara W. B. Trowbridge, of Detroit, Mich.
They had no children.

He organized the City National and the First National Banks, still in operation in Wichita Falls, Texas, and for a short time returned to Austin where he was in the bond and mortgage business until 1900 when he moved to Roff, then in the Indian Territory, now in Oklahoma, where he organized the Farmers Bank.

About six years later he left the banking business and for the remainder of his life was in the mortgage and real estate business at Roff.

When in the seventy-ninth year he wrote:

"I am glad to say I still *feel* young, am active mentally and physically and can easily walk ten or twelve miles and stand about as much work as ever. Am temperate and ever have been, never a user of tobacco nor addicted to strong drink. Have been busy all my life and much interested in all that goes on. Have accumulated very little, my life largely devoted to other things than money-making, and am better off, I reckon, than if I had a million dollars as a millstone around my neck.

"My library is my greatest pleasure, not a big one, but along lines that interest me, especially valuable in respect to literature of native authors of Spanish-American republics, Philippine Islands and West Indies. I have perhaps 1500 volumes in Spanish and about 500 volumes in French, (mainly French Revolution, Napoleon and the Ancient Regime), Italian, Portuguese, Catalan and Dialects of Spanish and French. I am fond of modern languages."

For a number of years after 1875 he was a member of the board of visitors of the U. S. Naval Academy, the first Texan so appointed. In the eighties his book "Southern Selections for Reading and Oratory" published in 1879 was widely distributed.

Colonel James died February 12, 1930 in Dallas, Texas, and was buried at Austin. Survived by his sister, Mrs. D. T. Iglehart, of Baird, Texas, and two step-daughters Mrs. C. C. Kinney and Miss Kathleen Trobridge, of Long Island, N. Y.

122. John Braxton Jarratt—1866.

Merchant—County Treasurer

Born December 3, 1843, at Jarratt, Sussex County, Va.

Parents: William Nicholas Jarratt, and Elizabeth A. Wilborn.

Grandparents: Nicholas Jarratt, and Mary (Polly) Brown, of Sussex Co. Captain Jones Wilborn, and Elizabeth Fannin (or Fennell).

On Jan. 1, 1862, the date on which the Institute reopened (it was suspended when the corps left in April 1861, to assist in drilling the

Confederate troops being mobilized in Richmond) he matriculated from Jarratt and was assigned to the fourth class. On May 27, 1862, he resigned at the request of his guardian, but returned on Dec. 15th of the same year and re-entered the fourth class.

He was second cadet corporal in Co. B at the battle of New Market, but resigned on January 30, 1865, to enter the Confederate States Army. In February he joined the 13th Virginia Cavalry, as a private, and was slightly wounded at the battle of Five Forks on the retreat from Petersburg to Appomattox Courthouse, where he surrendered with Lee's army.

He married Miss Gertrude Mary Adeline Jarratt, his first cousin, daughter of Thomas Jefferson Jarratt, of Petersburg, Va., and they had two children:
Dr. Robert Braxton Jarratt.
Gertrude Etta, who married John Hobbs Batte; one child, John H. Batte, Jr.

After the war Mr. Jarratt returned to his native county and engaged in the mercantile business at Jarratt, Va., which he conducted with success until he was elected to the office of county treasurer. As an evidence of his popularity as an officer and citizen, he was elected treasurer of Sussex county five times and served his county as such for nineteen years.

Mr. Jarratt's death occurred on December 9, 1906. His wife, who died on Oct. 22, 1912, was a sister of Walter Jefferson Jarratt, V. M. I., '68.

He was survived by his wife, two children, a grandson; two brothers Capt. B. F. and Wm. N. Jarratt, of Jarratt, Va.; and two sisters, Mrs. M. A. Applewhite, of Suffolk, Va., and Mrs. A. W. Whitehorn, of Greenesville, Va.

123. Thomas Garland Jefferson—1867.

"Died on the Field of Honor"

Born January 1, 1847, at "Winterham" in Amelia County, Va., the second child and eldest son of his parents.

Parents: John G. Jefferson, and Otelia M. Howlett of "Winterham," Amelia Co., Va.

He matriculated at V. M. I. from Amelia Court House, August 1, 1863. In the battle of New Market as a cadet private in Co. B he was mortally wounded and he died three days later, on May 18, 1864. He is buried beneath the New Market Battle Monument at V. M. I.

The most intimate account of his death was written by Sir Moses Ezekiel on July 23, 1904, and this he supplemented on September 3rd of that year. We quote from the former:

"I have again been prevented (by the retarded coming to Rome of those who were to see my colossal statue of Mr. Drexel in clay before casting it in bronze) from joining my old cadet comrades in answering the last roll call and receiving the medal, which, if still given to me, I should value above any earthly possession.

"After the battle of New Market was over and we who survived answered the roll call on the field I went in search of the wounded and found my room-mate and comrade Thomas Jefferson lying on the floor of a hut quite ex-hausted and wounded in the breast. It was night and I was without shoes, as I had been all day, and I went to the town of New Market and got a wagon and carried him to the house of Mrs. Clinedinst, who gave me a bed for him on the ground floor. She had two daughters Anne and Lydie. It was Sunday night late when I got him into bed and from that time up to Tuesday night, at about eleven o'clock, I never left him a moment or ever closed my eyes. A Mrs. Rupert, who lived in New Market, at whose house many cadets found both food and shelter was extremely kind to us all and gave me every possible help for my friend. I always hoped to save Jefferson and that last evening when he asked me to read from St. John, 'In my Fa-ther's house are many mansions' and then began to wander in mind, and thought that I was his mother, and then his sister, and finally asked me to make a light. It only then dawned upon me that all hope was past and (he was) in his agony. As our gallant color-bearer Evans was there with me, I sent up to call the family of Clinedinst (who had been as kind as it was possible for people to be all through those sad days) and they came down with candles in their hands whilst I had Jefferson in my arms, and he died. I washed and prepared him for burial and carried his mother a lock of his hair after we returned to Richmond."

124. Francis Smith Johnson—1867.

Lawyer

Born September 5, 1847, at Little Rock, Ark.

Parents: Robert Ward Johnson (1814-1879) U. S. Senator from Arkansas, 1853-61, then C. S. Senator; and Sarah Frances Smith.

Grandparents: Judge Benjamin Johnson, U. S. District Court of Arkansas from the creation of the Territory of Arkansas, in 1819, until his death in 1849, and Matilda Williams, of Franklin Co., Ky.
Dr. George W. Smith, and Sabina Dubbs, of Louisville, Ky.

He matriculated at V. M. I. March 5, 1864, from Jefferson, Ark., and was a cadet for the remainder of the session during which time he was a cadet private in Co. D. His brother, Benjamin S. Johnson wrote in 1908:

"He was one of the younger members of the corps detailed and left at the Institute as guard over the property. I remember his tell-ing me how hard he cried and begged to be taken along and permitted to go into the fight........ He remained a cadet in the V. M. I. until Hunter broke up the institution and destroyed the property. He then left the V. M. I. and joined the Confederate States army in North Carolina, becoming Adjutant of a newly organized North Carolina Regiment. The exact date of his enlisting, I cannot give, but he was in the battle of Greensboro, N. C., and surrendered when the final surrender took place. He then started on horseback from Greensboro, to rejoin his parents who had moved all their negroes and other property to a rented plantation near Waco, Texas, on the Brazos. He rode that distance on horseback accompanied by other comrades and joined his parents on the Brazos late in the month of August, 1865. He remained there until December, 1865, when his father sent him to Middletown, Conn., to prepare him for Yale under the care of Dr. Colton who had a preparatory school. After being with Dr. Colton two years he entered Yale in the year 1867, and remained there four years until he was graduated in 1871. He then went to the Law School of Columbia College, New York City, and after studying law there for two years he received his diploma and returned to Little Rock, Ark.

"Married Miss May Curran, in April, 1873, and immediately moved to California where he practiced law; returned to Little Rock, Ark., in the fall of 1882, and then opened his law office in partnership with myself and as assistant attorney for the St. L. 1. M. & S. Rwy. Co., in Arkansas, and the I. T. He continued to practice law faithfully and energetically until the day of his death, which occurred on the 22nd of September, 1902. He died very suddenly from heart trouble leaving his wife; one son, Robert Ward Johnson, Jr. (V. M. I. '01); and a younger daughter, Ada May Johnson, who is still (in 1908) single."

125. Porter Johnson—1867.

Farmer

Born Oct. 19, 1845, at Pruntytown, Taylor County, Va. (Now W. Va.).

Parents: Mortimer H. Johnson, (b. in Harrison County, W. Va.) and Eliza Dulaney Kemble (b. in Preston County, W. Va.).

Grandparents: Col. William Johnson, and Olive Waldo, of the Waldo family of New England who came over to this country in 1634.
William Kemble (b. in Burlington, N. J., father of William Elkanah Kemble, V. M. I., '53), and Margaret Hedgmond Dulaney, of Woodstock, Va.

When young Johnson matriculated at V. M. I. on Sept. 1, 1863, his parents were living at Brownsburg, Va. He was a cadet private Co. B at the battle of New Market and was wounded. The following letter written to his sister by him January 12, 1865, when the corps was quartered in the Alms House, Richmond, gives a picture of the times:

"I have now been from home over two weeks and not a line until I received your letter this morning. . . . I arrived safely here several days after I left home. Uncle Will (Dr. William Kemble, V. M. I. graduate of 1853) arrived several days ago. I got the things he brought. I am exceedingly obliged to mother for them. They were very nice indeed.

We are very poorly fixed here for study, twenty in a room, one small table, no chair or stools, but one gas burner attached to the side of the wall, instead of the center of the room, where it ought to be. There is but one little stove in the room and the meanest coal that you can imagine.

We have but two meals a day which is quite often enough of the kind, bread and beef for breakfast, and beef and bread for dinner. However, I am living and well. I have been to but two meals in the mess hall in the last four days.

I intend to leave here as soon as possible. I will have to cut my letter short as the gentleman who is going to carry it is in a hurry. I was on guard last night and set up until midnight reading Hiawatha, which will probably account for the enclosed lines. I was just thinking what I should write you about my stay in Staunton when these lines occurred to me. I expect they will cause some amusement for you. It is my first attempt at writing poetry and I am not certain that I succeeded very well, but it was written on the spur of the moment and under great difficulties. (His fears of it not being very good poetry were well founded.)

You must excuse all mistakes as I am writing in the dark nearly. Give my love to all and to all good night.

Your affectionate Brother.

P. S. Write soon and give me all the items of news and what you all think of my leaving here. (He means joining the army.) Uncle Porter (W. P. Johnson, Senator from Missouri) thinks I had as well leave."

On March 6, 1865, he did resign from the corps of cadets and joined the 8th Confederate Battalion (as 2nd lieutenant, Company "D"), commanded by Colonel Garnett Andrews. Johnson was captured at Salisbury, N. C., April 12, 1865, and imprisoned in the penitentiary at Nashville, Tenn., about three weeks; in the military prison at Louisville, Ky., about three weeks; and at Camp Chase, Ohio, where he remained until June 13, 1865, when all prisoners were paroled, when he returned to his home in Rockbridge County, Va.

In 1867 he married Rose M. Brown, daughter of Ludwell Harrison Brown, of Richmond, Va., and Margaret Cabell McClelland, daughter of Stanhope McClelland, of Nelson County, Va.

They had ten children: Fanny Kemble, wife of Vincent Costello, of Wheeling, W. Va.
Richard Mortimer (died 1916).
Ludwell Harrison.
Leake McClelland.
Edmonia Preston, wife of Chas. C. Beale, of Norfolk.
Olive McClelland, wife of Wm. E. Witt, Jr., of Baltimore.
Alice Lee, wife of T. M. Moreland, of Norfolk.
James Brown.
Waldo Porter (dead).
William Kemble (dead).

In May 1909 he wrote as follows:

"Unless we know from whom a man is descended, how are we to tell whether he has failed or not? Of course, we know in these latter days it is not who a man's ancestors were, but what has he done himself. Well, for the most of my life I have been an humble tiller of the soil—'I have also remained poor if I am honest.' We have at least obeyed the Scripture injunction, 'Be ye fruitful and multiply,' for we have raised to manhood and womanhood ten as fine children as any pair can boast of."

Mrs. Johnson died January 26, 1913 and he died June 9, 1917.

126. Henry Jenner Jones—1867.

"Died on the Field of Honor"

Born March 10, 1847, in King William Co., Va.

Parents: Thomas S. Jones, and Mary E. ——.

He matriculated at V. M. I. on August 13, 1863 from Aylett, King William County, by his guardian, James Leigh Jones, who was at the time connected with the Nitre and Mining Bureau of the Confederate War Department. In the battle of New Market while a cadet private in Co. D he was instantly killed by the explosion of a shell.

"At one discharge, Cabell, first sergeant of D Company, by whose side I had marched for months, fell dead, and with him fell Crockett and Jones. A blanket would have covered the three. They were awfully mangled by the canister. A few steps further on, McDowell sank to his knees with a bullet through his heart. Atwill, Jefferson, and Wheelwright were shot at this point. Sam Shriver, cadet captain of C Company, had his sword arm broken by a minie ball. Thus C Company lost her cadet as well as her professor captain." (The End of an Era, p. 302.)

Following a temporary interment by his comrades his body was brought to Lexington in 1866 and is now buried beneath the New Market Battle Monument at V. M. I.

127. Thomas Williamson Jones—1867.

Farmer—Teacher

Born January 8, 1847, in Brunswick Co., Va.

Parents: Rev. Edwin B. Jones, Episcopal minister of Brunswick Co., and Cornelia A. Campbell, of Nottoway Co., Va.

Grandparents: Dr. Thomas W. Jones, of Brunswick Co., and Mary Armistead Goode, of Mecklenburg Co., Va.
Dr. Archibald A. Campbell, and Sarah Elizabeth Epes, both of Nottoway Co., Va.

He matriculated from San Marino, at V. M. I. May 7, 1864 and four days later when the corps left on the New Market Campaign he was a cadet private in Co. B. He was left at the institute with the guard detail but took part in the Lynchburg Campaign a month later. He did not return the following session.

Married: Mary Elizabeth, eldest daughter of Thomas Branch, of Dinwiddie Co., Va. Their children were Edwin B. Jones, Elizabeth, and Cornelia C. Jones.

His brother S. G. Jones, of Rawlings, Va., married Delha Rebecca Bettie, the daughter of Claiborne Anderson Pope, V. M. I. '65, and his first wife Susan Alice Jones.

After the war he engaged in farming and teaching for the remainder of his life. He lived in Prince Edward County and there he died. He died at his home on January 19, 1913.

128. Walter Smith Jones—1867.

Lawyer

Born April 29, 1847, in Bedford Co., Virginia.

Parents: John Walter Jones, Bedford Co., and Elizabeth Lewis Smith.

Grandparents: William R. Jones, of Bedford Co., and —— Key, from Albemarle Co., Va.
William Smith, of Lewisburg, (W.) Va., who was a member of the constitutional convention of Virginia before the Civil War, and ——.

He matriculated at V. M. I. from Thaxtons Switch, Va., on April 1, 1864 and continued as a cadet until January 23, 1865 when he was granted a thirty day furlough on account of his health. He did not return to V. M. I. and in February 1865 he was commissioned a captain in the Confederate Army. He surrendered near Washington, Ga., on the Savannah river and was paroled at the close of the war. In the battle of New Market he was a cadet private in Co. C and was wounded.

He later entered the University of Virginia and studied law, practicing for some time at Bedford, Virginia. He gave up his practice years ago.

He was Assistant Adjutant of the United Confederate Veterans, and was at one time General of the Eastern Brigade. He was by birth and training a soldier. He was an honorary member of the Kiwanis Club of Louisville, Ga., a member of the Presbyterian church, and a Mason.

Married: December 20, 1874, Mary, daughter of Dr. —— Campbell and Mary Terry, of Campbell Co., Va., who died in 1901 survived by three of her seven children:
R. Clement Jones, of New York City.
May, wife of H. W. Burlingame, of Lowell, Mass.
Lettie, wife of Dr. S. T. R. Revell, of Louisville, Ga.

He lived in Louisville, Ga., about twenty years and on March 11, 1928 died at the home of his daughter, Mrs. Revell. Survived by his children and two brothers: R. Preston Jones, of Wytheville, Va., and Floyd Jones, of Johnson City, Tenn.

129. Wyndham Kemp—1867.

Lawyer

Born January 30, 1845, in Gloucester County, Va.

Parents: Judge Wyndham Kemp and Anne Louise Perrin, of Gloucester County.

Grandparents: Matthew Kemp, of Gloucester County, and Lucy Daniel, of Middlesex County.
Major William Kennon Perrin, and Fannie Burwell Page, both born in Gloucester County.

He served as an independent volunteer in the 26th Virginia Regiment, Infantry, C. S. A., Wise's Brigade, from May 1862 until he matriculated at V. M. I. on Dec. 30 of that year, from Gloucester C. H., and was admitted to the fifth class. The following session he took part in the battle of New Market as a cadet private in Co. B.

In the fall of 1864 young Kemp joined the 2nd Company of the Richmond Howitzers, Cutshaw's battalion, just in time to share in the disastrous retreat of the 19th of October, 1864, under General Early in the Valley. He was captured at the battle of Sailor's Creek on April 6, 1865, and was kept as a prisoner of war at Newport News, Va., until June 15, 1865.

Following the war he studied law in his father's office and when admitted to the bar, he went to Texas and located at Calvert, where he became a member of the firm of Davis, Beall & Kemp. In 1885 he removed to El Paso and was a member of the firm of Beall &

A note from

Mr. Thomas W. Davis

1839   Lexington

oldest state sup mil school

eng & teachers   4 yr

Stonewall Jackson

You can be

Barracks

honor system

Geo Marshall   # degrees

Museum

BA college   For study
         Taiwan

Rhodes Scholars   Thailand

exchanges
Medal of Honor   mil college

state-supports

citizen soldier

1500 # of cadets   Fac-student
               ratio

alumni support

Kemp, attorneys for the Southern Pacific Company and Galveston, Harrisburg, & San Antonio Railway Company.

Judge Kemp was for many years chairman of the El Paso bar committee. He was a member of the Society of Sons of the Revolution, also a member of John C. Brown Camp, Confederate Veterans, and an Odd Fellow. For a number of years he was City Attorney of El Paso and a member of the Public School Board. He was also chairman of the County Democratic Committee.

Wyndham Kemp was first married on Feb. 7, 1876, at Concord, N. C., to Mary Lewis Maury, daughter of Capt. William Lewis Maury, of Caroline County, Va.

There were two children of this union: Maury Kemp, attorney at law. Anne Perrin Kemp, who married Dr. Hugh S. White, of Lexington, Va. Their only child, Wyndham Kemp White, was graduated at V. M. I. in 1931.

On Feb. 14, 1888, at Snyder, Texas, he married secondly Mary Samuel Herndon. They had four children: John Page; Emily Wyndham; Herndon B.; and Roland Gordon.

Judge Kemp died suddenly (of a heart attack) February 9, 1909, at his home in El Paso.

130. William H. Kennedy, Jr.—1867.

Hotel Proprietor

Born September 15, 1843, in Westmoreland Co.

Parents: William H. Kennedy, hotel proprietor (Bollingbrook Hotel, Petersburg, and later lessee of the Farmville (Va.) Hotel), and M. J. ——

He matriculated at V. M. I. from Prospect Depot, Prince Edward Co., Va., August 1, 1863.

In the battle of New Market he was a cadet private in Co. "D." He returned the following session but resigned on January 19, 1865 to enter the C. S. Army, joined Mosby's Battalion, and served until the end of the war.

Following the war he was the proprietor of a hotel at Farmville for many years until his mind became impaired, he had attempted suicide twice, and he died under distressing circumstances by his own hand on December 27, 1877.

131. { Dent Poston King / Name changed to / Henry Dent King } —1867.

Farmer

Born about 1846 (he gave his age as 17 years when he matriculated).

Parents: William King, and Louisa Poston, who after the death of her husband married —— Morgan, of Saltville.

Grand-nephew of the pioneer William King, who owned the Salt Works at Saltville, Virginia, and who established at Abingdon, Va., the William King Academy.

He enlisted in Scott County, where he resided, in Capt. H. C.

Wood's company in April 1861, at the age of fifteen and later served with the Stonewall Brigade.

Receiving an honorable discharge from the Army he was entered at V. M. I. by Robt. F. Owens, of Hansonville, Russell Co., on May 4, 1863 from Scott County (as Dent Poston King) and was admitted to the fifth class. He was a cadet for two years and while a fourth classman was at V. M. I. with the guard detail when the battle of New Market was fought; at that time he was a cadet private in Co. D.

After the close of the war he went to Bristol, Va., where he resided for two or three years, and then moved to Russell County, where he owned a valuable estate. Having inherited an interest in the salt works at Saltville, Va., by careful management and good business methods he added materially to his wealth from year to year. He was a brave man, a man of fine intellectual qualities, and was noted for integrity in all his dealings.

He was unmarried, but his sister, Mrs. Morgan, and her daughter made their home with him. In 1901 he disposed of his holdings in Virginia and purchased the fine farm at Thomas' Bridge, Sullivan Co., Tennessee, which was part of the estate of Jonathan B. McClellan.

He was in a position to enjoy the fruits of his new possessions when ill health came upon him. He died at his home of Bright's disease July 19, 1904, aged 59 years and was survived by his two sisters, Mrs. Morgan and Mrs. Smythe, wife of Hon. Henry M. Smythe, former minister to Hayti. Interment was in East Hill Cemetery, Bristol.

132. William Myers Kirk—1867.

Physician

Born July 16, 1845, at Myers' Creek, Lancaster County, Va.

Parents: Rev. William Heath Kirk (b. at Marr's Hill, Lancaster County, Aug. 18, 1804) and Elizabeth Myers (b. at Myers' Creek, Lancaster County, Jan. 7, 1816).

Grandparents: Major John Kirk and Ann D. Heath.
Thomas Myers and Mary Ann Harris.

He was a student at Northumberland Academy before reporting for duty at the V. M. I. from Lancaster on July 25, 1863. He served as a cadet private in Co. D in the battle of New Market.

"We remained on the field to bury the dead, while General Breckinridge with the main army hastened on to Richmond. Two days later we received orders to follow. Our march back to Staunton was doubly terrible. Not only had we left many of our boys behind, but we were footsore and weary. At Staunton we were royally feasted and received clothing from the government. We were then transported on box cars to Richmond, and went into barracks at Camp Lee.

"On the evening after our arrival we were paraded in the Capitol Square and were addressed by President Davis. Hon. T. S. Bocock, Speaker of the House of Representatives, gave us the thanks of Congress for our gallant conduct, and the Governor presented us with a new State flag. It may be noted in this connection that we never carried a Confederate flag. We had gone into battle with our State flag from the Institute. Every figure on this flag had been riddled, except that of Washington.

"Not until we had been ordered into the fortifications on the Brook Turnpike did it dawn on us that we had done anything particularly worthy of praise . . ."

He continued with the corps until December 1864 when he was furloughed and returned home to prepare for the reopening of the Institute at the Alms House, in Richmond.

"While at home I went out one day in company with the 'Home Guard' and was captured in a skirmish with some Yankee raiders near Lottsburg, Northumberland Co., December 18th, 1864, and was taken to Fortress Monroe, and after being kept there for a week, was taken to Butler's H. Qs. at Bermuda Hundred on James river, where I remained for ten days and was then taken back to Fortress Monroe and was kept there until March 17th, 1865, when I was transferred to Point Lookout to be exchanged but was kept there until June 7th, 1865, when I was released and sent home. The following September I commenced to study medicine under Dr. Meriwether Lewis at Litwalton, Lancaster Co., Va. In October, 1866, I matriculated at the University of Maryland in Baltimore. I graduated from there March 1st, 1868 and located at White Stone, Lancaster Co., Va., which is still my home, and have practiced here for the last 44 years."

Quotations from a letter written by Dr. Kirk, March 10, 1910.

On November 22, 1871, he married Mary Josephine Lewis, only child of Joseph Henry Lewis and his wife, Lucy Robinson Latané, of Essex County, Va. No children were born to them but they adopted two orphan girls.

Dr. Kirk died July 11, 1918, in the 73rd year of his age.

133. Emmett Carter Knight—1867.

Tobacconist

Born March 14, 1848, in Nottoway County, Va.

Parents: Col. William Carter Knight, and Elizabeth Guerrant Dickinson, both born in Nottoway County. He married secondly Cleverine Thomas, dtr. of Benajah Thomas and Rhoda Lacy. Children of 2nd marriage: William O. Knight, Wray T. Knight, Sally (Mrs. Charles E.) Wingo, of Richmond; and Creed T. Knight, of Chicago.

Grandparents: John Hughes Knight, of Lunenburg County, and Sally Everett Carter, of Nottaway County.

Robert Dickinson, of Caroline County, and Mary Purnell Dupuy, of Prince Edward County.

After attending the school of C. P. Burruss, in Richmond, he matriculated at V. M. I. from Richmond on February 11, 1864. Three months later in the battle of New Market he was a private in Co. D and after leaving the institute he joined the reserves at Richmond and retreated with the Army to Appomattox.

Married: Josephine Mayo, daughter of George Mayo, of Cumberland Co., and Mary C. Jones, of Amelia Co.

Children: Cleverine Thomas, wife of Wm. R. Brown, of Paoli, Pa.
Martha Clinton, wife of Edward Hayes, of Morgantown, W. Va.
Sally Belle, wife of John E. Hill, of Mystic, Conn.

After the war he was a tobacco manufacturer and died in Washington, D. C., June 5, 1893.

—8

134. Wilson Kerr Lamb—1867.

Bookkeeper—Clerk

Born February 23, 1848, at Norfolk, Va.

Parents: William Wilson Lamb, at one time Mayor of Norfolk, and Margaret Kerr.

Grandparents: William Boswell Lamb (whose father Richard Lamb, served in the Continental Army), Mayor of Norfolk during the War of 1812, and ——.

He was entered at V. M. I. by Col. Wm. Lamb, then in Wilmington, N. C.; matriculated from Norfolk February 29, 1864 and was a cadet private in Co. C when the corps left on the New Market Campaign ten weeks later. At that time he was left at the institute with the guard detail and did not, therefore, participate in the battle. Later he took part with the corps of cadets in the Lynchburg Campaign.

The following session he returned to the institute and served from time to time with the corps in the trenches around Richmond until March 3, 1865, when he was granted a thirty-day furlough because of his health. Before the expiration of his furlough Richmond was evacuated and the corps disbanded.

After the war he was for several years a book-keeper and then served as clerk to his brother, Colonel William Lamb, who was Mayor of Norfolk from 1880 to 1886. While engaged in this work he died, unmarried, on July 10, 1884, aged 36.

135. Maurice Daniel Langhorne—1867.

Farmer—Real Estate Agent

Born August 16, 1847, in Roanoke Co., Va.

Parents: John Archer Langhorne, of Shawsville, Montgomery Co., Va., and Margaret L. Kent, of Montgomery Co., Va.

Grandparents: Maurice Langhorne, of Cumberland Co., Va., and Elizabeth Allen, of Prince Edward Co., Va.
Jacob Kent, of Wythe Co., Va., and Mary Buford, of Bedford Co., Va.

Entered V. M. I. August 21, 1863 and in the following spring fought with the corps of cadets in the battle of New Market as a private in Company "C." When the corps disbanded April 2, 1865 he joined the Confederate Army.

Married: October 17, 1877, Margaret Archer Kent, daughter of David Cloyd Kent, of Wythe Co., Va., and Elizabeth Ligon, of Powhatan Co., Va.
They had three children:
David Gray Langhorne.
Maurice Daniel Langhorne.
Eliza Kent Langhorne (deceased).

After the war he engaged in farming until 1889, when he moved to Pulaski and formed the real estate firm of Langhorne, Watson & Co. In the following year W. L. McGavock replaced Watson and the firm style was altered accordingly. He continued in the real estate business until his death, in Pulaski, on Sept. 26, 1900.

His brother Jacob Kent Langhorne, V. M. I. '66, was killed in battle near Brandy Station, Va., June 9, 1863.

136. James Septimus Larrick.

Teacher—Farmer—Surveyor

Born July 29, 1838, near Middletown, Va.

Parents: Joseph Larrick (b. 1782 near Middletown, Va.), and Mary Bell, who came to this country from Yorkshire, England, in 1829.

Grandparents: John Larrick (name originally spelled Larrique), who came to America from Alsace-Lorraine, France, about 1755, and Margaret Barrow, daughter of William Barrow, who came from Ireland and settled near Middletown, Va.

George Bell, who was converted to the Methodist faith under John Wesley, and who built the first Methodist church at Middletown, Va., soon after he settled there in 1819, and Mary Sigsworth, who died in England.

He worked on his mother's farm until the Civil War began. "Was elected 2nd Lieut. of a Cavalry Co. 1856, (James H. Drake, Capt.) of Stevens City, Frederick County, Va., where the company was mustered in. Members all from Frederick Co., Va., 100 strong. In 1859 the company received arms and was ordered to report to Gen. Lucius Davis at Charlestown, now W. Va. This my first military service was for the defense of any effort upon the part of the North to release 'Old John Brown,' at that time confined in the jail at Charlestown. The company did picket and scouting duty until Old Brown was hung Dec. 2, 1859, for treason.

"While at school at Front Royal, April 18, 1861, my company was ordered to Harper's Ferry to prevent, if possible, the burning of the U. S. Armory located there; we arrived at Harper's Ferry about daylight, morning of the 20th of April, 1861, after marching all night previously. We were stationed at Berlin Bridge, now Brunswick Station, B. & O. R. R. The Federal Army (Gen. Patterson, Commanding) was at Frederick City, Md.

"When Gen. Joseph E. Johnston vacated Harper's Ferry, the cavalry was formed into a regiment known as the First Regiment of Va. Cavalry, Lieut. Col. J. E. B. Stuart, Commanding, my company being Company 'A.' As soon as the 1st regiment was formed, it hastened to check Patterson's army which had crossed the Potomac River at Williamsport. We had almost daily skirmishing with the Federal Army until we were ordered to Manassas, 19th July, 1861. July 21st, 1861, about 2 o'clock P. M. the first regiment was ordered to charge the New York Zouaves. My captain and 1st Lieut. being absent, I was in command of my Co.; 1st Sergt. Holmes Conrad* (V. M. I., '58), 2nd in command; loss: 11 horses killed, no men. My horse was badly wounded (afterwards killed under me). I had many narrow escapes but was never captured or wounded.

"From Manassas and the Rappahannock, 1st regiment was ordered to Yorktown, Va., at which place my time of service expired (1 year). I resigned 19th of April, 1862. I rode from Yorktown to Lexington, Va., and

---

*Later Solicitor General of the United States. Contrary to his custom of making no public addresses, he delivered a carefully prepared historical address at V. M. I. on June 23, 1903, when the New Market Battle Monument was unveiled. His son, Capt. Robt. Y. Conrad, V. M. I., '05, was killed leading his troops in France in 1918; another son, Col. Bryan Conrad, is Asst. Director, Historical Division, of the Virginia Conservation and Development Commission.

reported to Capt. Polk, Sec'y, the only man I found about barracks. He informed me that the cadets were somewhere west from Staunton, Va., to check a force of Federals marching upon that city. Capt. Polk further informed me that the cadets would probably all be furloughed upon their return until the 1st of September, 1862, at which time I reported and was matriculated."

Young Larrick actually matriculated from Middletown, Va., on September 2, 1862, his age being recorded at that time as 22 instead of 24 years. He was the oldest cadet who participated in the battle of New Market and at the time was a private in Co. A although in the battle he served with the artillery section. He returned the following session and remained until January 18, 1865.

In 1871, he married Anna Cornelia Showalter (d. Feb. 10, 1925), of Frederick County Va. They had six children:
Frederick Joseph (V. M. I., 1894).
Sydney Guyer.
Charles Victor.
Richard Roy.
Cora Annette, m. Charles W. Hammack.
Barbara Augusta, m. Ernest T. Everley.

Captain Larrick was a school teacher, farmer, and county surveyor at Middletown for over twenty-five years. He fell dead (apoplexy) on March 14, 1911, while surveying on the farm of J. H. Pickeral, at Middletown.

137. Francis Tompkins Lee—1866.
Farmer—Tobacconist—Coal Operator

Born December 1, 1845, in Lynchburg, Va.

Parents: John Burwell Lee and Lilia Tompkins.

Grandparents: Beverly Lee and Rebecca Lee, both of Westmoreland Co., Va. Alexander Tompkins, of Caroline Co., and Elizabeth Byrd, of "Westover," Charles City Co., Va.

After preparatory instruction in Lynchburg; at William Dinwiddie's School in Albemarle County; and at Dr. Gessner Harrison's School in Nelson County, he matriculated at V. M. I. from Lynchburg May 29, 1862. At the time of the battle of New Market he was a cadet private in Co. D but in the battle he served with the Artillery Section.

"I served in campaigns of V. M. I. cadet battalion, first in mountain marches to Goshen, Covington and other Virginia points, to repel Federal raiders on the iron furnaces, marches of much severity in winter especially. Reaching Covington, Va., one winter's night, and accompanied by a regiment of Rockbridge County, Va., Home Guards, we next morning found Averill's Union Cavalry Brigade, 5,000 strong, camped on the opposite side of the town. . . . The cadet battalion and its two 3-inch pieces of artillery fell back twelve miles to Clifton Forge and held the mountain pass at that position several days, but the Federals did not advance farther and themselves retreated to West Virginia. I was one of a strong mounted detachment sent out from V. M. I. in 1863 to intercept deserters from General Lee's army making their way South along the mountains, but this proved more a frolic than otherwise; vastly different from the rapid mountain marches in severe weather. . . .
"While in Richmond we were marched to near Cold Harbor, Va., where

we were held with the reserves nearby while that terrific battle was being fought early one June morning, the roar of which I still vividly recall. It was just after this that the cadet battalion was presented by Governor Smith of Virginia with a new stand of colors to replace that shot to pieces at New Market. It was a brilliant scene in front of the Executive Mansion at Richmond; and these colors were carried until the close of the war. . . .

"Our services being again needed in the field, the corps encamped at Poe's Farm below Richmond, holding a portion of the lines of General Lee there for a considerable time, and gave some exhibition drills for instruction of that part of the army. Returning late in the fall to our barracks, we were again ordered in March, 1865, to the outer line of the army on the Darbytown Road, nine miles below Richmond, where we relieved Hood's Texas troops one dark night. Going out a quarter mile in front of the breastworks on picket next morning, we found a division of negro union troops in front of us. I was now the color sergeant of the corps, and, in Colonel Shipp's absence, looking after other troops then under his command, I had gone on picket with the battalion, but on his temporary return, he ordered me in and to remain in charge of his headquarters during his absence. In the afternoon three separate couriers brought sealed orders which I delivered to the Colonel on his return. He sent me at once to order the battalion off picket and we marched to Richmond. Having left no troops to oppose a Federal advance and finding the big guns on the interior line of works spiked, I then felt that Richmond was to be evacuated. We marched briskly and reaching the city before dark, found it in great confusion. We halted awhile at the Capitol Square, just opposite old St. Paul's Church, and then marched to barracks, and thence retreated west and with no supplies or money, it became necessary to disband and scatter in an effort to obtain necessary food. And thus the battalion disintegrated, a good many reaching Lynchburg after the surrender at Appomattox, and going thence to their homes after being paroled. Being with a small party and hearing the Yankees were near, I took the battalion colors from the staff, wrapped them around my body under my shirt, and thus brought them home to Lynchburg, Va., and after a year sent the colors to General Smith, Superintendent, at Lexington.

"The foregoing is mentioned mainly to show that the cadet battalion rendered arduous and much more service than I believe is generally known, and to show that its gallant record at New Market did not alone constitute its only response to the call of the South. . . ."

He continued at the institute until July 4, 1866 when he was graduated, standing fifth in his class and having the rank of cadet lieutenant.

Married: April 23, 1867, Lucy Harrison, daughter of Lorenzo Norvell, of Lynchburg, Va. They had five children:
Lorenzo Norvell.
Lelia Byrd (dec.).
Francis Marshall.
Mary, wife of Arthur H. Jennings.
John Burwell Lee.

He organized and for some years commanded the Lynchburg Light Artillery Blues.

After graduation he engaged in farming at "Springwood," the home of his ancestors and was later in the tobacco business. After 1890 he became interested in West Virginia coal properties and at the time of his death he was president of the Guyandotte and of the Sovereign Coal Companies.

He died in Lynchburg of pneumonia on July 12, 1918 and was survived by his wife and four children.

138. George Taylor Lee—1867.

Lawyer

Born March 8, 1848, at "Brookfield" (then about five miles from Richmond on the Brook Road) the home of his grandfather Taylor.

Parents: Charles Carter Lee (b. at Stratford in Westmoreland Co., 1798; grad. Harvard, 1819; lawyer, practiced in New York, West Virginia, Mississippi, and Virginia) and Lucy Penn Taylor (1828-1913).

Grandparents: General Henry ("Light Horse Harry") Lee (brilliant Revolutionary Soldier, Governor of Virginia, member of Congress) and Anne Hill Carter, his second wife.
George Taylor and Catherine Randolph, of Wilton, Va.

His parents moved from Brookfield, when he was about seven years old, to a farm "Windsor Forest," in Powhatan County on the James river about 25 miles from Richmond. He matriculated at V. M. I. from Fine Creek Mills, Va., on December 10, 1863 and later in the session served as a cadet private in Co. B and continued with the corps until Richmond was evacuated. After the evacuation of Richmond he went to his home in Powhatan County got a horse and joined the army of Northern Virginia near Farmville. He was on the battle field at Appomattox Court House, and saw Gordon's last charge but, though under fire in a small cavalry skirmish with the First Cavalry Brigade, he was not otherwise engaged in that battle and escaped from the field with that portion of the cavalry which had been placed between Grant's Army and Lynchburg. Soon afterwards he went to Richmond where he surrendered and was paroled.

In September, 1866, he went to Washington College, where he was a student for two sessions. In the Spring of 1870 he went to Hardy Co., West Virginia, where he remained two years, teaching, and studying law in the office of Homer S. Carr, in Moorefield. He was granted a license in 1872 but did not enter upon the practice of law for several years, spending the intervening time in teaching and other work.

In September, 1883, he returned to Lexington; received the degree of bachelor of law from the Washington and Lee University in 1884; and began the practice of his profession at Rocky Mount, Va. From there he moved to Lonoke, Ark., in the fall of 1887 and continued his practice.

Married: May 15 (New Market Day), 1888, Ella Marian, the widow of Dr. James J. Fletcher, and the daughter of William Goodrum. They had three children, two sons and a daughter.

In 1891, because of failing health, he moved to Johnson City, Tennessee, in order to live in a higher altitude. There he practiced law about 25 years and then returned to his old home at Fine Mills Creek where he remained until 1929 when, at the age of 81 years, he moved to the Confederate Home, in Richmond, where he is now living.

139. Robert Fleming Lee—1867.

Manufacturer—Clerk

Born February 13, 1849.

Parents: Col. Richard Bland Lee (born July, 1797, an officer of the U. S. Army, later in Confederate Army), and Julia Anna Manon(?) Prosser (of Richmond, Va.)

Paternal Grandparents: Richard Bland Lee (born Jan., 1761) and Elizabeth Collins (of Philadelphia, Penn.)

He was entered at V. M. I. by his father, Col. Lee then at Tarboro, N. C., and matriculated on March 5, 1864 from Fairfax County, Va. With one exception he was the youngest cadet in the corps at the time of the battle of New Market but he was not in the battle as he was on the detail left in Lexington to guard the institute. At the time he was a cadet private in Co. C. Later in the session he took part in the Lynchburg Campaign and was with the corps in the trenches around Richmond in the following fall until November, when he went to North Carolina — his resignation was accepted on February 4, 1865. He remained in North Carolina until the end of the war and then attended Mr. Ambler's school in Fauquier Co., Va.

He moved to Alexandria about 1867 and there he, with his nephew, operated a Barytes Mill. In later years he was a clerk.

He died in Richmond, Va., about November 23, 1913, and was buried in Ivy Cemetery, Alexandria.

140. Alexander Hamilton Leftwich—1867.

Public Utilities Service

Born Sept. 12, 1847, at Lynchburg, Va.

Parents: Augustine Leftwich (b. Bedford County, Va., March 4, 1794; served in the War of 1812), and Elizabeth Williams Clark (b. in Camden, S. C., July 6, 1812).

He matriculated at V. M. I. on January 14, 1864, and served as a cadet private in Co. B in the battle of New Market. He did not return the following session but was commissioned first lieutenant and sent to High Bridge, Va., as a drill master. From there he went to Charlotte, N. C. to the 6th Infantry, Sam Shriver of the New Market corps being his Company Commander; was captured at Salisbury by Stoneman's troops but escaped and went to the Catawba river and helped build a pontoon bridge to replace the railroad bridge which had been burned by the Federals.

The company "had strict orders from General Johnston to examine the paroles, so as to prevent desertions from his army. While on duty one night, about one o'clock, ambulances drove up and I called out the guard, wondering what it could be, and to my surprise found that it was Jeff Davis and his party, including his wife and a number of his cabinet, one of whom I talked to, General John C. Breckinridge, then Secretary of War, who commanded us at New Market."

A short time thereafter he was paroled at Hamburg, S. C. by General Upton. In the Spring of 1866 he went to Richmond and was employed with the firm of S. C. Tardy and Co. In 1868 he removed to Baltimore associating himself with the firm of Ricards, Leftwich and Company. The following year he was commissioned colonel of the 4th Infantry Regiment, Maryland National Guard.

On Dec. 7, 1871, he married Annie B. Shorter, of Alabama. Her father, Honorable Eli S. Shorter, was in Congress before the war, and her uncle, John Gill Shorter, was Governor of Alabama. They had five children:
Mrs. Edwin Bennett Young.
Mrs. T. J. Murphy.
Mrs. Hanson Robinson.
E. Shorter Leftwich (V. M. I., '98).
Clem S. Leftwich.

In the late eighties and early nineties he was president of the Spartanburg Gas, Electric Light, and Power Company, Spartanburg, S. C. He later filled the same position with the Bristol Belt Line Railway Company, Bristol, Tenn., and Va.

Colonel Leftwich died August 11, 1908, at his daughter's home in Baltimore, and his body was taken to Lynchburg, Va., where it was buried in the family lot.

141. Samuel Houston Letcher—1869.

Lawyer—State Senator—Jurist

Born January 4, 1848, in Lexington, Va.

Parents: John Letcher (War Governor of Virginia; member of U. S. Congress; member and president, board of visitors, V. M. I.), and Mary Susan Holt, of Rockingham Co., Va.

Grandparents: William Houston Letcher, and Elizabeth Davidson.
Dr. Richard Holt, and Elizabeth Shafer, of Rockingham County.

He attended the English and Classical Preparatory School conducted in Richmond by Frank H. Alfriend. While on a trip to Brazil he heard, in Rio, that hostilities between the North and the South had commenced and he often referred to the experiences* he encountered in reaching home, without passports through the Federal lines after he debarked at New York, as one of the most exciting events of his life.

As a boy of fifteen he served in the trenches around Richmond and on February 29, 1864 matriculated at V. M. I. A few months later he took part in the battle of New Market, where he was a cadet private on the extreme left of Co. D. At the close of the session he joined the army and served under General Early in the Maryland and Valley Campaigns. In December 1864, he was commissioned lieutenant in the Provisional Army of the Confederate States and ordered to South-Western Virginia, where he served until the close of the war with Gen. Robert Preston's Brigade.

In October 1865 he re-entered the Institute and was graduated

---

*See Confederate Veteran, October, 1928, Vol. 36, p. 370.

on July 2, 1869, standing 21 in his class and ranking as first lieutenant in Co. B.

After studying law in his father's office he was admitted to the bar in 1874 and became a member of the firm of Letcher, Maury, and Letcher, of Lexington.

In 1884 he was appointed a member of the board of visitors of the V. M. I., a service which continued for fourteen years and during the last ten years of which he was president of the board.

In 1897 he was elected to the State Senate and the following year, on the death of Judge William McLaughlin, he was appointed Judge of the (then) 13th Judicial Circuit Court of Virginia a position he filled with great credit and dignity until his voluntary retirement in 1912. He was succeeded by Judge Henry Winston Holt, V. M. I. '86.

In his later life he devoted his talent to preparing some memoirs of his father, but illness prevented completion of this work.

He died September 5, 1914, of Bright's disease and was buried in the family plot in Lexington. He never married and was survived by two brothers: Capt. John D. Letcher, V. M. I. '73, and Capt. Greenlee D. Letcher, V. M. I. '86, of Lexington; and four sisters (Elizabeth) Mrs. James A. Harrison, of Charlottesville; (Virginia) Mrs. W. LeConte Stevens, of Lexington; (Margaret) Mrs. Robert J. Showell, of Berlin, Md.; and Miss Fannie Letcher, of Lexington.

142. Norborne Clack Lewis—1867.

Physician

Born Sept. 21, 1846, at Lawrenceville, Va.

Parents: John H. Lewis and Rowena T. Robinson.

Grandparents: Nicholas Lewis and Martha Claiborne.
Clack Robinson and Emily Young.

He matriculated at V. M. I. on Jan. 2, 1864, and served as a cadet private in Co. B at the battle of New Market. Returning the following session, he was a cadet until Richmond was evacuated.

He was graduated in medicine at the University of Virginia 1867 and later at the University of New York. He practiced his profession for a short time in Petersburg, Va., with his kinsman, Dr. John Herbert Claiborne, later settling in Lawrenceville, Va., his parental home, where he enjoyed a large practice throughout his life.

On November 21, 1871, Dr. Lewis married Miss Murtis Rawlings (b. April 22, 1849; d. July 21, 1912), daughter of W. P. Rawlings of Diamond Grove, Va. They had two children:
Dr. William Herbert Lewis.
Mrs. Henry Lightfoot Heartwell. (Mrs. Heartwell was appointed sponsor-in-chief for the Virginia division of the United Confederate Veterans at the New Orleans reunion in April, 1923.)

He died March 3, 1905, at his home in Lawrenceville, after an illness of several weeks.

143. William Lynn Lewis—1867.

Farmer—Resort Proprietor

Born June 14, 1844, at Orangeburg, S. C.

Parents: Col. William Lynn Lewis, and Letitia Preston Floyd, daughter of Governor John B. Floyd of Virginia.

When he matriculated at V. M. I. on May 18, 1863, his parents were residing at Sweet Springs, Monroe County, (West) Va., he was admitted to the fifth class. As a cadet private in Co. A he took part a year later in the battle of New Market.

Later he joined the Confederates States Army as lieutenant of infantry and fought at Bentonsville, N. C., after General Lee's surrender at Appamottox, and was captured at Augusta, Ga., while on his way to join the trans-Mississippi army under General Kirby Smith. He returned to "Lynnside," old Sweet Springs, W. Va., the home of his ancestors, where he occupied himself with his farm. He was also proprietor of Old Sweet Springs Hotel, a popular summer resort.

On March 18, 1868, he married Miss Florence C., daughter of Major John Dooley, of Richmond, Va. They had four daughters:
Mary Lynn Lewis (died Nov. 26, 1915).
Mrs. Jarvis Keiley.
Mrs. Cary Breckinbridge.
Coralie Floyd Lewis.

Mr. Lewis died on April 9, 1908, at Old Sweet Springs, after a short illness following a stroke of paralysis. Among his survivors was a brother, John Floyd Lewis, V. M. I., '68, of Bay City, Texas (d. June 13, 1922).

144. Robert Nelson Locke—1867.

Merchant

Born March 6, 1847, in Lunenburg County, Va.

Parents: Rev. Thomas E. Locke, an Episcopal minister (b. Dec. 4, 1812; d. April, 1897), of Berkeley County, W. Va., and Lucy Armistead Nelson (b. June, 1822; d. Jan. 1, 1892), of Mecklenburg County, Va.

Grandparents: Meverell Locke, of Berkeley County, W. Va., and Rosalie McCleary, of Shepherdstown, W. Va.
Robert Carter Nelson, of Lunenburg County, Va., and Isabella Hopkins Wilson, of Hopkinsville, Ky.

He matriculated at V. M. I. from Oak Grove, Westmoreland County, Va., on Aug. 29, 1863, and was a cadet private in Co. D in the battle of New Market. Returning home on furlough in November 1864, he joined and served with Col. John G. Mosby's command until the close of the war.

On Oct. 30, 1876, he married Sally May Sutcliffe, daughter of John Edward and Fanny Herr Sutcliffe, of Louisville, Ky. They had one child:
Cora Sutcliffe Locke, m. Edwin Kirtley Milton, Nov. 11, 1902. Their two sons are: Edwin Kirtley Milton, Jr. and John Sutcliffe Milton.

His first business venture was in Martinsburg, W. Va., where he stayed but a short time, securing a position in Louisville, Ky., with the firm of R. H. Robinson Drug Company. Later he became treasurer of Grauman-Henchey-Cross Co., in Louisville. In 1905 he went to Memphis, Tenn., and made his home with his daughter until his death on September 8, 1912. He is buried in Cave Hill Cemetery, Louisville, Ky.

145. Thomas Samuel Lowry—1867.

Railroad Service

Born about 1846 (he was 17 years of age at matriculation), in Hanover County, Va.

Parents: Henry Samuel Lowry (son of Edward), of Hanover County, and Ann Jemima, daughter of Thomas Duke, of Louisa County, Va.

He matriculated at V. M. I. from Morris P. O., Hanover County, Va., Sept. 5, 1863, and was a cadet private in Co. D at the battle of New Market. The following session he resigned on March 17, 1865 to enter the Confederate Army.

"A few years after the close of the Civil War, he was taken with measles which left him in poor health. Thinking to improve it, he spent a year or more in Denver, Colorado, but all to no purpose; lived only a few weeks after arriving at his Kentucky home." (From a letter written by his cousin, R. Edward Lowry, of Verdon, Va., Aug. 3, 1904.)

Prior to his death he was clerk in the office of the superintendent of the Virginia and Tennessee (now Norfolk and Western) Railroad.

146. William James Lumsden—1867.

Physician

Born April 10, 1846, at Greensboro, N. C.

Parents: Rev. James D. Lumsden (b. in Edinburgh, Scotland), and Elmira Harris (b. in Rowan County, N. C.).

Paternal Grandparents: William Lumsden, and Agnes Youle, both of Dumfries, Scotland.

He received his preparatory education at the Crenshaw and Hardy Academy, located at what is now Blackstone, Va. He joined the Mathews County (Va.) Battery of Field Artillery in 1861 but was discharged in December, 1862 on account of ill health. On March 22, 1864, his father entered him at the Virginia Military Institute and he served as a cadet private in Co. D in the memorable battle at New Market on May 15th of that year. He was at Richmond at the time of the evacuation and from there worked his way to Greensboro to join the army of Gen. Johnston.

After the close of the war, he returned to Elizabeth City, N. C., joining his father on a farm in lower Pasquotank county. For a time he taught school. In March, 1869 he was graduated in medicine at the University of Maryland, and returned to Elizabeth City to begin the active practice of his profession. This marked the beginning of forty years of service to eastern North Carolina people to whom he became physician, friend, counselor and guide.

On June 29, 1874, he married Sarah L., daughter of W. W. Kennedy of Elizabeth City. They had no children.

Dr. Lumsden died on Oct. 14, 1914. Two years before he had suffered a fall and was crippled, for many months being confined to his room, in acute pain practically all of the time. His death was due to a stroke of paralysis.

He was a fellow of the American Medical Association and secretary of the Medical Association of the State of North Carolina.

147. George Kennon Macon—1866.

Lawyer

Born about 1846 (he was 16 years of age when he matriculated) in Henrico County, Va., about six miles from Richmond.

Parents: Miles Cary Macon, of Mt. Prospect, New Kent County, Va., and Frances Randolph Mütter, who was born in North Carolina but removed to Virginia when quite young, and made her home with Col. —— Adams at Indian Field on the York River.

Grandparents: Col. William Hartwell Macon, of Mt. Prospect, New Kent County, Va., and Hannah Selden.
Thomas Mütter and Ann Southall.

His father died when he was very young and his mother, sisters, and brothers lived in Richmond, Va. Young Macon received his preparatory education at the Academy of William H. Harrison in Amelia County, Va., where he achieved distinction in his classes and was the recipient of several prizes for conduct and scholarship. He matriculated at V. M. I. on August 14, 1862, giving his age as 16 years. He served as cadet 2nd corporal, Co. A in the battle of New Market where he was severely wounded by a piece of cannister which passed through one of his arms. By skilful medical attention and careful nursing, the arm was saved from amputation, but the effect of the wound was permanent. He was a cadet until Richmond was evacuated; then served in Gen. Johnston's army until the end of the war; returned to V. M. I. in the fall of 1865 and was graduated July 4, 1866, standing fourth in his class.

Following his graduation at the Institute, he taught in Rev. Phillips' Male Academy at Pass Christian, Miss. Upon being appointed assistant professor at V. M. I. in 1870, he resigned his position at Pass Christian and assumed his duties as an assistant professor at his Alma Mater. While performing these duties, he pursued the law course and received his LL.B. degree at Washington and Lee University, having the good fortune to be taught by Judge Brockenborough and the honorable John Randolph Tucker. Commencing the practice of his profession in the city of Richmond in 1872, he soon took a high stand at the bar.

Mr. Macon died on September 27, 1894, and was buried in Hollywood Cemetery in Richmond. He never married.

148. Robert Lewis Madison—Corps Surgeon.

Not a Cadet—Physician

Born February 22, 1828, at Woodberry Forest, Orange Co., Virginia.

Parents: Robert Lewis Madison, and Eliza Strachan, of Petersburg.

Grandparents: Gen. William Madison, youngest brother of President Madison, and Francis Throckmorton, Orange Co., Va.

His parents died when he was a youth and he was adopted by his uncle, Robert Strachan, who was then living in Petersburg, Va. When seventeen years of age he entered William and Mary College, from which he was graduated. He was a student at the University of Virginia, and received his medical degree at Jefferson College, Philadelphia. He practiced first in Petersburg and then removed to Baltimore.

On the 22nd of October 1859 he was unanimously elected by the Board of Visitors of the Virginia Military Institute, Mercer Professor of Animal and Vegetable Physiology Applied to Agriculture, and Post Surgeon of the V. M. I.

In the early part of the war, while the academic work at V. M. I. was suspended, he acted as surgeon in the Confederate Army and had charge, after the battle of Manassas, of a hospital at Orange Court House, Va.

When the institute reopened, following the period when the cadets acted as drill-masters in Richmond, he resumed his duties as Professor and Surgeon; accompanied the cadet battalion on all its military expeditions; and was present with it at the battles of McDowell and New Market.

He was the family physician of both General Robert E. Lee and Commodore Matthew Fontaine Maury, and attended each in his last illness.

Gifted with a cool nerve and a brave heart, when the occasion demanded coolness and courage, he had the tenderness of a woman which manifested itself in his unfailing sympathy in the suffering and sorrow of others.

He was twice married, first to Letitia Lee, great granddaughter of Capt. Ambrose Madison, brother of President James Madison; second to Helen Bannister, of Petersburg, Va., and had three sons: Monro, Robert Lee, and Edmond Bolling Madison, of Athens, Tenn.

In the closing days of the war, being on furlough without pay, he practiced medicine in Staunton and while there he suffered a severe attack of pneumonia which sowed the seeds of the disease which terminated his life. He died May 26, 1878, after long and severe illness and suffering and was buried in Lexington, Va.

149. Edmund Skinner Mallory—1867.

Lawyer

Born September 22, 1846, in Hampton, Va.

Parents: Col. Charles King Mallory (of the Confederate Army, born in Norfolk) and Martha A. Skinner, born in Edenton, N. C.

Grandparents: Charles King Mallory, Lt. Gov. of Va. during the War of 1812, and Frances Lowry Stevenson.
Edmund Blount Skinner and Emily Wood.

Matriculated at V. M. I. from Liberty (now Bedford) Va., on March 1, 1864 and ten weeks later as a cadet private in Co. A he took part in the battle of New Market. The following session he returned; on January 24th was appointed a cadet corporal in Co. A; and remained until the corps was disbanded on April 2, 1865.

In 1868 he was graduated in law at the Univerity of Virginia and the following year moved to Jackson, Tennessee.

Married: Sept. 18, 1872, Eugenia, daughter of John M. Parker of Jackson, Tenn.
They had two sons and two daughters: One daughter, Martha Skinner, died in infancy; the other daughter, Caroline Parker, died at the age of twenty-four; the oldest son, John Parker, was associated with his father in the practice of law, up to the time of his father's death, he then moved to Tucson, Arizona; the second son, Charles King, was graduated from the United States Naval Academy, and now lives in Syracuse, N. Y. (His son, Chas. King Mallory, Jr., V. M. I., '31.)

He practiced law in Jackson, Tenn., until the time of his death and at one time, was a candidate for Attorney General of Tennessee and also for Judge of the Court of Appeals.
Died in Jackson, Tenn. on August 19, 1903.

150. Charles Harrison Marks—1867.

Farmer—Lumber Manufacturer

Born August 15, 1846, at Burleigh, Prince George County, Va.

Parents: Edward Archer Marks, and Eliza Bryant, both of Prince George County.

Grandparents: Edward Marks, and Mary Harrison, both of Prince George County.
Thomas B. Bryant, of Raleigh, N. C., and Sarah Winfield Harrison, of Petersburg, Va.

He attended Prince George Academy before entering V. M. I. on August 11, 1863. He was a cadet private in Co. D at the battle of New Market and remained with the corps until Richmond was evacuated when he joined the Confederate Army, and was shot through the thigh during the last fight at Salisbury, N. C.

On April 29, 1870, he married Helen Peebles, daughter of Col. Richard M. Harrison and Rebecca Jane Peebles, of Huntington, Prince George County, Va. They had five sons and two daughters:
Wirt Peebles, physician at Claremont, Va. (d. Sept. 2, 1926). His wife, who was Helen Lee, survived him, as did their four sons, Edward H., Charles H., Walker Lee, Wirt P., Jr., and a daughter, Helen Roselyn Marks.
Charles H., farmer, m. (first) Lelia Blanche Adams, of Prince George Co.; (second) Virginia D. Mayes, of Sussex County.
Edward A., insurance agent, m. Mary Clark Blodgett, of Newark, N. J.
M. Harrison, minister, m. Sallie Watt, of Richmond, Va.
William H., farmer, Garysville, Va., m. Helen Fulton Figg, of Prince George County, Va.

Helen Peebles, m. Charles E. Harrison, of Gee, Va.
Rosa Eva, m. Edward Valentine Harrison, of Prince George, Va.

Mr. Marks was a farmer and engaged in the manufacture of lumber. He spent his entire life at Aberdeen, in Prince George county, Va., and there he died on June 23, 1896. His brother, John Alexander Marks, was a graduate of the Institute, Class of 1854.

151. Jacob Marks—Musician.

Bass Drummer—(Not a Cadet)

Born St. Augustine, Florida, about 1822.
Early in life he moved with other members of his family to Washington, D. C.
About 1848 he married Lucretia Lusby(?) in Washington, D. C. He was married three times, his third wife being the sister of his first wife.
Children: Henry, Julia, Emma and Cora.

He came to Lexington and was employed at V. M. I. as a drummer in the band and was one of the three musicians on the New Market Campaign.

After the war he moved to San Francisco, California. Died in Washington, D. C., in August 1912.

152. Alfred Marshall—1866.

Teacher—Civil Engineer

Born December 25, 1845, at Richmond, Va.

Parents: William Marshall, an Englishman, who for many years was the British vice-consul at Richmond, and Gertrude Virginia —— (a granddaughter of Bishop Richard Channing Moore, the first rector of Monumental Church in Richmond.

Matriculated at V. M. I. from Richmond, Va., on July 25, 1862, and stood 8 in a class of 125 as a fourth classman; on December 4, 1863 he was appointed a corporal and later in that session he took part in the battle of New Market as cadet second corporal in Co. D and at the end of the session he stood 5 in a class of 54. His second class year was passed in Richmond, he was second ranking orderly sergeant, and was interrupted when the city was evacuated.

Before returning to the V. M. I. he, with two other New Market Cadets—Glazebrook (Sketch No. 87) and Ross (Sketch No. 211), founded on September 11, 1865 the Alpha Tau Omega Fraternity. In his first class, or senior, year at V. M. I. he was the cadet captain of the single company of the session 1865-66 and was graduated with the third stand in his class on July 4, 1866.

The following year he served as adjutant and assistant professor of Mathematics and Tactics at V. M. I. Continuing his studies in the special school of mining engineering which had just been opened he was awarded the degree of Mining Engineer at V. M. I. in July 1868, being one of the first two graduates.

After serving as a civil engineer with the Chesapeake & Ohio Railroad he was in April 1870 appointed assistant engineer on the Mobile and Montgomery R. R. and it was while so engaged that he fell a victim of the dread scourge yellow fever.

He had been put in charge of the construction of that part of the railroad between Tensaw and Mobile, about twenty miles through swampy country.

He died in Mobile September 22, 1870 aged 25 years, and was buried in the spring of 1871 in Hollywood Cemetery in Richmond.

Throughout his last illness he was nursed by his old New Market comrade George Spiller (See Sketch No. 229) in fearless manner which won widespread admiration.

153. Martin Marshall—1867.

Lawyer

Born June 27, 1846, at Vicksburg, Miss.

Parents: Thomas Alexander Marshall (b. March 29, 1812; d. Dec. 6, 1893), of Vicksburg, Miss., and Letitia Miller (b. Feb. 19, 1824; d. Feb. 7, 1887).

Grandparents: Martin Marshall (1777-1853), a lawyer of Augusta, Ky., born in Fauquier Co., Va., fifth child of Rev. William Marshall, and Matilda Battaile Taliaferro.
Anderson Miller, of Frankfort, Ky., and a part owner of the first cotton seed oil mill ever built—it was in Natchez, Miss., and Elizabeth Bell, second dtr. of John and Frances Chapman Bell, of near Lexington, Ky.

He matriculated at V. M. I. on July 25, 1863, from Martin Co., Miss., his education prior to that time having been supervised by a private tutor. At the battle of New Market where he served as a cadet private in Co. D, he received a wound from which he never fully recovered—part of one knee was shot away.

"General John Echols (V. M. I., 1843) was a client of Marshall. A short while before the latter's death when the General was on a visit to him in Mississippi, he suddenly turned to Marshall and said, 'I have often wondered just what relation you are to little Marshall of the Cadet Corps who fell at New Market?' Marshall replied, 'I am the chap.' 'But,' rejoined the General, 'I saw that boy when he fell in battle shot to death.' Marshall replied, 'So did many others, but I didn't die though I was badly wounded and numbered with the killed for some time.' "

After the war he entered the University of Virginia where he was graduated in the law course. He settled in Vicksburg, Miss., and had a distinguished career.

On June 1, 1871, Martin Marshall married Mary Ella, daughter of John Bush, of Hinds County, Miss. They had five children: Letitia, Judith, Thomas Alexander, John, and Courtenay.

"Marshall first saw his future wife as he was driving to the station in his father's carriage to go to the University of Virginia in the fall of 1866. He made the coachman follow her up and learn who she was. He learned her name before he left the station, and immediately on his return home the next summer, he sought her hand and gained her heart."

He died September 17, 1895.

154. Thomas Staples Martin—1867.

Lawyer—U. S. Senator

Born July 29, 1847, at Scottsville, Va., where his father was a merchant and manufacturer.

Parents: John Samuel Martin (b. Fluvanna Co., Va.,) and Martha Ann Staples (b. Scottsville, Va.).

Paternal Grandparents: John S. Martin, and Mary Ann Haden, both of Fluvanna Co., Va.

His father on Sept. 5, 1863, in applying for the son's admission said, "He has been under the tuition of Mr. D. Pinkney Powers, for the last two years. Is now reading Horace; a very good French scholar; well grounded in Arithmetic; and now in Davies Algebra. . . . Is about five feet tall; generally healthy, but of delicate frame and constitution."

He matriculated at V. M. I. March 1, 1864 and was a cadet until Richmond was evacuated, April 2, 1865. With several other cadets he was ill in the institute hospital when the corps went on the New Market Campaign and, therefore, did not participate in the battle.* At the time he was a cadet private in Co. C; later he saw service with the corps in its military activities. In October 1865 he entered the University of Virginia and was there for two years, after which he commenced the study of law by reading at home. He was licensed to practice in 1869 and the remainder of his life was devoted to his profession, at the bar and in shaping national legislation. Older lawyers declared that he had the clearest legal mind of any lawyer in Virginia; his practice grew rapidly and he became the attorney for many corporations.

Married: Oct. 10, 1894, Lucy Chambliss Day, daughter of Col. Charles Fenton Day, of Isle of Wight Co., Va. She died January 7, 1915, and was survived by her husband and their two children:
Lucy Day Martin (d. June 11, 1927).
Thomas Staples Martin, Jr.
Their home was at "Monte Sano," on the Jefferson Highway just west of the University of Virginia.

He was a member of the board of visitors of several institutions (Miller Manual Training School, 1886; Univ. of Virginia, 1893; U. S. Naval Academy, 1905) but not until he successfully ran in 1893 for the office of U. S. Senator had he held public office, once installed he continued throughout the remainder of his life an extraordinarily useful public servant and statesman. In his campaigns he made very few speeches and yet, opposed in every election save the last, he ran successfully against such worthy opponents as Governors Fitzhugh Lee, Tyler and Montague; and Congressman Wm. A. Jones, V. M. I. '68.

He entered upon his senatorial duties March 4, 1895 and in 1911 he was elected minority leader of the Senate; with the advent of

---

*"When the battalion was ordered down the valley I was in the Hospital, having contracted a severe cold from lack of any heat in my room. When I recovered from the sickness I was retained as one of the guards at Barracks."

—9

Woodrow Wilson in 1913 he became the majority leader, a task which fell to his lot at a time when the work was truly colossal for it included the World War period.

He was the author of senate joint resolution No. 1, presented in April, 1917, which declared war on Germany. He was chairman of the Senate Appropriations Committee which during the war years prepared bills appropriating over fifty billion dollars, the largest amount ever appropriated by a legislative body in any country. One of the last three Confederate Veterans in Congress, he lent his great aid to his Alma Mater when Senator Dupont sponsored the bill reimbursing the Virginia Military Institute for the destruction of its property on June 12, 1864—on which date these gentlemen were both present, serving in opposing forces. He received the degree of Master of Arts from his Alma Mater in June, 1917.

The prodigious labor, performed without recreation or rest, of the war and post-war legislation undermined his health and, after an illness of about five months, on November 12, 1919, "he died as he would have wished to die—in harness, with faculties undimmed."

Death came in the hospital of the University of Virginia and his burial, attended by the great of the nation, was in the University cemetery.

Virginia has been fortunate in the calibre of her Senators. Martin, the "business senator" or the "busy senator," was the colleague of the great orator, John W. Daniel—the "Lame Lion of Lynchburg," who was succeeded by governor Claude A. Swanson, now secretary of the navy, who was in turn succeeded by Governor Harry Flood Byrd (grandfather Col. William Byrd, V. M. I. '49; brother Admiral Richard E. Byrd, V. M. I. '08; son Harry F. Byrd, Jr., V. M. I. '35; father-in-law James Bradshaw Beverley, V. M. I. '79). His own successor was the learned and stalwart Carter Glass All of these nationally respected gentlemen have ever appreciated the fundamental educational system, the mode of life, and the insistence on honor, integrity and industry for which the Virginia Military Institute has successfully stood for nearly a century.

155. William Bruce Martin—1865.

Lawyer—Jurist

Born September 18, 1846, at New Castle, Delaware.

Parents: General James Green Martin (b. in Elizabeth City, N. C.), a graduate of West Point, Brigadier General in the Confederate Army and General-in-Chief of the North Carolina troops, and Mary Anne Murry Read (b. in New Castle, Del.), great-granddaughter of George Read of Delaware, one of the signers of the Declaration of Independence.

Grandparents: Dr. William Martin, of Norfolk County, Va., and Sophia Daugé, of Camden County, N. C.
George Read, of New Castle, Del., and Louisa Ridgeley Dorsey, of Maryland.

Matriculated at V. M. I. from Raleigh, N. C., January 6, 1862 and served with the corps in all of its campaigns except the New Market Campaign. On February 11, 1864 he had been appointed a sergeant and at the time the corps was ordered away in May 1864 he was in the hospital recovering from a spell of illness. He was the fourth Cadet Sergeant in Co. C and was in charge of the detail left in Lexington to guard the Institute. The following session he was cadet second lieutenant in Co. C and remained with the corps until the evacuation of Richmond. He was graduated with the class of 1865 and stood ninth in his class.

After the war Judge Martin followed farming for a while, then clerked in a store, later taught school and finally began the study of law in the office of Judge Bailey, in Asheville, N. C. He became a licensed lawyer in North Carolina in 1867, and in the summer of 1868 established a law office in Norfolk, Va. He was at different times a member of the law firm of Duffield & Martin and Starke & Martin, the latter being a connection which lasted until his elevation to the bench. This occurred in 1895, when the Court of Law and Chancery was established in Norfolk for the relief of the Corporation Court, which, up to that time, had heard civil as well as criminal cases. Judge Martin was at that time recommended to the Legislature for the new judgeship by the Norfolk Bar Association. He was successively re-elected and always enjoyed the public's confidence and the respect and admiration of the members of the legal fraternity. As a jurist, he was invariably exact, fearless and impartial, his decisions always bearing the stamp of honor, integrity and deep regard for right and justice.

His popularity in Norfolk is attested by the fact that the voters three times chose him as City Attorney, a position which he filled with conspicuous ability, and he also served as a member of the City Council, where his influence was always strongly felt. Among lawyers of the State Judge Martin was long known as the learned author of an index-digest of Virginia decisions, a work that gained the unanimous and hearty support of attorneys throughout Virginia.

Judge Martin was active in church work throughout his life. He was one of the founders of St. Luke's Church, of Norfolk, and was a member of the vestry and board of trustees of St. Andrew's Protestant Episcopal Church, of which he was also one of the founders. He represented the diocese of Southern Virginia in the general convention on several occasions, and was treasurer of the Diocesan Missionary Society.

On June 25, 1878, he married Elizabeth Marchant, daughter of Colonel Lucien Douglass Starke, of Norfolk, Va.

Children: Elizabeth Starke.
James Green.
William Bruce, Jr.
Lucien Starke.
Lida Starke.
Marianne Read.
George Read Martin.

A grandson, James Green Martin, IV, was graduated at V. M. I. with the class of 1932.

Judge Martin died at 11 :00 P. M., May 13, 1921, at his home, 1122 Westover avenue, having been ill for several weeks. He is buried in Cedar Grove cemetery, Norfolk, Va. Mrs. Martin's death occurred on January 20, 1932.

156. Simon Blount Mason—1867.

Merchant—Railroad Service

Born about 1848 (he was 15 years and 4 months of age at matriculation), in Washington, D. C.

Parents: John Young Mason (b. April 18, 1799, in Greensville County, Va.; d. Oct. 3, 1859, in Paris, France; Attorney General in President Polk's cabinet; U. S. Minister to France under President Pierce) and Mary Ann Fort (b. Southampton County, Va., Oct. 31, 1803; d. July 1, 1870).

Grandparents: Edmund Mason, and Frances Ann Young.
Lewis Fort, and Eliza Harris Coleman.

He matriculated at V. M. I on February 27, 1864, from Hicksford, Va., a lad of a few months over fifteen years of age, and served as a cadet private in "B" company at the battle of New Market. The following session he was a cadet until the evacuation of Richmond.

"I will impose upon your good nature to tell you a little incident that occurred after leaving Richmond. With five other boys, having been separated from the command, we were captured very early one morning (near Hampden-Sydney College) by troops belonging to Genl. Bartlett's command, Hancock's corps, and we requested to be taken to him (he was afterwards, I think, Minister to Spain). He and his staff were just as kind to us as they could be and we messed with them; when we stopped that night to eat supper, I was at the Genl's. mess and the smell of ham and real coffee was delightful, but eating and drinking the same cannot be described. Now the funny part comes. When the colored cook and waiter handed me my coffee, he said, 'Why how you do, Marse Blount.' The General said, 'Mason he seems to know you,' and I replied, 'He should, as he belongs to us.' He then said, 'Do you want him?' and I replied, 'No, he never was any account.' There was a laugh." Mason remained with General Bartlett until the day after the surrender at Appomatox.

In 1872 he married Amanda G., daughter of John Enders, of Richmond, Va. They had four children: John Young Mason (dead).
Enders Mason (dead).
Simon Blount Mason, Jr., m. Mary Montgomery, daughter of Mrs. William Alexander Wylie.
St. George Tucker Mason (dead).

Following the war Mr. Mason engaged in mercantile pursuits and later entered the railroad business. He was assistant to the President of the Erie Railroad, with offices at 21 Cortlandt St., New York City, for many years. He died at his home in Ashland, Va., on January 16, 1921, and was buried in Hollywood cemetery, Richmond, Va. His death followed an illness of several days brought on by pneumonia.

A brother, St. George Tucker Mason, was in the class of 1865 at V. M. I., but was not a member of the New Market corps.

157. Reuben Maury—1867.

Farmer

Born August 4, 1847, at "Piedmont," Charlottesville, Va.

Parents: Jesse Lewis Maury, of "Piedmont," and Lucy J. Price, born in Pittsylvania County, Va. She had charge of a division of the hospital at Charlottesville during the Civil War.

Grandparents: Reuben Maury, who built "Piedmont" in 1806, and Elizabeth Lewis, daughter of Jesse Pitman Lewis, a soldier of the Revolution.

Stephen Price, of Albemarle County, Va., and —— Harper, of "Spring Hill," near Ivy Depot, Va.

He entered Major Jones's school in Charlottesville before he matriculated at V. M. I. on August 17, 1863. At the battle of New Market he served as a cadet private in Co. C.

Following the war, Mr. Maury returned to "Piedmont," which he inherited from his father, and was very successful as a farmer.

On December 14, 1910, he married Mrs. Bryan Houston (née Weyman), of Atlanta, Ga.

He died on January 2, 1923, and was survived by his mother (she died the following month) ; by his wife ; a brother, S. Price Maury ; and two sisters, Ellen, who married the Hon. James L. Slayden, member of the House of representatives from Texas for twenty-two years, and Jane, who married Albert Maverick, of San Antonio, Texas ; a nephew, Fontaine Maury Maverick, V. M. I. '16; and a nephew, Lewis Augustine Maury, V. M. I '13, a son of S. Price Maury.

158. Thomas William McClung—1867.

Farmer

Born March 8, 1847, in Greenbrier County, W. Va.

Parents: Major William McClung, a farmer of Blue Sulphur Springs, W. Va., and Elizabeth Wilson McClanahan, of Roanoke, Va.

Paternal Grandparents: Col. Samuel McClung, who served in the Revolutionary War, and Rebecca Bolland.

He entered V. M. I. on October 31, 1863, from Lewisburg, and was a cadet private in Co. D at the battle of New Market.

On Feb. 25, 1871, he marred Elizabeth Strother Estill, daughter of Floyd Estill and Susan Kincaid, of Lewisburg, W. Va.

They had nine children: William Estill (d. in Cincinnati, Ohio, March 15, 1920).

John Edgar, of Lewisburg, W. Va.

Thomas McClanahan and

Lawrence Floyd, of Frankfort, Ky.

Florence Elizabeth, m. Daniel S. Combs.

Agatha Estill, m. J. Marvin Watts, of Lewisburg, W. Va.

Lucy Withrow, m. Chas. Edwin Boone, of Ronceverte, W. Va.

Margaret Lynn McClung, of Lewisburg, W. Va.

Susan Rebecca, m. Gordon R. Worthington, of Jackson, Miss.

Mr. McClung spent his entire life farming and lived on the same farm where his father lived before him near Lewisburg, West Virginia.

He died December 23, 1921.

159. James William McCorkle—1867.

Merchant

Born February 13, 1841, at Fairfield, Rockbridge County, Va.

Parents: Samuel R. McCorkle, and Mary Ann Snyder, of Kerrs Creek, Rockbridge County, Va.

Maternal Grandparents: John Snyder, and Barbara ——, of Rockbridge County.

Before entering V. M. I. he "Volunteered at Braxton Courthouse, Virginia, (now West Virginia) ; mustered into service about April 20th, 1861. Elected Second Sergeant in Company "C" (Braxton Blues), Hansbrough's Battalion, and served in this capacity until the reorganization of the army in the spring of 1862. At this time was elected Second Lieutenant in the same company; at the same time the Battalion was placed in the 25th Virginia Infantry. Served as Lieutenant in the 25th until resignation in October 1862 to accept an appointment as cadet to the V. M. I., which was of some ten months standing. That is to say, the ten months covered the Valley Campaign and all of the movements of Stonewall Jackson until slightly wounded at the battle of Second Manassas, and placed in a temporary hospital at Middleburg, Loudoun County, Va. Was in the following battles: Greensboro River, fall of 1861; Alleghany Mountain, December 12th or 13th, 1861; McDowell, spring of 1862, and the different engagements in the Valley Campaign and back to the battles of Cross Keys, Port Republic, Seven Days Fight at Richmond, Cedar Mountain, and Second Manassas."

He matriculated at V. M. I. on Dec. 12, 1862, from Kerrs Creek, Va. and was admitted to the fifth class. The following session he took part in the battle of New Market as a cadet private in Co. B. He resigned from the corps of cadets on February 18, 1865, was commissioned First Lieutenant, and re-entered the active service. He was in command of his company (the Captain was absent) and on the morning of April 12, 1865, his regiment was ordered to Salisbury, N. C. In the attack of General Stoneman, McCorkle was captured and taken to prison at Camp Chase, Ohio. He was released from the prison hospital on June 11, 1865, but was not able to leave the hospital until July 4, 1865.

He married Annie E. Frazier, daughter of James P. Frazier of Bath County, Va. A daughter, Mrs. Gooch Vaught (?) of Roanoke, Va., survived him.

For many years he was a merchant at Middlebrook, Va., later removing to Roanoke, where he died on October 27, 1914.

160. William Hugh McDowell—1867.

"Died on the Field of Honor"

Born December 31, 1846, at Beattie's Ford, Iredell County, N. C.

Parents: Robert Irwin McDowell (b. 1813; was graduated from Hampden-Sydney College, Va., in 1832), of Mt. Mourne, N. C., and Rebekah Brevard.

Grandparents: Hugh McDowell, and Margaret, daughter of General Robert Irwin, both of Mecklenburg County, N. C.
Franklin Brevard and Margaret Jack Conner, both of Mecklenburg County, N. C.

He entered V. M. I. on August 22, 1863, from Mt. Mourne, N. C., and was assigned to the fourth class. He was killed on May 15, 1864, while serving as a cadet private in Co. B at the battle of New Market. When ordered to New Market, he was contemplating accepting a position upon the staff of General James Conner, his kinsman.

"In advancing from the ravine the Battalion was now and then protected by folds in the ground from the direct fire of the enemy. From the ravine to the close of the Bushong House is about half a mile. The cadets were exposed to direct fire the last half of this distance, losing three killed at this stage of their advance, the number including First Sergeant Cabell of D Co., and Privates Stanard and McDowell of B Co." (Mil. Hist. of V. M. I., p. 312.)

"A little removed from the spot where Cabell fell, and nearer to the position of the enemy, lay McDowell, it was a sight to wring one's heart. That little boy was lying there asleep, more fit, indeed, for the cradle than the grave. He was barely sixteen, I judge, and by no means robust for his age. He was a North Carolinian. He had torn open his jacket and shirt, and, even in death, lay clutching them back, exposing a fair breast with its red wound." (The End of an Era, p. 306.)

After temporary interment at New Market, his remains were brought to Lexington in May, 1866, and are now buried beneath the New Market battle monument at V. M. I.

161. John Williamson McGavock—1867.

Farmer

Born October 25, 1846, in Wytheville, Va.

Parents: Ephriam McGavock, of Wytheville, Va., and Abigail Jouet Williamson.

Grandparents: James McGavock and Mary Crockett.
Mathias Williamson and Frances Hargrave Jouet.

He matriculated at V. M. I. from Wytheville, on January 14, 1864. Four months later he took part in the battle of New Market as a cadet private in Co. C.

"I was in C company and being a tall boy for that company, my place was next to Capt. Hill. Not being prompt on the morning of the battle, I lost my place at the head of the company and took my place at the other end next to the colors. Poor Merritt took my place and was badly wounded along with Hill. . . . We went over the ground where some of our troops had been for we passed a number of killed and wounded. I recollect seeing far in advance of us a gallant Confederate. He was half reclining, evidently wounded. He was cheering all he could with one hand, and voice, holding himself up with the other. I saw many a bullet strike him and he was perfectly still when we passed him. We travelled a long while over ground where the Yankees had been, because I picked up a Yankee gun and was the first cadet to fire a gun (and that was accidently—the new gun being easy on trigger). . . . Although I was within a few feet of Cabell and Crockett when they were killed, yet I knew nothing about it until the battle was over. Crockett was from my county and was a close friend of mine. . . ."

The following session he returned and was a member of the corps until Richmond was evacuated.

On November 21, 1871, he married Emily Maria Graham. The children of
this union were as follows:
David Graham (b. Oct. 8, 1872), m. Evelyn Robins.
John Williamson (b. Nov. 21, 1873), county clerk of Wythe County, Va.,
m. Nannie F. Miller.
Ephraim (b. Nov. 25, 1874).
Martha Pierce (b. July 26, 1876).
Abigail Jouet (b. Nov. 19, 1877), widow of Montgomery W. Boyd.
James Hampton (b. Dec. 3, 1878), m. Bess Kelley.
Henry Parrish.
Margaret Mathews (b. April 14, 1884), wife of W. R. Crockett, of Pu-
laski, Va.
Mary Bell (b. July 14, 1886).
Mrs. McGavock died in 1889, and on June 17, 1891, he married secondly,
Jane Byrd Pendleton. Of this union there were the following children:
Emily Maria Graham (dead), m. Alcott Neary, of Rochester, N. Y.
Byrd Page (b. July 9, 1894).
Sarah Jackson (b. June 6, 1896), wife of John Allison, of Pulaski, Va.
Gurdon Pendleton (b. Nov. 15, 1898).
Stephen (b. Nov. 25, 1901).
Francis Nelson (b. March 2, 1907).

"After the war I was a student at Norwood School in Nelson County, Va.,
and from there went to the University of Virginia and studied in the academic department, graduating in Latin and French. I taught school for a
short period in Alabama and since then have been a farmer. My present post
office address is Max Meadows, Wythe County, Va., R. F. D."

The above was written some years ago by Mr. McGavock. He is
now (1933) living at his home in Max Meadows and owns extensive
blue grass tracts in the eastern part of Wythe County where stock
raising is a leading industry. He is a member of the Republican
party and has always been active in politics.

162. Newton McVeigh—1867.

Merchant

Born July 13, 1846, at Alexandria, Va.

Parents: James Harvie McVeigh, of Middleburg, Loudoun County, Va., and
Cynthia Aeiel Guest, of Maryland.

Grandparents: Jesse McVeigh, and his wife, Ann ——
Rev. Job Guest, and his wife, Elizabeth ——

He attended private school before entering V. M. I. on February
26, 1864. In the battle of New Market he was a cadet private in
Co. A. When the corps was disbanded in Richmond, McVeigh joined
Mosby's command in which he remained until the close of the war.

In 1877 he married Lillian Rosalind Tapscott (died June 9, 1922), daughter
of Benjamin Tapscott and his wife, Charlotte Wallace. They had two
children:
Charles Senff McVeigh (b. June 3, 1883).
Charlotte Wallace McVeigh (b. February 16, 1890).

Mr. McVeigh was engaged in the notions business as a traveling
salesman with headquarters in Richmond, Va., for some time. He
then removed to Baltimore and for many years was connected with

the house of Armstrong, Cator & Co. Member of the Travelers' Protective Association.

He died on June 21, 1904, in Richmond, Va., at the home of his mother-in-law, Mrs. Charlotte Tapscott.

163. Henry Johns Mead—1866.

Editor—Banking

Born about 1845 (he was 17 years of age when he matriculated), in Bedford County, Va.

Parents: Thomas Mead, county surveyor of Bedford County, and Mary A. Worsley, of Loudoun County, Va.

Grandparents: William Mead (born in Bucks County, Pa., but moved with his parents to Fairfax County, Va., in 1745; later settling in Bedford County) and Mary Shreve (a descendant of Truelove Shreve, the granddaughter of the famous Mary Dyer, who was hung in Boston during the early Colonial days because of her religious principles).

John Worsley (an Englishman who came to America in 1802 and bought an estate in Loudoun County, near Waterford, which he called "Hedgeland" on account of the beautiful thorn hedges he had around it instead of fences) and Elizabeth, daughter of Judge Joshua Daniel, of Virginia.

He matriculated at V. M. I. on November 26, 1862, from Liberty, (Bedford County), Va., and was assigned to the third class. He was entered by his guardian, Rev. John A. Wharton. In the battle of New Market he was a cadet private in Co. A and was wounded in the thigh. The following session he resigned on January 19, 1865 in order to enter the Confederate army.

On February 11, 1905, his sister, Mrs. Elizabeth Mead Hoffecker, of Wilmington, Delaware, wrote as follows:

"He was in William and Mary College prior to its closing, and then went to the V. M. I. He was a man of rare literary attainment. For several years he edited, and owned, the Warrenton Journal, Fauquier Co., Va. His health became very poor and he sold it, and returned to his home in Leesburg, accepted a position in the Loudoun National Bank and held it at the time of his death. He was offered the cashiership when Anthony Dibrell died, but would not accept it on account of his ill health."

Mr. Mead died very suddenly on June 27, 1894, in Leesburg, Va.

164. James Love Merritt—1867.

Farmer—Surveyor

Born about September, 1845 (at matriculation he was 17 years 11 months old).

Parents: W. H. E. Merritt and Elizabeth Willis Goode.

Grandparents: Henry Merritt and —— Walker.
John Bennett Goode and Permelia Hendricks.

Matriculated at V. M. I. from Lawrenceville, Va., on August 6, 1863 and later in the session was a cadet private in Co. C in the battle of New Market. In this battle he was severely wounded.* He did not return to the Institute the following session.

---

*In a few minutes a shell from one of Carlin's guns on Bushong's Hill

After the war he followed civil engineering for some years and then settled on his farm near Lawrenceville where he lived with his brother, Howard Jeffries Merritt, V. M. I. '68. For many years he was a Justice of the Peace and was held in high esteem by the bench, bar, and people of Lawrenceville.

He died at his home, unmarried, on March 18, 1911.

165. Collier Harrison Minge—1864.

Cotton Merchant

Born January 19, 1845, in Mobile, Alabama.

Parents: Collier Harrison Minge, of Weyanoke, Charles City County, Va. and Anna Maria Ladd, of Montpelier, Charles City County, Va.

Grandparents: John Minge and Sarah Harrison, both of Charles City County, Va. She was the daughter of Benjamin Harrison, of Berkeley, one of the signers of the Declaration of Independence.
Oliver Ladd, of Montpelier, Charles City County, Va., and ——

His paternal ancestors date back to the time of James Minge who was clerk of the House of Burgesses in 1676.

In 1836 his parents moved to Mobile, Alabama, from which place he matriculated at V. M. I. on August 2, 1860. As cadet Captain of Co. A he was the highest ranking officer in the corps. In the battle of New Market he commanded two three-inch rifled guns which were manned by cadets selected from the four companies. During the battle this section of artillery was detached from the corps and served directly under Major William McLaughlin, who commanded all the Confederate artillery at New Market. No sub-professor accompanied the artillery on this campaign, as had theretofore been customary. Captain Thomas M. Semmes, V. M. I., '60, who had been in charge of artillery instruction had been assigned to temporary duty on the staff of Major General Francis H. Smith, the Superintendent, on May 11, 1864. The Superintendent was indisposed at the time and did not leave Lexington with the corps on that date.

At graduation he was commissioned a second lieutenant and assigned as Adjutant to Wallace's Battalion and served at the Narrows of New River and at Chafin's Farm, below Richmond; assigned to the defences of the Stanton River Bridge and organized a battery of artillery for that service. In August 1864 he was commissioned Captain and transferred to the Dept. of the South; surrendered at Meridian.

On January 9, 1878, Captain Minge married Eva, daughter of Colonel Andrew Jackson Ingersoll and Mary Melvina Simms, of Mobile, Ala.
Children: Collier Harrison, Jr., V. M. I., 1900; m. (first) Theo Vance, of Shreveport, La.; one son, Collier Harrison, III; m. (second) Madie

---

burst just in front of the line, and Captain A. Govan Hill, Tactical Officer of C Company, and four cadets, Corporal Wise, J. S., D Co., Private Woodlief, P. W., Jr., B Co., and Privates Merritt, J. L., and Read, C. H., Jr., of C Co., were struck to the ground." (Wise's Mil. Hist. of V. M. I., p. 388.)

Frances Diggett, of Chicago, Ill.; a son, Robert Collier, and a daughter, Dorothy Louise, survived their father who died on June 6, 1918.
Ethel Ingersoll.
Mary Ingersoll.
Jeannie Dixey.

With his father-in-law, Captain Minge engaged in the cotton business in Mobile, the firm being Ingersoll, Minge & Co. Later he removed to New Orleans and continued in the same work with his brother-in-law, Mr. A. J. Ingersoll, Jr. About 1905 he retired from active business and made his home at Mississippi City. He was a member of most of the New Orleans clubs and was prominent in the carnival organizations.

His death occurred on December 5, 1915, in Hotel Dieu, New Orleans, following an attack of pneumonia. His body was taken to Mobile and interred in Magnolia Cemetery in that city.

His portrait in cadet uniform hangs in Jackson Memorial Hall.

Mrs. Minge died on December 15th, just ten days after her husband's death, and was survived by the following children: C. H., Jr., Mary, Mrs. R. M. Walford, of Shreveport, La., and Mrs. John Gedding, of Decatur, Ala.

166. James Hunter Minor—1867.

Merchant—Clerk of Court—Real Estate

Born March 7, 1848, at Orange Court House, Va.

Parents: Dr. James Hunter Minor (1818-1862), of Music Hall, Albemarle Co., Va., and Mary Watson Morris (1821-1903).

Grandparents: Samuel Overton Minor, and Lydia Laurie Lewis.
William Morris, and Nancy Watson, of "Sylvania," Louisa Co., Va.

Matriculated at V. M. I. from Cobham, Va., on September 11, 1863 and later in the session as a cadet private in Co. C was in the battle of New Market. He did not return to the institute the following session but enlisted in Carrington's Battery and served with it until the end of the war.

For several years thereafter he was a merchant until he was elected Recorder of Deeds for Audrain Co., Missouri, and served in that capacity and as deputy for fifteen years.

Married: May 31, 1880, Ida (died 1895), daughter of Jeptha Lake, of Farber, Mo. They had two daughters:
Mary Morris, who married Dr. Allie Adams, of Callaway Co., Mo.
Lucile.

In his later years he was in the real estate business in Mexico, Mo. There he died January 4, 1914 and was buried in Elmwood Place.

He was survived by his second wife and his two daughters: Mrs. Adams then living at Auxvasse, Mo., and Miss Lucile Adams, at Malta Bend, Mo.

His brother, Richard C. Minor, was graduated at V. M. I. in 1876.

167. Stephen Trigg Mitchell.

Rancher—Railroad Service

Born November 2, 1845, at "Wheatly," Bedford County, Va.

Parents: Robert C. Mitchell, born in Amherst County, Va., and Lucy Phillips, of Botetourt County, Va.

Grandparents: William Mitchell and Sally ——
Dr. Samuel Phillips and ——

He matriculated from Liberty (now Bedford) at V. M. I. on January 11, 1864, and at the battle of New Market was a cadet private in Co. C.

Following the close of the war, with three older brothers, he returned from the army to "Wheatly" in Bedford county where they studied under a tutor for one year. At the end of that year when but little more than twenty years of age, he went to Texas where he successfully worked as a rancher for several years. Returning to Virginia he married Mary, daughter of Lewis L. Barnes, of Richmond, Va.

He died in Scottsville, Albemarle County, Va., May 24, 1896, and was survived by his wife and two sons, Trigg and Beverly V. Mitchell. In August 1913 the latter was employed in the Treasury Department of the Norfolk and Western Railroad, Roanoke, Va.

As a matter of record, some members of this family spell the name "Michel."

168. David Guin Mohler—1867.

Real Estate

Born December 29, 1846, at "Mountain Home," Page County, Va.

Parents: Jacob Mohler (b. 1804; d. Jan. 22, 1880), of Page County, Va., and Frances Jane Grigsby (b. Feb. 11, 1812; d. May 6, 1848).

Grandparents: John Mohler (b. April 5, 1772, in Pennsylvania; d. April 17, 1835, in Rockbridge County, Va.), and Magdalene Rhinehart, of Pennsylvania.
Elisha Grigsby (b. 1774; d. 1847), and Elizabeth Porter.

He entered the 3rd Virginia regiment, Confederate Army, in 1861, at the age of fifteen years, in the Valley of Virginia. In 1862 he joined Van Dorn's Army at Holly Springs, Miss., and was on the retreat from Holly Springs to Grenada, Miss., and from there marched to Vicksburg. He served three months just before the fall of that city and was ordered to Knoxville, Tenn., where he served a few months under General Dabney H. Maury. From there he was ordered to Mobile, Ala., and saw service until December, 1863.

On January 13, 1864, he matriculated at V. M. I., and on May 15th of that year served as a cadet private in Co. "A" at the battle of New Market. Following the destruction of the Institute by General Hunter, he joined the corps of cadets at the Alms House in Richmond to continue his studies. Resigning his cadetship on February 1, 1865, he joined Mosby's command and remained with that organization until captured at Burks' Station, near Alexandria, Va., by the 8th Illinois Cavalry, April 12, 1865, just after the surrender of General Lee. He was confined in the Alexandria jail for a few days and then sent to "Old Capitol" prison in Washington, D. C., where he was held until May 15, 1865. Refusing to take the oath of allegiance to the United States government, he was sent to Elmira, N. Y., and remained there until July 3rd, when, after taking the oath required (the war being over), he was released.

On October 10, 1878, he married Laura, daughter of Samuel Lyell, of Baltimore, Md., and sister of Colonel John Warner Lyell, V. M. I., 1859. They had two sons, John Samuel and Arthur Douglas Mohler.

Mr. Mohler engaged in the real estate business in Alexandria, Baltimore and Washington, D. C. He died in Washington on June 5, 1917, and was buried in Arlington Cemetery.

His brother, Elisha Grigsby Mohler, was graduated at V. M. I. with the class of 1862.

169. Edwin Steptoe Moorman—1867.

Farmer—County Treasurer

Born September 5, 1845, in Campbell Co., Va.

Parents: Thomas Bowling Moorman, of Campbell Co., and Frances Elizabeth Goggin, of Bedford Co.

On August 1, 1863 he matriculated at V. M. I. from Yellow Branch, Campbell County, and later in the session served as a cadet private in Co. D in the battle of New Market, where he was wounded in the arm by a grapeshot.

In 1868 he married Sarah Lucinda Moorman, daughter of John Clark Moorman and Matilda Katharine Leftwich, both of Campbell County.

He engaged in farming throughout his life but took part in other activities. For two years he was U. S. Revenue Collector and for six years a justice of the peace. In 1887 he was elected county treasurer and so continued for a number of years.

He died suddenly at his home in Rustburg on April 16, 1912, survived by his wife and two children: Carlton Gilmer Moorman, of Roanoke, Va., and Mrs. Fannie Goggin Goolsby, of Marion, Va.

170. Patrick Henry Morgan—1866.

Lawyer—State Senator—Supt., U. S. Life Saving Service

Born Shawboro, N. C., July 31, 1844.

Parents: Joseph B. Morgan and Annie Lamb.

Paternal Grandparents: Miles Morgan and Lydia Burgess, of Camden Co., N. C.

After attending Indian Ridge Academy (N. C.) he matriculated at V. M. I. from Indian Town, Currituck Co., N. C., on April 29, 1862; repeated the work of the fourth class the following session; and as a third classman took part in the battle of New Market. At the time he was a cadet private in Co. A but in the battle he was attached to the artillery section. He did not return to the institute the following session.

July 19, 1865, he married Susan De Ford, daughter of William De Ford, of Camden Co., N. C. They had two children, Charles D., and Lillie Morgan.

Sept. 21, 1881, he married secondly, Bettie Ferebee, daughter of Edwin Ferebee, of Camden Co., N. C. They had four children, Bessie, Lattie, Joseph P., and Edwin F. Morgan.

After the war he studied law and was licensed to practice but never actively engaged in his profession—rather did he prefer to engage in various business pursuits, which he conducted with much success. Keenly interested in politics, he represented his district in the state senate in 1891-92, and was then appointed Superintendent of the 7th District, United States Life Saving Service (now the Coast Guard)' with headquarters at Shawboro, N. C. His district extended from Cape Henry, Va. to the South Carolina line. He held this position about twenty years, retiring one year before his death.

He died at his beautiful home in Shawboro, N. C., on August 27, 1917, one of the most substantial citizens of his community in business, politics, and the church. He was survived by his wife and three sons who live in Shawboro and by two daughters: Mrs. D. G. Cooper, Jr., of Henderson, N. C., and Mrs. R. W. Norman, of Salisbury, N. C.

171. Arthur Alexander Morson—1865.

Farmer

Born June 20, 1846, at "Hollywood," eight miles from Fredericksburg, Va., on the Rappahannock River.

Parents: Alexander Morson, of "Hollywood" and Maria May Berry, of "Berry Plains," on the Potomac River, near Mt. Vernon, Va.

Paternal Grandparents: Alexander Morson, and Anne Casson Alexander (daughter of William Pearson and Sarah Casson Alexander, of "Snowden"). See Sketch No. 173.

He was a nephew of James A. Seddon, Secretary of War, C. S. A.

Matriculated at V. M. I. by his guardian Dr. Hugh Morson, from Fredericksburg, on January 1, 1862 and was admitted to the third class. The following session he took part as a cadet private in Co. C in the battle of New Market. This class was graduated as of May 12, 1864 and he stood 16 among 24.

"I did not serve with the corps around Richmond, but was appointed a Lieutenant and Drill Master, and in this capacity served near Urbanna on the Rappahannock until after Lee's surrender, and was paroled at Ashland."

Married: May 1, 1878, Bessie Eppie, daughter of Louis Dameron, of Mississippi, near Jackson. They had thirteen children:
Arthur James.
Mildred Berry, who married Axel Frederic Youngling.
Hallie Taylor, who married Massie(?) Arthur Kennington, Jr.
Bessie Kate, who married Nathan I. Greene.
John Andrews.

Rosalie Vere, who married Weissinger O. Emerson.
Julie Dameron.
Hugh Blair.
Sara Frances.
William Todd.
Phillip Hull.
Margaret Priscilla.
Mary Roberta Alexander.

He engaged in farming all his life near Jackson, Mississippi, and was the proprietor of the Hermitage Creamery and Stock Farm (specializing in high grade Jersey milch cows) in the Van Winkle neighborhood.

On October 7, 1914 he died at his home from an attack of indigestion.

Said the Clarion-Ledger of Jackson:

"Mr. Morson was well known here, being rated among the most substantial citizens of the community. He is survived by a wife and twelve children."

His brother, Alexander Morson, was graduated at V. M. I. in 1853.

172. James Bruce Morson—1867.

Planter—Manufacturer

Born 1848, in Richmond, Va., in the house now known as the White House of the Confederacy, at that time owned by his father.

Parents: Hon. James M. Morson, of Richmond, Va., and "Dover," Goochland Co., Va., and Ellen Carter Bruce.*

Grandparents: James Bruce, of "Woodburn," and Elvira Cabell, his second wife.

He matriculated at V. M. I. on August 6, 1863, from Dover Mills, Va., and later in the session he served as a cadet private in Co. C in the battle of New Market. The following session he returned and was a cadet until the corps was disbanded in Richmond on April 2, 1865.

After the war he removed with his cousin, Tom Seddon to New Iberia, Louisiana, where the two operated a large sugar plantation until 1888 when they removed to Birmingham and he became connected with the Sloss Steel and Iron Co., of which company Mr. Seddon was the president. As Captain of Troop D, First Cavalry, Alabama National Guard, he was an able officer. Fraternally he was a member of the Knights of Pythias.

In the latter years of his life he was connected with the Alabama State Fair Association.

He married Claudia Marshall, of Louisville, Ky., a descendant of Chief Jus-

---

*Ellen Carter Bruce's sister, Sarah Bruce, married Hon. James Alexander Seddon, Secretary of War, of the Confederate States, and her brother, Charles Bruce, married Sarah Seddon, the sister of Hon. Jas. A. Seddon. The two sisters, Ellen and Sarah Bruce, were belles of Washington society, much admired for their beauty, charm, and character. Two poems addressed to them by John Quincy Adams, then president, are still preserved in the family.

tice Marshall, and they had two daughters, who met a tragic death by drowning in Alabama, and a son Thomas Seddon Morson.

Capt. Morson died at his home at "Fairview", Birmingham, Ala., November 11, 1914 after an illness of several months. Interment was in Louisville, Ky.

He was survived by his widow, son, and two sisters: Mrs. Leigh Robinson, of Washington, D. C., and Mrs. Wyndham R. Meredith, of Richmond, Va.

173. William Alexander Morson—1864.

Tobacconist—Farmer

Born February 2, 1843, at Fredericksburg, Va.

Parents: Arthur Alexander Morson, born at "Hollywood," near Fredericksburg, Va., and Maria M. Scott, born at "Oakwood," Fauquier Co., Va.

Grandparents: Alexander Morson, born 1761, near Fredericksburg, and Anne Casson Alexander, born 1781 at "Snowden," near Fredericksburg. (See Sketch No. 171.)

Judge John Scott, born at "Gordonsdale," near The Plains, Va., and Elizabeth Pickett, born at Warrenton, Va.

Matriculated at V. M. I. on March 27, 1862 from Richmond and was admitted to the third class. As a first classman he was Cadet Second Lieutenant of Co. A in the battle of New Market. Following the Lynchburg Campaign he was graduated with his class, standing 9 in a class of 14. Later he was a lieutenant in the Confederate army.

After the war he engaged in farming in Fauquier County, Va., at "Oakwood" his grandfather's place. In the course of time he went west and was a leaf tobacco broker in St. Louis, later in Cincinnati.

He married but we have no record of his wife's name.

On June 9, 1903 he died at Newport, Kentucky, and was survived by his widow and three children: Violet, William, and Gordon.

John Scott Morson, V. M. I. '65, was his brother, and his sister, Anne Alexander Morson, married General Scott Shipp, V. M. I. '59 (See Sketch No. 219.)

174. Gustavus Brown Wallace Nalle—1867.

Merchant—Farmer

Born March 29, 1846, at "Greenville," near Raccoon Ford, Culpeper Co., Va.

Parents: Philip Pendleton Nalle, of Stevensburg, Culpeper Co., Va., died Nov. 17, 1907, in his 92nd year, and Elizabeth Wallace of White Hall, King George Co., Va.

Grandparents: Martin Nalle, of Stevensburg, and Eleanor Madison Barbour, of Bloomingdale, Orange Co., Va. (a sister of James Barbour, who was Gov. of Va.; Pres. of the Senate; Sec. of War and Minister to Great Britain; and of Philip Pendleton Barbour, who was Speaker of the House of Representatives, and Justice of the Supreme Court).

Gustavus Brown Wallace, who served in the War of 1812, and ——

Matriculated at V. M. I. from Culpeper, Va., on August 17, 1863,

A TYPICAL CADET OF THE V. M. I. NEW MARKET CORPS

HON. SAM'L
MCD. MOORE'S
HOME

PORTER'S
LODGE

SUPT'S QUARTERS
AND
V. M. I. HEADQUARTERS

COL.
GILHAM'S
QUARTERS

COL.
WILLIAMSON'S
QUARTERS

BARRACK

LAUNDRY

HOSPITAL

MESS
HALL

THE VIRGINIA MILITARY INSTITUTE IN 1858

and later in the session he served as a Cadet Private in Co. D. The following session he was, on January 24, 1865, made a Cadet Corporal, Co. D, and continued his Cadetship until the corps was disbanded on April 2nd.

"We occupied the trenches on north side of James River, from which we were withdrawn on the night of the evacuation of Richmond and being cut off from the army of Northern Virginia by the destruction of the bridges at Richmond, were marched to Columbia, Fluvanna Co., Va., and there disbanded by Gen. Francis H. Smith . . . on April 4, 1865."

Married: December 10, 1872, Nannie Hull, daughter of Colonel John Porter. They had seven children, two of whom died in early youth.

"With an old Yankee mule and horse, without money or provisions, planted and cultivated a crop of corn. In September, 1865, borrowing the necessary money I matriculated at the University of Virginia. Returning home in 1866, I taught school, 1866-67. In 1868, with borrowed capital, I commenced the mercantile business (at Raccoon Ford) and continued in this business until 1905."

Moving to Culpeper, Va., in 1905, lived there although continuing to engage in farming until his death, February 27, 1926, after a lingering illness of several months.

For many years he was a vestryman of old St. Paul's Episcopal Church at Raccoon Ford and a director of the Culpeper National Bank.

He was survived by his wife, five children (William Crump Nalle, of Alexandria, Va.; Dr. Brodie Crump Nalle, of Charlotte, N. C.; Philip Porter Nalle, of Fort Myers, Fla.; Fenton Mercer Nalle and Mary Hart, wife of Frederick Power Hudgins, of Culpeper, Va.), and six grandchildren.

175. William Nelson—1865.

Lawyer

Born April 25, 1845, in the "Nelson House," Yorktown, Va., the last of the Nelsons born in this house.

Parents: William Nelson, of Yorktown (always called York or "little York," by the Nelsons, who settled there in 1700), and —— Whiting, a widow née Shield.

Grandparents: William Nelson (son of Thomas Nelson, Governor of Virginia and signer of the Declaration of Independence) and Sarah Burwell Page, of Rosewell, Gloucester Co., Va. (oldest daughter of Governor John Page, of Virginia).
John Shield, and ——

He matriculated at V. M. I. from Yorktown, April 1, 1862 and continued as a cadet until March 20, 1865, shortly before the corps was disbanded. In the battle of New Market he was second cadet sergeant in Co. D. Later on his class was graduated as of May 12, 1864 and he was the second distinguished graduate of his class and first lieutenant of Co. D.

After the war he studied law and practiced in New York with the firm of Alexander and Greene, whose offices were in the old Equita-

—10

ble Life Assurance Building at 120 Broadway — at that time the tallest building in New York.

Because of ill health he left New York on advice of his physician and settled in Austin, Texas, in the fall of 1871. There he built a home and sent for the slave, Priscilla, who had taught him to read. She came, brought her two children, and later was remembered in her young master's will—buying a home with her legacy. An echo from an ended era.

Married: Molly, the daughter of Judge Thomas Duval, of Austin, Texas. She was the granddaughter of Governor Duval of Florida. They had no children.

He died in St. Louis, September 10, 1877, en route from Virginia to his home in Austin, Texas, where he was buried. Survived by his wife and two sisters, Mrs. (Fanny) Mercer and L. Page Nelson.

176. Nelson Berkeley Noland—1870.

Civil Engineer—Farmer

Born September 19, 1846, in Hanover County, Va.

Parents: Colonel Callender St. George Noland (a lieutenant in the U. S. Navy in Mexican and Seminole wars, a lieutenant colonel of artillery in Confederate States service, stationed on James River), and Mary Edmonia Berkeley.

Grandparents: Major William Noland, of Aldie, Loudoun County, Va., and Catharine Callender, of Carlisle, Penn.
Thomes Nelson Berkeley, and Elizabeth Edmonia Churchill.

Before entering V. M. I. on July 29, 1863, from Verdon, Hanover County, Va., Mr. Noland attended Christian's School in Richmond. He was admitted to the fourth class at V. M. I. and served as a cadet private in Co. C at the battle of New Market. He was on the right flank of the company, next to the colors. The following session he was a cadet until Richmond was evacuated.

On October 18, 1895, he wrote the following notes about the events immediately preceding the charge of the cadets:

"I noticed just in front of my company an orchard and a dwelling house, and I think it was about here that the enemy's fire was most destructive to our Battalion. We went through the yard very close to the house, and it seems to me that a short distance beyond this house we were ordered to lie down behind the remnant of a worm-fence, about two rails high. Noticing Shriver, Cadet Captain of C Co., going further to the front, I followed him, and when about 30 yards in front of the line I saw him fall, or, as I supposed at the time, lie down for protection. At that I dropped as flat as I could in a furrow, and with my face close to the ground I could see a clear space next to the earth under the cloud of smoke, and right in front, covered by the smoke like a tarpaulin, I could see emerging the felloes and 12 inches of the spokes of what I think may have been the wheel of a Yankee gun.

"As well as I can make it out, my position was right between the Cadets and the Yankee battery and line of battle. The distance between the fence-row occupied by the Cadets and the Yankee front could not have been more than 200 yards.

"The fire was furious at this time. It seemed to me I saw pieces of paper caught up and swept towards us by the currents of air set in motion by the projectiles, and the boughs of a large tree immediately in my front were all stretched out and swaying towards us. I believed I was bound to get killed, but I did not want to get killed out of ranks, so I made a spurt back to the line and scuttled in behind 2 rails alongside of some fellows.

"Whilst lying here with the air literally filled with Yankee missiles, each one of which seemed to miss me only by a scant sixteenth of an inch, I noticed the Color Sergeant of a body of troops on our left and rear, jump up, and along with the Color Guard run to the front and establish himself upon the prolongation of our line.

"In a second a number of his regiment were running to the front and grouping themselves around him. I saw them falling like jackstraws, on their backs, faces, sides and knees. Then the flag, which had been perfectly erect in the centre of the group, dipped almost to the ground, but some one had it up again in a moment. Then the regiment arose with a yell and rushed into line.

"Just then some fellow jumped up right near me, and by his voice I knew him to be Evans, our Color Sergeant. He sang out in a powerful, clear voice; 'Captain Wise, take command! Col. Shipp has fallen!' In the same second I saw Captain H. A. Wise spring to the front with drawn sword (as did Captains Preston and Robinson) and give the order to rise—then, I think, charge."

He returned to the Institute in the fall of 1868, entered the second class and was graduated on July 4, 1870, standing 37 in a class of 52 who were graduated on that day. He took the civil engineering course.

Following his graduation he served as a rodman with the Chesapeake and Ohio Railway Company and then left for Peru to accept a position with the Peruvian Hydrographic Commission. We quote from a letter written by Mr. Noland on August 4, 1904:

"In regard to my experiences in South America, Admiral John Randolph Tucker was at the head of the party. The object of the exploration was to find the head of steamboat navigation on the Amazon River, or some tributary thereof, nearest to the city of Lima, Peru, and best suited as the eastern terminus for a proposed railroad to be built from Lima across the Andes Mountains. My position in the party was that of civil engineer and topographer. We ascended the Amazon and its tributaries 3167 miles from the Atlantic Ocean, in boats, and located a suitable terminal point. We penetrated a region never before visited by white men, and had several encounters with cannibal Indians. Whilst engaged in this work I had yellow fever."

Returning to Virginia and finding the field of his endeavors limited, he, in 1875, went to Colorado and spent seven years as a mineral surveyor in the mountains of that state.

In 1883 he married Elizabeth, daughter of William T. and Alice Cornelia Mayo, of Ashland, Va. She died a few months later.

After several business ventures he removed to "Edgewood," Offley P. O., Hanover County, Va. With the exception of a short time when he was an assistant engineer on the Richmond, Fredericksburg and Potomac Railroad, he engaged in farming and developing certain water power in the vicinity of his farm. He was author of "Travels on the Amazon River."

Mr. Noland died at "Edgewood" on March 2, 1913 and was buried in Hollywood cemetery, Richmond. Among those surviving was a sister, Miss Margaret B. Noland, of Richmond and "Edgewood;" a brother, Fenton, of "Airwell," Hanover County; and William Churchill, a brother, of Richmond.

177. Archibald Waller Overton—1866.

Merchant—Banker

Born Nov. 11, 1845, in Fayette County, near Lexington, Ky.

Parents: Captain Dabney Carr Overton and Eliza Dorothia Harris, the latter of Louisa County, Va.

Grandparents: Waller Overton, one of the first settlers of Kentucky, and Martha Ragland.
  Captain Frederick Harris and Catherine Smith, of Fredericks Hall, Va. Captain Harris was a member of the Virginia Assembly of 1806; also captain in the War of 1812.

Both of his parents having died, young Overton, when ten years of age, was taken to Virginia to be under the care of his mother's family, among whom was Capt. David B. Harris, afterwards General Harris, a distinguished engineer officer of the Confederate Army. It was by Captain Harris that young Overton was entered at the V. M. I. on Aug. 25, 1862. He was a private in Co. C, and served with the cadet artillery at the battle of New Market.

On July 4, 1866, he was graduated at the Institute, standing 7 in a class of 11.

After leaving the Institute he engaged in the tobacco business at Fredericks Hall, Louisa County, Va., and continued in this for about two years.

On March 11, 1874, he married Miss Laura Ellen Harris, daughter of Nathaniel W. and Ellen Mullock Harris, of Louisa County. They had one son, Waller Mullock Overton.

In May 1887, Mr. Overton moved to Kentucky and accepted a position as bookkeeper in the Farmers Bank at Henderson. In three years he removed to Frankfort to accept a similar position with the Farmers Bank of Frankfort. He was promoted through the various ranks until he became cashier in 1904.

His death, which occurred February 29, 1920, was a tragic end of a noble life. It was the result of serious injuries by fire, death relieving his sufferings within a few hours. He was one of the early initiates of the Alpha Tau Omega fraternity.

Dabney Carr Overton, a brother of the subject of this sketch, was a member of the class of 1873, V. M. I.

178. Francis Walker Page—1866.

Musician—Invalid

Born July 20, 1845, at Cobham Grove, Albemarle County, Va.

Parents: Francis Walker Page, and Ann E. Cheeseman, of Albemarle County, Va.

Paternal Grandparents: Dr. Mann Page, and Jane Frances Walker, of Keswick, Albemarle County, Va.

On September 17, 1862, he was entered at the Institute by his mother, Mrs. Ann E. Page, of Bentivoglio, Albemarle County, Va. (his father having died when he was one year old). He was a cadet private in Co. A at the battle of New Market while a third classman and the following year he returned but staid only a short time, or until February 7, 1865. As a cadet his health was poor, necessitating furloughs in the latter part of 1863 and 1864 and in the first month of 1864 and 1865.

Following his withdrawal from V. M. I., he did not attend school again in this country but spent several years in Germany perfecting himself in music. He became an accomplished pianist but in 1886 his mind became affected and in that year he entered the Western State Hospital, in Staunton, Va., where he died on January 5, 1901.

He never married.

His uncle, William Wilmer Page, was a cadet at V. M. I. in the class of 1856.

179. Philip Nelson Page—1866.

Argentine Cattle Dealer

Born May 2, 1847, in Washington, D. C.

Parents: Captain Thomas Jefferson Page, U. S. Navy (later in Confederate States Navy), of "Rosewell," Gloucester County, Va., and Benjamina Price, of Loudoun County, Va.

Grandparents: Mann Page, of "Rosewell," and Elizabeth Nelson, of York County, Va.
Col. (or Major) Price, U. S. A., of Loudoun County, Va., and ——

He matriculated at V. M. I. January 9, 1862, from Yorktown, Va., and served as a cadet private in Co. C in the battle of New Market. The following session he resigned on January 26, 1865 as he had been appointed a "cadet in the C. S. A."

On December 15, 1905, he wrote:

"On leaving the dear old V. M. I. in the summer of 1864, I applied to the Secretary of War (Mr. Seddon) and was endorsed by Brigadier General Montgomery D. Corse for active service, and received the appointment to General Corse's staff as aidedecamp, with whom I served subsequently until the end of the war. I was made a prisoner along with him and the remnant of the brigade on the fatal field of Sailor's Creek just a day or two before the surrender at Appomattox. I was sent with others to Johnson's Island, Lake Erie, and released in June, 1865, on the general amnesty. The night Lincoln was killed we were in the old capitol prison, Washington, en route to Johnson's Island.

"On being released I went to Italy to join my father and family, and after a short stay with them, left for South America, where I have ever since resided, with occasional visits to Europe."

Mr. Page made a comfortable fortune as a cattle dealer in Argentina but lost it when Baring Brothers bank in England failed after the Argentine "bouleversement". In October, 1923, his address was Estancia Palmer, Estacion Ubajay, Republica Argentina, S. A.*

---

*For recent information, see following Sketch No. 295 in this book.

180. John Ross Patton—1867.

Banker

Born Nov. 8, 1846, in Danville, Va.

Parents: William S. Patton, a prominent banker of Danville, and Catherine A. Ross.

Grandparents: Dr. James D. Patton and Mary Fearn.
John Ross and Mary Meriwether Allen.

After preparing at the Danville Military Academy he matriculated at V. M. I. on March 8, 1864. Two months later he took part in the battle of New Market as a cadet private in Co. B. He did not return the following session.

After the war he returned to Danville, went into the banking business with W. S. Patton Sons & Co., and was a member of the firm at the time of his death.

He died in Danville, Va., June 26, 1877, aged 33 years.

181. William Macfarland Patton—1865.

Civil Engineer—Professor—Author

Born August 22, 1845, in Richmond, Va.

Parents: Hon. John Mercer Patton (distinguished lawyer, member Virginia Legislature, member of Congress, Lt. Gov. and Acting Governor of Virginia) and Margaret (Peggy) French Williams, of Culpeper Co., Va.

Grandparents: Robert Patton (a native of Scotland and merchant of Fredericksburg, Va.) and Anna Gordon, daughter of General Hugh Mercer, who was mortally wounded at the battle of Princeton in 1777.
Isaac Hite Williams, eminent lawyer, and Lucy Coleman, daughter of Capt. Philip Slaughter, of the Revolution.

He matriculated at V. M. I. from Culpeper, Va., on January 1, 1862; was a cadet until the corps was disbanded in Richmond on April 2, 1865; and was graduated with third stand in the class of 1865. In the battle* of New Market he was fourth cadet sergeant in Co. B.

On three occasions he was called to the faculty of his alma mater. From 1867 to 1870 he was assistant professor of Latin and French; during this period he did graduate work in engineering and received the degree of Mining Engineer. Then followed four years in the West Indies and in Central America on engineering projects.

In 1873 he returned to V. M. I. and became professor of Civil Engineering and related subjects—the title varying somewhat over this nine year period of service. He had succeeded General G. W. Custis Lee as head of the Civil Engineering course at V. M. I., when Gen. Lee was called to the presidency of Washington College (now

---

*Six of his brothers were in the Confederate army, among them were: Col. John Mercer Patton, V. M. I., '46; Col. George Smith Patton, V. M. I., '52, killed in battle at Winchester; and Col. Waller Tazewell Patton, V. M. I., '55, killed in battle at Gettysburg.

Washington and Lee University) to succeed his father, General Robert E. Lee.

In the field of practical engineering he was engineer of the Mobile and Birmingham Railroad; chief engineer of the Louisville, St. Louis, & Texas Railroad; engineer in charge of bridges across the Susquehanna, Schuylkill, Ohio, Warrior, Tombigbee, and Mobile rivers; engineer of sewers for a number of cities, and other important works.

Married: January 7, 1875, Annie Gertrude (1852-1921), daughter of Samuel F. Jordan and Elizabeth Leibert, of Rockbridge Co., Va.

In 1888 he returned to V. M. I. as professor of Civil Engineering and allied subjects and remained two years after which, while regaining his impaired health, he wrote two valuable books: "A Treatise on Foundations" (1893), and "A General Treatise on Civil Engineering" (1894).

In 1896 he was appointed Professor of Civil Engineering and Dean of the Engineering School of the Virginia Agricultural and Mechanical College, the name of which was in that year enlarged by adding "and Polytechnic Institute", and continued in this work until his death. Patton Engineering Hall at V. P. I. was named for him.

Col. Patton was succeeded in the Civil Engineering department at V. P. I. by Col. Robert Athelstan Marr, V. M. I. '77, and his colleague on the faculty there was Lingan Strother Randolph, V. M. I. '80, professor of Mechanical Engineering.

Colonel Patton died May 26, 1905 at the home of his brother-in-law, J. E. A. Rose, V. M. I. '83, in New York City, where he had been under treatment for cancer of the stomach. Interment was in Lexington, Va.

He was survived by his wife and six daughters: (Sallie T.) who m. Dr. John E. Williams, dean V. P. I., Blacksburg, Va.; (Margaret French) who m. Colonel Thomas A. Jones, V. M. I., '98; (Virginia Mercer) who m. Winston B. Davis, of Blacksburg; (Nannie Marie) who m. Stuart Magruder Spiller, of New York; and Misses Agnes T. and Lucy J. Patton; a brother, Hugh Patton, of Lynchburg, Va.; and a sister, Mrs. Eliza P. Gilmer, of Chatham, Va.

182. Alexander Spotswood Payne—1867.

Insurance

Born July 9, 1845, in Lynchburg, Va., youngest son of his parents.

Parents: Dr. Robert Spotswood Payne, physician of Lynchburg and first president of the Medical Society of Virginia, and Frances Russell Meem.

Grandparents: John G. Meem, a merchant and bank president of Lynchburg and former owner of the famous "Mt. Airy" estate near New Market, and Elizabeth Russell, of Abingdon, Va.

Alexander Spotswood Payne, of "New Market," Goochland Co., later moved to Ivy Creek, near Lynchburg (son of Archer and Martha Dandridge* Payne), and Charlotte Boyce.

---

*Daughter of Col. Nathaniel West and Dorothea Spotswood Dandridge; granddaughter of Governor Spotswood of Virginia.

Prepared at the Westwood Military Academy, near Lynchburg, of which Col. J. T. Murfee, V. M. I. '53, was one of the principals; then to New London Academy, when it consolidated with Westwood, and remained until it suspended in 1861, when he transferred to Washington College.

Matriculated at V. M. I. on May 11, 1863 and the following session repeated the fourth class (he having taken but two months work with that class in his first session) and while doing so he was a cadet private in Co. A in the battle of New Market.

He had transferred to V. M. I. on May 11, 1863, and "a few days after by dint of persuasion and a loan of a uniform, I was permitted to fall in with the battalion as escort at the funeral of General Jackson. From that time was with the corps of cadets until the final break-up at Richmond that black Sunday in April, 1865, when the battalion was withdrawn from the fortifications on the Charles City Road (most of us were in the rifle pits in front of the same at the time), marched back to barracks at the Richmond Alms House and there disbanded and instructed by General Smith to meet him in Lynchburg. With several other comrades, by walking most of the way, we reached that place on Saturday following. Securing my horse, with Cadet M. D. Langhorne, we started westward with the idea of joining General Joe Johnston's army, but after reaching Montgomery County and finding the Confederacy hopelessly disbanded, I returned home. Not being able to return to the V. M. I. on account of General Hunter's barbarism in burning the barracks, was sent to the University of Virginia, October, 1865, where I took the academic course for two years, which closed my scholastic career."

Married: June 15, 1887, at St. Johns Church, Liberty (now Bedford), Va., Nora Burks (d. 1915), daughter of Judge Edward Callohill Burks (late of the Supreme Court of Virginia) and Mildred Elizabeth Buford.

After the war he was for some years in the railroad service and then engaged in tobacco manufacturing. For most of his life, however, he was in the insurance business in Lynchburg.

For a number of years he took an active interest in military affairs and was Captain of the "Fitz Lee Troop", now disbanded.

Captain Payne died of heart disease at his home on College Hill, in Lynchburg, October 2, 1910 and was buried in the family square at the Presbyterian Cemetery. Survived by his wife; a daughter, Nora Burks Payne; and one brother, John M. Payne, of Amherst, Va.

183. David Stuart Peirce—1866.

Lawyer

Born August 17, 1846, in Pulaski Co., Va.

Parents: James N. Peirce, of Wythe Co., Va., and Anne Dabney Stuart.

Grandparents: David Peirce, and Mary Bell, of Wythe Co.
Judge Alexander Stuart (U. S. Judge in Illinois and Missouri; Circuit Judge in Missouri, and later speaker of Missouri legislature; died in 1832 in Staunton while on a visit to the family of his deceased brother, Judge Archibald Stuart), and Anne Dabney, his first wife.

He matriculated at V. M. I., from Saltville, Va., November 3, 1862, and was a cadet until the corps was disbanded in Richmond on

April 2, 1865. While a third classman he took part as a cadet private in Co. D in the battle of New Market and was there wounded.

After the war he attended the law school of the University of Virginia in 1865-66; was awarded the orator's medal by the Jefferson Society; and received the degree of B.L. in 1866.

Married: Bettie Lawson Boyd, of Wytheville, where he located after graduation and remained throughout his life.

A successful lawyer and advocate his reputation was firmly established in 1875 when as junior counsel he appeared in the chancery case of Thomas L. Preston vs. W. A. Stuart, Palmer, et als.

In the presidential election in 1876, when he was a democratic elector, his oratory placed him among the principal political speakers of the state. Gifted with a musical voice, vivid imagination, a keen sense of humor, quickness of perception, and a fund of common sense, to which he added legal ability of an unusual order he was an advocate to be valued and an antagonist to be respected.

Secretary and General Manager of the Lake Spring Land and Improvement Co., of Wytheville; and a member of the board of visitors of the V. M. I. from January 1, 1891 to his death on December 3, 1893.

He was survived by his wife and one son, Robert Lawson Peirce.

184. Robert Aldridge Pendleton—1867.

Wholesale Hardware

Born October 29, 1847, near New Glasgow, in Amherst Co., Va. All early letters show the initial C. between his middle name and surname.

Parents: Robert Aldridge Pendleton, Sr., a lawyer and clerk of the Amherst Co. Circuit Court from 1855 to 1894, and Louisa Elizabeth Pierce, born in Amherst Co. and died in 1865.

Maternal Grandparents: Col. Jonah Pierce, a soldier of the War of 1812, and Sallie Cheatwood.

Matriculated at V. M. I. from Cobham, Amherst Co., Va., September 12, 1863 and later in the session he was a cadet private in Co. A. in the battle of New Market, where he was wounded in the head by a piece of schrapnel. After a short period in the V. M. I. hospital he joined the corps in Richmond but was soon recalled when Hunter's raiders advanced southward. The following session he returned and remained until the corps was disbanded on April 2, 1865.

Married: In 1870, Virginia Elizabeth, daughter of Col. Charles A. Mantz, then editor and proprietor of the St. Louis Times, and Caroline Hickman (b. 1826 in Williamsport, Pa.). They had three children:

Charles M., Virginia, and Blanche.

In 1868 he went to St. Louis and began as stock clerk with A. F. Shapleigh Hardware Co. (now Norvell-Shapleigh Hardware Co.). He soon became the company's foremost traveling salesman and for twenty-five years represented it in northern Missouri. He knew every hardware dealer in Missouri and southern Illinois. In 1901 he joined the selling force of the Witte Hardware Company, with which he remained until his death on April 18, 1911 at his home in St. Louis.

He was survived by his wife and three children.

After his death the following letter, written in 1903 by L. W. Wimbish (See Sketch No. 279), was found in his papers:

"I received a V. M. I. catalogue the other day and imagine my surprise when I found your name and address. W. H. Kennedy (See Sketch No. 130) told me many years ago that you were dead. I have not seen you since you, with blood streaming down your face, sent me on to the front and a message to your loved ones in case you died. Let's renew old acquaintance."

185. William Wood Pendleton—1867.

Invalid

Born Dec. 24, 1845, in Cincinnati, Ohio.

Parents: Col. Edmund Pendleton, a lawyer born in Amherst Co., Va., who practiced in Cincinnati, New Orleans, and Lexington, Va., and Cornelia M. Morgan, of Cincinnati, Ohio.

Paternal Grandparents: Dr. Micajah Pendleton, and Louisa Jane Davis.

He matriculated at V. M. I. July 26, 1862 from New Orleans, La., where his parents then resided. While repeating the work of the fourth class he took part in the battle of New Market as a cadet private in Co. C. The following year he returned but resigned on March 20, 1865 and joined the Washington Artillery, C. S. A., and continued in the army until the surrender at Appomattox.

He came out of the army with his health shattered and died, unmarried, in 1870. His father, Col. Edmund Pendleton, was graduated with the class of 1842—the first class to be graduated at V. M. I. His brother, Ephraim Morgan Pendleton, was graduated at V. M. I. in 1877.

186. James Gabriel Penn—1866.

Tobacco Manufacturer—Capitalist

Born November 14, 1845, at Penn's Store, Patrick County, Va.

Parents: Thomas Jefferson Penn, of Danville, Va., and Catharine Lucinda Penn.

Grandparents: James Penn and Mary Leith.
Greenville Penn and Martha Read.

After preparing at the Greenville Academy, which was named for his grandfather, he matriculated at V. M. I. on September 27, 1862, from Penn's Store, and served as a cadet private in Co. B in the battle of New Market.

On July 5, 1904, Mr. Penn wrote as follows:

"I left the corps of cadets while they were encamped in the trenches around Richmond and was detailed a lieutenant in one of the companies of a regiment organized by Colonel Tucker, and assigned to the army of General Joseph E. Johnston. I remained with this regiment until the surrender. I came to Danville in 1868 and entered the mercantile business under the firm name of Peyton, Penn & Co. Sold out my interest in same in 1870 and in 1872 formed the copartnership of Pemberton and Penn, commission merchants for the purchase of leaf tobacco. My partner, Mr. Pemberton, died in 1873, but I have conducted the business under the old firm name for 33 years and am still at the head of it. We have done a large and successful business, making close and intimate relations not only with large firms in this country, but also in foreign markets. I am at present President of the Commercial Bank, Danville, Va., Vice-President of the Dan River Power and Manufacturing Co., large stockholder and director in the Riverside Cotton Mills, director in the Merotock Manufacturing Co., director in the Danville Storage Co., and also interested in other minor enterprises."

Mr. Penn was married twice. His first wife was Sarah Elizabeth, daughter of Thomas W. Pemberton, of Richmond, Va. After her death he married Sallie, daughter of David S. Johnson, of Madison, Georgia, in 1885.

He died on August 27, 1907, and was survived by two sons:

John Pemberton, V. M. I., '98, born November 21, 1875, married Nellie Cummings, of Danville; their children are: John Pemberton, Jr., Marie Alice (m. John Dillard Watt, of Reidsville, N. C.), and Kitty Frantz.

James Gabriel, Jr., V. M. I., '98, born April 18, 1877, married Kathryn Boyd, daughter of Robert C. Boyd, of Charlotte County, Va.

He had two daughters: Mary K., wife of Barnes Rucker Penn; and Annie Lee Penn.

187. William Edward S. Perry—1867.

Farmer

Born July 4, 1846, at Liberty, Bedford County, Va.

Parents: Oliver H. Perry, and Rachel, daughter of John Claiborne, of Rockbridge County, Va.

He matriculated at V. M. I. on August 1, 1863, and was a cadet private in Co. B at the battle of New Market. He resigned his cadetship on February 6, 1865, to enter the Confederate States Army.

In 1868 he left Virginia and went West, locating in the State of Missouri. While there he married Miss Emma Lee, of Missouri. In 1879 he returned to Bedford county, Va., hoping to regain his health, but died on October 29, 1880, a victim of consumption. "After his death his widow and children—three boys and one girl—returned to Missouri. A few years later Mrs. Perry died in Missouri, and the children were sent to her brother, Mr. Horace Lee, of Yuba City, California. Later one of the sons died. When last heard of, the eldest son, Oliver, and the daughter, Sadie, were living in Yuba City."

188. Thomas Key Phelps—1867.

Farmer

Born September 21, 1847, on the Keyton plantation, Bedford County, Va.

Parents: Thomas Jefferson Phelps (b. December 28, 1826), of Bedford County, and Malinda Perkins Key (b. July 9, 1811), widow of William Nelms. She died February 12, 1894.

Grandparents: Thomas Phelps and Nancy Carter.
Captain Thomas Key (b. August 15, 1779; d. April 29, 1818), and Docia Preston.

His early life was spent on the old family place, "Keyton," and his early education was received at the neighborhood school, from which he went to Sunnyside Academy, then conducted by Rev. A. Eubank.

He matriculated at V. M. I. from Liberty (now Bedford) on March 1, 1864 and in the battle of New Market six weeks later, he served as a cadet private in Co. D. The following session he was with the corps until it disbanded in Richmond on the eve of the evacuation of that city. During this same period his father was serving as a soldier in Company F, Southside Dragoons.

Mr. Phelps married Elizabeth, daughter of Dr. Benjamin Hammond Moulton, a practising physician at Davis Mills, Va. Eleven children were born to Thomas Key Phelps and his wife, as follows:

Thomas Hammond, M.A., Randolph-Macon College.
James Key, of Bedford County, Va.
William Richard, m. Mildred May Davis, of Dinwiddie County, Va. Col. Phelps is principal of Randolph-Macon Academy at Bedford, Va.
Wilbur Moulton (dead).
Sarah (died at the age of nine).
Hattie May, of Roanoke, Va.
Lucy, of Roanoke, Va.
Ruth, wife of Dr. G. W. Southerland, of Rocky Mount, Va.
Margaret Elizabeth, widow of Dr. Samuel Leonidas Rucker, of Moneta, Bedford County, Va.
Ella Docia, of Bedford County, Va.
Laura, of Bedford County, Va.

After the close of the war, he returned to "Keyton" and went to work on the farm, bent upon retrieving, to some extent, the fortune of the family. By industry and skill he succeeded and became the owner of the old home. He was a member of the county school board, and a director of the Peoples National Bank, of Bedford, at the time of the organization of that institution. He was active in church and Sunday School work, and long served on the Board of Stewards of the Methodist Church.

Mr. Phelps died in a hospital in Roanoke, Va., on Sunday, December 27, 1925, and was survived by six daughters and three sons.

189. Samuel Travers Phillips—1867.

Lawyer

Born March 14, 1847, in Urbana, Maryland.

Parents: Rev. Richard Henry Phillips, D.D., an Episcopal minister, founder of the Valley Female Seminary, now Stuart Hall, Staunton, Va., and Eleanor Thom.

Grandparents: Captain Samuel Phillips, of Fredericksburg, Va., and Sarah

Reuben Thom and Eleanor ——

On February 26, 1864, he matriculated at V. M. I. from Staunton, Va., and was assigned to the fourth class. He served as a cadet private in Co. B at the battle of New Market where he was wounded.

Following the war young Phillips attended the University of Virginia, studying the sciences, modern languages, English literature and philosophy, and was graduated in a number of subjects in 1867. He then began the study of law under Judge Hugh W. Sheffey. After a year of study and reading he entered the law school at the University of Virginia in 1868 and was graduated with distinction in one session and received his B. L. diploma July 1, 1869, and began the practice of his profession at the Staunton, Va., bar, July 9th of that year. On May 6, 1870, he was elected commonwealth's attorney of Staunton, being the first appointee to that office in the city of Staunton. He was made captain of the West Augusta Guards when that body reorganized in 1874.

Great and tragic sorrows came to him and he determined to try his fortune at the bar elsewhere, and at the time of his death, September 27, 1877, was on the eve of his departure to California where he hoped to enter anew the career of a lawyer.

On March 3, 1932, his portrait was presented to the City of Staunton by his grandnephew, Charles Phillips Blackley, V. M. I. '31 to be hung on the walls of the corporation court room.

A brother, Reuben Triplett Phillips, attended the Institute for two years with the class of 1866.

190. Andrew Pizzini, Jr.—1865.

Merchant—Pioneer Electric Traction Magnate

Born September 24, 1846, in Richmond, Va.

Parents: Juan Pizzini, a native of the Isle of Corsica and for many years the Italian consul in Richmond, and Celeste Eulalie Pizzini, of French descent, her parents being refugees from Martinique.

As a schoolboy he entered the Confederate army as a private in Co. D, First Virginia Infantry, the company being commanded by Capt. Griswold and the regiment by Col. P. T. Moore. With this regiment he went to Manassas and served with it until discharged by order of the Sec. of War, in Sept. 1861, so that he might enter V. M. I. He matriculated December 31, 1861 and continued with the corps until his graduation, standing sixth in his class. He took part in all the campaigns of the corps and at the battle of New Market was a cadet orderly (1st) Sergeant of Co. B. In this battle he was slightly wounded by a sabre cut and carried the scar throughout his life.

"The men were falling right and left. The veterans on the right of the cadets seemed to waver. Colonel Shipp went down. For the first time, the cadets appeared irresolute. Some one cried out, 'Lie down!' and all obeyed, firing from the knee—all but Evans, the ensign, who was standing bolt upright, shouting and waving the flag. Some one exclaimed, 'Fall back, and rally on Edgar's Battalion!' Several boys moved as if to obey. Pizzini, the first sergeant, of B Company, with his Corsican blood at the boiling point, cocked his rifle and proclaimed that he would shoot the first man who ran. Preston, brave and inspiring in command of B Company, smilingly lay down upon his remaining arm, with the remark that he would at least save that. Colonna, cadet captain of D, was speaking low to the men of his company

words of encouragement, and bidding them shoot close. The Corps was being decimated." (End of an Era, p. 302.)

In June 1864 he was promoted to Second Cadet Captain, commanding Co. D, and as such surrendered at Richmond in April 1865.
Prior to the final session and while on summer furlough he took part
in the Seven Days battles around Richmond and in the fall of 1864
raised a company composed largely of ex-cadets and served in the
trenches at the battle of Fort Harrison, etc., until the corps was
again assembled.

Married: Anna Gertrude Davis (1848-1917) of Richmond. They had six
children.

For seventeen years after the war he was a merchant and then
turned to the electrical field when the development of electric
lighting and electric traction was an infant industry. He took an
active part in establishing the first commercially successful electric
street railway in the world,* the Clay Street line in Richmond, and
thereafter secured lighting and power franchises from the city and
developed the field of electric current for lighting and manufacturing purposes. As president, general manager and part owner of the
Electrical Street Railways Light and Power Companies of Richmond, he continued his labors until 1900, when he retired from active
business. Thereafter, he devoted his time to his real estate and
other investments.

He continued his interest in military affairs and was Captain of the
Richmond Light Infantry Blues from 1882 to 1885; was a member
of the City Council for six years and president of that body; president of eight corporations and a director in many others, industrial
and financial, including the Merchants National Bank and the Met-
ropolitan Bank of Richmond.

Captain Pizzini died at his home in Richmond on January 31, 1913
after a brief illness—one of the most highly esteemed, influential and
enterprising citizens of Richmond.

He was survived by his wife; three sons, William B. and Albert
A. Pizzini, of Richmond, and Andrew J. Pizzini, V. M. I. '00, of
New York City; and three daughters, (Lucille) Mrs. Alexander M.
Paul, of Boston; (Anne) Mrs. William McK. Barbour, of Los
Angeles, later New York City; and (Estelle) Mrs. George E.
Sprague, of Lynn, Mass.

191. John James Audubon Powell—1867.

Lawyer—Legislator

Born September 23, 1846, at "Melrose," Henrico County, near Yellow Tav-
ern, Va.

---

*The chief engineer on the construction of this railway was Andrew Lang-
staff Johnston, V. M. I., '72; and prominent among the legal advisers was
John S. Wise, V. M. I. '66 (See Sketch No. 282) who became a leading authority in this field.

Parents: Dr. John Norment Powell, of Henrico County, Va., and Mary Catherine Wright, of Westmoreland County, Va.

Grandparents: John Powell, of King William County, Va., and —— James Cox Wright, of Westmoreland County, Va., and ——

Prior to his entrance at V. M. I., he attended Roanoke College for a short time. During his stay there, he, with other students, volunteered under Captain Holland and was sent to guard New River Bridge on the then Virginia and Tennessee Railroad. On February 19, 1864, he entered V. M. I. from Richmond and less than three months later served as a cadet private in Co. B at the battle of New Market. The following session he resigned on February 22, 1865 and served with Mosby's Rangers until that famous organization was disbanded.

On November 9, 1871, he married Annie S. (d. April 5, 1927), daughter of Ferdinand Jones, of Orange County, Va. They had six children:

J. Norment Powell, general counsel for the Carolina, Clinchfield and Ohio Railroad; died July 9, 1916.

——, wife of Thomas M. Carter, of Mississippi.

Ferdinand, of Johnson City, Tenn.

Mary Claughton.

Annie Marion, wife of Dean W. T. Hodges, of William and Mary College.

Junius, who attended Washington and Lee University.

After the war for several years Mr. Powell farmed in Henrico county, and in 1869-'70, he attended law lectures at the University of Virginia, receiving his LL.B. from that institution. He practiced his profession in Fluvanna county and represented that county in the legislature during the sessions of 1885-86 and the extra session of 1887. In 1889 he moved to Wythe county where he engaged in the practice of law and was mayor of the town of Wytheville, Va. At one time he was librarian of the Supreme Court of Appeals.

Mr. Powell died at his home in Wytheville on Friday, October 24, 1930.

192. Frank Preston—(Captain).

Not a Cadet—Professor

Born September 1, 1841, at Lexington, Va.

Parents: Colonel John Thomas Lewis Preston (b. April 25, 1811; d. July 15, 1890), and Sarah Lyle Carruthers (b. February 26, 1811; d. January 4, 1856), of Rockbridge County, Va.

Grandparents: Captain Thomas Lewis Preston, lawyer and member of Virginia legislature, of Lexington, Va., and Edmonia Madison, daughter of Mr. Edmund Randolph.

William Carruthers and Phoebe Alexander, both born in Rockbridge County, Va.

When sixteen years of age, he entered Washington college, now Washington and Lee University, and completed a four years' course with much credit. He had planned to go to Virginia, had, indeed, matriculated at that University, when the war broke out and he immediately offered his services to his State, and eventually received his commission in a volunteer regiment. His services with the regular army terminated at the battle of Winchester where he fell with an arm shattered by a minie ball, and a great gash in his side from a bit of shell. So badly was his arm injured that amputation of that member was necessary to save him. Accordingly, the operation was performed in Winchester. Later Winchester, with all the wounded Confederates who could not be moved with the army, fell inside the Federal lines by reason of an advance of the Union forces.

The Federal surgeons, with unlimited medical supplies, soon made young Preston more comfortable than he had been even with his own friends. Soon after his capture, however, and before his wounds had begun to heal, he took advantage of the carelessness of the hospital guard to escape to the home of a sympathetic Confederate lady. He remained under her roof for several days, until news came of the approach of a Yankee search party, then drove over to Lexington.

Compelled by the loss of his arm to resign his commission, he accepted a position as Instructor of English, Latin, and Tactics at the Virginia Military Institute. The Institute then had three hundred names on its rolls, and was each year sending a hundred or more young men to officer the raw Confederate recruits. Safe to say, few of them left the grim walls of barracks without being influenced for the better by Captain Preston, the tactical officer of Co. "B". Witness two incidents of the battle of New Market:

"Before we left our camp something occurred that even now may be a solace to those whose boys died so gloriously on that day. In the gloom of the night, Captain Frank Preston, neither afraid nor ashamed to pray, sent up an appeal to God for protection to our little band. It was an humble, earnest appeal that sunk into the heart of every hearer. Few were the dry eyes, little the frivolity, in the command, when he had ceased to speak of home, of father, of mother, of country, of victory and defeat, of life, of death, of eternity. Those who, but a few hours later, heard him commanding 'B' company in the thickest of the fight, his already empty sleeve showing that he was no stranger to the perilous edge of battle, realized as few can, how the same voice can at one time plead reverently and tenderly and at another pipe higher than the roar of battle." (J. S. Wise, "The End of an Era," p. 293.)

"I remember distinctly the fact of our lying down in this position, because I was immediately next to Captain Preston, who, having lost one of his arms at the first battle of Manassas, protected the other as well as he could by keeping it under his body." (F. L. Smith, letter, Mch. 27, 1909.)

He returned with the corps to V. M. I. and continued his work at the Institute until the advance of the Union forces made necessary the retreat and finally the disbanding of the cadet battalion.

Feeling the need of a profession, Captain Preston took up the study of languages and literature at Berlin, and returned after the year abroad to accept the chair of modern languages at William and Mary College. He was spared to the pursuit of his vocation only one year. His death on November 19, 1869, followed a lingering illness of consumption, to the ravages of which disease he more easily sucsumbed since his old wound in the side had never fully healed. Interment was in Lexington.

The V. M. I. Barrack in Ruins

Temporary Barrack of V. M. I. Cadets, December, 1864, to April, 1865

193. James Brainerd Preston—1867.

Farmer

Born December 3, 1845, near Abingdon, Va.

Parents: John Fairman Preston, born near Abingdon, Va., and Jane Rhea, born near Blountville, Tenn., a daughter of Samuel Rhea.

Matriculated at V. M. I. from Abingdon on August 17, 1863 and later in the session was a cadet private in Co. B. The following session he returned but resigned on March 1, 1865 to enter the Confederate army.

Writing in after years of the battle of New Market he said:

"I was slightly wounded but never reported it. I had a little Testament in my left vest pocket. A spent ball hit the Testament and I was unconscious for a short time. When I regained my consciousness I was washing my hands in a mud-puddle. I still had my gun and followed on. When the enemy rallied there were about 40, I think, who took shelter behind a log cabin, near an old barn under which were a good many of the enemy in hiding, that we afterwards took as prisoners. . . . Little John L. Cocke picked up a haversack of crackers; a stray bullet cut one side strap and they fell to the ground. He said, 'Did you see that d—— thing take my rations.'"

On October 13, 1866 he was commissioned by the Governor of Virginia 2nd Lieut., 125th Reg't, 17th Brigade and 5th Division of the Virginia Militia.

Married: Hattie Bryan, daughter of Seaton Garland Tinsley (both born near Richmond, Va.). They had one child, Seaton Tinsley Preston.

He was a farmer and lived near Abingdon until he moved to Bristol, Va., where he was living at the time of his death on October 21, 1922. He was survived by his son who was at the time residing in Pikeville, Ky.

194. Thomas Wilson Preston—1867.

Bookkeeper

Born December 28, 1846, at Abingdon, Va.

Parents: Robert Robinson Preston (b. in Kentucky; lived at Abingdon, Va., where he was a banker; d. February, 1866), and Elizabeth McDonald Cummings (b. in Washington County, Va., d. March, 1885).

Grandparents: Walter Scott Preston, and Anne Montgomery, both of Kentucky.

James Cummings, and Mary Campbell, both of Washington County, Va.

Young Preston matriculated at the Institute on January 4, 1864, and served as a cadet private in Co. B at the battle of New Market. The following session he returned but resigned on February 17, 1865 to enter the Confederate army.

In 1866 Mr. Preston moved from Abingdon, Va., to Greenville, Miss., and later lived at Brandon in that State. In 1879 he went to Vicksburg where he spent the remainder of his life.

In St. Louis, Mo., on August 4, 1880, he married Mary Ella, daughter of Winchester Bledsoe Shelby, of Brandon. They had one son and four

—11

daughters. His wife and one daughter died in a fever epidemic in Vicksburg about 1915. The records do not give this daughter's name. The children surviving their mother were:

Shelby, of Memphis, Tenn.
Nell Cummings, of Washington, D. C.
Margaret, wife of Mr. —— Keefe, of Vicksburg, Miss.
Marian Douglas, also of Vicksburg.

Mr. Preston was a bookkeeper for many years, being associated with the Louis Hoffman Hardware Company in Vicksburg.

He died suddenly on February 20, 1925, at his home in Vicksburg.

195. Ferdinand Bowman Price—1867.

Railroad Service

Born December 27, 1846, at Washington, D. C.

Parents: William Ferdinand Price, born in Christiana, Del., and Amelia Morgan Cox, born in Philadelphia, Pa.

Grandparents: Isaac Price, born in Delaware, and Martha Roberts, born in Maryland.
William Cox and Sarah Corfield, both born in Philadelphia, Pa.

Matriculated at V. M. I. from Richmond, Va., on March 2, 1864 and ten weeks later as a cadet private in Co. C fought in the battle of New Market. He remained in the corps until the end of the session and then became a courier on the Staff of General G. W. C. Lee, serving from the fall of 1864 until the end of the war.

Married: Mary, daughter of Dr. Frank W. Hancock, of Richmond, Va., a surgeon in the Confederate army. They had four children:

Mary Hancock.
F. Bowman, Jr.
Virginia Bell.
Pemberton Morris Price.
The first two children were born in Charlottesville, Va.; the last two in Philadelphia.

From 1866 to 1868 he represented a tobacco manufacturing company in Baltimore, Md., after which he entered the transportation service and so continued for the rest of his career. From 1868 to 1871 he was employed in the office of the General Freight Agent of the Philadephia & Reading Railroad in Philadelphia; left that service to become chief clerk to the General Freight & Passenger Agent of the Atlantic Coast Line, Wilmington, N. C.; transferred in the latter part of 1871, as chief clerk with the same company at Portsmouth, Va.; from December 18, 1874 with the Clyde Steamship Company, Philadelphia; January 1, 1878 appointed agent of the Richmond & Danville Railroad in Philadelphia; in November 1880 he was appointed Philadelphia Agent of the Associated Railways of Virginia and the Carolinas; May 1894 appointed agent of Southern Railway in Philadelphia and so continued, becoming one of the best known men in railroad traffic circles.

He maintained a home at Haymarket, Va., and there he died January 23, 1917 after a long illness. He was survived by his wife, four children, and a sister, Mrs. G. A. Lyell, of Richmond, Va. His wife died in Alexandria, Va., on February 3, 1925.

196. William Norvell Radford—1867.

Farmer

Born at Lynchburg, May 9, 1846 (oldest child).

Parents: Lieut. Edmund Winston Radford (2d Va. Cav.) ; killed leading a gallant charge at Manassas, July 18, 1861, leaving wife and eight children; educated at Washington College, and Anne Norvell.

Grandparents: William Radford, educated at Washington College, and Elizabeth Moseley.
William Wiatt Norvell, and Anne Harrison.

Prepared at New London Academy, Campbell Co., and matriculated Jan'y 7, 1864 from Forest Depot. Four months later he served as a cadet private Co. D in the battle of New Market. Later he served with Gen. G. C. Wharton.

Following the war he was a farmer and took care of the family until his death, October 4, 1872, at the family homestead—"Ashwood", Bedford County. He never married.

Great-uncle of W. G. Wills, Jr., '19.

(From his sister, Mrs. Arthur P. Gray, Amherst, Va.)

197. Charles Carter Randolph—1870.

Episcopal Minister

Born April 18, 1846, at his father's home, "The Grove," south of Warrenton, Va.

Parents: Capt. Charles Carter Randolph, of Fauquier Co., Va., a soldier of the War of 1812, and Mary Ann Fauntleroy Mortimer.

Grandparents: Col. Robert Randolph, of "Eastern View," a soldier of the Revolutionary War, and Elizabeth Hill Carter, of "Shirley," Charles City Co., Va.
Dr. Charles Mortimer, of "Cedar Grove," Stafford Co., near Fredericksburg, Va., and ——

In 1862 he joined Co. F, 6th Va. Cavalry, of which his brother-in-law was lieutenant. That year he saw service in the Valley and at the battle of Port Republic, first met "Stonewall" Jackson, who dropped his glove in passing over a stile. Randolph picked it up, handed it to Jackson and was asked "are you a warrior, sir?" He replied "Yes, sir." After that battle Jackson took him on as a special courier—one who carries verbal messages only. It took a little time to arrange his discharge from the cavalry and his first battle service in his new role was at Malvern Hill. He carried dispatches for Jackson at Second Manassas and at Sharpsburg (Antietam), where he rode all day carrying dispatches through that bloody battle. Speaking of Sharpsburg, Gen. J. E. B. Stuart said "a young lad named Randolph, from Fauquier, about twelve years*

---

*Really sixteen but small in stature.

of age, brought me several messages from General Jackson under circumstances of great personal peril and delivered his dispatches with great clearness and intelligence." Because of his youth Jackson arranged for his entrance to the V. M. I. and he matriculated February 12, 1863 from Charlottesville, being entered by Mrs. Mary B. Ball. He was admitted to the fifth class and the following session as a cadet private in Co. C he took part in the battle of New Market. There he was desperately wounded and lost the hearing in one ear. Three days before this his oldest brother, Capt. Robert Randolph, of the Black Horse Company of Fauquier County, was killed in battle near Richmond.

"Randolph too was shot when we were shoulder to shoulder. He had just said smiling, 'There's no use dodging, boys, if a ball's going to hit you, it'll hit you anyway' when he fell. I thought he was dead but I found him at night in the hospital." (Sir Moses Ezekiel, letter, July 23, 1904.)

Because of his wound he did not return to V. M. I. until the fall of 1866, when he re-entered with his brother, Norwood Beverly Randolph, and they were both graduated in 1870, standing 39 and 46 respectively in their class.

After teaching two years he entered the Theological Seminary at Alexandria, and was graduated in 1876. As deacon he served Christ Church, Mathews County, and after being ordained to the priesthood in 1877 he assisted at St. Thomas' Church, Baltimore Co., Md. In 1878 he was called to Woodville Parish, Botetourt Co., with churches at Fincastle, Buchanan, and Eagle Rock—there he remained for 19 years, with the exception of two years as rector at Americus, Ga. In 1899 he became the rector of Moore Parish in Campbell Co., Va., with churches at Evington, Rustburg, and Lynch Station—a devoted ministry of seventeen years which was terminated by his retirement in November 1916.

Married: First, Sallie Turpin, daughter of William Anthony, of Botetourt Co., Va.; she died a little over a year later. Their only child, Anthony, died in 1899, aged 18 years. Secondly, Sarah Blair McGuire (d. 1919), daughter of Rev. William McGuire and Mariette Heber Alexander, of "Caledon," King George Co., Va. They had five children, one of whom died in infancy.

After his retirement he continued to supply churches until the fall of 1924. He died at his home in Richmond, where he had been living since 1919, on May 14, 1925. He was survived by his four children: Bessie Carter Randolph and Mary Mortimer Randolph, of Richmond; Charles C. Randolph, Jr., V. M. I. '12, of Columbia, S. C.; William McGuire Randolph, of El Dorado, Ark.

Fellow clergymen of his in Virginia who were his first cousins were: Rt. Rev. Alfred Magill Randolph, Rev. Buckner Randolph, and Rev. Landon Mason. He was a younger brother of Mrs. Robert Dabney Minor (Landonia Randolph) of Richmond who died in 1912.

198. George Edward Raum—1867.

Traveller—Artist—Egyptologist—Author

Born August 22, 1846, at Charles Town, West Virginia.

Parents: Dr. William Rippey Raum and Elizabeth Moody.

Grandparents: John Raum and Catherine Rippey, of Shippensburg, Pa., daughter of Capt. Wm. Rippey, who served in the Revolutionary War. Rev. John Moody and Elizabeth Crawford.

Married: In 1882, Mary C. Woodward, daughter of R. B. Woodward, of San Francisco, Calif. She accompanied him on his travels over the world. They had no children.

The extraordinary career of this old cadet might well fill a book. The following digest was written by him in 1896:

"After John Brown's raid upon Harper's Ferry, the prelude of the Civil War, talked with Brown and his followers—Cook, Coppic, Stevens, Hazlett, Green, and Copeland, and saw them all hung, being a member of the Letcher cadets, a boy company of Charlestown, who stood guard at the gallows. When the State of Virginia seceded from the Union, joined Capt. John Avis's company and marched to Harper's Ferry demanding the surrender of the Arsenal, but it was evacuated and burnt by U. S. troops.

"Became courier and scout at Headquarters of Gen. Jos. E. Johnston and was by his side when he was wounded at the battle of Seven Pines, or Fair Oaks. Took part in battles around Richmond, Fredericksburg, Winchester, Gettysburg, etc.

"Being ill with pneumonia had to give up field duty and was recommended by General T. J. (Stonewall) Jackson for a cadetship at V. M. I.; was near him when he died at the Chandler House at Guinea Station."

(He matriculated at V. M. I. on February 13, 1864 and three months later served as a cadet private in Co. A in the battle of New Market. The following session his name was dropped from the rolls on February 6, 1865, because of absence in army service.)

"After the V. M. I. was burned by order of Gen. Hunter, received a furlough and became attached to the army advancing on Washington, D. C., and escaped capture at Middletown, Md., by running through a private house. Having captured (Aug. 12, 1864) near Charlestown, (West) Va., some U. S. soldiers with dispatches and letters for Sheridan's army, besides two sutlers, was afterwards surrounded and captured by the 6th New York Cavairy under Major Wm. E. Beardsley, tied (Aug. 13) and about to be shot near Berryville, Va., when released by Mosby's Rangers. The Rangers also captured 200 prisoners, 800 animals, and burned 75 wagons. In one wagon there was a safe, said to contain one million dollars in U. S. currency to pay off Sheridan's army, which could not be broken open or carried off.

"Joined Mosby's Rangers and was with them until the surrender. Was wounded near Charlestown and Winchester. Captured at same places and escaped.

"After the war engaged in commercial, mining, and railroad business in Charlestown, New Orleans, New York, and San Francisco.

"In 1882 started on an extensive tour of the world (20 years) to visit many uncivilized and most of the civilized countries. Studied art (painting) in Paris at Julians under Bougereau and Ferrier.

"Was in Alexandria, Egypt, after its capture by the English, and the battle of Tel-el-Kebier, when Arabi Pasha was vanquished and his army made prisoners by Lord Wolseley. Had a private audience with the Pope at Rome; attended the coronation of the Tzar of Russia; was attacked by Arabs at the Dead Sea in Syria. Escaped from being sacrificed before the Golden Idol in India; took refuge in a temple from a mob in China; was stopped near Mt. Everest from entering Thibet; and was photographed on an iceberg at the Muir Glacier in Alaska.

"While in Africa met Sir Samuel Baker, the great African explorer; General Gordon, who was afterwards killed by the Mahdi, at Omduran; Henry M. Stanley, who found Mr. Livingstone; the Hon. Cecil Rhodes, the great diamond king; and accompanied General Kitchener to Nubia when he defeated the Khalifa and took Khartum.

"In 1885 was commissioned Colonel of Engineers.

"Excavated in Africa and in February, 1896, uncovered the great Sphinx at Gizeh, finding a portion of its beard and Stone Cap, or Crown.

"Edited and had translated "Matilda," or the Crusade preached by William of Tyre.

"Author of 'A Tour Around the World,' 'A Visit to the Desert of Sahara and the Buried Cities of Timgad and Lambessa,' and 'Constantine, Tunis, and the Ruins of Ancient Carthage.' "

He has hundreds of trophies, among which he especially treasures a collection of eighty-six gold and silver Japanese coins, many of them more than 500 years old.

He was formerly manager and part owner of the old Woodward's Gardens, San Francisco, and while travelling collected objects for it throughout the world; in 1931 he was negotiating for the establishment of an East Bay museum.

He has been living in Berkley, California, since 1906, but because of an automobile accident which caused partial paralysis and loss of sight he has been much handicapped in the literary work in which he has been engaged.

199. Charles Henry Read, Jr.—1867.

Architect

Born about 1846 (he was 17 years and 2 months of age when he matriculated), in Richmond, Va.

Parents: Dr. Charles Henry Read, of New York State, pastor of the United Presbyterian Church, Richmond (the only one burned in the evacuation fire of April 3, 1865), from March, 1849, until he retired from active service there in October, 1887 (died in 1900), and Trephena L. ——, died January, 1898.

He matriculated at V. M. I. on August 29, 1863, from Richmond, Va., and at the battle of New Market served as a cadet private in Co. C. The musket he used at New Market is in the V. M. I. museum. Near the muzzle the barrel is bent at a considerable angle and shows clearly where the shell which bent it struck.

"This musket was knocked off my shoulder by a piece of the same shell that wounded Prof. A. Govan Hill, Sub Capt. of 'C' Co., Jno. S. Wise, Merritt, and myself. I was struck over the right eye and Dr. Geo. Ross sewed up the wound on the porch of the Hinkey House immediately in rear of our line and while it was going forward into the fight."

Married: M——, daughter of David Levy (afterwards David Levy Yulee), agriculturist, congressman, and United States senator from Florida. They had a son who was living in Washington in 1904 and to whom, through his mother, his father's New Market "Cross of Honor" was sent.

He was an architect and practiced his profession in Richmond.

He was to have provided the design for the pedestal of the New Market Battle Monument at V. M. I. but his health broke down and in 1900 he had to abandon this work. Although the last years of his life were spent in an endeavor to regain his health he had made arrangements to attend a reunion at V. M. I. in 1904 but death came a few days before. He died June 19, 1904, survived by his wife and son.

Mr. Read's only sister, Emma, wife of Judge Charles R. Ball, of Leesburg, Va., died October 7, 1918.

200. Alexander Fletcher Redd—1865.

Baptist Minister—Professor

Born about 1846, in Mecklenburg Co., Va. (he was 16 years of age at matriculation).

Parents: W. S. Redd, and Fannie T. Daws, of Mecklenburg Co., they had three children and she married secondly, C. L. Doggett, of Clarksville, Va.

Matriculated at V. M. I. from Boydton, Va., on January 1, 1862 and was admitted to the third class. The following session as third cadet sergeant in Co. C he took part in the battle of New Market. On December 31, 1864 he was promoted to be cadet second lieutenant and continued in the corps until the evacuation of Richmond.

After a year at the University of Virginia he attended the Philadelphia Polytechnic Institute and the Southern Baptist Theological Seminary in South Carolina.

Married: First, Mary Pope, of Petersburg, Va., and secondly, Belle King, of New Orleans, La. His two children, Fletcher and Florence, died young.

In 1868-69 he was assistant professor of Latin at V. M. I.; was later pastor of a Baptist Church in Raleigh, N. C.; professor of Chemistry at Chapel Hill, N. C. and from there transferred to Mercer University, Georgia. He was particularly interested in mineralogy and electrical research.

He died in Alabama February 28, 1906 where he had been a professor at Howard College.

201. Washington Franklin Redwood—1867.

Bank Cashier

Born July 22, 1845, in Mobile, Ala.

Parents: William Henry Redwood of Mobile, Ala., and Louisa Virginia Anderson.

He matriculated at V. M. I. on March 21, 1863, from Mobile, Alabama, and was admitted to the fifth class. The following session he took part as a cadet private in Co. B in the battle of New Market. Returning to the Institute he was appointed the fourth corporal in Co. A, and remained with the corps until it disbanded.

"We left Richmond the morning it was evacuated, in the early hours, and went up the canal to Cartersville, walking from there to Danville to which place the Confederate government had been removed. From Danville we commenced our homeward journey."

He married Ella Jane (b. June, 1854, in Providence, R. I.), daughter of Dr. Thomas D. Thompson and Sarah Jane Bowers. They had four sons, three of whom were living in 1910: William, Richard B., and Nelson.

Mr. Redwood spent the greater part of his life in the banking business in Macon and Brookville, Miss. Being stricken with paralysis, he moved back to Mobile and made his home with his son, R. B. Redwood. He died there on January 22, 1929.

A brother, John Tyler Redwood, V. M. I., '65, died in July, 1862, from wounds received at the battle of Cold Harbor, June 27, 1862.

202. John Jett Reid—1867.

Farmer

Born July 12, 1846, at Woodville, Rappahannock County, Va.

Parents: Joseph Reid and Cora Virginia Walden.

Grandparents: Walter Botts Reid, whose ancestors were Scotch, landing at Dumfries, Va., in the early part of the 17th century, and Mary Anne Reid, daughter of Captain Joseph Reid, of Washington, Va.

Captain William Walden, of Rappahannock County, Va., and Frances Anne Moore.

Being a schoolboy in 1861 and too young for the army, he rendered service to the Confederacy by collecting arms which were shipped to Richmond and remodeled for the army. After the evacuation of Manassas in 1862, he went with his parents to Bedford county where he was a member of the Bedford Reserves. During the session 1863-64, he left the New London Academy and entered V. M. I. on March 17, 1864, from Lynchburg, Va. At the battle of New Market two months later, he served as a cadet private in Co. D. On March 16, 1865, he resigned his cadetship to enter the Confederate States Army.

In 1867, he married Lucy Penn Rodes, of Lynchburg. His file shows the names of two daughters: Mrs. Dr. James G. Brown, of Woodville, Va., and Mrs. E. P. Brownton, of Los Angeles, Calif.

After the war, he returned home to assist his father in the mercantile business and farming.

Mr. Reid engaged in farming all his life and in 1903 his address was Scrabble, Rappahannock County, Va. After a short illness he died on November 14, 1907.

203. George Francis Reveley—1866.

Died young

Born June 18, 1843, at Appomattox, Va.

Parents: George Francis Reveley and Margaret Robertson.

Maternal grandparents: David Robertson and Elizabeth ——.

He was entered at V. M. I. on August 19, 1862, by his mother, Mrs. M. Reveley, of Nebraska, Appomattox County, Va., and at the battle of New Market served as a cadet private in Co. D. He remained with the corps until it disbanded on the eve of the evacuation of Richmond. On March 1, 1865, he was appointed cadet sergeant in Co. D.

He died on October 20, 1867, at his home in Appomattox.

Two brothers attended the Institute—William Wirt, '62, died October 24, 1865, from effects of military prison life; and David Robertson, '65, Treasurer of Virginia from 1882 to 1884, died November 30, 1900, at Timber Ridge, Rockbridge County, Va.

204. Jesse Douglas Richeson—1867.

Lead Mining, etc.

Born about 1846 (he was 17 years and 4 months of age when he matriculated).

Parents: Colonel William A. Richeson, wealthy tobacco grower of Amherst County, Va., who represented that county in the General Assembly, and —— Douglas.

He matriculated at V. M. I. on January 9, 1864, from Amherst Courthouse and took part in the battle of New Market as a cadet private in Co. B, and continued with the corps until the evacuation of Richmond.

In 1865 he went to Missouri and was employed by the Collier White Lead and Oil Company, of St. Louis, of which his uncle, Thomas E. Richeson, one of the most prominent citizens in St. Louis, was the president.

He married but the name of his wife does not show on his record. In after years his mind was affected and he died in 1882.

A brother, Thomas Varland Richeson, was a member of the Class of 1871.

205. Lucien Cincinnatus Ricketts—1867.

Lawyer—Prosecuting Attorney

Born August 22, 1847, at Guyandotte, W. Va.

Parents: Dr. Gerard Compton Ricketts (b. November 27, 1821), and Virginia Everett (b. April 23, 1826), of Guyandotte, W. Va.

Grandparents: Elijah Ricketts and Elenor ——.
Colonel John Everett (b. February 15, 1788, in Albemarle County, Va.; d. July 14, 1871, at Guyandotte, W. Va.), and Sallie Woodson (b. 1785 in Albemarle County; d. 1855 at Guyandotte).

He was a student at Marshall College, Huntington, W. Va., before the war broke out. In 1861, he entered the Confederate States Army under General Albert Gallatin Jenkins, with whom he served until he was entered at V. M. I. on August 22, 1863, by his father, Dr. G. C. Ricketts. Captain Waller R. Preston, of

Blacksburg, Va., is shown subsequently as his guardian. At the battle of New Market he was a cadet private in Co. C.

"On that occasion (at the battle of New Market) I was detached from the company to serve personally with Gen. Scott Shipp, then commandant of the battalion. As a matter of history . . . at the time we were about to engage the enemy, Gen. Jno. C. Breckinridge, commanding, gave orders for all mounted officers to go into the charge dismounted and not deeming that the order applied to me, and being mounted, rode into the battle on horseback, being the only person on horseback on the firing line of the cadets or elsewhere along the line until Gen. Breckinridge and his staff later appeared."

Colonel Francis L. Smith (sketch No. 226) wrote on February 8, 1910:

"I would like to see some mention of 'Cooney' Ricketts for I thought he acted with great gallantry, mounted on Shaw's horse, riding ahead and in front of the corps when we became engaged with the enemy. I was put on that horse (after being wounded of course) and rode him into New Market."

On the day following the battle he carried the report of Colonel William Gilham, who accompanied the corps of cadets on the campaign as acting superintendent, to Gen. Francis H. Smith, superintendent, who had been indisposed and remained in Lexington. He reached Lexington on May 17th, with the first news of the battle, which was fought on May 15th. Ricketts continued his cadetship until February 17, 1865.

On May 16, 1871, Mr. Ricketts married Fannie Leonora, daughter of John George Miller and Sarah Asenith, of Barboursville, W. Va.
Children: Sarah Virginia (b. February 20, 1872), dead.
    Cora Bell (b. October 21, 1873), wife of S. G. Worden of Los Angeles, Calif.
Ella Evalyn (b. December 27, 1876), wife of H. Roland of Guyandotte, W. Va.
    John George (b. September 5, 1880), of Huntington, W. Va.
    Luciene Eugenia (b. January 6, 1884), dead.

He read law in the office of his uncle, Honorable Laban T. Moore, and was admitted to the bar in 1869. He was twice prosecuting attorney of Cabell County and was land examiner for the national government under the Cleveland administration.

Mr. Ricketts died on September 18, 1906, at his home in Guyandotte. Camp Garnett, United Confederate Veterans, of which he was a member, had charge of the funeral services.

206. Robert Ridley—1866.

Railroad Service

Born September 27, 1844, in Southampton County, Va.

Parents: Robert Ridley, of Southampton County and Ann Eliza Blunt, of Greensville County, Va.

Grandparents: Thomas Ridley and Mary Wright, both of Southampton County.
    John Norfleet Blunt, of Southampton County, and Sally Peterson, of Greensville County.

He was entered at V. M. I. by Thomas Ridley and matriculated from Jerusalem, Southampton Co., Va., on January 7, 1862. The following session he repeated the fourth class and while a third classman he participated in the battle of New Market as fourth cadet corporal, Co. C.

"I was with the corps until late in December, 1864, when I left for home to prepare to join the 13th Virginia Cavalry, but was prevented from doing so by a long spell of sickness which lasted until the close of the war." He had been promoted to be first line sergeant of Co. B in June, 1864.

He married Lucy Ann, daughter of Charles Fox Urquhart and Eliza Blount Hill, of Southampton Co., Va. The names of their children are:
Thomas Urquhart Ridley.
Ann Eliza, wife of —— Pretlow.
Mary Antoinette, wife of —— Frank.

After the war he engaged in farming for a number of years and in 1882, he moved to Portsmouth, Va., where he was employed in the auditing department of the Seaboard Railroad and was with that railroad and its successor, the Seaboard Air Line Railway, for many years.

Mr. Ridley died on April 18, 1913, at his home, 810 Riverview Avenue, Portsmouth. He was a member of the Masonic lodge and Stonewall Camp of Confederate Veterans.

His brother, Norfleet Blunt Ridley, attended the Institute with the class of 1868.

207. John Roane—1867.

Medical Student—Died young

Born January 8, 1849, at "Uppowac," King William Co., Va.

Parents: James Roane and Mary C. Waring.

Grandparents: John Roane, member of Congress (1809-1837) and of the Constitutional Convention (1829-30), and Elizabeth Brockenbrough. Horace Waring and Isabella Roane.

He matriculated at V. M. I. on July 25, 1863, from Ayletts, King William County, Va., and the following session participated in the battle of New Market as a cadet private in Co. B. Only one cadet, Lewis S. Davis, who was in the battle, was younger. Another cadet, Robert F. Lee, who was in the corps but not in the battle, was younger.

"In 1865, he went to Richmond and began the study of medicine but died in June, 1867, when only eighteen years of age, just as he was ready to pass his medical examination."

208. Thomas Beverly Robinson—1856.

Teacher

Born February 29, 1836, in King William County, Va.

Parents: Captain Thomas Robinson (b. June 10, 1813) and Mary Susan

Hoomes (b. August 19, 1817; d. May 8, 1900). They were married at Orange Courthouse, May 11, 1835.

"After being taught at his home by his mother until the age of 12 or 13, he went to the Rumford Academy in his home county and remained there until 1853, when he entered V. M. I. as a State cadet on August 8th," and on September 5th, was assigned to the third class. He was graduated on July 4, 1856, standing 10 in a class of 33.

After attending the University of Virginia he returned to V. M. I. as assistant professor of Mathematics (1862-63), with the rank of lieutenant and the following session was promoted to the grade of captain. In the battle of New Market he was the tactical officer in command of Co. D.

When the cadets were ordered back to Lexington from "Carter's Farm in June, 1864, he was sick and did not return to the army for some weeks. Then he formed a company called the 'Brunswick Greys.' He, with four brothers, remained in the field until the surrender of General Lee at Appomattox. The year after the war he came to Lancaster County, Va., where he taught school for 8 or 10 years."

During the Civil War he was at one time Captain in the 21st Virginia Regiment. In his later life he was a major in the Virginia militia.

He married Fannie Moore Hull, daughter of Peter and Jane Moore Hull, of Northumberland County. Mrs. Robinson died on January 19, 1910, leaving three children: Fannie Hull, Mary Hoomes, wife of —— Sadler, of Lancaster, Va.; and one son, Thomas Beverly Robinson.

He died at his home in Nuttsville, Va., October 25, 1895, and was buried at White Chapel in Lancaster County. His grave is marked by a Confederate stone.

209. Peter Wilson Roller—1867.

Farmer

Born January 9, 1848, at Mt. Crawford, Va.

Parents: Josiah S. Roller, Mt. Crawford, Rockingham County, Va., and Martha J. Burgess.

He entered V. M. I. on September 2, 1863, from Mt. Crawford, and during that session served as a cadet private in Co. C at the battle of New Market; "from there to Richmond, to Lynchburg and back to Lexington when the Institute was burnt. I went back when the corps was moved to Richmond and was called all around Richmond several times. So you see I was a regular 'war' cadet."

Mr. Roller spent his entire life on his farm near Mt. Crawford, in the Shenandoah Valley.

On October 30, 1912, he married Bessie, daughter of Isaac Marshall. They had three children:
Virginia Wilson.
Elmer Josiah.
Oscar Woodward Roller.

After an illness of two weeks he died on Friday, September 17, 1926, at his home. He was buried at Bridgewater, Va., "and his casket was lowered with a wreath of green tied with the colors of V. M. I." He was survived by his wife and three children.

210. George McNeill Rose—1867.

Lawyer—Legislator

Born June 5, 1846, at Fayetteville, N. C.

Parents: John M. Rose (b. September 17, 1815), and Jane Strange McNeill (b. February, 1821).

Grandparents: Duncan Rose and Annie McAden.
George McNeill and Elizabeth Kirkland.

In 1860-62, he attended Davidson College, N. C., and on August 8, 1863, he matriculated at V. M. I. from Fayetteville, N. C., and was assigned to the fourth class. At the battle of New Market he was a private in Co. C, and remained with the corps until June 1864, following the return of the cadets from Richmond and the Lynchburg Campaign. He then joined the Confederate army and was first lieutenant and adjutant of the 66th North Carolina Regiment, Kirkland's Brigade, Hoke's Division. At the battle of Bentonsville he was slightly wounded and later surrendered with General Johnston's army.

After the war, he entered the University of North Carolina and was graduated in June, 1867.

On December 16, 1869, Mr. Rose married Augusta Jane, daughter of Augustus Steele, of Fayetteville, N. C. They had eight children:
Jane Augusta, wife of Hon. B. A. Morgan, of Greenville, S. C.
Augustus Steele, physician (now dead), m. Jean Evans.
John M., m. Bertie Alston.
George McNeill, Jr., lawyer, m. May Kirkland Crow.
Charles Grandison, lawyer, m. Irene Lacy.
Mary.
Thomas Duncan, m. Lila Williams.
Julius Gray (died in infancy).

During the sessions 1876-77, 1880-81, and 1883-84, Mr. Rose was a member of the General Assembly of North Carolina. In 1880-81, he was Speaker pro tem, and Speaker in 1883-84. He practiced law in Fayetteville for many years in addition to his services in the State Legislature.

About 1922 he was stricken with paralysis in his right side and incapacitated for further active work. His death occurred on Sunday, June 15, 1924, at his home in Fayetteville, N. C., where he spent his entire life.

211. Erskine Mayo Ross—1865.

Lawyer

Born June 30, 1845, on his father's plantation "Bel Pré," in Culpeper Co., Va.

Parents: William Buckner Ross and Elizabeth Mayo Thom.

Grandparents: George Ross, of "Elk Spring," Culpeper Co., Va., and ——
    Farish.
John Thom (a Colonel in the Virginia forces in the War of 1812 and a
    son of Alexander Thom, who was a Highland soldier in the battle of Cul-
    loden and later emigrated to America) and Abby DeHart Mayo, of "Pow-
    hatan Seat," near Richmond, Va.

He matriculated at V. M. I. July 25, 1860, from Brandy Station, Va., and later in the session went to Richmond with the
corps of cadets, under Major (later "Stonewall") Jackson to drill
recruits at Camp Lee. In July, 1861, he was assigned to the "Irish
Battalion," of the Provisional Army of Virginia, of which his uncle, J. Pembroke Thom, was captain, and was with them through
the Valley Mountain Campaign and at the battle of Cedar Run
where he was complimented for personal bravery by "Stonewall"
Jackson. In the fall of 1862, he re-entered the Institute and the
following session, as cadet first (orderly) sergeant of Co. A, he
fought in the battle of New Market. He returned to V. M. I. in
the fall of 1864, and stayed until the corps was disbanded the following April. In that period he was cadet captain of Co. A (the
highest ranking cadet officer), and at graduation he stood 14 in
his class.

With two other New ,Market cadets (see sketches 87 and 152),
he founded the Alpha Tau Omega Fraternity on September 11,
1865. At that time he was a clerk in ˜Crenshaw & Company's
mercantile establishment in Richmond. At the invitation of his
uncle, Cameron E. Thom, a captain on Gen. J. E. B. Stuart's staff
and a practicing lawyer in Los Angeles, he moved to his home and
office—arriving in California May 9, 1868. Said he in 1904:

"I at once commenced the study of the law, part of the time only at night,
as at times I had to do other work during the day to make both ends meet;
was admitted to the Bar the latter part of 1869; was fairly successful at the
Bar; in 1879 was elected a Justice of the Supreme Court of California, and,
drawing one of the short terms, was, in 1882, re-elected a Justice of the same
court, for the full term of twelve years; in 1886 resigned my seat on the Supreme Bench of California, and resumed practice at Los Angeles, in partnership with the late Senator Stephen M. White; a few months afterwards I
was appointed by President Cleveland, United States District Judge for the
then newly-created Southern District of California; in 1895, during Mr.
Cleveland's second term, I was appointed by him United States Circuit Judge
for the Ninth Judicial Circuit, which position I still hold."

In 1912, he became a member of the Circuit Court of Appeals
for the Ninth Judicial District and so continued until his retirement in 1925, when President Coolidge wrote commending him on
a "record which will long stand as a memorial to a just and fearless and able judge."

Married (first) May 7, 1884, Inez H. Bettis, of Los Angeles, and they had
    one son, Robert Erskine Ross, born March 30, 1875. Mrs. Ross died
    in 1908.
Married (second) in 1909, Ida Hancock, widow of Major Henry Hancock,
    the engineer who planned the modern city of Los Angeles. She died in
    1913.

His portrait hangs in the V. M. I. Library together with those of his two brothers: Dr. George Ross, V. M. I. '59 (see sketch No. 212), and Col. John DeHart Ross, V. M. I. '59. A nephew, George Erskine Ross, was a member of the Class of 1904 at V. M. I.

Judge Claude T. Reno, National Historian of the Alpha Tau Fraternity, wrote of Ross's inspiring life:

"A judicial career which covers almost fifty years cannot be summarized in a few sentences. Indeed the life of a judge does not easily lend itself to historical narrative. His work is performed out of the sight of the vast public and ordinarily only the profession appreciates its real import. His monuments are not more durable than the musty and dust-collecting books in which his opinions are published. Unless he serves in the formative period of the life of a people or in the hour of a great crisis, his name is writ in water. Judge Ross, fortunately for his fame, served in the Supreme Court of California when a new and radical constitution was passing the ordeal of judicial interpretation and in the United States Courts when a host of important and far reaching questions were clamoring for solution. It is too early for the final verdict, but his intellectual gallantry, his great learning, his luminous expositions, his devoted and earnest love for the truth, his unspotted reputation mark him for a high place in America's select circle of judicial immortals. He wrote a score of opinions which every well-read lawyer must know. Reference has already been made to the railroad strike cases.* To them must be added the Stanford case, which involved the validity of the will creating Stanford University; the Cuddy contempt case, a breath-taking performance in its day; the Noyes and McKenzie cases, which furnished the basis for Rex Beach's best seller, The Spoilers; the Chinese exclusion cases, which reversed settled public policy; and the Southern Pacific cases through which the government recovered millions of acres of public land. In the famous Buckley case his dissenting opinion acquired a position in the legal literature of the country never accorded to the majority decision. The dissenting opinion is the law of the land."

In this brief sketch we must omit stirring examples of his personal courage—some on the field of battle, one during the anti-Chinese riots in Los Angeles when with drawn revolver he quelled a murderous and incendiary mob.

Near Los Angeles he operated an immense ranch, using the most modern methods of farming and among other enterprises he founded Glendale, now a large and thriving city.

Judge Ross died in Los Angeles December 10, 1928, and was survived by his son. In addition to bequests to members of his family, his will disposed of the following property: $40,000 to the Virginia Military Institute; $5,000 to the Alpha Tau Omega

*When in the reign of terror which swept to the Pacific Coast following the Pullman strike in Chicago, Judge Ross, on June 9, 1894, took the country by storm and crystallized public opinion. Charging a grand jury in quiet and even tones but with obvious determination, he said: "It is of the first importance that the law be in all things and at all times maintained. This is especially true in times like the present when there seems to be abroad in the land a spirit of unrest and in many cases a defiance of law and order. Every man should know that whatever wrongs and grievances exist, no matter in what quarter, can only be corrected through lawful means. The great mass of the American people are law-loving and law-abiding and will never tolerate any high handed or unlawful attempts to correct wrongs, real or imaginary."

Fraternity; $100,000 to the American Bar Association, the annual income to be paid as a prize for the best discussion of a subject to be by it suggested at its preceding annual meeting; $20,000 to the Children's Hospital of Los Angeles; $5,000 to the Salvation Army of Los Angeles; $5,000 to the Orthopaedic School-Hospital for Crippled Children of Los Angeles; $20,000 to the Pilgrimage Play in the City of Los Angeles; $50,000 to the Memorial Home for Girls in Richmond, as a memorial to his mother and his sister, Mary Cameron Ross Buford. The residue of the estate was left to three Protestant Episcopal churches in Richmond (St. Paul's), Los Angeles (St. Paul's), and San Francisco (Grace).

212. George Ross—1859.

Physician—Professor

Born October 22, 1838, at "Berry Hill," in Culpeper Co., Va., the residence of his grandfather, Col. John Thom.
For parents, etc., see sketch of his brother, Erskine M. Ross, No. 211.

On July 30, 1856, he matriculated at V. M. I., from Brandy Station, Va., and on July 4, 1859, he was graduated, standing 12 in a class of 29. The following October he began the study of medicine on the eastern shore of Virginia in the office of his uncle, Dr. Wm. Alexander Thom; then, after a year's further study he was graduated with the degree of M.D. at the University of Virginia in 1861.

Married in February, 1863, Annie Elizabeth, the eldest child of James Alexander Beckham and Frances Jackson Alcocke, both of Culpeper Co., Va. They had two daughters. Mrs. Ross died January 31, 1921.

While a student at the university he helped to organize a company of students known as the "Southern Guard," and marched with it as first lieutenant to Harper's Ferry when Virginia seceded, but the governor refused to enlist the company in the permanent forces and ordered it back to university, where Ross aided in organizing a training school for military instruction. An endeavor to organize the "Piedmont Artillery" came to naught because of lack of ordnance and so in December, 1861, he entered the Confederate Army as Asst. Surgeon, and was assigned to the Banner Hospital, in Richmond. In the spring of 1862 he organized Crew's Factory Hospital and there remained as executive head until transferred to Chimborazo Hospital. In June, 1863, he reported to the Army of Northern Virginia, then near Gettysburg, and was put in charge of the Reserve Hospital of the Third Corps after which he was transferred to the Staff of Gen. A. P. Hill, as Assoc. Medical Director of his corps—as such he was present at the battles of Bristow Station and Mine Run and the skirmishes around Culpeper C. H. and Liberty Mills.

He was detached from the army and on Jan. 11, 1864, reported to the V. M. I. as Assistant Surgeon and as such was present on the battle field with the corps of cadets at New Market; after the battle, he accompanied the corps to Richmond and the following fall served with it in the trenches around Richmond; while it was at the Alms House; and was with it when it was relieved on the evacuation of the city.

Following the war Dr. Ross returned to Richmond and practiced his profession until his retirement, a few years before his death. He was a Lecturer in the Summer School of the Medical College of Virginia for eight years, filling the chairs of Anatomy and Minor Surgery; later he organized the chair of Obstetrics at the University College of Medicine, in Richmond, and after his active duties continued to be the Professor-Emeritus of Obstetrics.

He was a member of the first Board of Health organized in the State, appointed by Gov. Walker; a member of the board of visitors of V. M. I. for three years following Jan. 1, 1887; a 32d degree Mason.

In May, 1886, he organized the surgical service of the Richmond and Danville R. R. Co., and was its Chief Surgeon until 1896, when he resigned. He afterwards served for many years as Consulting Surgeon of its successor, the Southern Railway.

He was the author of a book of verse "Gathered Leaves" and among his contributions to medical literature may be mentioned, "The History of Spinal Injuries without Fracture," "Tetanus," "A Manipulative Mistake," "Internal Hemorrhoids," and "The Congeners of Phagedena, and its Treatment with Turpentine."

His portrait hangs in the V. M. I. Library.

Dr. Ross died March 31, 1926, aged 88, at the home of his son-in-law, William H. Palmer, Jr., V. M. I., '86, in Richmond, Va. He was buried in Hollywood Cemetery following services at St. Paul's Church, of which he was the Senior Warden and long a vestryman. He was survived by his daughters, (Fannie) Mrs. William H. Palmer, Jr., and (Hattie), Mrs. Charles B. Antrim, both of Richmond, and his brother, Judge Erskine M. Ross (See Sketch No. 211).

213. Lawrence Royster—1866.
Accountant—Clerk of the Courts

Born January 14, 1841, in New Kent County, Va.

Parents: John Woodson Royster and Susan Bacon Wilkinson.

Grandparents: Littlebury Royster and —— ——.
William Wilkinson and Susan Bacon Savage.

After serving in the Richmond Greys, he was entered at the Institute on February 5, 1862, by his mother, Mrs. S. B. Royster, of Richmond, Va. After repeating the work of the third class, he was appointed first cadet corporal in Co. A, the highest military office in his class, and as such served in the battle of New Market. "We retired for the night in a church; but we had scarcely fallen asleep,

—12

when we were aroused to get up and go to the front; the usual roll not being sounded as we were too near the enemy." In June, 1864, he was promoted to be the third ranking orderly sergeant in the corps, and the following session he resigned on March 31, 1865, two days before the corps was disbanded, and joined the 43rd Cavalry under Mosby.

In 1867 he married Alice Josephine, daughter of John Ridley and his wife, Mary Ann Gardner. They had one son, Lawrence Thomas Royster, a physician and surgeon, who, in 1923, was elected professor of pediatrics (diseases of children) in the department of medicine at the University of Virginia.

Starting at first as a farmer, he was then a bookkeeper and for many years was Clerk of the Courts of Norfolk, Va., a position to which he was elected following a great reform movement in the city. At the time the Court of Law and Chancery and the Corporation Court had not been divided.

He was past commander, Grice Commandery No. 16, Knights Templar of Virginia.

He died at his home in Norfolk on December 1, 1907.

214. Thomas Meldrum Rutherfoord—1867.

Capitalist—Tobacconist

Born June 5, 1848, in Richmond, Va.

Parents: Samuel J. Rutherfoord and Frances C. Watson.

Paternal Grandparents: Thomas Rutherfoord and Sarah Winston.

Before entering V. M. I. he was a member of Co. G, 34th Va. Battalion, local defense troops, Richmond, Va. He matriculated at the Institute on January 29, 1864, from Mattoax, Amelia County, Va., and less than four months later served as a cadet private in Co. C at the battle of New Market. The following session he resigned his cadetship on March 30, 1865, three days before the corps was disbanded and then joined Co. G, 3rd Regiment and was assigned to the staff of General John B. Gordon, commanding the 2nd Corps of the Army of Northern Virginia, as courier (being under age), and surrendered at Appomattox Courthouse on April 9, 1865. During the session 1865-66, he attended the University of Virginia.

On April 16, 1872, he married Laura, daughter of James Thomas, Jr., of Richmond, Va. They had three children:
James Thomas (V. M. I., '93), died February 1, 1933.
Laura, wife of George D. Mayo, of Richmond.
Gwendolyn.

For many years Mr. Rutherfoord was a member of the R. A. Patterson Tobacco Company, and was also a member of the board of directors of the First National Bank of Richmond, Va. He was the first president of the Hermitage Golf Club, was once president of the Westmoreland Club, and was a member of the Country Club of Virginia.

After an illness of many weeks he died April 2, 1914, at his home, 112 East Grace Street, and was buried in Hollywood Cemetery, Richmond, Va. He was survived by his wife, three children, and six sisters: Misses Jane and Sarah Rutherfoord and Mrs. Etta R. Wheat, of Richmond; Mrs. Lettie Goodwin, of Wytheville; Mrs. George Bernard, of Petersburg; and Mrs. Lewis E. Harvie, of Danville.

215. George Andrew Seaborn—1866.

Soldier—Killed in Battle

Born November 6, 1845, in Sussex Co., Va.

Parents: Capt. James Seaborn (born March 4, 1777, in Sussex Co., Va.; soldier in War of 1812; giant in size, weighed 384 lbs.) and Susan Avant, born in Sussex Co.

Grandparents: —— Seaborn (found at sea after a shipwreck when he was a child too young to know his name; his parents were lost; rescuers cared for him, and gave him the name —— Seaborn) and Susan Thorp. —— Avant and —— Lofton, of Culpeper Co., Va.

He matriculated at V. M. I. on August 11, 1862, from Jarratt, Sussex Co., Va., and was entered by L. W. Mason. He was a cadet for two years and while a third classman he was a cadet private in Co. A. In the battle of New Market he was with the cadet artillery section.

On leaving the Institute he joined Co. H, 13th Virginia Cavalry, and was killed in battle at Dinwiddie Court House on April 8, 1865, the day before General Lee surrendered.

216. Carlton Shafer—1864.

Lawyer—Legislator

Born April 3, 1844, near Leesburg, Loudoun Co., Va., the second of ten children.

Parents: Frederick William Shafer (born near Darmstadt, in Germany, and came to America in 1835) and Susanna Lezear.

He matriculated at V. M. I. July 25, 1860, from Leesburg and was a cadet until his graduation on June 27, 1864, when he stood second in his class. His military record at V. M. I. can best be traced from the Chronological Table in this book. While a cadet he was a corporal, an orderly sergeant, and in the battle of New Market he was the third cadet captain, commanding Co. B. When the corps went to Richmond in April, 1861, he was assigned as drillmaster to the "Livingston* Guards," of Polk Co., Texas. After graduation he was commissioned second lieutenant in the provisional

---

*When the New Market monument was dedicated in 1903 he was accosted by a gentleman in Lexington, who asked if he was the man who had trained this organization, whereupon Shafer showed him a carbuncle ring engraved "L. G. to C. S." The questioner had served on the committee which selected the ring forty-two years before and presented it in appreciation of his services.

army and was detailed to guard the salt works, at Saltville, Va., and continued on this duty until the end of the war.

With Jos. E. Packard, he established a school for boys in one of the buildings on the court house green in Leesburg. This was discontinued in 1867, when he became professor of mathematics in Frederick College, at Frederick, ,Md. He studied law; began to practice in Frederick in 1871; and continued the active practice of his profession for twenty-two years. During this period he was a school examiner; a member (1886) of the Maryland House of Delegates,* and served as chief clerk of that body for three terms after 1888.

Married: November 19, 1884, Sara, daughter of Dr. George Lafferty Andrew and Catherine Piatt, of La Porte, Indiana. Dr. Andrew, a grandson of George Lafferty of Virginia, was during the Civil War an officer in the U. S. Sanitary Commission, an organization supported by the benevolence of northern people to provide comfort for Federal soldiers. Mrs. Shafer wrote numerous articles for magazines and two books, "The Day before Yesterday" and "Beyond Chance of Change."

In 1893 Shafer removed to Baltimore where he had been appointed chief clerk to the Collector of Internal Revenue of the Sixth District (Maryland, Delaware, District of Columbia, and the Eastern Shore of Virginia) and so continued until 1900 when he was appointed Collector of Water Rents and Licenses for the City of Baltimore.

Never robust, he always suffered from the effects of pneumonia contracted while serving at the salt works during the war and this compelled him to change his place of residence. In May, 1904, he formed a partnership with ex-judge Wm. B. Biddle, a well-known lawyer of northern Indiana who had been Major in the 73d Indiana Volunteers, and they practiced law in La Porte.

His portrait hangs in the V. M. I. Library.

He died April 26, 1906, and following services in All Saint's Church, of which he was senior warden, he was buried in Pine Lake Cemetery at La Porte.

His dignity, courtesy, loyalty, and gentlemanliness had won the hearts of the people among whom he lived and Patton Post of the G. A. R. attended his funeral in a body. On the base of the celtic cross over his grave appears his name and his military record—the only Confederate soldier there buried.

His wife died in an automobile accident October 19, 1913. They had no children.

217. William Brenton Shaw—1865.

Lawyer—State Senator

Born September 15, 1843, at Indian Ridge, in Currituck County, N. C.

*He wrote that four V. M. I. cadets were members of this body at the time, three of them New Market cadets: Thos. G. Hayes, Baltimore City; T. Herbert Shriver, Carroll Co.; Carlton Shafer, Frederick Co.; and Edwin Gott, '71, Anne Arundel Co.

Parents: Col. Henry M. Shaw, of the 8th N. C. Regiment, C. S. A., who was killed in battle near New Berne, N. C., February 1, 1864, and Mary Trotman.

Grandparents: Rev. John A. Shaw, and Elizabeth Mutchmore, who came to North Carolina from Newport, R. I.

Ezekel Trotman, a Scotchman, and Emily, daughter of Colonel Peter Daugé (now written Dozier) of the 10th N. C. Regiment in the Continental line under Washington.

"I was prepared for college at the old Indian Ridge Academy in Currituck County, N. C., under Prof. J. T. Lassell, finishing the course in June 1861, and on July 4, 1861, I was commissioned by the Governor of North Carolina as drillmaster and ordered to report to my father for duty. I was then engaged in drilling various companies of his regiment until January, 1862, when my father made me decline a commission as lieutenant in one of the companies, and sent me to V. M. I."

He matriculated on January 9, 1862, from Indian Town, N. C., and as a second classman he was second cadet sergeant of Co. A and color bearer of the corps but sickness prevented him from taking part in the New Market Campaign and Evans carried the colors in the battle. At the end of the session he was promoted to be first lieutenant of Co. A. At graduation he stood 22 in his class of 24.

It was his misfortune to be absent when the corps engaged in battle at New Market and he was thus deprived of first-hand knowledge of the details of that campaign but he was an eloquent orator and at the meeting of the Alumni Association on June 21, 1904, forty years after the battle, he made the speech conferring upon Mrs. E. C. Crim the name of "The Mother of the New Market Corps" and presented to her a "cross of honor" similar to those given to the other members of the New Market Battalion organization.

He married Jennie, daughter of Edwin Ferebee of Camden County, N. C. They had three sons and two daughters.

"After graduation, civil engineering was my choice of professions, but I found so little demand for my services just after the war that I read law under my uncle, Colonel L. D. Starke who had survived the war and taken up his practice. I was licensed by the Supreme Court in 1868, but did not undertake active practice until 1874, from which time forth I have devoted my whole time to the practice of law in the State and Federal Courts (of North Carolina).

"I represented the 1st district of North Carolina in the State Senate in 1874 and 1875 but declined a re-election. I was also appointed State's Attorney in my district and held that office during the litigation between two claimants."

In 1905 Mr. Shaw and his wife moved to Madison, Wisconsin, to be with their two sons who were established in business in that city. He entered upon the practice of his profession but the following year he suffered a severe illness and just as he seemed to be improving, his wife became very ill and he was compelled to return to Henderson, N. C., his old home. Mrs. Shaw died in 1907.

On December 24, 1908, he died suddenly at the residence of his son, H. M. Shaw, in Oxford, N. C. He was found dead in his room, partially disrobed, sitting in his chair, with a book in his hand. He was survived by the following children: Henry M., Mrs. Richard J. Corbitt, Mrs. Bessie Strouse, William B., and Edwin F. Shaw. He was buried in Henderson, by the side of his wife.

218. John Hardy Shields—1867.

Merchant

Born September 23, 1846, in Lynchburg, Va.

Parents: Col. John Camden Shields (first commander of the 1st Company, Richmond Howitzers, to which was assigned the two howitzers and two six pounders of the old V. M. I. cadet battery; later Editor of the Richmond Whig) and Martha Mahala Hardy, of Campbell Co., Va.

Grandparents: Joseph Shields, Nelson Co., Va. Served as Captain in the War of 1812, and Elizabeth Camden, of Rockbridge Co., Va.
Chesley Hardy, of Campbell Co., Va., and Martha Mahala Johnson, who was an aunt of Gen. Thomas Rosser.

He matriculated August 11, 1863, from Richmond, Va., when he was 16 years and 10 months old and later in the session was a cadet private in Co. C at the battle of New Market. The following session he was a cadet until Richmond was evacuated.

After the war he was connected with hardware house of Donnan & Co., Richmond, Va. He married Elizabeth Lee Donnan.

He was killed in a railroad collision near Prospect Station, N. & W. R. R. on May 19, 1875.

Two of his brothers were V. M. I. cadets: William Thomas Shields, '71, a member of the board of visitors 1899 to 1908; and Orville Shields, '80.

219. Scott Shipp—1859.

Soldier—Educator
In Command of Cadets at New Market.

Born August 2, 1839, at Warrenton, Va. (Spelling of name changed from Ship to Shipp about 1883.)

Parents: Captain John Shipp, and his third wife, Lucy Blackwell Scott, who later married Dr. Henry M. Clarkson, of Boone Co., Mo.

After attending Mrs. Franklin's School, the Warren Green Academy, and the Warrenton High School, his mother went to Missouri to live and he entered Westminster College, Fulton, Mo., in 1852. At the end of the junior year he was employed as a rodman and assistant engineer on the North Missouri Railroad and was so engaged for the year 1855-56. He matriculated at V. M. I. on August 14, 1856, from Columbia, Fauquier Co., Va.; was entered by Dr. H. M. Clarkson; and was admitted to the third class. He was graduated July 4, 1859, standing 4 in a class of 29 and having the rank of cadet first lieutenant of Co. B.

His three-year cadetship was but the forerunner of a service to

V. M. I. extending over 61 years—with a few minor exceptions an unbroken service. At graduation he was commissioned lieutenant and was assistant professor of mathematics and latin; the following year he transferred to latin. During these years he studied law at Washington College, a course which was interrupted by the war but which he later resumed and in which he was graduated in 1866. He was immediately admitted to the bar but never practiced.

The history of his life is largely the military history of the V. M. I. before the World War, and a voluminous book has been written on that theme. He was with the corps of cadets at John Brown's Execution and on every subsequent campaign with the exception of one which occurred while he was in service with troops. On all campaigns after 1861 he was in command of the cadets and this, of course, includes the New Market Campaign. The following quotations pertain to one phase of the battle of New Market:

"The advance was thus continued until having passed Bushong's house, a mile or more beyond New Market, and still to the left of the main road, the enemy's batteries, at 250 or 300 yards, opened upon us with canister and case-shot, and their long lines of infantry were put into action at the same time. The fire was withering. It seemed impossible that any living creature could escape; and here we sustained our heaviest loss, a great many being wounded and numbers knocked down, stunned, and temporarily disabled. I was here disabled for a time, and the command devolved upon Captain H. A. Wise, Company A. He gallantly pressed onward. We had before this gotten into the front line." (War Records, Series 1, Vol. 37, part 1, pp. 90, 91.)

"About the middle of the orchard, Colonel Shipp was knocked down, and, we thought, mortally wounded. Here for the first and only time our line was broken. Even then these brave boys did not retreat, but ran forward thirty yards where in confusion, yet still together, we lay down behind a fence, and began for the first time to fire upon the enemy." (Capt. Frank Preston, letter May 19, 1864.)

"It was at this point of the advance, after he had corrected the alignment of the Battalion by marking time, just beyond the Bushong House, that the Commandant, always in front, was struck on the left shoulder by a heavy but spent fragment of shell, and literally swept from his feet. For a time he was apparently stunned, though he was not wounded except very slightly in the face, probably by a tiny piece of shell." (Mil. Hist. of V. M. I., p. 313.)

When the Corps went to Richmond in April, 1861, he remained at the Institute in charge of 47 cadets who had been left because they had been considered too immature to act as drillmasters. But in a very short time he reported at Camp Lee in Richmond as Asst. Adjutant-General with the rank of Captain. Soon afterwards he was appointed a major in 21st Virginia Infantry, the regiment of which Col. Wm. Gilham, who had been commandant of cadets, was the colonel. When it was decided to re-open the institute on January 1, 1862, Shipp was appointed commandant of cadets and was directed by the Secretary of War to report as such. These orders were modified to enable him to participate in Jackson's wintry Romney Campaign. Repeated attempts to engage in active duty thereafter were of no avail but in addition to the cadet campaigns he did serve for a short time by utilizing a sixty day leave which started on July 28, 1863. Then the man who could not be spared from his duties in shaping the embryo officers of the Confederacy joined Co. H, 4th Virginia Cavalry, then on the retreat from Gettysburg, and served with it during his leave as a private soldier—mostly on the line of the Rappahannock River.

After the corps was quartered at the Alms House in Richmond, it was called to active service twice. On March 11, 1865, Colonel Shipp commanded the corps on the line of battle between the Canal and the Westham Road, several miles west of Richmond, expecting to be attacked by Federal cavalry, under General Fitzhugh, which Sheridan sent down from Columbia. The attack did not materialize and the corps was withdrawn in two days. On the night of April 1, 1865, the cadets under his command were ordered to occupy Field's abandoned works on the Charles City Road, and just after sunrise they relieved the last of the Confederate infantry and assumed command of this section of the line. The cadets were in the rifle pits on April 2nd within speaking distance of the enemy, the only troops at this point between Richmond and the Federals, when they were relieved late that afternoon by a squadron of cavalry. That night the evacuation of the city commenced. Col. Shipp returned to Lexington for a time and about sixty days later was paroled in Richmond.

Married: August 19, 1869, Anne Alexander, daughter of Arthur A. Morson, of Richmond, Va., and sister of William A. Morson. (See Sketch No. 173.) They had three children:

Elizabeth Scott (d. 1901), wife of Col. N. Beverley Tucker, V. M. I., '88, professor at V. M. I. until his death.

Lucy Scott, wife of Benjamin Huger, V. M. I., '93, of Lexington, Va.

Arthur Morson Shipp, V. M. I., '97, Colonel in the U. S. Army.

Mrs. Shipp died February 25, 1884.

He continued as commandant and as professor of the various branches of tactics until January 1, 1890, when he became superintendent with the rank of brigadier-general. Almost immediately he was appointed a member of the board of visitors of the United States Military Academy and four years later he served in a similar capacity at the United States Naval Academy, of the latter board he was president.

During his administration the last of the debt incurred to rebuild the Institute after its destruction in 1864 was liquidated; numerous additions and improvements were made in the physical plant and the academic courses; and the size of the corps increased from 199 to 310.

On June 30, 1907, General Shipp resigned the active direction of the Institute and spent the remainder of his days as Superintendent-Emeritus. A trip around the world supplemented former travel in Europe. In 1867 he carried the proposal to Commodore Matthew Fontaine Maury, then exiled in London, that he accept the Chair of Physics at V. M. I.,—Maury accepted, reported the following year, and was a member of the faculty until his death in 1873.

Among the many honors conferred on Gen. Shipp was the degree of LL.D. by Washington and Lee University and the presidency of the newly created Agricultural and Mechanical College at Blacksburg, Va. The latter was in 1880 and he actually held the position for four days or until he found that his condition that he be consulted in the selection of his faculty would not be fully complied with.

Gen. Shipp, the trainer of several generations of young citizens, was admired and respected by all who knew him. He was not beloved by the cadets but the same traits which forbade the love of youth compelled it of those same men as they reached maturity. A stern disciplinarian, he was absolutely impartial, just, and fearless. His actions were always based on the right, as he saw it, and never on what might be popular.

His portrait, full length in uniform, hangs in Jackson Memorial Hall at V. M. I.

General Shipp died at his home in Lexington at 10:15 p. m., December 4, 1917 and following services at Lee Memorial Church, of which he was a vestryman, he was buried in Lexington. He was survived by his son, daughter, and three grandchildren: Scott Huger, V. M. I., '22, Elizabeth Huger, and Benjamin Huger, V. M. I., '34.

220. Samuel Sprigg Shriver—1864.

Farmer—Legislator

Born January 9, 1843, at Wheeling, W. Va.

Parents: Jacob Sherman Shriver, and Eliza Hay McElheran.

Grandparents: Daniel McElheran, and Amelia Hay, daughter of Col. Hay of Gen. Washington's Staff.
David Shriver, Fayette Co., Maryland, and Eve Sherman.

He matriculated at V. M. I. on January 1, 1862, from Staunton, Va., and was admitted to the third class. As a first classman he was the fourth cadet captain, commanding Co. C, at the battle of New Market. At graduation he stood fourth in his class. In the battle of New Market he was struck on the elbow of the left arm by a piece of shell which knocked him down. Recovering his feet he continued to lead his company until a musket ball struck the same elbow and forced his retirement. His arm was stiff for the rest of his life. After recovering from the wound he was detailed as inspector of arms in the Ordnance Department, at Richmond. He was then put in command of the "Galvanized Corps," as it was called, in North Carolina.

After the war he studied law in the office of Hon. Charles Russell, in Baltimore, and was admitted to the bar but did not practice. He moved to his plantation in Mintonsville, Nansemond Co., Va., about 1868. There he engaged in farming for the remainder of his life—highly respected among his people whom he represented in the Virginia Legislature in 1877-78.

He died, unmarried, on August 17, 1881, at Suffolk, Va.

221. Thomas Herbert Shriver—1867.

Farmer—Legislator—Banker

Born February 14, 1846, at Union Mills, Carroll County, Md.

Parents: William Shriver (b. December 23, 1807, at Union Mills), and Mary M. J. Owens, of Littlestown, Penna.

Paternal Grandparents: Andrew Shriver (b. November 7, 1762, on Little Pine Creek, Md.), and —— ——.

When he was preparing for college, the War between the States started, and on June 28, 1863, Shriver joined Company K, 1st Maryland Cavalry, and participated in the battle of Gettysburg and also took part in a number of cavalry engagements in Northern Virginia. Because of his youth he was detailed to the Virginia Military Institute, matriculating on September 1, 1863. During that session he was a cadet private in Co. C, but at the battle of New Market was detailed with the artillery.

He remained with the corps of cadets until it disbanded in Richmond on the eve of the evacuation of that city, at which time he rejoined the 1st Maryland Cavalry which refused to surrender at Appomattox. They disbanded to meet at Waynesboro, Va. The regiment was reorganized and marched down the Valley to Cloverdale, Va., intending to join General Johnston in the Carolinas, but were met by General T. T. Munford who informed them of the surrender of Johnston and the collapse of the Confederacy. Issuing an address, General Munford disbanded this regiment as the last organized troop of Virginia. Young Shriver was paroled at Staunton, Va., June 23, 1865.

"After the war he returned to Baltimore, Md., and entered mercantile pursuit for a time. Was clerk in bank, assistant receiving teller; then traveling salesman. In 1876 he formed co-partnership with his brother, B. Frank Shriver, under the firm name of B. F. Shriver & Co., as general manager. They engaged in farming, milling, and canning fruits and vegetables, which business grew to be one of the largest in the United States. He was twice elected to the Maryland Legislature, 1878 and 1880; elected to Maryland State Senate in 1884; and was appointed Deputy Collector of the Port of Baltimore in 1886 under President Cleveland. Served on Governor's Staff as Brigadier General and Commissary General, having been appointed by Governors Henry Lloyd and Elihu E. Jackson. He was Vice-President and Director of the Westminster Deposit & Trust Co., and President of the Westminster (Md.) Hardware Co. Also President of the Union Mills Savings Bank of Union Mills, Carroll County, Md., and for many years a member of the State Central Committee of Maryland."

In February, 1880, he married Elizabeth R., daughter of Robert Lawson, of Catonsville, Md. The names of their children are Hilda, Joseph N., Robert T., and William H. Shriver.

In 1916 General (he derived this title from having served on the staffs of Governors Lloyd and Jackson of Maryland) Shriver suffered a stroke of paralysis, and died on December 31, 1916, survived by his four children, all of Westminster, Md.

He was a devout Roman Catholic; an active member of the Knights of Columbus, served as Grand Knight in the Westminster Commandery; and an intimate friend of Cardinal Gibbons, who delivered the eulogy at the funeral which was held at St. John's Catholic Church, Westminster.

222. Sanford Bernard Skaggs—1866.
Teacher

Born June 16, 1845.

Parents: Edward R. Skaggs (a merchant, who died at Blue Sulphur Springs, Greenbrier Co., West Va., in December, 1874) and Catherine Duffy (died at Summerville, W. Va.).

He matriculated at V. M. I., January 10, 1862, from Blue Sulphur Springs; repeated the work of the fourth class; and while a third classman fought in the battle of New Market as a cadet private in Co. A.

After the war he taught school. He died of consumption on May 18, 1868, aged 23 years.

He never married and his New Market Cross of Honor was sent to his first cousin (nearest of kin), Howard C. Skaggs, Clerk of the Circuit Court of Greenbrier County, Lewisburg, W. Va.

223. William Lane Slaughter—1867.
Real Estate—Insurance

Born November 18, 1847, at Fredericksburg, Va.

Parents: Montgomery Slaughter (b. at "The Hermitage," Culpeper County, Va.), and Eliza Lane Slaughter (b. at "Rose Hill," Rappahannock County, Va.).

Grandparents: William Slaughter, of Rappahannock County, Va., and Harriet Ficklen, of Stafford County, Va.
Philip Slaughter and Eliza Lane, both of Rappahannock County, Va.

He entered the Institute on September 1, 1863, from Fredericksburg, and was a cadet private in Co. C at the battle of New Market. The following session he was with the corps until Richmond was evacuated.

On February 5, 1873, he married Hannah Battaile, daughter of Hay Battaile Hoomes, of Fredericksburg, Va. They had no children.

After the war Mr. Slaughter followed the profession of a civil engineer. Later he became a member of the firm of Slaughter and Griffin, real estate and insurance agents, at Fredericksburg.

He died on May 18, 1905, after a brief illness, and was survived by his wife, one brother, Philip M. Slaughter, of Richmond, Va., and two sisters, Mrs. H. L. Bressler, of Washington, D. C., and Miss Fannie Slaughter, of Fredericksburg, Va.

224. Charles Henry Smith—1867.

Railroad Agent

Born November 22, 1845, at Brownville, Jefferson County, N. Y.

Parents: Colonel Larkin Smith (b. April 9, 1814, at Fredericksburg, Va.; d. December 4, 1884, at San Antonio, Texas), graduate of West Point, class of 1835, Colonel in U. S. A., wounded at Battle of Mexico, Quartermaster Department, C. S. A., and Catherine Storrow Brown (b. August 14, 1821, at Brownville, N. Y.; d. January 23, 1894, near Drakes Branch, Va., at the home of her daughter, Mrs. Woods).

Grandparents: Charles Henry Smith (b. December 10, 1785; d. Aug. 22, 1849, at Norfolk, Va.; son of Larkin Smith, member of Virginia House of Burgesses), U. S. paymaster at Norfolk, Va., and Evelina Coleman, daughter of William Scandreth Stone and Milly Richards.
General Jacob Brown (b. May 9, 1775, in Bucks County, Pa.; d. February 24, 1828), general-in-chief of the United States Army (1821 to 1828), and Pamela ——.
He was a distant cousin of J. R. Triplett. (See Sketch No. 249.)

He entered the Institute on August 6, 1863, from Richmond, Va., where his father was serving with the quartermaster department of the C. S. A., although his home was at Drakes Branch, in Charlotte county. He was a cadet private in Co. C at New Market.

"I charged with Co. C till I was wounded by a bursting shell. In five or ten minutes I was with the line of battle again and in less than five minutes was again dropped to the ground with three or four other boys by concussion—none of us hurt. My wound was fortunately only a bruise; only pained me for a week or two. . . .

"I gave up my cadetship the night of the evacuation of the city of Richmond. I was at the Alms House just prior to the evacuation. I was with the boys when we were camped few miles from Richmond, and marched with them through Rocketts and Main Streets that fearful, sad night. I was on one of the canal boats that left the city that same night. I threw away in the water my gun, belt, cartridge box and canteen before starting. I ran up to a relative's house on Franklin Street to get some money to buy something to eat while on my rush home. A Mr. Haxall came to the door. I told him my wants. He said, 'Why, Charlie, I have $1000 all in $100 denominations. I can spare you $500 but it isn't worth a d——! Don't you see the people making bonfires out on the street? They are burning it.' I took the $500 and spent it $100 at a time at farm houses on my route home, dividing cornbread, butter, ham, eggs and buttermilk with my comrades, five of them. These boys all left me along the road at different turning-off places, except one, who accompanied me to within five miles of home when he too stopped. I have often wondered if any of those boys remember that tramp—all of us in our cadet uniforms.

"I did not join the army—remained at home a while then went to St. Louis, Mo. In 1869 I went to Georgia, engaged in mercantile business. When the Southern Railway was building, I took the agency at Buford, Ga., holding the position of station agent there for thirty-two years."

Mr. Smith married Julia Frances, daughter of Joseph T. Garner, landowner and planter of Georgia and Alabama. They had three children:

Charles Henry Smith, Jr., graduate in law at Athens, Ga.; with Southern Broom Manufacturing Company, Atlanta, in 1919.

William Larkin Smith, bookkeeper and stenographer; in business in Atlanta in 1909.

Pamela Brown Smith, music teacher.

He died on October 22, 1917.

225. Edward Harvie Smith, Jr.—1867.

Civil Service—Merchant

Born October 25, 1845, at Village View, Dinwiddie County, Va.

Parents: Dr. Edwin Harvie Smith, chief surgeon at Chimborazo Hospital during the Civil War, C. S. A.; later U. S. consul to Naples, and Anne Anderson.

Grandparents: Hon. John Hill Smith (Captain of Williamsburg Troop in War of 1812; son of Larkin Smith, Colonel in Revolutionary War, and Mary E. Hill) and Mary Cary Ambler (daughter of Col. John Ambler and Mary Cary, of Jamestown Island).

Edward Anderson, Major in the War of 1812, and Anne Gilliam.

He entered V. M. I. on July 19, 1862, from Richmond, Va. At the battle of New Market while repeating the work of the fourth class he served as a cadet private in Co. A. and was wounded. On July 1, 1864, he was appointed a second lieutenant and ordered to drill reserves stationed at High Bridge, which he did until he resigned and rejoined the cadets at Richmond in October of that year and continued his cadetship until he was "appointed second lieutenant, 1st of April, 1865, and ordered to Andersonville as drillmaster, but did not go as I was with the Corps of Cadets below Richmond when it was evacuated."

On October 25, 1870, he married Nina, daughter of James Nelson, a prominent lawyer of Richmond, Va. They had three children:

William Gay, cashier of U. S. Custom House, Richmond.

Nina Ambler, wife of Charles Clifton Cox, of Waverly, Va.

Ann Gilliam, of Richmond.

"Manufacturer of tobacco, 1871-73. Appointed Inspector of Public Works for the District of Columbia, March 1, 1873. Resigned in March, 1874, to accept the position of Deputy Clerk, U. S. District Court, Eastern Division of Virginia. Resigned in July, 1876, to accept the position of U. S. Tobacco Inspector for the Third Internal Revenue, District of Virginia. Appointed by Hon. John Sherman, Secretary of Treasury. Held the position until October 1, 1885, when the office was abolished. Was Judge of Election for ten years, and one term Chairman of the Board of Election Commissioners for Richmond, Va. October 15, 1885, appointed Weigh Master by Gov. Wm. E. Cameron, to fill unexpired term and held the position until end of term. Was not a candidate for reappointment."

In 1887 Mr. Smith was with the firm of J. H. Chataigne & Co.,

Directory Publishers, with offices at 1100 East Main Street, Richmond, Va.

He died at the Soldiers' Home in Richmond on March 23, 1912.

226. Francis Lee Smith—1867.

Lawyer—Legislator

Born October 6, 1845, at Alexandria, Va., the third son of his parents.

Parents: Francis Lee Smith, one of the leading lawyers of Alexandria, and Sarah Gosnell Vowell.

Grandparents: John A. W. Smith, of Warrenton, Va., and Maria Love Hawkins (dtr. of Capt. John Hawkins, Adjt. 3rd Va. Reg't, Continental Army, and Alice Corbin Thomson, who was the dtr. of Dr. Adam Thomson and Lettice Lee, dtr. of Philip Lee, of Md., and Elizabeth Sewall. Philip Lee being the grandson of Richard Lee, the Emigrant to Virginia in 1641).

John Cripps Vowell (born in London, England, 1767, and died in Alexandria, Va., 1852) and Mary Jaquelin Smith (born at Shooters Hill in Middlesex Co., Va., 1773 and died in Alexandria, Va., 1846; dtr. of Augustine Smith and Margaret Boyd).

He matriculated at V. M. I. on January 4, 1862, from Alexandria and was on Oct. 5, 1862 required to repeat the work of the fourth class but because of ill health he dropped out for a year. On December 3, 1863, he was re-admitted as a fourth classman and later in that session he was a cadet private in Co. A where he was wounded twice within a few moments. He was shot in the chin, the ball entering his mouth, shattering his jawbone and coming out of his neck, just missing the carotid artery and the jugular vein. Another shot entered his shoulder and broke his collar bone—this Minie ball was later mounted and is in the V. M. I. Museum. Ricketts, who was the only mounted cadet, put him on his horse and he rode back to New Market for treatment. At the end of the session he was promoted to be seventh ranking corporal in the corps and continued his cadetship until Richmond was evacuated.

After the war he studied law with his father, a lawyer of the old school, and in 1867 was admitted to the bar. He was corporation attorney for the city of Alexandria, 1871-72; member of the Virginia State Senate 1879-83; member of the Virginia Constitutional Convention, 1901-02, and there following an inspired address embodied a provision in the Constitution for the preservation and perpetuation of the Virginia Military Institute. He was a member of the Board of Aldermen of Alexandria 1885-87; of the Board of Visitors of the V. M. I. 1885-88, 1903-04 and 1906-10; and Board of Directors of the Citizens National Bank of Alexandria 1887 to 1904.

Married: November 20, 1871, Janie Lindsay, daughter of Major William T. Sutherlin, and Jane E. Patrick, of Danville, Va. Two children died in infancy and their third child, Janie Sutherlin Smith, died October 31, 1904. Mrs. Smith died August 24, 1876.

His interest in military affairs never waned and he was Captain of the Alexandria Light Infantry 1878; Major of the 3rd Regiment Virginia Volunteers 1881; and Lieut. Colonel of the same regiment in 1882.

His clientele was wide and he was retained as attorney by many financial and other corporations, including the Pennsylvania Railroad, Southern Railway and Washington Southern Railway Companies.

Col. Smith died at his home, 510 Wolfe St., Alexandria, Va., August 25, 1916, aged 71 years.

He was survived by two sisters, Miss Margaret Vowell Smith, of Alexandria, and Mrs. William Everard Strong, of New York City; and a nephew, Courtland H. Smith, Jr., V. M. I., '98. Two of his brothers were V. M. I. cadets: John Jaquelin Smith, '57, and Clifton Hewitt Smith, '61. A bronze memorial tablet to the memory of Colonel Smith hangs in the Jackson Memorial Hall at V. M. I.

227. William Taylor Smith—1867.

Rancher

Born April 26, 1844, in Clarksburg, Va. (now W. Va.).

Parents: Col. Augustine John Smith (b. April 29, 1802, in Alexandria, Va.), and Louisa M. Wilson (b. September 22, 1811, in Clarksburg, now West Virginia).

His parents were both dead at the time he matriculated at V. M. I., and he was entered in March 6, 1862, by his brother, Augustine Jacquelin Smith, of Harrison county, Va. At the battle of New Market, while still a member of the fourth class and a cadet private in Co. C, he served with the cadet artillery section as a driver. His conduct under fire resulted in his promotion at the end of the session to be first cadet corporal in Co. B. His cadetship continued until March 31, 1865, two days before the corps disbanded, when he resigned to enter the Confederate army.

Following the war he drifted west and for a time lived in the Indian Territory. In 1905 he was a resident of Texas.

The following information was received in 1909 from his brother Mortimer W. Smith:

"Married but name of wife unknown, as he went to Texas many years ago. Do not know whether there were any children. Has not been heard from for over twenty years. Do not know whether he is living or dead."

In 1910 Edward Hill Pritchett, '80, of Bonham, Texas, wrote:

"There used to live in this county (Fannin) near Ravenna a man by the name of W. T. Smith, who was a member of the New Market Corps. He went into the army from the Institute and served during the remainder of the war, and drifted to Texas after the war. I have lost track of him for the last two or three years and do not know where he is. . . . He married once or twice."

His father was a member of the V. M. I. board of visitors from Harrison county from 1855 to 1858.

228. John Franklin Sowers—1866.

Stockman—Farmer

Born April 23, 1846, at "Lakeville," Clarke County, Va.

Parents: John W. Sowers and Mary Elizabeth Mitchell, of White Post, Clarke County, Va.

Grandparents: James Sowers and Elizabeth Kerfoot, of Clarke County, Va. William Mitchell and Matilda ——, of Warren County, Va.

"At the time he matriculated at V. M. I., he resided with his parents at their home, 'Farnley,' Clarke county, and with his father, in a private conveyance, drove up the historic Shenandoah Valley to Lexington." He entered the Institute from White Post, Clarke Co., Va., on September 4, 1862 and as a third classman served as a cadet private in Co. D at the battle of New Market. He remained with the corps until the end of the session, following the Lynchburg Campaign. Returning to "Farnley," he joined Colonel Mosby's command and served until the end of the war.

In 1881 he married Mary Hamner, daughter of James H. and Mary Baker Thomson, of Frederick, Md. They had one son: John Thomson Sowers, born June 12, 1882.

Mr. Sowers spent his life in his native county where he was a successful stockman and farmer, being one of the largest landowners in Clarke county.

He died on May 19, 1915.

229. George Spiller—1866.

Civil Engineer

Born December 5, 1845, in Nelson Co., Va.

Parents: James Madison Spiller, and Caroline Kyle.

Grandparents: George Spiller, and Mary Spears. Barclay Kyle, and Jane McDonald, Botetourt Co., Va.

After attending Wm. S. Reid's school in Amherst County he matriculated at V. M. I. on January 1, 1862, from Fincastle, Va. Typhoid fever caused him to lose a year but in the fall of 1863 he took part as a third classman in the battle of New Market as a cadet private in Co. A. He was slightly wounded in the head in the battle but continued his cadetship until graduation on July 4, 1866 when he stood ninth in his class. He was appointed a sergeant in Co. C on March 1, 1865.

Before the war a branch library was maintained at V. M. I. by a debating society called the Society of Cadets. George Spiller was cadet librarian at the time of Hunter's Raid when the library, records, and books were destroyed by fire. Two books were saved by him, the "Life of Patrick Henry," by William Wirt, and Volume 6 of Moore's Poems. These two books were sunk with a packet-boat in the C. & O. Canal, but were eventually recovered and taken to Texas. Through the interest of Sidney Briggs, class of 1923, who was a special agent for the Aetna Fire Insurance Co., of Dallas, Texas, Col. Spiller restored them to V. M. I., where they are preserved in the museum.

After graduation, George Spiller's father gave him the store and mill known as "Gilmore's Mill" in Rockbridge Co., Va., where he was in business until May, 1870, when he and his classmate, Alfred Marshall, went to Alabama as civil engineers. Marshall soon fell a victim to yellow fever. Spiller slept with him the night before he was taken ill and nursed him like a brother until he died. Marshall was a founder and Spiller the sixth initiate of the Alpha Tau Omega fraternity.

In 1879 he married Belle Loving, daughter of Mr. J. C. Loving, who resided on a ranch in Lost Valley, in what is now Jack County. They made their home in Jackson, Tennessee, in 1881, but returned to Fort Worth, Texas, in 1883, and a year later moved to Jacksboro.

After Marshall's death he went to Louisiana and thence in 1871 to Texas, where he engaged in engineering in Houston. In 1873 he was surveyor for the Houston and Great Northern Railway. In 1876 he became official surveyor of the Young Land District, which comprised virtually all of Northwest Texas, exclusive of the Panhandle. He located the land which the State of Texas granted to the public schools. He was official surveyor of Jack county from 1894 to January, 1931, and was succeeded by his son, Kyle Spiller. For many years he operated the Spiller Abstract Company and in connection with this work was in the insurance business.

After an illness of three years, in the last year of which he became blind, he died April 14, 1931, and was buried in Oakwood cemetery. He was survived by his wife, a daughter, Miss Carrie Belle Spiller of Santa Barbara, Calif., and eight sons, six of whom were his pallbearers:

E. B. Spiller, Secretary and General Manager of the Texas and Western Cattle Raisers Association; James Spiller, Panhandle; Kyle Spiller, Jacksboro; William M. Spiller, Albany, N. Y.; George Spiller, Cleveland, Ohio; Col. Hampden Spiller, attorney, 1010 First National Bank Building, Forth Worth, Texas; Major Oliver L. Spiller, a graduate of the U. S. Naval Academy and an officer of the U. S. Army; and John L. Spiller, Ventura, California.

230. William Hickman Spiller—1867.

Merchant—Town Treasurer

Born April 4, 1847, at Wytheville, Va.

Parents: William Hickman Spiller (b. October, 1800, in Lancaster County, Va.; d. about 1854), and Susan Crockett.

Grandparents: James Spiller, and Catherine Markham, daughter of Captain Francis Smith, an extensive landowner in Hanover and Louisa Counties, Va. He was an officer in the Continental Army in the Revolutionary War, was captured by the British and died a prisoner of war.

Joseph Crockett, and Susan, daughter of John Montgomery, a native of England, who came to Virginia in 1732.

—13

William Hickman Spiller matriculated at V. M. I. on July 28, 1862, from Wytheville, Va., and in the battle of New Market served as a cadet private in Co. A, while repeating the fourth class. He continued his cadetship until January 27, 1865 and later served as a Captain in King's Battery.

After the war he returned to his home at Wytheville and worked on the farm. In 1866 he entered Washington College at Lexington and was graduated in 1870 with the degree of Bachelor of Arts. He did not, however, enter professional life.

On November 23, 1870, he married Cynthia McComas, daughter of Colonel Thomas Jefferson Boyd and Minerva Ann French, of Giles County, Va. Of this union there were eight boys and three girls:
William H., Thomas Boyd, Sue Montgomery, Robert Kent, Minnie Milton, Frank Markham, Stuart Magruder, Josephine Preston, Donald Douglas, Ernest McComas, and Edwin Bright.

Mr. Spiller engaged in the mercantile business in Wytheville, dealing in dry goods, notions, men's furnishing goods, boots and shoes. In the Spring of 1899 he went to Roanoke and for seven years was treasurer of the Becker Grocery Company, wholesale dealers in staple and fancy groceries, cigars and tobacco. Selling out his interest in this firm, he returned to Wytheville where he was elected town treasurer. About 1915 he suffered a stroke of paralysis and was forced to retire from active duty.

He died suddenly at his home in Wytheville on Saturday, April 27, 1918. His widow and the following children survived: Dr. William H. and Donald Spiller, of New York; Lieutenant Colonel R. Kent Spiller, of Washington, D. C.; Thomas Boyd Spiller, of Baltimore; Mrs. Frank Morton Williams, of Mobile, Ala.; Lieutenant Ernest M. Spiller, in France; Captain Edwin B. Spiller, of the U. S. Coast Artillery; Stuart M. Spiller, of Tokyo, Japan; Miss Susan and Frank M. Spiller of Wytheville.

231. Clay Stacker—1869.

Lawyer—Civil Engineer

Born January 11, 1847, at Cumberland Iron Works, Stewart County, Tenn. (He matriculated as H. C. Stacker. The first initial was dropped during his cadetship.)

Parents: Marinus Stacker (b. in Pennsylvania), and Maria Richmond (b. at Nashville, Tenn.).

Grandparents: Samuel Stacker, and Elizabeth Beltzhoover, of Pennsylvania. Barton Richmond, and Deborah Briggs, of Connecticut.

He attended Stewart College in Clarksville, Tenn., and was in school in Paris, France, when the war broke out. Returning to America, he was entered at the Virginia Military Institute on July 25, 1863, by Colonel William B. Richmond, of Clarksville, Tenn. At the battle of New Market he served as a cadet private in Co. B. He continued his cadetship until January 9, 1865. In June 1864, he had been promoted to be the second ranking cadet corporal in the corps. After leaving the Institute he served as a private in the Second Kentucky Infantry.

"He was one of the escorts to accompany President Davis on his departure from Richmond, after Lee's surrender, accompanying him as far as Washington, Ga. When the escort here was deemed too large for safety, he offered to be one of ten to escort and guide the President until he should make his escape. But the beardless youth was too young for this hazardous duty and his offer was courteously declined. When the last pay roll of the Confederacy was made up, out of the $26.00 which fell to him in the final disbursement, he preserved one of the sacred treasure with this inscription: 'Presented to Clay Stacker, one of the last followers of Jefferson Davis, Washington, Ga., May 4, 1865.'" (From Mrs. Stacker, Sept. 13, 1910.)

In the fall of 1866 he returned to the Institute, entered the third class, and on July 2, 1869, was graduated with ninth stand in his class.

On September 11, 1872, in the Presbyterian Church in Lexington, Va., he married Grace Winthrop, daughter of Rev. John W. Pratt, and Mary Grace Crabbe. Her father was at the University of Alabama as minister and professor when it was burned by the Federals late in the Civil War. He became pastor of the Lexington Presbyterian Church soon after the war.

The Stackers had five children: Patrick Lewis, Edwin, Clay, Maria, wife of —— Ellis, and Grace Pratt, wife of —— Coulter.

Major Stacker was city engineer of Clarksville, Tenn., and engaged in the practice of law there. "He was a faithful and honored Odd Fellow, serving a term as Grand Master of the State of Tennessee. Was Captain of Company H, First Tennessee Regiment, at the time of the labor troubles in the coal regions of East Tennessee and responded promptly to the Governor's call on the militia to quell the disturbances. Was always devoted to the memory of the Lost Cause, being at the time of his death Brigadier General of the Third Division of Confederate Veterans of Tennessee. He was also at this time Captain of the Citizens Volunteer Guards, organized to protect the City of Clarksville from destruction by the 'Night Riders,' during the famous tobacco war of 1904-1908.

"Constant exposure to damp air during the night watches, the overburden of responsibility, the prolonged suspense and the intense excitement caused by the raids of the 'Night Riders,' culminated in a severe heart trouble which ended his life."

He died at his home in Clarksville, Tenn., September 13, 1908. Mrs. Stacker died on February 25, 1931.

A brother, Samuel Stacker, attended the Institute for three years in the class of 1871.

232. Jaqueline Beverly Stanard—1867.

"Died on the Field of Honor"

Born about 1844 or 1845 (he was 18 years of age when he matriculated), in Orange County, Va.

Parents: Beverly Stanard and Ellen Taliaferro.

Grandparents: William Stanard, of Stanardsville (now county seat of Greene County, Va.), and Elizabeth Branch, of Powhatan County, Va. Hay Taliaferro, and —— Taylor.

He matriculated at V. M. I. on January 20, 1863, from Orange Courthouse, Va., and the following session, while repeating the fourth class, he took part in the battle of New Market, as a cadet private in Co. B.

Cadets Stanard, Redwood and Woodlief had been assigned under Cadet John S. Wise, corporal of the guard, to remain with the baggage-wagon. However, when the battle was imminent the wagon was left in charge of the black driver and these cadets rushed into the fray. Redwood alone came out unscathed.

After the corps had passed the Bushong House and reached the orchard, between the house and the line of the enemy, the effect of the artillery and musketry fire was terrific "in fact, almost all our loss was here." "In this fatal orchard" Stanard and Jefferson were mortally wounded and were removed to houses in the town.

Later in the afternoon John S. Wise, who had been slightly wounded in the first stage of the battle set out in search of his comrades. His search was successful but as he later wrote:

"I had come too late. Stanard had breathed his last but a few moments before I reached the old farmhouse where the battery had stood, now converted into a hospital. His body was still warm and his last message had been words of love. Poor Jack! Playmate, room-mate, friend—farewell.

"Standing there, my mind sped back to the old scenes at Lexington when we were shooting together in the 'Brushy Hills;' to our games and sports; to that day, one week ago, when he had knelt at the chancel and was confirmed; to the previous night at the guard-fire when he confessed to a presentiment that he would be killed; to his wistful, earnest farewell when we parted at the baggage-wagon, and my heart half reproached me for ordering him into the fight. The warm tears of youthful friendship came welling up for one I had learned to love as a brother; and now, thirty-four years later, I thank God that life's buffeting and the cold-heartedness of later struggles have not damned the pure fountains of boyhood's friendship. A truer-hearted, braver, better fellow never died than Jacquelin B. Stanard." (The End of an Era, p. 307.)

A sad reflection is that Stanard had resigned his cadetship on January 29, 1864, but eight days later he was restored by the board of visitors.

Following a temporary interment his body was brought to V. M. I. in 1866, and now lies with four of his comrades beneath the New Market Battle Monument.

233. Richard Staples.

Musician—Kettle Drummer (Not a 'Cadet)

He was one of the three musicians who accompanied the corps of cadets on the New Market Campaign.

After the war he returned to V. M. I. but left during the session 1866-67, being succeeded by musician Evans.

Very little is known of him except that he died in Washington, D. C. about 1875, it is believed unmarried.
His "New Market Cross" is in the V. M. I. Museum.

234. Alexander Hugh Holmes Stuart, Jr.—1867.

Died While a Student

Born May 14, 1846, in Staunton, Va.

Parents: Alexander Hugh Holmes Stuart (b. April 2, 1807, in Staunton; attended William and Mary College and the University of Virginia; prominent lawyer; member of the Virginia House of Delegates; U. S. Congressman; member of the board of visitors of the University of Virginia; died February 13, 1891, in Staunton), and Frances Cornelia Baldwin, of Staunton, Va.

Grandparents: Judge Archibald Stuart, member of Convention which ratified the United States Constitution, president of the Virginia Senate, and judge of the General Court of Virginia, and Eleanor Briscoe, of Frederick County, Va.
Judge Briscoe Gerard Baldwin, an officer in the War of 1812 and member of the Supreme Court of Appeals of Virginia, and Martha Steele Brown. (Their sons, Col. Briscoe Gerard Baldwin, Chief of Ordnance of the Army of Northern Virginia, and James William Baldwin, were graduated at V. M. I. in 1848 and 1849 respectively.)

He entered V. M. I. on August 4, 1863, from Staunton, Va., and served as a cadet private in Co. D at the battle of New Market. He remained with the corps until it was disbanded in Richmond on the eve of the evacuation of that city. At the close of the war he entered the University of Virginia where he distinguished himself in scholarship.

During his second year at the University, he contracted typhoid fever and returned to his home where he died on July 6, 1868.

He was a first cousin of John A. Stuart. (See sketch No. 235.)

235. John Andrew Stuart—1865.

Farmer

Born October 4, 1843, in Augusta County, Va.

Parents: Archibald Patterson Stuart (b. 1799; d. 1866), and Josephine Theresa Xaupi, of New Orleans, La. (?)

Grandparents: Judge Archibald Stuart, president of the Virginia Senate and Judge of the General Court of Virginia, and Eleanor, daughter of Colonel Gerald Briscoe, of Frederick County, Va.
John Andrew Xaupi, and Josephine Zano (or Orso).
"Count Jean André Xaupi de Jan (after getting to America dropped the 'de Jan') was born in France, banished from that country during the Rebellion (age not known). His wife, Miss Josephine Theresa Orso, was born on the Island of San Domingo. Count Xaupi de Jan fled with his family from this island in the time of the insurrection, and, but for the timely warning of a negro slave, would have met the fate of most of the white people of that island. In his little skiff with his family and his faithful servant, after being out two or three days, spoke a vessel bound for the port of New Orleans where most of his children were born."

John Andrew Stuart matriculated at V. M. I. on July 19, 1860, from Staunton, Va. At the close of his fourth class year he "marched with the corps to Camp Lee, Richmond, in April 1861. Upon the disbandment of the corps in July, returned home and entered the 52nd Virginia Infantry as drillmaster and remained until February 1862." After being in service in West Virginia, he was taken down with fever and was sent home. Unable to return to duty in the field, he re-entered the Institute to complete his course. He was made a sergeant on February 11, 1864, and at once was placed above all other sergeants in his company, for three months later he was first (orderly) sergeant of Co. C at the battle of New Market and was wounded in the right leg. Rejoining the corps at Richmond in October, 1864, he remained until the evacuation of that city, serving as third ranking cadet captain (Co. B). At graduation he stood 13 in a class of 24.

He married Mrs. S. Pauline Carpenter (née Loving), daughter of General William G. Loving and Anna C. Perrow, of Lovingston, Nelson County, Va. They had no children.

In 1866, Mr. Stuart went to Missouri and engaged in farming and teaching for three years. He returned to Virginia and farmed in Augusta county, later removing to Lowry, Bedford county. He served as constable, magistrate, and school trustee of his county at different times and for two years was a member of the State Board of Agriculture.

He died on February 13, 1908, at Lowry, Va. He was a first cousin of Alexander Hugh Holmes Stuart, Jr. (See sketch No. 234.)

236. John Tabb—1867.

Teacher

Born October 5, 1846, in Alexandria, Va.

Parents: Dr. John Prosser Tabb and Rebecca Lloyd, of White Marsh, Gloucester Co., Va.

Grandparents: John Tabb and Evelina Matilda Prosser.
John Lloyd and Anne Harriott Lee.

He matriculated at V. M. I. on January 5, 1864, from Gloucester C. H., Va., and was a cadet private in Co. B. when the battle of New Market was fought but he did not accompany the corps. Years later he wrote:

"I was not in the battle because I was desperately ill in the hospital at Lexington with typhoid pneumonia at the time. When the cadets came back, covered with glory, I was distressed nearly to death that I, poor unfortunate boy, had been out of it all, and really it has been a life long subject of regret with me."

The following session he continued his cadetship until the evacuation of Richmond and, as a volunteer, joined the Division commanded by Major General William Mahone, V. M. I., '47. A few days later at the battle of Sailor's Creek he was taken prisoner. At the suggestion of the Sergeant of the section which captured him he was taken, with five fellow cadets, to General Bartlett personally, "Who kept us with his staff and treated us with distinguished consideration (as being cadets), and after the surrender, gave us passes signed by General Grant to go to our homes."

After the war he became a student at the University of Virginia and graduated in 1867.

"In 1868, I settled on my farm, Summerville, in Gloucester Co., Virginia, and established The Gloucester Academy for Boys, which has been in successful operation ever since, except during my residence of four years in Baltimore as principal of a boys' school there."

In 1868 he married Judith Coleman, of Halifax Co., Va. She died in 1880 and in 1882 he married Mary James, of Gloucester Co., Va.

He died July 3, 1921, survived by his wife, two daughters, Mrs. T. E. DuVal and Miss Mary Lee Tabb, of Gloucester; and three sons, John Tabb, Jr., of Richmond; Joseph James Tabb and Warner Throckmorton Tabb, of New York City.

237. John Ford Tackett—1868.

Merchant

Born April 22, 1847, Fredericksburg, Va.

Parents: John E. Tackett and Sophia Ford, both born in Stafford Co., Va.

Grandparents: John T. Ford, Stafford Co., Va. and —— Gregory, Williamsburg, Va.
Charles Tackett, Prince William Co. and Mather Anne Barber, Stafford Co., Va.

He arrived at V. M. I. just as the corps was leaving on the New Market Campaign and was left at the Institute with the guard detail. He did not actually matriculate until May 16, 1864, probably due to the confusion of the times. He entered from Richmond and on the return of the corps was assigned to Co. B.

The following session he repeated the work of the fourth class and continued his studies until July 3, 1868, when he was graduated with seventh stand in a class of eleven graduates.

He married Nannie Fendall, of Alexandria, Va., and they had two daughters.

After the war he engaged in merchandising in Richmond and then, for many years, he was the senior member of the firm of Tackett and Marshall, which conducted a large dry goods house in Alexandria, Va. On the death of his partner, he disposed of his interest in the business and moved to Norfolk where he became a partner of the long established dry goods house of Russell & Simcoe, the firm style being changed to Russell, Simcoe & Tackett. In his last years he conducted a dry goods brokerage business in Alexandria.

He died suddenly in the garden of his home, 211 So. Asaph

Street, Alexandria, on March 30, 1908, of heart failure. Survived by his wife and two daughters.

His brother, Charles Edward Tackett, V. M. I., '69, was a member of the V. M. I. board of visitors from 1908 to his death in 1910.

238. Alonzo Hunt Tardy—1867.

Merchant—Lumberman

Born December 25, 1847, in Campbell County, Va.

Parents: William H. Tardy (b. in Virginia; d. 1872), Confederate States Army, and Catherine Anthony (d. 1850).

He matriculated at V. M. I. on March 10, 1864, from Arnold-town, Campbell County, Va., and was entered by B. F. Tardy. Two months later he took part in the battle of New Market as a cadet private in Co. B.

"My military experience practically ended with Lee's surrender though I was at Greensboro, N. C., at Johnston's surrender also, having gone there to join Johnston's army.

"After the war I went to Leesville Academy (in Campbell County, Va.) for two years. I then was engaged in mercantile business eight or ten years at Hot Springs, Bath County, Va., then six or eight years in Pittsylvania County; then eight or ten years in coal and lumber business in Danville, Va."

Mr. Tardy married Ida Temple, daughter of Colonel Jesse Spinner Burks (V. M. I., '44) and Charlotte Thomson, of Bedford County, Va. They had no children.

In 1895 he moved to St. Louis, Mo., and for about twenty-two years was buyer for the Garetson-Greason Lumber Company of that city. Later, about 1917, he organized a lumber firm of his own.

He died at the Jewish Hospital on February 14, 1925, having been a patient at the hospital for five months, and was buried in the Bellefontaine cemetery in St. Louis. Mrs. Tardy died February 13, 1920.

239. Charles Beverly Tate—1866.

Teacher—Editor

Born February 18, 1847, in Wythe County, Va.

Parents: Charles Campbell Tate, of Smyth County, Va., and Elizabeth Friel Graham, of Wythe County, Va.

Grandparents: Gen. Charles Tate, who fought in the battle of King's Mountain, and Mary Campbell, of Virginia.
James Graham and Nancy Montgomery, of Virginia.

He entered the Institute on October 8, 1862, from Max Meadows, Va., and at the battle of New Market, while a cadet private in Co. C, he was detailed to serve with the cadet artillery section.

He continued his cadetship until the evacuation of Richmond, at which time he was a member of the second class and a sergeant in Co. B, having been appointed to the office on January 5, 1865.

He reached Lynchburg a few days before the surrender at Appomattox and acted as adjutant of the forces collected there.

For two years following the war, he attended the Norwood School in Nelson County, Va.

In 1878 he married Mary Frances, daughter of Colonel William L. Martin and Mary Lawson, of Lebanon, Wilson County, Tenn. They had no children of their own but Mrs. Tate reared the three orphan children of her brother, Colonel William M. Martin, a gallant Confederate officer of Lebanon.

Captain Tate taught school for six years in Tennessee and for twenty-four years in Virginia. He was principal of the Sub-Collegiate School, at (Bufordville), Montvale, Va., for thirteen years. In 1901 he became editor and owner of the News-Review of Pulaski, Va. In 1915, Captain Tate's address was Draper, Va.

On April 1, 1923, Mrs. Tate, who had been custodian of the tomb of General Robert E. Lee on the campus of Washington and Lee University since June 11, 1920, died at the Stonewall Jackson Memorial Hospital in Lexington. Following her death Professor Tate returned to Pulaski where he made his home with relatives until April, 1925, when he entered the Soldiers' Home in Richmond, Va., to spend his remaining days among his comrades. He had not been back to Richmond since he was honorably discharged from the Southern Army—a period of over sixty years.

He died in Richmond July 10, 1925, and was buried at Fort Chiswell, in Wythe County, beside his wife and in the cemetery where lie his father, mother, sisters and four brothers, two of whom gave their lives for the Confederacy; one of them, William Hanson Tate, V. M. I., 1861, was killed at the battle of New Market. Thomas Leonidas Tate, V. M. I., '66 (twin brother of the subject of this sketch, was a member of the V. M. I. Board of Visitors from July 1, 1906, to June 30, 1918. He died on December 9, 1925). Thomas G. Tate, '77, now employed in the office of the Attorney General of Virginia, is a first cousin.

240. Blair Dabney Taylor—1866.

Surgeon, U. S. Army

Born January 15, 1848, in Caroline County, Va., one of eleven children.

Parents: Edmund Taylor (b. Nov. 2, 1822; d. Sept. 21, 1880), V. M. I., '44; lieutenant C. S. A.; (farmer in Caroline and Orange Counties) and Susan Morris Dabney, of Campbell County, Va.

Grandparents: Dr. John Taylor (b. Sept. 7, 1784; d. Aug. 8, 1853; educated as a physician in Edinburgh, Scotland) and Lucy Gregory Woodford (born at Windsor, Caroline Co., 1793; died 1832).

John Blair Dabney, of Campbell County, Va., and Elizabeth Lewis Towles, of Appomattox Co., Va.

He matriculated at V. M. I. on July 25, 1863, from Marysville, Va., and was admitted to the third class. Later in the session as a cadet private in Co. C he took part in the battle of New Market and the following session continued his cadetship until the evacuation of Richmond.

After the war he attended the University of Virginia and received the degree of M.D. in 1869; the following year he received the same degree from New York University, and was then an interne in Bellevue Hospital, New York City.

On June 26, 1875, he was appointed Assistant Surgeon in the U. S. Army and his subsequent promotions were as follows: Captain and Asst. Surgeon, 1880; Major and Surgeon, 1893; Lieut. Colonel and Department Surgeon General, 1902; Colonel and Asst. Surgeon General, 1908. Retired at his own request after thirty years of service, April 30, 1911.

Married: November 12, 1872, Mary Elizabeth, daughter of Robert Allen, of Bedford Co., Va. They had two children:
Donald Allen Taylor, a contract surgeon in the army, who died at Ft. McPherson, Ga., Oct. 16, 1899.
Mary Blair Taylor.

He took part in Custer's expedition against the Sioux in 1876, and at various times served in the Dakotas, Texas, Indian Territory, Minnesota, and at Honolulu. During the Spanish-American War he was in command of the General Hospital at Ft. McPherson, Ga.; organized a base hospital and is said to have employed the first women nurses used by the government in the military organizations. From 1902 to 1906, he was in command of the Army and Navy General Hospital at Hot Springs, Arkansas, and then was Chief Surgeon of the Cuban Army of Pacification (Dec. 1906 to March 1908). The remainder of his active career was passed as Chief Surgeon of the Department of the Gulf, with headquarters in Atlanta, Ga.

He continued to live in Atlanta after his retirement and died there on October 29, 1930, aged 82. He was survived by his daughter, Miss Mary Blair Taylor.

241. Carrington Taylor—1867.

Civil Engineer

Born December 1, 1845, at Staunton, Va.

Parents: Edwin M. Taylor (born in New York City; came to Virginia about 1845 as a civil engineer and engaged in building the James River and Kanawha Canal; later associated with Col. Claude Crozet in constructing the Virginia Central, now the Chesapeake & Ohio, Railroad and was engineer in charge of the construction of the Blue Ridge tunnel at Afton. As an architect in Staunton, he designed the wings of old Trinity Church; the Virginia Female Institute, later called Stuart Hall; the Virginia School for Deaf and Blind, etc.; later cashier of the Bank of the Valley) and Jane Eleanor Kinney (d. 1886), of Staunton.

Grandparents: Najah Taylor and Susan C. ——
William Kinney, of Staunton, and Rebecca P. ——

He matriculated at V. M. I. on August 4, 1863, from Staunton, and later in the session took part in the battle of New Market as a cadet private in Co. C. The following session he continued his studies until January 30, 1865 when he resigned to enter the Confederate Army. In June 1864 he was promoted to third corporal of Co. C.

"After the war he chose the profession of engineering for his life work, and served most efficiently under Major H. D. Whitcomb, chief engineer, in building the extension of the Chesapeake and Ohio Railroad, until his early and lamented death."

He died in Richmond, Va., October 28, 1875.

242. John Eugene Taylor—1867.

Lawyer

Born about 1847 (he was 17 years of age when he matriculated), at Manchester, Va.

Parents: Dr. Samuel Taylor, of Manchester, and —— Brown.

He was entered at the Institute by William G. Taylor, matriculating on February 9, 1864, from Richmond, Va. Three months later while a member of the fourth class, he participated in the battle of New Market as a cadet private in Co. B.

After being graduated from the University of Virginia where he took the academic course, Mr. Taylor attended the Richmond College law school, from which he received his degree in June, 1871.

Following the completion of his law course, he was mayor of Manchester, Va. He later removed to New York City and for twenty-five years was a law partner of ex-Governor Westmoreland Davis, V. M. I., '77. He died, unmarried, at the Chelsea Hotel, in that city, on September 22, 1919. His body was taken to Richmond and buried in Hollywood cemetery.

243. William Chamberlyn Taylor—1867.

Editor—Real Estate

Born September 23, 1844, in Richmond, Va.

Parents: William Pinckney W. Taylor, of Charles City, Va., and Margaret Fadley (of Leesburg, Va., later Washington, D. C.).

He matriculated at the Institute on June 25, 1862, from Richmond, Va., where his father was a well known shoe merchant. While repeating the fourth class, he was a private in Co. C, but at the battle of New Market on May 15, 1864, he was detailed to serve with the cadet artillery. Having been promoted to be third corporal in Co. B he continued as such until the evacuation of Richmond, when he joined Colonel Mosby in the Valley of Virginia just before Lee's surrender, and in October, 1865, returned to Richmond and engaged in the shoe business with his father.

On October 28, 1868, he married Celeste M. D., daughter of Juan Pizzini,

of Richmond, Va., and sister of his New Market comrade, Andrew Piz-
zini (see Sketch No. 190). They had five sons.
Robert William (dead).
Charles Maurice (dead).
Howard Chamberlyn (dead).
Charles Kingston.
Otis Manson.

"In 1871, he engaged in newspaper business as a local editor in
which he remained until 1890. He then went into the real estate
business, continuing in same until his death which occurred on
April 27, 1892."

244. Peter Chevallie Temple—1866.

Farmer

Born April 25, 1844.

Parents: William Henry Temple, Chesterfield County, Va., and Caroline
Frances Gilliam, Sussex County, Va.

Grandparents: Robert Temple, Middlesex County, Va., and Elizabeth Sky-
ren, Hampton, Va.
Carter Gilliam and Elizabeth Green Hancock, both of Sussex County, Va.

He matriculated at the Institute on January 1, 1862, from Richmond, Va., and the following session repeated the fourth class.
While a third classman and a private in Co. A he took part in the
battle of New Market—serving with the cadet artillery section in
the battle. He continued with the corps until the evacuation of
Richmond, having been promoted to the grade of sergeant on December 31, 1864, and then joining Lee's army on the retreat, surrendered at Appomattox.

Mr. Temple spent his entire life in Chesterfield county where
he farmed his estate, "Campfield." He died there, unmarried, on
February 9, 1910. Interment was in the Temple burying ground
at "Ampthill," Chesterfield county.

245. Knox Thompson—1867.

Physician—Legislator

Born January 25, 1848, at Darvills, Dinwiddie Co., Va.

Parents: Dr. William Field Thompson, and Mary Ellen Cousins.

[NOTE: Two brothers of R. H. Cousins (see Sketch No. 50), Hillary Allan Cousins, '75, and Matthew E. Cousins, '78, were born at Darvills, in Dinwiddie Co., Va.]

Grandparents: William B. Thompson, and Prudence Mann, of Amelia Court
House, Va.
Capt. William Henry Cousins, of Dinwiddie Co., Va., a soldier in the War
of 1812, and Martha Robinson.

As a boy he attended Winfield Academy which at that time was a
well-known institution of learning located on his father's farm.

He matriculated at V. M. I. on January 16, 1864, from Crimea,
Va., and four months later as a cadet private in Co. C he fought in

the battle of New Market. The following session he returned and continued his cadetship until Richmond was evacuated. In 1866 he entered the University of Virginia and from there he went to St. Mary's Academy, Baltimore, where he was graduated in medicine on March 5, 1868.

On October 30, 1883, he married Lulie Willie Gee, daughter of William R. Gee, of Dinwiddie Co., Va., and Jane Parke Boisseau.

He located at Dinwiddie Court House, Va., and practiced the profession of medicine there until his death on March 19, 1894.

Dr. Thompson frequently held positions of trust in the county government and represented his people in the general assembly, (1891 to 1894), of which body he was a member at the time of his death. He was buried at his old homestead "Oak Grove," near Darvills.

His brother Norborne Field Thompson, V. M. I., '67, was a captain in Drewry's Heavy Artillery, C. S. A.

246. Augustus Pembroke Thomson—1866.

Physician—Fruit Grower

Born January 11, 1847, at Summit Point, Jefferson Co., (West) Va.

Parents: John A. Thomson, born at Berryville, Va., Jan. 4, 1805, and Mary E. Scott, born at Locust Grove, Bedford Co., Va., Oct. 2, 1821.

Grandparents: Dr. John Thomson, Berryville, Va. (born at the Glebe Land, Fauquier Co.), and Lucy Rootes Throckmorton.
Beverly R. Scott, of Bedford Co., Va., and Almira L. Anderson, of Bedford Co., Va.

He matriculated November 4, 1862, from Summit Point, (West) Va., and recalled as the most indelible event of his fourth class year his part in escorting the remains of General "Stonewall" Jackson from the canal boat to his section room at the Institute, where the body lay in state. In the following year he was a cadet private in Co. A but in the battle of New Market he served with the cadet artillery section as No. 1 on one of the pieces. "I did not witness the charge of the corps" . . . "We were merged under the command of Major McLaughlin just before the battle and were engaged the whole day, camping on the battlefield after the battle at the foot of Rude's Hill." At the end of the session he was promoted to be fourth line sergeant in Co. D and continued his cadetship until January 7, 1865, after which he joined Stewart's Horse Artillery and surrendered at Greensboro, N. C., with Gen. Jos. E. Johnston's army.

He married Elizabeth McIlhaney, daughter of James McIlhaney and Elizabeth Johnson, of Hillsborough, Loudoun Co.

After the war he studied medicine at the University of Virginia (1866) and continued his studies at the University of Maryland where he was graduated. He practiced his profession for a time but devoted most of his life to farming and fruit growing, being one of the pioneers in the fruit growing industry in the lower Shenandoah Valley counties.

Dr. Thomson died at his home on October 4, 1920.

He was survived by his wife and seven children: John Thomson, of Warren Co., Va.; James M. Thomson, publisher of the New Orleans Item, who married Genevieve, the daughter of Champ Clark, Speaker of the House of Representatives; Paul Jones Thomson, V. M. I., '04, manager of The New Orleans Item; Mary Scott, Dorothy, and Imogene Thomson, and Mrs. Washington Berry Grove. Also two sisters: Mrs. E. G. Booth, of Williamsburg, Va., and Mrs. Paul Jones, of Huntsville, Alabama. A brother, James Walton Thomson, '64, and a half brother, John Throckmorton Thomson, '50, attended V. M. I.

247. Francis Iselin Tomes—1867.

Died young from effects of military service

Born about 1847 (he was 15 years of age when he matriculated), at Nashville, Tenn.

Parents: Rev. Charles Tomes (born in England), Rector of Christ Church, Nashville, and Henrietta Coleman Otey.

Grandparents: Francis Tomes, of England, and —— ——
Rt. Rev. James Hervey Otey (born in Bedford Co., Va.), Bishop of the Diocese of Tennessee, and —— ——

He matriculated on January 15, 1863, from Memphis, Tenn., where his widowed mother had made her home with her father after war was declared. He was admitted to the fifth class and the following year while a cadet private in Co. C, he remained at the Institute with the guard detail when the corps left on the New Market campaign.

He served in the trenches around Richmond with the corps in the fall of 1864 until the furlough of December tenth. On December nineteenth he wrote concerning an extension of his furlough but there is no record that he returned thereafter.

His sister, Margaret A. Tomes, wrote as follows:

"He with others was set to digging trenches (near Richmond) and owing to the hardships, he took a violent cold which settled on his lungs. He went North just after the surrender and died at Canterbury-on-the-Hudson the following summer (1865), I think, or during the year."

248. Anderson Clay Toms—1867.

Transportation Service

Born March 12, 1848, at Norfolk, Va.

Parents: Anderson C. C. Toms, of Perquimans Co., N. C., and Mary Eliza Ramsay, of Pasquotank Co., N. C.

Grandparents: Benjamin Toms and Martha Wilson, of Perquimans Co., N. C. Dr. Richard Henry Ramsay, of Lynchburg, Va., and Jacamine Hunter Boush, of Kempsville, Princess Anne Co., Va.

He was entered by his mother and matriculated on April 21, 1864, from Norfolk, Va. He was assigned to Co. C as a cadet private but was left at the Institute with the guard detail when the corps left on the New Market campaign three weeks later. He returned to the institute the following session and remained until Richmond was evacuated. In arranging for his return on December 28, 1864, his papers were signed by his guardian, R. H. Toms.

"After the war, he began the study of medicine with Dr. J. J. Shannonhouse, near Elizabeth City, N. C., but later feeling it incumbent on him to assist in the support of his mother and sister whose all was swept away by the war, he went to Galveston, Texas, where, while engaged in the transportation service, he contracted yellow fever and died August, 1867." (From his sister, Mrs. Emily Toms Innerarity.)

249. John Richards Triplett—1866.

Manufacturer

Born May 11, 1845, in Richmond, Va.

Parents: William Stone Triplett and Ann O. Jenifer, both of Richmond, Va.

Grandparents: John Richards Triplett and Louisa Stone.

Hon. Daniel Jenifer (of Charles Co., Md.; Member of Congress from Maryland for many years and United States Minister to Austria under Presidents Harrison and Tyler), and Eliza Campbell.

He matriculated at V. M. I. on April 18, 1862, from Richmond, and the following session repeated the work of the fourth class. In the battle of New Market he fought with the corps as fourth cadet corporal in Co. D, to which office he had been promoted on Feb. 11, 1864, and was wounded in the battle. At the end of the session he was promoted to third line sergeant of Co. C. On February 1, 1865, he resigned his cadetship and entered the Confederate army as aide-de-camp on the staff of Gen. S. M. Barton; was later commissioned as lieutenant and served until the end of the war.

He married Sarah Lyon Ross, a daughter of William H. Ross and Mary Amanda Lyon, of Mobile, Ala., and a sister of Jack F. Ross, V. M. I., '73. They had four children:

Mary Amanda, wife of E. Dargan Ledyard.
Sallie Ross, wife of Charles A. Hall.
Nannie Jenifer Triplett.
Helen Lyon Triplett, died in 1911.

After the war he was a student at Lausanne, Switzerland, for two years. On his return from Europe he entered the iron industry and was associated with the Old Dominion Iron and Nail Works Co.

He died May 28, 1882, and was buried in Richmond, Va. Survived by his wife, who died in Mobile February 28, 1920; four daughters; and three sisters, Mrs. Thomas R. Price (wife of the professor of English at Columbia University) of Lewisburg, West Va.; Mrs. Philip Haxall and Mrs. Meredith F. Montague, of Richmond, Va.

250. John Liggat Tunstall—1867.

Farmer

Born November 14, 1845, in Lynchburg, Va.

Parents: Whitmell Pugh Tunstall, of Lynchburg, Va., and Mary M. Liggat.

Grandparents: William Tunstall and Sarah Pugh.
Alexander Liggat and Mary Lynch.

His father died before he matriculated at V. M. I. on September 23, 1862, from Lynchburg. He was entered by Mrs. Mary M. Brooks. As a third classman he took part in the battle of New Market as a cadet private in Co. D and was promoted to be third line sergeant in Co. A at the end of the session. He continued his cadetship until he was graduated on July 4, 1867, when he stood 7 in a class of 11.

He married Florence L. Massie (d. March 4, 1912), daughter of William Massie, of Nelson County, Va., the second son of Major Thomas Massie, of the Revolutionary War. They had two children:

Dr. William Massie Tunstall, of Lovingston, Va.
Corinne Tunstall, who married Charles Waring, of Washington, D. C.

After the war he was a farmer in Nelson County, Va., and died there March 24, 1877, in his thirty-second year.

After his death Mrs. Tunstall married, secondly, on February 23, 1879, Judge John Dunscomb Horsley (V. M. I., '68), a law partner of Senator Thomas S. Martin. Judge Horsley died in 1909 and his wife died three years later, survived by the following children: Catherine Dunscomb, Bland Massie, Thomas Staples Martin, and Eliza Perkins Horsley.

251. Richard Baylor Tunstall—1867.

Lawyer

Born July 1, 1848, at Norfolk, Va.

Parents: Dr. Robert Baylor Tunstall (1818-1883; physician of Norfolk) and Elizabeth Walke Williamson.

Grandparents: Alexander Tunstall, cashier of the Farmer's Bank, in Norfolk, and Elizabeth T. Baylor.
Thomas Williamson and Anne McC. Walke.

He received his early education at the Norfolk (Military) Academy and at Wm. R. Galt's school. On April 6, 1864, he was entered at V. M. I. by Mrs. J. L. Henderson, of Columbia, Va., and the following month he took part in the battle of New Market as a cadet private in Co. B. In writing of the campaign and the trip to Richmond which followed it he said:

"My recollection is very distinct that we went to Richmond on freight cars. I recall especially that on going to Richmond on these cars there was some mishap at Charlottesville, where we were delayed for quite a time, and where, I might mention incidentally, we emptied all the ice cream saloons of their 'goodies.'"

In 1865, Mr. Tunstall went to the University of Virginia, from which he was graduated with the degree of master of arts in 1868. Following his graduation he taught at the Norwood School for a year and then returned to the University of Virginia, completing the law course and receiving his LL. B. degree in one year. He engaged in the practice of law in Norfolk for a year when he went to New York where he practiced for twelve years, most of the time as a member of the firm of Kaufman, Tunstall and Wagner. Later he organized the firm of Grimball and Tunstall.

On December 18, 1878, he married Miss Isabelle Marcein Heiser, of New York City. They had five children.

Returning to Norfolk in 1883, he formed a partnership with his brother-in-law, Alfred P. Thom, under the firm name of Tunstall and Thom, the firm being reorganized in 1900, when Wm. H. White, V. M. I. '67 (see Sketch No. 275), became a partner, and thereafter known as White, Tunstall and Thom. This firm in turn was succeeded in 1905 by the firm of White, Tunstall and Willcox, and upon its dissolution in 1907, Mr. Tunstall, by reason of failing health, retired from the practice of law.

He supervised the organization of the Norfolk Railway and Light Company, of which he was for many years general counsel and a director.

Mr. Tunstall died at his home, 530 Pembroke Avenue, Norfolk, on October 11, 1919, and was survived by two sons, Robert Baylor Tunstall, Asst. General Counsel, Chesapeake and Ohio Railway, of Richmond, and Dr. Cuthbert Tunstall, ear, nose and throat specialist at the University of Virginia.

252. Charles William Turner—1867.

Lawyer—Adjutant General, Montana

Born June 8, 1846, at New Town (now Stephen City), Va.
(When he matriculated he signed his name as C. W. *H.* Turner. The *H* was not used in after life.)

Parents: Augustus John Turner (b. in Spartanburg County, S. C.; d. May 1905), music director at the School for the Deaf, Dumb and Blind, at Staunton, Va. (he organized the Stonewall Band in 1855), and Catherine Montrose Aby (b. in Frederick County, Va.).

Grandparents: Samuel Turner (b. near Coulter's Ford, S. C.), and Mahalah Chapman, of Spartanburg County, S. C.
Jonas Aby (b. in Germany), and Barbara Hulett, of Frederick County, Va.

He was a courier in "Stonewall" Jackson's brigade before matriculating at V. M. I. on April 15, 1864, from Staunton, Va. One month later her took part as a private in Co. C in the battle of New Market.

After the war he engaged in mercantile pursuits, first in Staunton, Va., and later in Baltimore, Md. Having studied law he went West and settled in Montana where he practiced his profession.

—14

In 1879, he married Emma, daughter of Noah Armstrong, of Seattle, Wash. They had two sons—Armstrong Memory Turner and Charles William Turner, Jr.

He was appointed Adjutant General of Montana by Governor Leslie, and organized the militia of that State about 1886.

In 1889, General Turner removed to Seattle where he successfully practiced law until he died by the hand of an assassin on January 7, 1907.

253. Etheldred Lundy Turner—1867.

Clerk of County and Circuit Courts

Born April 27, 1847, at Hicksford, Greensville Co., Va.

Parents: Joseph Turner, clerk of the County Courts (1841-56) and member of the Virginia Legislature, and Mary Peebles Mason, of Hicksford, Va.

Grandparents: Person Turner (a native of England) and Nancy ——. Peyton Mason (a soldier of the Revolution) and Martha Ann ——.

He was entered at the Institute on January 26, 1864, by his guardian, Augustus C. Butts, of Petersburg, Va., and assigned to the fourth class. As a cadet private in Co. B he left Lexington with the corps when it went on the New Market Campaign, but because of sickness he was left in Staunton and did not take part in the battle.

On December 19, 1876, he married Mrs. Ellen P. Wilson (née Walker), widow of James B. Wilson of Isle of Wight County, Va. There were three children: Mary Ellen; E. Peyton, who succeeded his father as clerk of the courts of Greeneville Co.; and P. W. Turner, cashier of the Merchants and Farmers Bank, of Emporia, Va.

In January 1867, he was appointed Deputy Clerk and in 1870 was appointed Clerk of the County and Circuit Courts of Greensville County, Virginia, and was periodically re-elected without opposition until his death on January 24, 1900. Said Judge Trumbull: "He was a good and true man in every relation of life, loved and honored by all; was a prominent Mason and Deputy for this district many years; was considered at the time of his death the best clerk in Virginia."

254. Edward Magruder Tutwiler—1867.

Civil Engineer—Coal and Iron Operator

Born October 13, 1846, at Palmyra, Fluvanna County, Va.

Parents: Colonel Thomas Harrison Tutwiler (b. October 18, 1818, at Seven Islands, Fluvanna Co., Va.), and Harriet Magruder Strange (b. February 13, 1822, at "Oak Hill," near Palmyra), sister of Col. John Bowie Strange, V. M. I., '42. Strange was the first cadet to go on guard when the cadets relieved the old Lexington Arsenal guard of soldiers on Nov. 11, 1839.

Grandparents: Martin Tutwiler, of Harrisonburg, Va., and Maria Shores, of Fluvanna Co. Colonel Gideon A. Strange (b. near Palmyra), and Harriet Magruder (b. near Union Mills, Fluvanna Co.).

He was entered at V. M. I. on January 13, 1864, by his father, then Captain Tutwiler, C. S. A., and was living at that time in Lexington, Va. Four months later he took part in the battle of New Market as a cadet private in Co. D. His recollections of the campaign were printed in the Richmond Times-Dispatch, June 23, 1912, from which the following has been extracted:

"The first day we marched to Midway . . . as we had no tents, we improvised a rude shed built of poles and leaves; then we built a nice fire in front . . . there was a fearful thunder storm. . . . We had camped near a Presbyterian church, so we opened a window and climbed through it into the church, where we found nice cushions in the pews. We soon slept where many a good follower of Calvin had slept before us. . . . The next morning we were on the march again. . . . At last, we reached our camping place, about one mile south of Staunton. The next day . . . in order to get our proper place in the marching column, we had to pass some of the regiments of old soldiers, and they jeered us considerably, singing 'Rocky bye, baby' and calling us 'New issue', etc. . . . My classmate, chum, and roommate, A. H. H. Stuart, Jr., of Staunton, was in the same company—Company D. . . . When General Hunter afterwards attacked Lexington Stuart was sick, so I took him to the house of my father, who lived at the time in Lexington. . . . (On May 15th) we began the march in the mud and rain. About 9 o'clock we deployed to the left of the road and halted when opposite New Market. I looked down at the road leading into New Market and saw a number of our negro cooks and servants walking into the town. Just at this time the Federal batteries shelled . . . I never saw such a precipitate retreat as our negroes made. . . . There were a number of ridiculous incidents. One of my company, Clendinen who was near me, suddenly started to the rear. At first I thought he was showing the white feather, but in a few minutes he came running back, and holding up a pair of new shoes, said, 'I found them.' He had them tied to his cartridge-box belt and the string broke; but shoes were scarce, and he could not afford to lose them, even if bullets were falling thick and fast around him. Hugh Fry, of Company C, called to a big fat Dutchman to surrender, and when he did not do so, shot him in the leg because he was too tender-hearted to kill him. . . . Presently, however, the command was given to rise and charge. Then it was that we rushed for the battery. We shot down the horses. The Federals served the guns until we got right on them. . . . I will read* you what its captain, Von Kleiser, thought of our conduct: 'Damn that cut. I wish it had been lower and taken my head off. Just think of it, will you? An officer who has fought under the Emperor, losing his every gun! That is the fortune of war, however, and I don't mind the loss so much as I do the fact that those Napoleons were taken from trained soldiers by a lot of school boys.' . . . About this time we saw a Federal colonel on horseback, trying to lead a riderless horse from the field of battle. Some of the cadets from Company A, who were nearest to him, started in pursuit. Cadet Garrett† was the swiftest runner. As soon as the colonel discovered that he was pursued, he let go the led horse, but Garrett gained on him; . . . Garrett raised his gun with the bayonet on it as a javelin and hurled it after the retreating officer. The bayonet pierced his shoulder and he immediately stopped and surrendered. . . . I afterwards talked to the prisoner, who proved to be Colonel Lincoln,‡ a cousin of the President. We kept

---

*The source of this remark of Von Kleiser's is not given. In after years there has been much discussion about the number of guns taken by the cadets in this battle.

†Tutwiler's article uses the name of Cadet Kennedy here. Kennedy was in Company D on the opposite flank of the battalion. See Sketch No. 83.

‡Lieut. Colonel (afterwards Brigadier General) Wm. S. Lincoln, of the

up the pursuit until we were ordered to desist. Stuart and I learned that our roommate McDowell had been killed while we were charging the battery, so we got permission to hunt for his body. It was not long before we found him . . . with the help of two other cadets we placed him on an oil cloth and took him to a nearby house. I wrote to his relatives in Morehead, N. C., giving an account of his death."

The following session he returned to the Institute and was a cadet until Richmond was evacuated. After the war he completed his course and was graduated on July 4, 1867, with the sixth stand in his class—at the time he was a cadet first lieutenant.

Having completed his course in civil engineering at the Institute, he taught school in Maryland for two years. Then he became a civil engineer, which profession he followed with success in the States of Pennsylvania, West Virginia, Virginia, Kentucky, Ohio, Georgia, Alabama and Mississippi, attaining the position of Chief Engineer of the Miami Valley Railroad in Ohio, and Principal Assistant Engineer of the Georgia Pacific Railway in Georgia, Alabama and Mississippi.

In July 1883, he became Superintendent of the Sloss-Sheffield Steel and Iron Company in Alabama. He remained in this position until 1889, when he began to operate his own coal mines. He became President of the Tutwiler Coal, Coke & Iron Co., Birmingham, Ala., on its formation in November 1893. When the company's holdings were sold in 1906, they included some of the most important interests in the district.

On April 11, 1876, he married Mary, daughter of Dr. Thomas R. W. Jeffrey, of Crittenden, Ky. They had three children: Temple W. Tutwiler; Edward Magruder Tutwiler, Jr.; and Herbert Tutwiler, V. M. I., '02 (b. Feb. 9, 1882; m. Mary Eastburn Addison, daughter of Arthur D. Addison and Minnie Chewning, of Eastville, Va.).

On July 11, 1887, he married, secondly, Margaret, daughter of John W. Chewning, who lived near Shadwell, Albemarle County, Va.

About the first of May, 1924, he was stricken with pneumonia and was confined to his room for four months. In the hope that a trip might restore his strength he sailed with Mrs. Tutwiler in December, 1924, for the Orient where they visited his son, Temple, head of the Tata Iron and Steel Co., in India.

Returning from India, he died aboard the "Empress of France" midway between Japan and the Hawaiian Islands on April 19, 1925. His portrait hangs in Jackson Memorial Hall at V. M. I.

255. John Nottingham Upshur—1867.
Physician
Born February 14, 1848, at Norfolk, Va.

Parents: Dr. George Littleton Upshur (d. Sept. 19, 1855, aged 33 years), of Northhampton County, Va., and Sarah Andrews Parker (d. in Richmond, Va., Aug. 29, 1910, in her 88th year).

34th Massachusetts Infantry. Wounded and taken prisoner at New Market (Official Records—Series 1, Vol.. XXXVII, Part 1, pages 84 and 85).

Grandparents: John Evans Nottingham and Elizabeth Upshur.
(Dr. George L. Upshur had his name changed by Act of Legislature to his mother's maiden name, by advice of maternal uncles, Judge Abel Parker Upshur and Captain George P. Upshur, to prevent extinction of the Upshur name.)
Dr. Jacob G. Parker and Anne ——.

After his preliminary training at the Norfolk Academy, he was entered at the Virginia Military Institute by Dr. W. A. Thom from Richmond, Va., on November 12, 1863, and at the battle of New Market served as a cadet private in Co. C, and was wounded in the right leg. He was unable to return to the Institute on account of the severity of his wounds. (See Surgeon's Report in Sketch No. 271.)

After the war he studied medicine at the University of Virginia and at the Virginia Medical College, graduating from the latter in ,March 1868. He began to practice his profession in Richmond April 1, 1869, after having been a resident physician at Howard's Grove Hospital, near that city, during the year following his graduation. He engaged in general practice and in connection with the performance of the duties of a large private patronage, he was very active in advancing the interests of the medical fraternity of Virginia.

He became a charter member of the Virginia State Medical Society in 1870, and was chairman of its executive committee from 1900 until 1902, and president of the Society for the year 1902-03. He was also an honorary fellow of the Tri-State Medical Association of the Carolinas and Virginia, and was its secretary in 1900-01 and president in 1901-02. He was also honorary fellow of the State Medical Society of West Virginia. He became a member of the Richmond Academy of Medicine and Surgery, was its first vice-president in 1896 and its president in 1897. In the Medical College of Virginia he was professor of Materia Medica and Therapeutics from 1884 until 1894, and clinical lecturer on diseases of women and children from 1884 until 1892. In 1894, he was professor of the practice of medicine in the same institutions and professor emeritus in 1899. He was a member of the ninth International Medical Congress in 1887, and of the first Pan-American Medical Congress in 1893. He was medical examiner for the Equitable Life Assurance Society and attending physician to the Female Humane Association. Dr. Upshur read many papers before the State Medical Society and wrote much for publication in scientific journals. Member of the Beta Theta Pi fraternity.

His first wife was Lucy, eldest daughter of Right Reverend Francis M. Whittle, Bishop of the Episcopal Church in the diocese of Virginia. She died August 7, 1876, leaving one son, Dr. Francis W. Upshur, of Richmond.

On December 11, 1879, Dr. Upshur married Elizabeth Spencer, daughter of William Spencer Peterkin and Emma Meteer of Baltimore, Md., and the children of the second marriage are:
William Peterkin, V. M. I., '02, Colonel, U. S. Marine Corps.

Elizabeth Nottingham, wife of George J. Benson.
Alfred Parker, V. M. I., '04, physician, New York City.

He was a member of the V. M. I. Board of Visitors from January 1, 1903 until June 30, 1906. In June 1903, he was chosen by his comrades as their orator on the occasion of the dedication of the New Market Battle Monument.

Dr. Upshur died on December 10, 1924, at his home, 1103 West Franklin Street, Richmond, Va., after an illness of two weeks. He was survived by his widow, three sons and one daughter. He was a member of St. James Church of Richmond, and served as one of its vestrymen for many years and until his death.

256. Wilberforce Veitch—1867.

Salesman

Born November 6, 1846, in Baltimore, Md.

Parents: Eldridge Roberts Veitch (b. Sept. 20, 1811, in Alexandria, Va.; d. 1867), Methodist minister, and Elizabeth Manning Ching, of Devonshire, England.

Grandparents: William Veitch and Rachel Page, both born in Prince George Co., Md.

Thomas Ching and Grace Manning Shepherd, of Devonshire, England.

"In 1857 and a portion of 1858, my father was stationed at the Methodist Episcopal Church at Annapolis, Md., and during that time I was a student in the primary department of St. Johns College. During that time the military feature was added to the institution and being too small to carry a gun, I was made a marker. In the spring of 1858 my father was appointed presiding elder of Rockingham District with residence at Staunton, Va. Soon after going there Captain Robert Lily organized a military company of boys known as the 'Junior Blues.' To this I belonged."

He also attended the Staunton (Military) Academy until the cadets disbanded. In the fall of 1861, Rev. Clifton C. Wheat opened a boys' school and he was a student there until March 29, 1864, when he matriculated at V. M. I. from Staunton, Va.; was assigned to the fourth class; and was a cadet private in Co. B.

"I remember well the morning of May 11, 1864, the beating of long roll early and our tumbling down stairs, falling into ranks, roll call and the detail of the men who were to remain as a guard for the property of the State and cadets. As I remember, it consisted of twenty-one. I was one of them. Tried hard to have it changed but could not. The Battle of New Market we heard of about a week after it took place and we were all filled with sorrow at the loss of the brave boys who fell there. I recall the return of the corps from Richmond on the afternoon of June 10th and on account of the rumor that Gen. Hunter was advancing from Staunton, nearly all of us slept in front of barracks that night. The next morning Hunter began to shell the property and after changing our position once or twice, we marched out of the grounds and halted again just outside Washington College grounds. . . . Soon after we resumed our march heading for Balcony Falls where we camped that night on the top of the mountain. . . . We remained around there for a day or two, then proceeded to Rope Ferry where we took boats and reached Lynchburg the next morning."

He remained with the corps until the evacuation of Richmond. "I reached home one week after leaving Richmond which was the 9th of April, 1864, the day on which Gen Robert E. Lee surrendered. This terminated my connection with the Virginia Military Institute.

"I went into commercial life after things had resumed shape. For nearly two years I lived in Montgomery County, Maryland, at Brookville. Spent several months in Baltimore and on the 27th of April, 1868, started for Chicago. Obtaining a position with Field, Leiter & Company, I was connected with the retail for nearly eight years. On February 1, 1876, went into wholesale, most of my time being spent in the linen department. I organized for the house a railway supply department, of which I became the head.

"On April 30, 1918, I celebrated my 'Golden Jubilee', having finished fifty years of continuous service. I had many pleasant things done for me on that occasion, and was presented by Mr. John G. Shedd, President of Marshall Field & Company, with a beautiful gold medal studded with diamonds, in recognition of my fifty years of service."

Mr. Veitch left Chicago on July 10, 1920, and having spent a month at Warm Springs, Va., went to Staunton where he was a patient at the Kings Daughters' Hospital. He died in that city, unmarried, on May 4, 1921.

257. William Latham Venable—1867.

Tobacconist—Insurance

Born April 26, 1847, at Farmville, Va.

Parents: Joseph E. Venable, tobacconist, of Prince Edward County, Va., and Mary Dunnington, of Lynchburg.

Paternal grandparents: Robert Venable and —— Bradley, of Lynchburg.

He entered V. M. I. on January 18, 1864, from Petersburg and four months later served as a cadet private in Co. D at the battle of New Market. The follownig session he was a cadet until Richmond was evacuated and some of his experiences on the way home were recorded by his son from dictation in a letter written on May 28, 1917:

"My father tells me that he walked from Richmond to Walker's Ford, his sister's home, taking a couple of cadets with him. . . . After he had stayed there for a week or two he decided he had better get back to Petersburg to let his father and mother know where he was. They went into Lynchburg and started walking down the Norfolk & Western tracks, begging each train that passed to give them a lift, only with the reply, 'You darned Johnny Rebs, you made me walk for four years, now you can walk for four.' He got within about 25 miles of Petersburg, and one of the Union officers hollered to him, 'Come on boys, I will ride you as far as possible on this train,' so we finally came into Petersburg on a freight car."

Mr. Venable attended school for two years after leaving the Institute and then went into the leaf tobacco business and was prominently identified with this industry in Petersburg, Va., until 1916.

In April 1872 he married Mary Lamar, daughter of Thomas Leiper Patterson and Louise A. Sprigg, of Cumberland, Md. They had four children: Joseph Ewing (d. October 9, 1918), V. M. I. 1899, m. June 14, 1916, Vir-

ginia Alexander, daughter of Marcus Bull, of Petersburg. They had
one son, William Latham Venable, named for his grandfather.
Bessie F.
Helen, wife of George W. Plummer.
Leiper, wife of Dr. J. Gordon Rennie (decd.), all of Petersburg, Va.

In 1916, Mr. Venable conducted an insurance business in Petersburg and his son was manager of the firm.

He died on August 5, 1928, at his home, 403 W. Washington St.,
Petersburg, and was buried in Blandford cemetery in that city. At
the time of his death, Mr. Venable was a director of the National
Bank of Petersburg, having served at one time as vice-president of
that institution.

258. Charles Duy Walker—1869.

Episcopal Clergyman—Author

Born September 7, 1848.

Parents: Rev. Cornelius Walker (clergyman, author, Professor in the Virginia Theological Seminary) and Margaret Jane Fisher, of Richmond, Va.

Grandparents: William Woodson Walker, and Mary Walker (a first cousin;
an adopted child called Mary Barnes).
James Fisher, Jr., of Richmond, and Elizabeth Montgomery Mc——.

He matriculated at V. M. I. April 16, 1864 from Richmond and
served as a cadet private in Co. C in the battle of New Market
where he was severely wounded. Although he never completely
recovered from the effects of his wounds he returned to the Institute in the fall of 1866, and was graduated on July 2, 1869, at the
head of his class. At the time of his graduation he was cadet first
lieutenant in Co. C.

For two years after his graduation he taught at V. M. I. He
was commissioned lieutenant and in 1870-71 taught mathematics,
the following session he was acting Assistant Professor of Chemistry.

In 1872, he founded Beta Theta Pi, the magazine of that fraternity and edited it until 1874—a "pioneer" in fraternity journalism. His editorial abilities lead to his selection as the author of a
585 page book, issued in 1875 by J. B. Lippincott & Co., of Philadelphia, to which the title "Memorial, Virginia Military Institute"
was assigned. It contained biographical sketches of 161 of the 259
V. M. I. cadets who lost their lives in the Civil War. The book was
dedicated to Gen. William H. Richardson, Adjutant General of Virginia, whose name was subscribed to the diploma of every V. M. I.
graduate for the first thirty-seven years after its foundation. The
actual work of compiling these sketches was completed in 1873 while
he was a student at the Theological Seminary, at Alexandria, Va.,
where he began his preparation for the Episcopal ministry in 1872.

Married: —— —— and they had a daughter Mary, who was born about six
weeks after her father's death and who married Charles E. Dallam, of
Henderson, Ky. About 1885, Mrs. Walker married Rev. L. W. Rose, of
Henderson, Ky.

He was ordained in 1875 and became the Rector of Amherst Court House Parish and remained there until his death from typhoid fever on September 23, 1877.

He is buried in Ivy Hill Cemetery, Alexandria, Va., and a tablet was erected to his memory in his only church.

259. Charles Pinkney Walker—1867.

Farmer

Born latter part of 1847 (he was 16 years and 9 months of age when he matriculated), in St. Marks, Florida; he was the youngest son of his parents.

Parents: Major Nat. Walker (d. in 1860) and Mrs. —— Spencer, whose maiden name was —— Moseley, a sister of Alexander Moseley. She died when her son Charles was about 15 months old.

His parents died when he was very young and in the spring of 1860 he and his brother, Jeff, were sent to make their home with their uncle, Alexander Moseley, who lived at Howardsville, Va.

After several efforts to enter the army he matriculated at the Virginia Military Institute from Howardsville, on February 13, 1864, and as a cadet private in Co. B he took part in the battle of New Market, where he was slightly wounded in the left side. His brother, Lieutenant Jeff Walker, was killed in the battle of Chancellorsville.

After the battle his uncle provided a cavalry outfit and allowed him to join Colonel Mosby's command with which he served until the close of the war.

He returned to Florida in 1865, and, finding that his father's property had been lost, he started a fish and oyster business with his kinsman, W. H. Walker, near St. Marks, Fla., which they conducted successfully for several years.

In the spring of 1874 he married Nannie Handley, of Thomas Co., Ga., where her father had moved from Emanuel Co., Ga.

After the death of his wife in 1880, he moved to Leon Co., Fla., and thence to Lloyds, Jefferson Co., Fla., where he engaged in farming and the timber business until his death on March 23, 1888. He was survived by two sons, Jeff Moseley Walker, of Tallahassee, Fla., and Charles Pinkney Walker, Jr., an officer of the U. S. Army.

260. Robert Emmett Waller—1867.

Lawyer—County Judge

Born December 10, 1846, in Spotsylvania County, Va.

Parents: Dr. Nelson S. Waller and Mary Hampton DeJarnette, of Spotsylvania Co.

Grandparents: Absalom Waller, of Spotsylvania Co., and —— ——. Captain Elliotte DeJarnette, of Caroline Co., Va., and —— ——.

He matriculated at V. M. I. on August 7, 1863, from Lewis's Store, Spotsylvania Co., Va., and while a fourth classman served as a cadet private in Co. C at the battle of New Market. "I was with the corps at Richmond when it was disbanded, and did not join any other command. I did not attend any university after leaving the V. M. I."

He was married twice, his first wife was Constance G., daughter of William G. Cazenove, of Alexandria, Va. They had no children.

He married secondly, Kate B., daughter of Captain Thomas R. Dew, of Spotsylvania; one daughter, Nannie Maria Waller.

After the Civil War he read law and was elected County Judge for the county of Spotsylvania in 1879, which position he held continuously until February 1, 1904, when that office was abolished. He then engaged in farming. In July 1913 he was appointed Commonwealth's Attorney of Spotsylvania to succeed T. Stokeley Coleman. He also served for some years as a member of the School Trustee Electoral Board of that county.

Judge Waller died at his home in Partlow, Va., on August 8, 1916.

A brother, William Judson Cary Waller, was a member of the Class of 1868 at V. M. I.

261. N. Tiernan Walton—1867.

Merchant

Born about 1845 (he was 18 years of age when he matriculated).

He had experienced some war service before he was entered at the Institute on January 2, 1863, by N. W. Walton, of Richmond, Va. While repeating the work of the fourth class, he served as a cadet private in Co. C at the battle of New Market. The following session he was a cadet until the evacuation of Richmond and after January 24, 1865 he served as clerk to the adjutant.

Less is known of him than of any member of the New Market Corps. He lived in Philadelphia about twenty years and died there November 2, 1918.

He operated a book store which was not successful and despite all efforts of his old comrades to assist him he seemed to shrink away. His Cross of Honor was taken to him by F. B. Price (see Sketch No. 195) and in his last years he was aided by Mr. Benjamin Duke (in an anonymous and generous way through his representative, Mr. Alexander H. Sands, Jr., of New York City) for whom he had worked or with whom he had been associated in former years.

He would never talk or write of his past life, other than to record in 1903 the roll of his cadet company and the names of those he remembered in the battle. It is believed by those who knew him that he never married and, so far as is known, no kinsman survived him.

262. George William Ward, Jr.—1867.

Lawyer—Judge—Editor

Born July 31, 1847, at "Rosemont," Frederick County, Va.

Parents: George William Ward (b. in Culpeper Co., Va., and moved to Winchester), and Julia Anne Funsten.

Grandparents: Colonel Daniel Ward, of Culpeper, Va., and —— ——. Oliver Funsten, of Clarke Co., Va., and Margaret —— , who were natives of Ireland.

He matriculated at V. M. I. on March 8, 1864, from Greenwood, Va., and two months later as a cadet private in Co. D fought in the battle of New Market.

He entered the University of Virginia in the fall of 1865; remained during the sessions of 1865-66 and 1866-67; and was graduated in some of the academic schools. After leaving the university he studied law at the Winchester Law School (formerly Judge Tucker's) and was licensed to practice his profession at the Winchester bar.

On December 10, 1878, he married at Knoxville, Tenn., Elizabeth Arthur Preston, of Abingdon, Va., a native of New York City, who with one daughter, Rosalie Garnett Ward, survived him.

In 1871 he removed to Springfield, Mo., and after a short residence there returned to Virginia and located in 1874 at Abingdon where he became prominent in the practice of his profession and in politics. He was twice (1884 to 1887) elected attorney for the Commonwealth in Washington county, Va., and was twice (1880 and 1887) appointed judge of the court of that county. He held this office at the time of his death which occurred January 22, 1897.

From 1884 to 1887 he was a member of the Board of Visitors of V. M. I. For a time he edited the Abingdon *Virginian* and later the *Southwest Examiner.*

263. Lloyd Washington—1867.

Merchant

Born November 2, 1846, at "Blenheim," Westmoreland County, Va.

Parents: Lawrence Washington, of Westmoreland Co., and Sarah Tayloe Washington (b. at "Heywood," Westmoreland Co., April 14, 1800).

Grandparents: Henry A. Washington, of Westmoreland Co., professor of history and political economy at William and Mary College, and —— —— William Augustine Washington, of Westmoreland Co. (oldest half-nephew of General George Washington and one of the executors of his will; buried in the Washington tomb at Mt. Vernon), and Sarah Tayloe, his third wife, of "Mt. Airy," Richmond Co., Va., sister of John Tayloe, owner of Octagon House, Washington, D. C., which was used as the "White House" in 1812 when the City of Washington was burned by the British.

He matriculated at V. M. I. on August 29, 1863, from Westmoreland, Va., and during that session took part in the battle of New Market as a cadet private in Co. B. "I accompanied the corps to Camp Lee, and the intermediate line of entrenchments around Richmond; was corporal* in Co. B. When the cadets were recalled to

---

*On June 27, 1864, he was promoted to fourth Corporal in Co. B.

Richmond to resume their studies, after having been furloughed, I resigned, and joined Mosby, and was with him at the time of Gen. Lee's surrender at Appomattox."

In 1865 he went to Chicago and entered the mercantile business. He is retired and is now living at the Windermere Hotel, 56th Street and the Lake, in that city. He is unmarried.

Two brothers, John Tayloe Washington, '43, and Robert James Washington, '61, attended V. M. I.

264. William Pryor Watson—1867.

Merchant—Farmer

Born January 10, 1847, in Warren Co., N. C.

Parents: John Watson, and Mary G. Pryor.

Grandparents: William Watson, born in Warren Co., N. C., and Frankie Norsworthy, born in Norfolk, Va.
William E. Pryor (of same family as General Roger A. Pryor) and Mildred ——. They were Virginians and moved to North Carolina.

He matriculated at V. M. I. August 8, 1863, from Warrenton, N. C. Later in the session he served as a private in Co. A, at the battle of New Market where he received a wound in the right arm below the elbow. The following session he resigned on March 6, 1865 to enter the Confederate army.

After the war he carried on a successful mercantile business in the town of Warrenton, North Carolina, under the firm name of Parker & Watson until his death, May 2, 1883.

He did not marry and his New Market Cross of Honor was sent in 1904 to his nearest of kin, his sister, Mrs. G. W. Purefoy, of Warrenton, N. C.

265. John Samuel Webb—1867.

Civil Engineer—Farmer

Born July 24, 1845, in Prince George County, Va.

Parents: Samuel Gibson Webb, an Englishman, who after the war was postmaster at Chuckatuck, Va., and Katherine Heath.

Grandparents: Hardiman Dunn Webb, a native of England, and Celia Robinson.
Colonel Richard Heath, State Senator for many years, and Mrs. Rebecca Baird.

He matriculated at V. M. I. August 7, 1862, from Disputanta, Prince George County, Va. As a third classman he took part in the battle of New Market, serving as a member of the cadet artillery section to which he had been detailed. Normally he was a cadet private in Co. D. The following session he returned to the Institute; was promoted to be a cadet sergeant in Company C on March 1, 1865; and continued as such until April 2nd.

"I remained at the Alms House until the Evacuation of Richmond closed the Institute, when I started to Greensboro, N. C., to become a very young Lieutenant, or Adjutant in Gen. Alexander's Artillery Command. Gen. Lee having surrendered, we hoped to join Jos. E. Johnston's army which we (my roommate, Adams, and myself) found was negotiating with Gen. W. T. Sherman terms of surrender, when we reached Greensboro, and we surrendered."

He remained at home in Petersburg for a year; returned to the Institute in the fall of 1866; and was graduated in 1867 with eleventh stand in his class and the rank of cadet quartermaster.

After graduation he accepted a position as statistician under General Wm. Mahone on the Atlantic, Mississippi, & Ohio R. R., and then transferred to the engineering field work forces at the time engaged in making the Cumberland Gap Survey. Then followed experience on projects in Tennessee, Kentucky, Ohio, and the west, of public highway construction and of railroad and mining engineering. Several times was he resident engineer and in charge of a division on the C. & O., the N. & W., and the C. C. & C. Railroads; was locating engineer, then chief engineer of the Atlantic & Danville R. R.; 1885-86, chief engineer of the Great Western Air Line R. R. from Charlotte, N. C., to Norfolk, Va.; general inspecting engineer, in 1900, for the R. P. & C. Rwy., and in 1903, was resident engineer on the Seaboard Air Line Railway at Piedmont, Ala.

Returning to his native county, he lived at Disputanta and engaged in farming, he owned land and timber tracts in Prince George and Surry Counties. His engineering work continued in connection with electric traction projects and the Argus Mines, a gold mining project for which he was consulting engineer.

He invented and, on March 8, 1905, patented, the "Combined Railjoint and Chair" for making "a continuous rail."

On December 26, 1919, he died in the Petersburg Hospital, Petersburg, Va.

266. Levi Welch—1864.

Rancher

Born July 8, 1842, at Charleston, Kanawha County, Va. (W. Va.).

Parents: John Welch (b. December 24, 1789, in Washington County, Pa.; d. April 16, 1856), and Julia Putnam McFarland (b. December 16, 1806, in Ohio; moved to Charleston, W. Va., when about 13 years of age; d. December 1, 1890).

Grandparents: George Welch and Hannah White.
James Clark McFarland, son of Major Moses McFarland (a soldier of the Revolution), and Sarah Devol, daughter of Jonathan Devol, who was a Colonial soldier.

As a boy, Levi Welch was a pupil, first, of Dr. Henry Ruffner, and later of his son, David L. Ruffner. "He was a member of the Kanawha Riflemen, commanded by Captain George S. Patton,* several years before the Confederate war, and who were mustered

---

*Graduated at V. M. I. in 1852. Killed in battle at Winchester, Va., June 19, 1864.

into service, May 8, 1861, as State troops. A few weeks afterwards the 22nd Regiment was formed and Captain Patton was made Colonel, commanding. On the 17th of July at the battle of Scary Creek, fifteen miles below Charleston, Lieutenant James Clark Welch, the brother of Levi Welch, was killed, gallantly sighting one of his pieces. Health failing the latter, he was honorably discharged and appointed a State cadet in the Military Institute, Lexington, Va., which he entered on March 1, 1862, from Upper Falls Coal River, Kanawha county, Va.

"While on furlough from the Institute, visiting his old company, the battle of Dry Creek occurred, Col. Patton commanding the Confederates and Genl. Crook the Federals. During the fight Levi Welch, acting as aide-de-camp on Patton's staff, was ordered to carry a dispatch from Col. Patton to the extreme end of the Confederate lines. Instead of taking a circuitous route for safety, he passed between the lines whilst fighting was at its heat, and escaped unhurt."

Porter Johnson, '67 (Sketch No. 125) wrote of him as follows:

"Upon his return to duty, the General of the troops with which he served, wrote Gen. Smith, Superintendent of V. M. I., a very complimentary letter speaking in the highest terms of Cadet Welch's conduct. I recall the fact that Gen. Smith read this letter to the corps of cadets and that we were all proud of the honor he had done himself and the Institute of which he was a member."

In the battle of New Market he was detached from his company, he was second lieutenant of Co. B, and put in charge of one of the 3-inch rifles in the cadet artillery section. A few weeks later was graduated with seventh stand in a class of fourteen.

After the war he lived for several years in Louisville, Ky., holding the position of bookkeeper in several large mercantile houses and in the fall of 1869 he removed to California.

On February 22, 1872, he married Mary I. Small (d. Sept. 27, 1882), of California. They had four children:
George Henry Welch, born Dec. 25, 1872, died in infancy.
Cornelia Susan, wife of Dr. William J. E. Middleton, of Grass Valley, Calif.
Henry William, and John Welch.

Mr. Welch remained in California until September 1890, when he leased his ranch and returned home bringing his family with him. He died February 11, 1901, in Charleston, W. Va.

267. Charles Edward Wellford—1865.

Secretary, C. & O. Rwy.

Born March 29, 1844, at Fredericksburg, Va.

Parents: Dr. Beverly Randolph Wellford and Mary Alexander Casson.

Grandparents: Dr. Robert Wellford and Catharine Gates.
William Alexander and Sarah Casson.

He matriculated at V. M. I. on January 27, 1862, from Richmond, Va., and was a cadet private in Co. D, at the battle of New Market.

After the war he went into business until 1872, when he became a civil engineer in South Carolina and Alabama. He was for several years Private Secretary to General W. C. Wickham, Vice-President, C. & O. Rwy., and then became Secretary of the Chesapeake & Ohio Railway with offices in Richmond, Va., and so continued until his death.

Mr. Wellford died, unmarried, April 16, 1912, at Burgh Westra, Gloucester county, Va., the home of his niece, Mrs. T. R. Marshall. His body was taken to Richmond and interment was in Hollywood Cemetery.

268. Charles Macon Wesson—1867.

Lawyer—Editorial Writer

Born July 15, 1847, in Brunswick County, Va.

Parents: William H. Wesson (b. in Brunswick Co.) and Maragret A. Palmer (b. in Charlotte Co.).

He was a student at the Virginia Collegiate Institute, Portsmouth, Va., before matriculating at V. M. I. on August 14, 1863, from Norfolk, Va. At the time his father's address was Summit, N. C. While a fourth classman he took part in the battle of New Market as cadet private in Co. B. The following session he was on January 9, 1865, detailed as clerk to the adjutant, the order stating that he was to be on the same footing as the private secretaries of the superintendent and commandant. Fifteen days later he was relieved and appointed a corporal in Co. B, and continued his cadetship until Richmond was evacuated.

"With four other cadets I was captured near Hampden-Sydney College, Va. We were kept prisoners for a few days but General P. H. Bartlett, commanding 5th Army Corps, U. S. A., upon our word of honor not to attempt to escape gave us the privilege of his mess, and we slept in his staff officers' quarters until General Lee surrendered. Then General Bartlett gave us a certificate to go home. No oath was required of us. His chaplain, Father Egan of Notre Dame Church, Washington, gave me a ten-dollar greenback bill, the first I ever saw, to help me homeward, which was a distance of upwards of one hundred and seventy miles."

After the war he was a student at Randolph-Macon College, later attending the University of Virginia from which he received his LL. B. degree in 1868.

On November 10, 1869, he married Caroline Moye, daughter of William Francis Dancy, of Edgecombe, N. C., and resided in Tarboro for several years. They had three children:

Charles Macon Wesson, Jr., formerly Colonel, U. S. A.; vice-president American Clay Machinery Co., of Bucyrus, Ohio, in 1919; m. Anne Dunbar, daughter of General George B. Davis, U. S. A.

——, wife of Madison Brown, of Centerville, Md.

Laura Wirt, wife of Samuel White, of New York.

After practicing his profession in Richmond he took up journalism and for a long time was connected with the old Richmond Times in a responsible position, and his contributions to the press for many years, both in poetry and prose, attracted general attention. In 1915 his address was Fine Creek Mills, Powhatan County, Va., the home of his forefathers.

He died in Richmond, Va., January 5, 1924. The honorary pall-bearers were Colonel Joseph Button, General Charles J. Anderson, Dr. John N. Upshur, James B. Harvie, Mark Hankins, Dr. George Ross and Rev. C. C. Randolph, all survivors of the battle of New Market except Colonel Button, a member of the V. M. I. Board of Visitors. Captain Wesson was buried in old St. Luke's church-yard, Powhatan county.

269. Cary Weston—1864.

Real Estate

Born about 1844 or 1845 (he was 17 years of age when he matriculated).

Parents: John Cary Weston (1824-1896), and Jane Parks (d. 1869), both born in Norfolk, Va.

He matriculated at V. M. I. January 11, 1862, from Norfolk, and was admitted to the third class. On September 24, 1862, he was relieved from his duties in the superintendent's office on account of having been appointed cadet sergeant-major. The following session he was the cadet adjutant and as such fought in the battle of New Market. About two weeks after the battle he was graduated with twelfth stand in his class. He was then appointed drill master with the rank of lieutenant in the C. S. A.

The war over, he became general agent of the Dismal Swamp Land Company.

He married Julia Paul, daughter of Samuel W. Paul of the old firm of Paul & Pegram, dry goods merchants. They had one daughter, Julia Paul, who died May 22, 1887. His widow married Dr. Thomas B. Ward, of Norfolk, who died in April, 1885.

He died of scarlet fever after an illness of four days on February 24, 1871, aged 26. His portrait in cadet uniform hangs in the Jackson Memorial Hall at V. M. I.

270. John Edward Wharton—1866.

Engineer—Lawyer

Born April 8, 1845, in Bedford Co., Va.

Parents: Rev. John Austin Wharton (attorney, judge, and Episcopal clergyman; born in Bedford Co., Va.; died in 1888, aged 85 years) and Isabella Brown, born in Berkshire Co., Mass., in 1811. Died 1895.

Grandparents: John Wharton, of English descent, and Sallie —— Lyman Brown and Fannie ——

He matriculated at V. M. I. December 31, 1861, from Liberty (Bedford), Va. After repeating the work of the fourth class he took part, as a third classman, in the battle of New Market at which time he was a cadet private in Co. B. His cadetship continued until February 1, 1865, when he resigned to enter the Confederate army.

After the war he studied law and practiced his profession in Bedford, Va.

In 1882, he married Mattie Logwood, daughter of Lee McClintock, of Bedford. They had two daughters:
Mary Virginia Wharton.
Isabelle Bertrand Wharton.

In 1883 he removed to the State of Washington, where he was engaged in various engineering enterprises for about four years. Returning to Virginia he was employed in the engineering department of the Norfolk & Western Railroad for about thirty years. During this time his home was in Roanoke, where he was a communicant of St. John's Episcopal Church.

He died at his home, 316 Mountain Avenue, S. W., Roanoke, October 24, 1917 and was buried in Longwood Cemetery, Bedford, Va.

271. Joseph Christopher Wheelwright—1867.

"Died on the Field of Honor"

Born November 26, 1846, in Westmoreland County, Va.

Parents: Dr. Frederick D. Wheelwright (one of the first to volunteer in the 20th Virginia Cavalry and later surgeon in the same regiment, in which his sons Thomas and Frederick also served), of Westmoreland County, Va., and Maria L. ——

He matriculated at V. M. I. on August 29, 1863, from Westmoreland County, Va., and later in the session as a cadet private in Co. C took part in the battle of New Market and was mortally wounded. At which stage of the battle he was wounded has not been definitely established but after the Federal army had been driven from the field he was borne from the battle ground by his comrades and was later taken to Harrisonburg to the home of Dr. Newman, whose family ministered to his comfort with the most tender solicitude.

On June 1, 1864, Col. R. L. Madison, Surgeon of the V. M. I., wrote from Lexington to the Superintendent, then in Richmond:

"I arrived here last evening and brought Capt. Hill and cadets Gibson and Marshall in an ambulance from Staunton. Capt. Hill and cadet Marshall are doing very well, but Cadet Gibson is still in a critical condition and I am afraid will yet suffer amputation of his leg notwithstanding all my efforts to the contrary. I was left in New Market in charge of several wounded cadets, but brought all of them to Harrisonburg except White, T., who is still at Dr. Meem's and improving. I wrote you from Harrisonburg and again from Staunton, but as I received no reply to either letter I presume you did not receive them.*

"There were ten (10) cadets severely wounded, viz., White, T., Wheelwright, Darden, Atwill, Garnett, Upshur, Randolph, Macon, Gibson and Marshall. Of these the first is at Dr. Meem's. Poor Wheelwright is at Dr. New-

---

*These letters not located.

—15

man's in Harrisonburg and although receiving the most skillful attention and the most affectionate kindness, will probably die, if indeed he is not already dead. Cadet Upshur I left in Staunton doing very well, at the house of a relative, Capt. Bailey, Commissary of the Post. All the others (except those I brought here) are rapidly improving and I gave each a 30 days furlough and they went off to Lynchburg on the cars on Tuesday (May 31st).

"In regard to cadet Gibson I must confess I feel much anxiety. His wounds are severe and not doing well. He is a noble boy and has shown more fortitude than any one I ever saw. His father was to see him in Staunton but went away on the second day. He has an aunt residing near Goshen. I have given you these particulars as in duty bound and also because I know the deep interest you take in the welfare of our wounded, and I desire to know what your wishes are in respect to myself. Whether to remain here and attend Capt. Hill, and cadets Gibson and Marshall, or report to you in Richmond. I do not think it advisable for me to leave Mr. Gibson unless there is a prospect of the corps being in another engagement, but of course will obey cheerfully any order you may give.

"My wife desires her respectful regards to you. Remember me kindly to Col. Ship and to the Captains. Also to Dr. Ross and accept for yourself the high consideration with which, I remain."

The best medical skill proved unavailing and death came June 2, 1864, the day after Colonel Madison's report was written.

Following a temporary interment, his remains were brought to Lexington in 1866 and now rest beneath the New Market Battle Monument at V. M. I.

272. John Sproul White—1867.

Merchant—Farmer

Born March 14, 1846, in Lexington, Va.

Parents: William White and Frances Sproul, of Augusta Co., Va.

Grandparents: —— White and Ann (?) Johnston.
John Sproul, of Augusta Co., Va., and Matilda Scott.

After attending Washington College in 1862-63, he matriculated at V. M. I. on February 15, 1864, from Lexington, Va., and three months later as a cadet private in Co. B, he took part in the battle of New Market.

Early in life he went into the mercantile business with his father. The business proved confining and ill health compelled him to devote much of his time to farming. In 1893 he moved to Augusta County and gave his entire time to farming until 1900, when he moved to Clifton Forge. There he at first operated a drug store and later became cashier of the Alleghany Ore & Iron Company. A few months before his death he purchased the grocery business of Hawkins Brothers.

He died, unmarried, on September 1, 1904, of typhoid fever at the Chesapeake & Ohio Hospital in Clifton Forge. Interment was in Lexington, Va.

He was survived by one brother, Arch S. White, of Lynchburg, Va., and two sisters: Mrs. Anna White Irwin, wife of H. D. Irwin, and Miss Scottie White, of Minneapolis, Minn.

273. R. Joseph White—1866.

Merchant

Born about 1843 (he was 19 years of age when he matriculated), in Aberdeen, Miss.

Parents: Zachariah Johnston White (born in Rockbridge County, Va.; educated at Washington College 1822-23; removed to Aberdeen where he was a merchant; returned to Virginia in 1854; sheriff of Rockbridge County; died April 20, 1871), and Eliza Jane Williams, of Aberdeen.

Before entering the Institute he attended Jacob Fuller's Preparatory School and Mr. Estill's School, in Lexington. He matriculated at V. M. I. on September 3, 1862, from Lexington, Va., and the following session while a third classman, he served as a cadet private in Co. D, at the battle of New Market. He remained with the corps until Richmond was evacuated and then joined Gen. Joseph E. Johnston's command under Colonel McLaughlin.

Following his graduation from the Business College, in Baltimore, about 1870, he engaged in the mercantile business with his father in Lexington until the latter's death in 1871. Closing out his Lexington establishment, he went to Fulton, Missouri, where he continued his career as a merchant.

Married twice. First, Miss Mattie McDonald, of Sherman, Texas. One daughter, Maggie, married and living in Texas in 1913.

Second, Miss Alice McDonald, sister of his first wife. There were five children by the second marriage, four of whom were living in 1913.

Mr. White died in Texas November —, 1894.

274. Thomas Wilson White—1867.

Farmer

Born September 19, 1846, at Abingdon, Va.

Parents: William Young Conn White and Margaret Jane Greenway, of Abingdon, Va.

Grandparents: Col. James White and Elizabeth Wilson.
John C. Greenway and Margaret Cowan.

He was a student at the Abingdon Male Academy before he matriculated at V. M. I. on August 18, 1863, from Abingdon, Va. During that session while a member of the fourth class, he served as a cadet private in Co. A in the battle of New Market. He was desperately wounded in that fight by a grape shot which shattered the bone of his right leg just below the hip joint, and was lamed for life. "He was captured by General Hunter between New Market and Mt. Jackson and held prisoner for three days." (The captivity was probably after he left Dr. Meem's residence—see surgeon's report in sketch No. 271. Ed.)

He entered the University of Virginia in 1865 to take the medical course but ill health brought about by his wound forced him to abandon this profession and he returned to Abingdon and engaged in farming.

He married Eliza Armstrong, daughter of Hon. James King Gibson, of
Abingdon, Va., and they had the following children:
Margaret, wife of Arthur P. Wilmer, of Richmond, Va.
James Gibson.
Mary Gibson, wife of J. Clark Carpenter (decd.), of Johnson City, Tenn.
Elise Wilson (d. Oct. 8, 1918), wife of Victor S. Paine.
Sarah Given, wife of Marvin Gorham, of Detroit, Mich.
Dr. Thomas Wilson, Jr. (V. M. I., '03, m. Lucy C. Skelton, of Richmond,
Va.; d. Oct. 2, 1929).
Gilbert Greenway (V. M. I., '10, m. Frances, daughter of Mrs. Anna Dos-
ser Pierce, of Johnson City, Tenn.), of Detroit, Mich.

Mr. White died suddenly at his farm eight miles from Abingdon
on July 23, 1907. He was survived by all his children except
James Gibson White; also by his brother, John Greenway White,
V. M. I., '66 (d. Sept. 6, 1907), and his sister, Mrs. T. P. Trigg,
both of Abingdon. Two grandsons attended V. M. I., James Clark
Carpenter, Jr., '29, and Gilbert White Carpenter, '35.

275. William Henry White—1867.

Lawyer—District Attorney—Railroad President

Born at Deep Run, in Norfolk County, Va., April 16, 1847.

Parents: William White (b. June 1821, Norfolk Co.) Col. 14th Va. Inf'y,
of Pickett's Division, and Henrietta Kemp Turner (b. April 30, 1821,
King William Co., Va.).

Grandparents: William White, served in War of 1812, and Love Old, both
of Norfolk Co.
James Frazier Turner (of Bath Co.) and Mary Quarles (of King William
Co.).

Prepared at a private school in Richmond; then after a short period in college he entered V. M. I. Jan. 19, 1864, from Petersburg
and remained until the corps was disbanded April 2, 1865.

He took part in the battle of New Market as a cadet private in
Co. A, and after March 1, 1865, served as secretary to the commandant.

In the fall of 1865 he entered the Univ. of Va. and after leaving,
being still under age, he served with the Clerk of Norfolk Co. until 1868—when he secured his license to practice.

Married: 1st, Nov. 4, 1869, Lucy Landon Carter Minor, dtr. of Dr. Lewis
Willis Minor (son of Dr. John Minor, of Fredericksburg, Va.) and
Lucy Landon Carter, of Willis Hill, Va.
Children: Eloise Isabelle White, m. O. G. Hinton, of Petersburg, Va.
Dr. Wm. H. Landon White, of Knoxville, Tenn.

2nd, March 10, 1880, Emma Gray, dtr. of Benjamin C. and Susan E. Reid
Gray, of Richmond, Va.
Children: William H. White, Jr.—attorney.
Emma Gray White, m. William R. Trigg, Jr., of Richmond, Va.

He began to practice law in Portsmouth and the following year
(1869) became Commonwealth's Attorney of Norfolk Co., and then
served in the same capacity for the City of Norfolk. In 1873 he
formed a partnership with Judge Theodore S. Garnett, which con-

tinued for more than twenty years, to 1895. A democrat, he was appointed in 1900 U. S. District Attorney for the Eastern District of Va. and continued to serve through much of McKinley's term. He was a member of the firm of White, Tunstall, & Thom, one of the leading law firms of the South, from 1900 until 1907. Tunstall was an old New Market Corps comrade (See sketch No. 251). In 1907, he was elected president of the Richmond, Fredericksburg, & Potomac R. R., in which position he served until his death.

He was a brilliant lawyer, a polished speaker, and a distinguished executive. When he took over his last task following the stormy agitation over the executive control of the Richmond-Washington line he was hailed as the "great pacificator." His record justified the tribute and the intricacies of the problems of taxation and of the re-charter of the company were successfully solved. During his administration the road was double-tracked and the monumental Broad Street Station, at Richmond, was built. A sentimental act was the acquisition of the property at Guinea Station on which stands the house in which "Stonewall" Jackson died.

He was a member of the V. M. I. Board of Visitors from January 1, 1888, to December 31, 1890, and from January 1, 1894, to December 31, 1896; he served in a similar capacity at the Univ. of Va. for many years.

In 1917 the alumni contributed funds to erect stables at V. M. I. so that field artillery and cavalry units might be added. The plan was that each alumnus would contribute what he earned on May 1st. In sending in his contribution Mr. White wrote on the accompanying card:

> "I regard the V. M. I. as an institution as useful in Peace as in War. No other country has its equal" (5-1-17).

The necessary fund was raised but because of the World War, which the United States entered while the alumni were being circularized, the mounted units were not established until 1919. Prior to that time the fourth classmen served as horses and drew the cannon.

He died in Richmond August 5, 1920, after an illness of several months, and was buried in Hollywood Cemetery.

276. Henry Colgate Whitehead—1866.

Treasurer of Traction Company—Accountant

Born July 23, 1845, at Norfolk, Va.

Parents: John Boswell Whitehead, merchant, of Norfolk, and Emily Arnold Herman.

Grandparents: Nathan Colgate Whitehead, of Southampton Co., Va., and Elizabeth McPherson.
Henry Herman (born in Germany), and Emily Arnold, of Suffolk, Va.

He matriculated at V. M. I. January 9, 1862, from Norfolk, and the following session repeated the work of the third class. The cadets were on duty in the summer months in those days and on July 8, 1863 he was assigned to special duty in the office of the post adjutant.

"In May 1864, I was a member of Co. B and a private, being at the time in the 3rd class, but when the cadets were ordered to Staunton and from there up the Valley to New Market, I was assigned to the section of artillery (2 guns) under the command of Cadet Captain C. H. Minge. I participated in the battle of New Market on May 15, 1864, with the artillery detachment and was wounded while assisting in serving one of the guns during one of the many 'warm' times we experienced during that day. I was struck by a piece of shell on my left collar bone. I was knocked several feet from the gun, my uniform torn and I was considerably bruised—not, however, sufficiently to compel me to leave the field—the result of the blow having been felt more for several weeks after than under the immediate excitement at the time." His cadetship continued until the evacuation of Richmond in April, 1865.

After the war Mr. Whitehead engaged in mercantile pursuits for a time, later holding the office of treasurer of the Norfolk City Railway Company, before it merged into the Virginia Railway & Power Company.

In 1868 he married Margaret Walke, daughter of Walter Herron Taylor and his wife, Cornelia Cowdery, of Norfolk, Va. They had four children: Cornelia Wickham, wife of Rev. Robert S. Coupland; Emily Arnold, wife of Rev. Edward W. Gamble; John B. Whitehead, Ph.D., Johns Hopkins University and associate professor of electricity in that university; and Hugh Grigsby Whitehead, cashier of the Virginia Bank & Trust Co., Norfolk, who married Rena Burwell.

In 1903 Mr. Whitehead was secretary-treasurer of the Consolidated Turnpike Company of Norfolk, and in 1909 he was with the Norfolk Chemical Company, Inc., distillers and manufacturers of tar products. He retired as an accountant about 1916 and died at the home of his son, Hugh G. Whitehead, Cambridge Crescent, Larchmont, Norfolk, April 19, 1920.

A brother, Hugh Grigsby Whitehead, was graduated at the V. M. I. on July 4, 1872, and died four months later, November 3, 1872.

277. John Coyle Whitwell—Not a cadet.

Assistant Quartermaster and Commissary on the New Market campaign.

Born October 17, 1828, at Washington, D. C.

Parents: John George Whitwell and Anna Wood.

He married, first, in 1850, Augusta, daughter of Augustin Newton, of Alexandria, Va. There were two daughters: ——, wife of George C. Heard, of Los Angeles, California, and ——, wife of William E. Middleton, of Washington, D. C.

His second wife was Margaret Smith, daughter of Samuel Miller, of Washington, D. C. By this marriage there were two sons: Sanford Nesbit and George Miller Whitwell, who, in 1909, were both connected with the Washington Gas Light Company.

Captain Whitwell was in charge of the Commissary Department at V. M. I. from 1862 to 1864. He was specifically mentioned in the order issued May 11, 1864, in which the corps of cadets was directed to join Major General John C. Breckinridge. Paragraph two of that order reads: "Captain J. C. Whitwell will accompany the expedition as Assistant Quartermaster and Commissary, and will see that the proper transportation, etc., is supplied."

On January 27, 1910, General Scott Shipp wrote as follows:

"At the outbreak of the war, he (Whitwell) was in the mercantile business in—I think—Brooklyn, N. Y. I do not know when he came South; I think not until 1862. He came to the Institute in 1862 and was there until the close of the war. I do not think he had other military service than at the Institute. I saw him once after the war. He was then a merchant in Washington, D. C."

After the war he returned to Washington, D. C., and was secretary of the then Great Falls Ice Co. of that city, which afterwards merged into the American Ice Co. He was prominent in local musical circles, having a fine baritone voice. For many years he was musical director at the Central Presbyterian Church of Washington (the first Southern Presbyterian Church in the city), of which he was one of the founders and a deacon until his death on April 13, 1882.

D. C. B. Wilson.

Name changed. See 12. Daniel Cary Barraud.

278. Richard Grey Wilson—1867.

Merchant

Born July 21, 1846, in Surry County, Va.

Parents: Richard Farmer Wilson (born in Isle of Wight Co., Va.), and Ellen Douglas Grey (born in Southampton Co., Va.).

Grandparents: Dr. George Wilson, and Mary Anne ——, both of Isle of Wight Co., Va.

He attended Mr. Wm. H. Harrison's School at Amelia, Va., and Hampden-Sidney College before entering V. M. I.

On October 6, 1863, he matriculated at V. M. I. from Surry County, Va., giving his father's address as Box 931, Richmond, and his occupation as "Treasury Department." He was assigned to the fourth class and during that session took part in the battle of New Market as a cadet private in Co. B. At the end of the school year his stand in his class was 82 in a class of 187. The following session he returned to the institute but was on furlough from January 18 to February 1, 1865 because of sickness.

After the war he moved to Richmond where he engaged in the hardware business. He never married, and died on December 16, 1901.

His New Market "Cross of Honor" was sent to his brother, Charles H. Wilson, of Hampton, Va., on December 4, 1909.

279. Lewis Williams Wimbish—1867.

Farmer—County Treasurer

Born September 28, 1847, at Boydton, Va.

Parents: Lewis Williams Wimbish (b. at Houston—now Halifax, Va.), and Mary Jane Townes (b. in Boydton, Va.).

Grandparents: Colonel John Wimbish, clerk and sheriff of Halifax Co., Va., for many years, and Rebecca Williams, daughter of Colonel Joseph Williams of the U. S. Army.
Colonel William Townes, a soldier in the War of 1812, and Lucy Macklin, of Mecklenburg Co., Va., a daughter of Major —— Macklin.

He matriculated at V. M. I. April 1, 1864, from Clarksville, Va., and was entered by William Townes. Six weeks later he took part in the battle of New Market as a cadet private in Co. A. The following session he returned and remained until Richmond was evacuated, whereupon he went to General Joseph E. Johnston's army.

After the war he went to Texas and Mexico where he remained for three years. Returning to Virginia, he lived the rest of his life at Phillis, Mecklenburg Co., engaged in farming and operating a mill. During this time he served as sheriff, county treasurer, and justice of the peace.

He married Lucy Townes, a daughter of Colonel William Townes, Jr. (member of the Virginia State Senate) and Emmet Barksdale. They had eight children: Dr. W. T. Wimbish, of Clarksville, Va., Lewis W., Lucy Townes, Nannie Barksdale, Claiborne Barksdale, Mary Emmet, Joseph Hopkins, and Charlotte Rebecca.

He died August 22, 1914, and was buried at Mays Chapel, near his home.

280. Samuel Griffin Wingfield—1867.

Lawyer—Mayor of Lynchburg, Va.—Clerk of Court.

Born October 17, 1846, at Bellevue, Bedford County, Va.

Parents: Hon. Gustavus A. Wingfield (d. February 18, 1888), Judge of the fifth judicial circuit of Virginia, and Charlotte Griffin (d. 1855), of Bedford Co.

Grandparents: Lewis Wingfield, of Bedford Co., and —— ——.
Dr. Samuel Griffin, of Bedford Co., and —— ——.

Before entering V. M. I. he attended Mt. Laurel Academy in Halifax County, Va., for two years. He matriculated at the Institute on May 30, 1863 and a year later took part in the battle of New Market as a cadet private in Co. A. The following year he returned to the Institute and continued his cadetship until January 19, 1865.

After the war he served for a time as deputy in the clerk's office of Bedford county and later occupied a similar position in Lynchburg. In 1880 he was elected Mayor of that city but retired in 1882 to enter the law class of the University of Virginia. He was elected president of his class and was graduated with the degree of Bachelor of Laws.

On October 17, 1887, he married Sallie Lewis Alexander, a daughter of John Dabney Alexander (county clerk of Campbell Co., Va.) and Mary Pannill, and a sister of his New Market comrade, William Kirkwood Alexander (see Sketch No. 4). They had two children:

Samuel Griffin Wingfield, Jr., with the Curtis Publishing Co. of Philadelphia.

Dorothy, wife of J. K. Irving, Jr., of Howardsville, Va.

Mr. Wingfield practiced law but a short time before he was elected clerk of the corporation court of Lynchburg, a position which he filled with credit during several terms until his death November 12, 1901.

A brother, William Lewis Wingfield, was graduated at V. M. I. with the class of 1859.

281. Henry Alexander Wise—1862.

Soldier—Educator

In command of cadets during their charge at New Market

Born May 18, 1842, in Accomac Co., Va. (a brother of Louis C. Wise, see Sketch No. 283).

Parents: John Cropper Wise and Anne Finney, both of Accomac Co., Va.

Grandparents: Maj. John Wise and his second wife, Sarah Corbin Cropper (daughter of General John Cropper, of the Continental Army). (See Sketch No. 282.)

Col. John Finney, who served in the War of 1812, and Margaret Bowman.

The early years of his life were spent in Accomac and Princess Anne counties, and in Norfolk, Va. He attended both public and private schools in these counties (a boarding school at London Bridge, Princess Anne Co., Va., and the Norfolk Academy of which Rev. Robert Gatewood, V. M. I. '49, was the principal).

On September 2, 1859, he matriculated at V. M. I., from Norfolk and was admitted to the third class. At graduation he stood ninth in his class.

On April 21, 1861, he went with the corps of cadets under the command of Major Thomas J. Jackson, to Richmond, in the military service of the State of Virginia, and was assigned to the duty of drilling volunteer companies assembled at the camp of instruction at the Fair Grounds (Camp Lee). This service he continued at Ashland, and at Gauley Bridge in western Virginia until May, 1861, when he was appointed Adjutant of the 46th Virginia Regiment of Infantry, Wise's Brigade.

He served with this command in the early operations in western Virginia, participating in the battles and skirmishes of the Brigade. In February 1862, Wise's Brigade was transferred to the eastern part of the State to the command of Gen. Huger. The 46th Virginia was stationed at Naggs Head, North Carolina, and constituted a part of the force assigned to the defence of Roanoke Island. When the Burnside Expedition attacked the island, several companies of the 46th Virginia under the command of Major W. H. Fry were sent to the island to assist Col. Shaw in its defence. The members of these companies, Wise being among them, were made prisoners when the island was surrendered, held for two or three weeks, and then paroled at Elizabeth City. Wise then went to Norfolk, Va.

While on parole he was appointed by the Board of Visitors of the Virginia Military Institute an Assistant Professor of Mathematics and Latin in that institution, where he remained until he was exchanged.

During the time he was on parole, his old commander of the 46th had him appointed Adjutant of his battalion of Scouts, Couriers and Guides, attached to the headquarters of General Lee. In this capacity he never served but remained at the Institute and took part in the various operations of the corps in defence of the Valley of Virginia.

The first year he taught he was commissioned a lieutenant; the following session he was promoted to the grade of captain and as such was the tactical officer in command of Co. A of the corps of cadet in the battle of New Market. When Col. Shipp was wounded Captain Wise took command of the cadet battalion on the battle field.*

"Captain Henry A. Wise relates to this day how the fragment of a shell having shot away all his garments from one particular place, he hunted around desperately for clothes enough to sit on. Account given to the author: 'I remember well when you lost your coat-tail and the seat of your trousers.' " (Turner's New Market Campaign, p. 105; numerous references in cadets' letters to this incident.)

"It seems to me that I can see you now, tall, handsome, and soldierly-looking, as you ran down the Cadet line with sword drawn, until you reached our center, very near where the colors were carried by Evans, when you said: 'Get up from here and give the Yankees hell.' " (R. E. Waller, letter, May 26, 1909.)

---

*As the representative of the New Market cadets in Richmond, Preston Cocke wrote to Capt. Wise on June 1, 1894, that at a recent meeting they had decided to request him (Wise) to write the history of the New Market Campaign—the Richmond members of the New Market Corps agreeing to raise the funds for its publication and to render any required help necessary in gathering source material.

Captain Wise accepted this responsibility on July 3, 1894, and gathered a tremendous amount of data from all those, whose addresses were known, who had taken part in the campaign. In 1899, however, he reported that he felt his effort inadequate and preferred to have the history written by a non-partisan. In the course of time (1909) E. Raymond Turner, a graduate student at Johns Hopkins University and later Professor of European History at the University of Michigan, was selected to write the history and all data which had been accumulated was turned over to him. Prof. Turner's book "The New Market Campaign" was published in 1912, the Richmond Alumni Association of the V. M. I. joining with the New Market cadets in defraying the cost of publication. To Captain Wise, however, is due the everlasting glory of collecting the data while it was possible to gather it from participants. It was characteristic of the man who commanded the corps of cadets in its famous charge and who trained and inspired the youth of the great city of Baltimore for over forty years, that his inate modesty should overcome his personal courage and scholarly attainments and cause him to deliver the results of his labor to another for interpretation and publication. After the publication of Prof. Turner's book all letters, sketches, etc., were turned over to the Virginia Military Institute for preservation.

"Manifestly, they, the cadets, must charge or fall back. And charge it was; for, at that moment, Henry Wise ('Old Chinook', beloved of every boy in the command) sprang to his feet, shouted out the command to rise up and charge, and, moving in advance of the line, led the Cadet Corps forward to the guns. The battery was being served superbly. The musketry fairly rolled, but the cadets never faltered. They reached the firm greensward of the farmyard in which the guns were planted. The Federal infantry began to break and run behind the buildings. Before the order to limber up could be obeyed by the artillerymen, the cadets disabled the teams, and were close upon the guns. The gunners dropped their sponges, and sought safety in flight. Lieutenant Hanna hammered a gunner over the head with his cadet sword. Winder Garret outran another and lunged his bayonet in him. The boys leaped upon the guns, and the battery was theirs. Evans, the color-sergeant, stood wildy waving the cadet colors from the top of a caisson." (The End of an Era, p. 302.)

He resigned his position at V. M. I. on February 4, 1865, effective March 15, 1865, and reported for duty to Captain John Donnell Smith, commanding a battery of artillery in Huger's Battalion, Longstreet's corps, in which he had been appointed a lieutenant. In this capacity he took part in the engagements of the battery, serving on the lines near the Howlett House; took part in the battle of Sailor's Creek, and was surrendered with General Lee's Army at Appomattox C. H.

After the surrender Capt. Wise went to Princess Anne Co., Va., where his parents resided, finding employment on a farm for a short time, and afterwards engaged in teaching school for a year in Princess Anne Co., Va. He then went to Norfolk and was for three years an instructor in the Norfolk (Military) Academy, of which Rev. Robert Gatewood, V. M. I. '49 was the Principal. In 1870 he moved to Baltimore and became principal of Male Grammar School No. 4. After serving five years in this position, he was appointed Assistant Superintendent of the schools of that city. In 1883, upon the resignation of the Superintendent, Henry E. Shepherd, he was made Superintendent of the schools, and for more than seventeen years discharged the duties of that position (Superintendent of Public Instruction). In 1900, he became First Assistant Superintendent of the schools of the city, from which position he was retired, at his request, on the 30th of September, 1911.

His portrait hangs in Jackson Memorial Hall at V. M. I.

Captain Wise returned to Norfolk and lived there the remainder of his life. He died at the Boissevain Apartments, 520 Boissevain Avenue, Norfolk, Va., on July 11, 1918, after an illness of several months and following services at St. Luke's Episcopal Church he was buried in Elmwood Cemetery in Norfolk.

He never married and was survived by a sister, Mrs. Annie Wise Craft, of Norfolk, and a brother, Dr. John C. Wise, Medical Director, U. S. Navy, retired, of Washington, D. C.

282. John Sergeant Wise—1866.

Lawyer—Congressman—Author

Born December 27, 1846, at Rio Janeiro, Brazil, where his father was at the time Envoy Extraordinary and Minister Plentipotentiary from the United States.

Parents: Henry Alexander Wise (of Accomac Co., Va.; born December 3, 1806; left an orphan at a tender age; died September 14, 1876; Governor of Virginia January 1, 1856 to January 1, 1860; Brigadier-General, C. S. A.) and his second wife, Sarah Sergeant (died in October, 1850).

Grandparents: Major John Wise (of Accomac Co., Va.; lawyer; Speaker, Virginia House of Delegates) and his second wife, Sarah Corbin Cropper (see Sketch No. 281).

Hon. John Sergeant (distinguished lawyer of Philadelphia, Pa.; member of Congress many years; candidate for Vice-President of the United States on the ticket with Henry Clay in his first candidacy. Son of Jonathan Dickenson Sergeant and Margaret Spencer) and Margaretta Watmough (daughter of James Horatio Watmough, a merchant of Philadelphia, and Ann Carmick).

His father returned in August, 1847, to his home at Only, near Onancock village in Accomac County, Va., and in the village John started to school under a Mr. Maxwell. After his father became Governor, he attended the school of Rev. J. Ambler Weed, in Richmond, and afterwards that of William Dabney Stuart. In 1859 he went to the home of his sister, Mrs. Plummer Hobson, near Dover Mills in Goochland County, and while there he attended the school conducted by the Rev. Jacob Denison Dudley, who was Rector of Hebron Church. In 1860, upon his retirement from office, Governor Wise bought "Rolleston", a plantation near Norfolk, and that year John attended a private school at the home of Thurman Hoggard, presided over by (later Reverend) Landon R. Mason.

At the outbreak of the war, his father entered the army, having been commissioned a brigadier-general, and John returned to school in Goochland. On September 3, 1862, he matriculated at V. M. I., from Richmond. The following session, while in the third class, he took part in the battle of New Market as third Cadet Corporal in Co. D and was slightly wounded and retired from the field early in the engagement.

"Up to this time I was still corporal of the guard, in charge of the baggage-wagon, with a detail of three men. . . . We had not been relieved in the general bustle and confusion. My orders were to remain with the wagons at the bend in the pike. . . . When it became evident that a battle was imminent, a single thought took possession of me, and that was, that I would never be able to look my father in the face again if I sat on a baggage-wagon while my command was in its first, perhaps its only, engagement. . . . My oration . . . ran about this wise: 'Boys, the enemy is in our front. Our command is about to go into action. . . . I shall join the command forthwith. Anyone who chooses to remain may do so.' All the guard followed. The wagon was left in charge of the black driver. Of the four who thus went, one was killed and two were wounded." (J. S. Wise, "The West Point of the Confederacy," p. 468.)

That afternoon after the Battle

"I entered the town, and found it filled with soldiers, laughing and carousing as light heartedly as if it were a feast, or a holiday. In a side street, a great throng of Federal prisoners was corralled; they were nearly all Germans. Every type of prisoner was there, some cheerful, some defiant, some careless, some calm and dejected. One fellow in particular afforded great merriment by his quaint recital of the manner of his capture. Said he, 'Dem leetle tevils mit der vite vlag vas doo mutch fur us; dey shoost smash mine head ven I was cry zurrender all de dime." (The End of an Era, p. 304.)

At the end of the session he was promoted to be the fourth line sergeant in Co. B but he did not serve as such for he received a commission as second lieutenant and drill master. And so the remainder of the summer was spent in and about Petersburg with his father's command, and in October he reported at Dublin Depot in southwestern Virginia to drill a regiment of reserves. On arrival there he found the regiment marching to Saltville, and participated in the battle the next day in which Burbridge was repulsed. The following spring he was assigned as Adjutant to Major F. J. Boggs, commanding the artillery defences of the Richmond and Danville Railroad, and carried to Danville the last dispatch sent by General Lee to President Davis. Turning south, he joined Johnston's army at Greensboro, N. C., and remained with the staff of Gen. Carter Stephenson until Johnston's surrender. He then went to Richmond, and thence to Philadelphia, where he spent part of that summer at the home of General George G. Meade, who married his mother's sister, Margaretta Sergeant, and in October went to the University of Virginia, where he remained two years, graduating in Law under John B. Minor and in Moral Philosophy and Political Economy under William H. McGuffey.

Married: November 3, 1869, Evelyn Beverly Douglas, the daughter of Hugh Douglas and Nancy Hamilton, of Nashville, Tennessee. They had five sons, all of whom attended the V. M. I., and two daughters.

In 1867 he began the practice of law and after his marriage he formed a partnership with his father which lasted until the death of General Wise in 1876. From 1876 to 1879 he was a member of the board of visitors of the V. M. I.

His first participation in politics was in 1873, when he unsuccessfully opposed the election of Gen. Bradley T. Johnson to the Virginia Senate; in 1880, as independent candidate for congress against his cousin, George D. Wise, was defeated; in 1881, appointed U. S. District Attorney, Eastern Virginia, by President Arthur; in 1882, elected Congressman on the Readjuster ticket over John E. Massey; and in 1885, as Republican candidate for Governor, was defeated by General Fitzhugh Lee.

In 1878 Captain Wise was chosen to command the Richmond Light Infantry Blues which at that time left the First Virginia Infantry and was reorganized as an independent command. Dr. Thomas Nelson Page, the author and later Ambassador to Italy, was the first lieutenant, and T. Ritchie Glazebrook, V. M. I. '70, was first sergeant. He restored the ancient distinctive uniform to this well known organization. His brother, Capt. O. Jennings Wise, while leading the Richmond Blues was killed at the battle of Roanoke Island.

Early in his professional life he became connected with the concern (See Sketch No. 190 and footnote page 158) which built the first electric street railway. This brought him into contact with northern interests then engaged in developing the infant industry of electrical power. In 1888 he removed to New York City as General Counsel of the Sprague Electric Railway & Motor Company; in 1892, was attorney for the Edison General Electric Company; in 1893, was attorney for the General Electric Company and that year was a law partner of Dallas Flannagan, V. M. I. '87. Some years later his sons, Henry and John, were his law partners.

He was leading counsel in the great controversies between the Street Railways and the Telephones, a litigation extending over twenty-seven states of the union and at one time taking him to England. He was employed in several large railroad reorganizations and in the cases to test the constitutionality of the new (1902) Constitution of Virginia.

An authority on electrical law, his address delivered before the New York State Bar Association at Albany on "Electricity in the Highways" attracted much attention and was used as a text-book in American and foreign universities. In the midst of his duties he found time to become an author and wrote "Diomed, the Autobiography of a Dog" (1898) ; "The End of an Era" (1899) ; "The Lion's Skin" (1905) ; "Recollections of Thirteen Presidents" (1906) and "Citizenship", the same year. In addition to his books he wrote for the magazines and his article on "The West Point of the Confederacy" published in the Century Magazine in January, 1889, attracted wide attention.

On many occasions his ready and eloquent oratory recounted the deeds of the New Market Cadets and his visits to the Institute, as a member of the board of visitors and to see his sons, extended over such a long period that he was well known to all who wore the Cadet gray during his span of life.

In the last six years of his life he was practically an invalid. He moved back to Virginia and, in his home, "Kiptopeake", near the shores of the Atlantic Ocean, in Northampton County, surrounded by his books, his dogs, and his memories, he spent his declining years. His last winter was spent in a hospital at Bryn Mawr, Pa., and on his return home he stopped by the summer home of his son, Henry, near Princess Anne, Md., pneumonia set in and he died there on May 12, 1913. That night four hundred men prominent in public life, especially at the bench and bar, assembled in New York City to honor his son, at whose home he died, on the occasion of his retirement from the office of United States District Attorney.

He was buried in Hollywood Cemetery, Richmond, Va., on New Market Day.

He was survived by his wife and the following children: Hugh Douglas Wise, V. M. I., '91, Colonel, U. S. Army; Major Henry Alexander Wise, V. M. I., '94, lawyer, New York City; John Sergeant Wise, Jr., V. M. I., '95, lawyer, New York City; (Eva Douglas) Mrs. Perrine Barney, of Cape Charles, Va.; Colonel Jennings Cropper Wise, then Commandant at V. M. I., now a lawyer in Washington, D. C.; Miss Margaretta Wise; and Byrd Douglas Wise, V. M. I, '06, of New York City.

283. Louis C. Wise—1865.

Civil Engineer—Real Estate

Born July 23, 1844, in Norfolk, Va.

Parents, etc.: See Sketch (No. 281) of his brother, Henry A. Wise.

He matriculated at V. M. I. January 9, 1862, from Norfolk, and continued his cadetship until the evacuation of Richmond. At graduation he stood 19 in his class and was first lieutenant in Co. C. While in the second class he took part in the battle of New Market, where he was twice wounded and at which time he was second Cadet Sergeant in Co. C.

"During the charge, when just on the outer edge of the apple orchard, when the fire from artillery and small arms was quite rapid, I saw Louis Wise stagger and fall. I at once went to him. In a few minutes I found that he could walk with my aid, and assisted him back a short distance somewhat out of the line of the heaviest fire, there I found that he was not dangerously wounded yet suffering considerable pain.

"I recall that about this time the firing in front slackened notably and soon became less and more remote, and I then felt sure that the fight had been won and quickly; it appeared to me to have been not more than 15 or 20 minutes after Wise was wounded. Thus, I was not 'in at the finish,' which has ever since been a source of regret to me. I then went with Wise to the house where our blankets had been left where he received necessary attention to his wounds." (Letter of G. B. W. Nalle, dated June 15, 1909.)

In a letter written about the same time, April 26, 1909, Wise said: "I know that when we marched down the Valley Pike after the battle, that all the old Confederate veterans lined both sides of the road and cheered us to the echo. It was the proudest day of my life."

After the war he went to Mexico and was engaged as a civil engineer in the construction of the Imperial Mexican Railroad from Vera Cruz to the City of Mexico. In 1866 he moved to Texas and spent the remainder of his life in that state. He was principal of the Bastrop Academy and later was commissioned major in the Fourth Texas Infantry and was Assistant Adjutant General of the State of Texas.

Married first Winifred Cornick Wright, daughter of Dr. James P. Wright, of Princess Anne County, Va. She died January 9, 1873, leaving an infant child, Mary Moncure Wise, who died June 22, 1873, aged 6 months.

Married secondly, in January 1876, Jeanette H. Porter, daughter of Rev. A. A. Porter, a Presbyterian minister of South Carolina. She died in January, 1877, leaving an infant son, Henry A. Wise, who died January 4, 1904.

In 1882 he married Barbara Cornick Scott, his third wife, a daughter of Captain James Scott, of Princess Anne County, Va. They had two sons: John C. Wise, born 1884, who was associated with his father in business, and Louis Scott Wise, who practiced law in Abilene.

In 1880 he surveyed in the Indian country large bodies of land for the Houston & Great Northern Railroad and from 1881 to 1893 conducted a general land and surveying agency in Abilene. From 1894 to 1903 was chief of the Topographical Department of the General Land office of the State of Texas and lived in Austin.

He returned to Abilene in 1904 and conducted a real estate and insurance business, the firm style being Louis C. Wise & Son. In addition to the real estate brokerage business he also operated a cotton plantation.

He died August 6, 1911, in Abilene and was buried there, survived by his wife and two sons.

284. James Etchison Witt—1867.

Teacher

Born September 16, 1845, in Bedford County, Va.

Parents: William Henry Witt, farmer, of Bedford Co., and Rebecca Grigsby.

Paternal Grandparents: John Witt and Mildred Howard.

He attended the Sunnyside High School, Rev. Alex. Eubank, principal, before entering V. M. I. On August 21, 1863, he signed his name in the matriculation book, but the rest of the data was not filled in. He returned on November 3, 1863, when he matriculated from Liberty, Bedford Co., Va., and was admitted to the fourth class. During that session he took part in the battle of New Market as a cadet private in Co. D.

"In the autumn of '64 we were ordered to Camp Lee, Richmond, where we remained for a time, resuming academic duties in the Alms House, Richmond, where we pursued our studies during the winter of '64-'65. Fearing a draft and probably a denial of the privilege of choosing a command, a requisition being made for recruits to the army ranging from the age of 16 to 60 years, a goodly number of the cadets resigned (2-6-1865), I among the number. I boarded a train going to Petersburg where I joined an artillery battery, receiving a furlough home for a short period to prepare to be a full-fledged soldier. Before the expiration of the furlough, General Lee surrendered. Thus ended my military as well as my educational career."

On December 12, 1866, he married Fannie Triplette, daughter of Pleasant Bond, of Bedford Co., Va. The names of their children in the order of their birth are as follows:

Rosa Lillian, wife of Ernest Claude Marshall, of Roanoke, Va.
Mary Alice, died June 26, 1895.
James Eugene, farmer, Bedford City, Va., m. Eula Adams.
Luther Henry, farmer, Bedford City, Va., m. Eva Rice Goode.
Eva Mae.
Fannie Elizabeth, wife of Edward Ellis Lloyd, of Roanoke, Va.
Bertha Irene, wife of Walter W. Wingo, of Lynchburg, Va.
Howard Bond, unmarried, who resides in Lynchburg, Va.

On August 25, 1904, he wrote:

"I trust that I have been fairly successful in working myself to the front rank in my profession—holding a professional certificate—having taught as second principal for a number of terms in the graded school in the county seat of my native county, and at other times and places as principal. Complimentary to my long experience in teaching and my knowledge and acquaintance of text books, I have on more than one occasion been chosen as a member of the county committee for the selection and adoption of text books for use in the schools of our county, and have for many years, at the instance of each succeeding superintendent of schools of our county, assisted in conducting examinations of teachers."

In 1911, Mr. Witt was principal of the Clinch Valley Institute, a three-room school in Tazewell Co., Va.

Having taught for half a century he retired and at present is making his home with his daughter, Mrs. E. C. Marshall, 815 Patterson Avenue, S. W., Roanoke, Va.

285. Hunter Wood—1865.

Lawyer

Born November 2, 1845, in Albemarle County, Va.

Parents: Dr. Alfred C. Wood, physician, and Martha Walker Rogers, both of Albemarle Co.

Grandparents: Thomas Wood and Susan Irvin.
Dr. James B. Rogers and Margaret Wood, all of Albemarle Co., Va.

He matriculated at the Virginia Military Institute on July 18, 1862, from Charlottesville, Va., and was admitted to the third class. While a second classman he was fifth cadet sergeant in Co. A, and received a penalty on May 7th suspending him from his office for a period of two weeks but the New Market Campaign took place within that period. The record is not clear as to whether he actually took part in the battle or not and his letters make no mention of the campaign. He was graduated with eleventh stand in a class of 24.

After the war he took the law course at the University of Virginia and in 1867 moved to Hopkinsville, Kentucky, where he practiced his profession during his entire lifetime. In 1870 he was elected county attorney of Christian county, and in 1874, Commonwealth's Attorney. For ten years he was master commissioner, and during President Cleveland's administration was collector of internal revenue in the second Kentucky district.

Mr. Wood made a specialty of corporation law and represented many large corporations. He was one of the founders of the Kentucky *New Era,* which paper he owned for many years.

On December 16, 1868, he married Rosalie Nelson, daughter of John R. Green. Their children are:
A. Walker Wood, owner of the New Era, Hopkinsville, Ky.
Hunter Wood, Jr., city judge of Hopkinsville.
Hugh Nelson Wood, of Louisville.
——, wife of J. Rogers Barr, of Hopkinsville.
——. wife of Edmund A. Chavanne, of New Orleans. La.

—16

Following an attack of influenza, Mr. Wood died of pneumonia on May 29, 1920, at his home in Hopkinsville, survived by his widow and five children.

286. Henry Thomas Wood—1867.

Farmer

Born September 24, 1844, on James River, near Old Locust Bottom Church, Botetourt County, Va.

Parents: Samuel Davis Wood (b. in Bath Co., Va.) and Panthea Anderson Davis (b. in Prince Edward Co., Va.).

Grandparents: Thomas Wood and Sarah Anderson Davis (both born in Bath Co.).
Henry Davis and Eliza —— (both born in Prince Edward Co.).

He matriculated on September 2, 1862, from Locust Bottom, Botetourt county, Va., and was assigned to the fifth class. The following year as a cadet private in Co. A he took part in the battle of New Market. While the corps was in Richmond he resigned and entered the Confederate Army as a Forage Master in Gen. W. L. Jackson's command. "He was captured between Clifton Forge and Covington, Va., made his escape in Covington, rejoined his command and remained with it until the close of the war."

On November 1, 1865, he married Nannie, daughter of William Anderson, of Botetourt Co. Children:
Georgiana, wife of C. H. Marks, of Cincinnati, Ohio.
Emma, wife of James Wright, of Glen Wilton, Va.
Clara, wife of Samuel Noel, of Iron Gate, Va.
Alva B., of Baldwin, Botetourt Co., Va., m. Dora Robinson.
Ashby, of Glen Wilton, m. Willie Deisher.
Henry, of Glen Wilton, m. Mamie Simpson.

After the war he engaged in farming with his father, near Baldwin, Va., where he died on February 13, 1879. Mrs. Wood later married Mr. Stuart Agee, of Baldwin.

287. Julian Edward Wood—1866.

Physician

Born May 3, 1844, in Currituck County, North Carolina.

Parents: William E. Wood (b. 1813 in North Carolina) and Sophia M. Trotman (b. 1826 in North Carolina).

Grandparents: William E. Wood and Ann ——.
Ezekiel Trotman and Emily ——.

He matriculated at V. M. I. on January 9, 1862, from Hickory Grove, Norfolk county, Va., where his father was engaged in farming, and was admitted to the fourth class. He repeated the work of the third class and at the battle of New Market he was second cadet corporal in Co. C and was a member of the color guard.*

---

*The Shield and Diamond, the magazine of the Pi Kappa Alpha Fraternity, carries in the April, 1933, issue an article, by Dr. Freeman H. Hart, of Hamp-

At the end of the session he was made first line sergeant in Co. A. Resigning his cadetship on February 1, 1865, he was commissioned a first lieutenant in the North Carolina troops and assigned to General James Martin's brigade as a drillmaster, serving in that capacity until the end of the war.

In 1867 he attended the University of Virginia where he studied medicine for one year. Having taken one term in Baltimore, he was graduated in medicine in 1869. He began the practice of his profession in his native county, Currituck, and then went to Princess Anne Co., Va.

Returning to North Carolina, in 1874, he married Mary J., daughter of James Chamberlain Scott, of Elizabeth City. They had two children:
Mae Wood, who married A. H. Worth.
William E. Wood, of Alaska.

Dr. Wood was the organizer of the Pasquotank Rifles which won first prize at the Raleigh (N. C.) exposition. "He was later colonel of the first division of the North Carolina naval reserves, serving with distinction and honor both to himself and the companies of which he was the leader. . . . Dr. Wood was one of eastern North Carolina's leading physicians, being widely known throughout the State among the medical fraternity."

He died at his home in Elizabeth City on June 2, 1911, and is buried in Hollywood cemetery there. He was survived by his wife and two children.

288. Martin Birney Wood—1867.

Lawyer—Judge of County Court

Born about 1845 or 1846 (he was 17 years 8 months old when he matriculated), at Pleasant Hill, Scott County, Va.

Parents: James O. Wood (b. December 13, 1806, in what is now Scott County, Va.; d. July 22, 1874; commissioner of revenue; and clerk of the County and Superior Courts) and Ann Elizabeth Godsey.

Grandparents: Henry Wood (b. May 18, 1773; d. February 4, 1859; county magistrate and member of the Virginia Legislature) and Sally Lawson.
John Godsey and Julia Jett.

"I was born at Pleasant Hill, the old homestead. I was sent to the 'Old Field' schools at a very early age. I learned to read and write at eight. Even at that early age books of travel and history gave me great pleasure. My father possessed few books, but these I read assiduously. I read and reread the 'Tales of Peter Parley' and 'Parley's Common School History.' I read and studied 'Mitchell's Geography' about this time. No one taught or encouraged me. I

den-Sydney College, concerning the founders of the fraternity. Julian Edward Wood was one of the founders and the article states "it is now partially established that at least two of the Founders of Pi Kappa Alpha participated in that famous battle (New Market)"—the other being James B. Sclater, who was in the battle but not in the cadet battalion. Another founder, Littleton Waller Tazewell was in the Class of 1868 at V. M. I.

read all the books of fiction I could get. In those days they had high bedsteads with curtains around them, and as father required all to work in the fields, often I would hide under the bed and read. I read all the Patent Office reports I could get.

"In 1858 I went to school at Fall Branch in Tennessee. I studied English grammar, arithmetic, algebra, Latin, and Greek. I continued there for more than a year. In the spring of 1860 I went to school at Jonesville, Va. In 1861 I was clerk in a store for A. J. Litton, at Stickleyville, in Lee County, at one hundred dollars a year.

"In March, 1862, I joined Stonewall Jackson's command in the valley of Virginia. I was wounded at the battle of Sharpsburg, September 17, 1862. It was a long time before I could walk. I then went to the Virginia Military Institute,* where I remained till it was burned by the Federal general, Hunter, in 1864.

"In August, 1865, my father was elected clerk of the County Court of Scott County. I was made his deputy. In 1869 he was relieved of the office by the military authorities. I then studied law and was licensed to practice. In May, 1870, I was appointed clerk of the county, and in November of that year I was elected by a large majority for the term of six years." (From the "History of the Wood Family in Virginia," written by Judge M. B. Wood, September 20, 1876.)

When the battle of New Market was fought he was a cadet private in Co. D but he was left with the guard detail at the Institute because the old wound in his leg prevented him from marching.

On September 26, 1872, he married (first) Kate Mildred, daughter of Joel Dinwiddie and Jane Smithson, a grand niece of the celebrated William Smithson, of England, who gave his fortune—a half-million dollars—to found the Smithsonian Institute at Washington. They had two daughters and one son. Mrs. Wood died April 11, 1890.

On February 15, 1894, Judge Wood married (second) Mrs. Mary A. Benton, daughter of Thomas Farish Williamson, of North Carolina. There was one child of this union—Mary, born September 10, 1896, died 1898.

Following his six-year term as county clerk, Mr. Wood declined to be a candidate for re-election, and in 1881 he was elected judge of the county court of Scott county, in which capacity he served about six years. He was a member of the V. M. I. Board of Visitors, from 1882 to 1884.

Judge Wood died at his home in Bristol, Va., on November 17, 1908, of rheumatism. He was survived by his wife and the following children: Mrs. C. D. Caldwell, of Bristol; Mrs. Homer Kinsey, of Roanoke, and Henry Clinton Wood, II, V. M. I., '91. Also by three brothers: Major H. C. Wood and William Morison Wood, V. M. I., '67, of Bristol (See sketch No. 290); and Captain James Harvey Wood, V. M. I., '64, of Washington, D. C.

---

*He matriculated on September 8, 1863, from Estillville, Va.

289. Philip Southall Wood—1867.

Lawyer—Commonwealth's Attorney

Born July 13, 1848, at "Selma," the residence of his grandfather in Amelia County, Va.

Parents: William Richard Wood, a lawyer who lived at "Seven Oaks," in Chesterfield Co., Va., and Lucy Henry Southall.

Grandparents: Alfred Wood, of "Seven Oaks," near Goode's Bridge, Chesterfield Co., and Tabitha Ligon.
   Dr. Philip Turner Southall, and his second wife, Elizabeth Webster, of "Selma," Amelia Co.

He received his early education at Washington Academy, Amelia, and on January 28, 1864, he was entered at the V. M. I. from Farmville by his uncle, Professor Stephen O. Southall, of the University of Virginia. The following May he took part in the battle of New Market as a cadet private in Co. A, and continued to be a cadet until January 14, 1865, when he resigned in order to enter the Confederate Army.

After the war he entered the University of North Carolina. Leaving there before graduation, he read law under Major Willis Dance, of Powhatan Co., and was admitted to the bar in 1868 a short time before he was twenty-one years old.

On February 16, 1876, he married Emma Pride, daughter of John Pride and Julia Franklin Steger (d. in Richmond, May 16, 1919), of Amelia Co. They had four children who survived both parents:
   Richard Henry Wood, of Amelia.
   Julia Pride, wife of Rev. S. O. Southall, of Dinwiddie, Va.
   Philip Southall Wood, of Amelia.
   Lucy Henry Wood, of Richmond, Va.

In 1869 or 1870 he was elected attorney for the Commonwealth of Amelia Co. This position he held at the time of his death, having been re-elected for the third time just before his death. He died July 24, 1884, in Amelia, and was buried in Hollywood cemetery, Richmond.

290. William Morison Wood—1867.

Merchant

Born December 21, 1845, near Gate City, Scott County, Va.

Parents, etc. See sketch of his brother, Judge Martin B. Wood (Sketch No. 288).

He matriculated at V. M. I. on March 3, 1864, from Glade Springs, Va., and was admitted to the fourth class. At the battle of New Market he served as a cadet private in Co. A. He did not return the following session but wrote on March 20, 1865, to find out when the corps would next assemble.

On March 1, 1893, he married Lavenia Haden, widow of S. B. McClellan and daughter of Robert Gillespie Haden and Czrena Hamilton, of Red River Parish, La.

Children: William Haden, civil engineer at Johnson City, Tenn., m. Agnes Bryant, of Rogers, Ark. She died Sept. 11, 1932.
Harold Edison, certified public accountant, Richmond, Va.; m. Ruth Perkins, of Orange, Va. They have two sons—Harold, Jr., and Billy.
Juliette Elizabeth, wife of Joseph L. Parrish, of Old Hickory, Tenn. They have one son.

Following the war Mr. Wood went into the mercantile business, and for many years owned and operated the Wood Grocery Company, at 24 Sixth Street, Bristol, Tenn.-Va. Mrs. Wood died on March 7, 1927, and since that time he has lived with his children. At present he is making his home with Mrs. Parrish at 901 Clark Street, Old Hickory, Tenn.

291. Jonathan Edwards Woodbridge—1865.

Mechanical Engineer—Naval Architect

Born January 16, 1844, at Richmond, Va.

Parents: Rev. George Woodbridge (born in 1804, at Worthington, Mass.; graduated at West Point July 1, 1822; resigned from the service June 30, 1828; studied theology at the Seminary at Alexandria, Va.; rector of Monumental Church, Richmond, for 45 years; died February 14, 1878) and Rebecca Nicolson (born June 1805, at Richmond, Va.; died 1880).

Grandparents: Jonathan Woodbridge (born 1766; lawyer and brigadier general of the militia of the State; died 1808) and —— ——.
Andrew Nicholson, of Richmond, Va., and Judith Diggs.

He matriculated at the Virginia Military Institute on January 1, 1862, from Richmond, Va. When he was a second classman he was cadet sergeant major, the highest ranking non-commissioned officer in the corps, and in that capacity served in the battle of New Market. His portrait in cadet uniform hangs in the V. M. I. Library.

"'At-ten-tion-n-n! Battalion forward! Guide Center-r-r,' shouted Shipp, and up the slope we started. From the left of the line, Sergeant-Major Woodbridge ran out and posted himself forty paces in advance of the colors, as directing guide, as if we had been upon the drill-ground. That boy would have remained there, had not Shipp ordered him back to his post; for this was no dress parade. Brave Evans, standing six feet two, shook out the colors that for days had hung limp and bedraggled about the staff, and every cadet leaped forward, dressing to the ensign and thrilling with the consciousness that this was war." (The End of an Era, p. 298.)

At the end of the session he was promoted to cadet adjutant and continued his cadetship until the evacuation of Richmond. At graduation he stood 10 in a class of 24.

"On Saturday night, April 1, 1865, the cadets were called from their barracks in Richmond to go on the lines below the city, taking the place of Lee's veterans who had been withdrawn to the south side of the river. As adjutant of the corps, I took out the last order to evacuate the lines below Richmond. After marching into the city Sunday night to our barracks, we were at once disbanded and told to take care of ourselves. This was Sunday night about 10 o'clock, April 2nd. I with several other cadets started at midnight to make our way to join Genl. Lee. I got up to the army at Appomattox late Saturday evening. On Sunday morning I learned of the probability of surrender, so went to Lynchburg, thinking a stand might be made there.

"The autumn of 1865 (September) I went to Chester, Penna., entering the shipbuilding yard of Reany Son & Archbold, afterward the Delaware River Iron Shipbuilding and Engine Works, rising to be the Superintending Engineer of the works, covering a period of 20 years.

"In 1885 I entered the U. S. Government service in civil capacity.

"For forty years I was employed as naval architect and mechanical engineer during which time I engaged in the construction of many of the largest and finest vessels of the American Merchant Marine, as well as most of the great fighting ships of the United States Navy.

"On May 23, 1876, I married Louise, only daughter of John Odenheimer Deshong, a wealthy and influential citizen of Chester, Penna. No children. I have resided in Chester since 1865.

"In April 1905 I retired from active work and have devoted my time to my private affairs and travel."

He is now living at 1401 Potter Street, Chester, Penna.

292. Pierre W. Woodlief, Jr.—1867.

Merchant—Insurance

Born about 1846 (he was 17 years of age when he matriculated).

Parents: Pierre W. Woodlief, merchant, of New Orleans, La., and —— ——.

He matriculated at V. M. I. on February 6, 1863, from New Orleans, Louisiana. While repeating the work of the fourth class (he was not at the Institute between August 6, 1863 and February 15, 1864) he served as a cadet private in Co. B at the battle of New Market. He was wounded in this battle, and quoted below is a short account of the incident written by his comrade, George T. Lee (sketch No. 138):

"At this point we got into thick fire and several of the boys were struck as we advanced. A circumstance which impressed this on my mind is this: shortly before reaching the house Woodlief was struck and fell out of ranks. He was close to me, and as he fell to the ground seemingly in much pain, I asked Captain Preston if I had not better go to him; but he ordered me to stay in ranks. I was on the right of B and close to Preston, so I had no difficulty in saying what I did to him. However, before the few words were ended, we had passed several steps beyond where Woodlief fell, as we were advancing quite rapidly."

He returned the following session and continued his cadetship until the evacuation of Richmond. On January 21, 1865 he was granted a 20-day furlough because of illness.

In 1885 Mr. Woodlief was with Neumegen, Zacharias & Co., wholesale and retail dealers in dry goods, clothing, etc., at Weatherford, Texas. In 1889 he was Manager, Western District, of the Provident Savings Life Assurance Society of New York, with his office at Fort Worth, Texas.

On September 15, 1913, William Alexander Robertson, of Ope-
lousas, La., who served in the same regiment with Woodlief during the Spanish-American War, wrote as follows:

"P. W. Woodlief in his old age enlisted in the 2nd United States Volunteer Infantry (Volunteers at large), better known as 'Hood's Immunes,' commanded and organized by Duncan B. Hood, a son of General Hood. The
regiment was mustered in during May and June, 1898, for service in the Spanish-American War under the call for volunteers at large outside of the National Guard. Woodlief was mustered in as 2nd Lieutenant of Company M,
a crack company composed of Cincinnati boys. The other companies of the
regiment were from New Orleans, the country towns of Louisiana, and Texas.
The regiment left New Orleans for Santiago, Cuba, on July 28, 1898, on the
S. S. 'Berlin', served ten months in Cuba, principally on garrison duty in the
Provinces of Santiago and Holguin, and on May 22, 1899, sailed from Gibara,
Cuba, on the U. S. transport 'Logan,' landed at New York, and was finally
mustered out at Camp Meade, Harrisburg, Penna., on June 22, 1899. It saw
no active service during the war, arriving in Cuba at about the time peace was
declared or just afterwards, and being thereafter used for garrison and police
duty during the surrender and deportation of the Spaniards and afterwards.

"Lieutenant Woodlief was first promoted to First Lieutenant and in that
capacity served as Adjutant for several months at the Port of Gibara, where
a portion of the regiment was stationed. Subsequently he was promoted to a
Captiancy, but I do not remember to which company he was assigned. He was
in very bad health after the regiment was brought to Holguin, preparatory to
embarkment for New York, during the first part of 1899, and after its muster
out at Camp Meade, Penna., he went to Covington, La., the location of Camp
Caffery where the regiment was mustered in originally, and there died, some
time during 1899, I think."

293. Zachary Taylor Woodruff—1867.

Physician

Born June 22, 1847, in Tuscaloosa, Alabama.

Parents: David Woodruff and Eliza Antoinette Bell, of Tuscaloosa, Ala.
    (Their daughter, Virginia Hortense, married Maj. Gen. Robert E. Rodes,
    V. M. I. '48).

He matriculated at V. M. I. on December 11, 1863, from Tuscaloosa, Alabama, where his father was a bookseller. Later in the
session he took part in the battle of New Market as a cadet private
in Co. A; went with the corps to Richmond a few days later; and
after the corps returned to Lexington and the session was ended he
"joined the corps of cadets at the University of Alabama and remained at that institution until Croxton's raid in April 1865. Croxton burned all of the University buildings and then took the men,
young and old, and confined them in the court house. Woodruff
was one of the unfortunate captives. He with a number of others
was surprised at a wedding; even the groom was carried off with
the rest. . . ."

After the war he studied medicine and received his M. D. degree
from Tulane University in 1868. He practiced in Alabama until
1872 and then moved to Vicksburg, Miss. In 1877 he was appointed city physician.

"He never married and died on July 17, 1878, the year of the terrible scourge of yellow fever. He came home to Tuscaloosa to be nursed by his loved ones and is buried in the cemetery here."

294. John Wesley Wyatt—1864.

Teacher

Born August 9, 1839.

Parents: Benjamin Wyatt, farmer, of Campbell County, Va., and Catherine Penn Armistead.

He received his preparatory education in Mr. Thomas J. Gordan's school in Buckingham Co., Va. He matriculated at V. M. I. on August 11, 1860, from Campbell Courthouse, Va., and was admitted to the fourth class. As a second classman he was one of the cadet first-sergeants and in the battle of New Market he was the cadet battalion quartermaster. Two other cadets (Larrick and Boggess) who were in the battle were older.

"I was struck on the leg below the right knee by a canister shot which had sufficient force to mash through my clothing and my flesh to the bone of my leg, causing a wound somewhat painful but not dangerous. Shortly after this, Cadet Captain Shriver was wounded and I succeeded to the command of the company.

"While in camp near Richmond I made the report to Col. Shipp, of the part which Company C bore in the battle, but in reporting the wounded, did not include myself for two reasons: first, I did not belong to the company; second, I was not disabled and did not leave the field. The report is made now for the first time."*

On July 14, 1864, he married Hannah Catharine, daughter of Dr. George Hall Leitch, of Madison Courthouse, Va. They had ten children: Frank Barbour and Richard Hall, of Fort Worth, Texas; Ethel and Thomas Louis, of Lynchburg, Va.; Bessie Leitch, wife of John W. Jenks, of Bedford Springs. Va.; and the following who are now dead: George Armistead, Mary Penn, Samuel Madison, Benjamin, and Mary Catharine.

"After the war he started a private school in Lynchburg. On July 17, 1872, he was elected principal and professor of mathematics and natural sciences in the Lynchburg High School, which place he held until his death on July 3, 1891."

One of the grammar schools in Lynchburg is named for Mr. Wyatt.

295. William Tilton Yarbrough—1867.

Tobacconist

Born January 1, 1846, at Richmond, Va.

Parents: William J. Yarbrough, a tobacconist, of Richmond, and Ophelia Gathright, of Frazier's Farm, Henrico Co., Va.

---

*Many cadets were slightly wounded in the battle but minor wounds like this one were frequently not included in the official reports.

He attended private schools in Richmond before matriculating at V. M. I. on August 28, 1862, from that city. While repeating the work of the fourth class, he was a cadet private in Co. A and because of ill health was left at the Institute with the guard detail when the corps went on the New Market Campaign. After the destruction of the barracks in Lexington in June 1864, he was detailed to Richmond in the department of the C. S. A. Provost Marshal (General Gardner) until the evacuation of that city.

In June, 1873, he married Mary Virginia, daughter of Dr. William S. McChesney, of Staunton, Va. They had two children:

William McChesney.

Daisie, wife of Dr. B. B. Ranson, of Maplewood, N. J.

In 1870 he became a member of the firm, W. J. Yarbrough & Sons, manufacturers of all styles of twist, fancy bright, and black tobaccos, of Richmond.

He died at his home there on January 27, 1895, survived by his wife and two children, and is buried in Hollywood cemetery, Richmond.

179. Philip Nelson Page.

(Continued from page 149)

After the type had been set and the paging completed, the following item from Concordia, Argentina, appeared in the newspapers of April 13, 1933:

"Philip Nelson Page, oldest American inhabitant of Argentina, who left the Virginia homestead of his family and came to South America in 1865 when the Confederacy lost the War Between the States, is going home.

"Eighty-six now, he has lived a cattle raiser's life in northern Argentina since he quit the United States as a lad of 18 after Lee's army, in which he served as an orderly, surrendered to Grant.

"He has become a livestock grower of means, but he has long since lost touch with other Pages who did not stray so far from the ancestoral estate, Rosewell, on the York River.

"In his declining years he thinks of his native land. So he has asked for a renewal of the sheep-skin passport issued to him by President Lincoln's secretary of state, William H. Seward—it expired 66 years ago—and this year, or next, or whenever he gets his affairs in shape, he will start back to Virginia.

"His father, Thomas Jefferson Page, owned land here in Entre Rios province. Thus Philip had a surer destination than most of his comrades when several hundred of them decided after the war that Argentina, Brazil, or Uruguay offered a brighter future to a young man than the South. He left the United States in October, 1865, on a boat that got him to Argentina in the following year. A brother, now dead, joined him.

"He wrote to the home folks, and they to him, for some time but gradually these links were broken and for years he has known of his family only by what is told in a genealogy issued in the 80's. From it he ascertains that his cousin was the late Thomas Nelson Page, author and American ambassador to Italy under Woodrow Wilson.

"Philip Nelson Page was born in Washington, D. C., in May, 1847. He is still healthy and active, although his hearing is failing."

Promotions in the Battalion of Cadets Six Weeks after the Battle of New Market

Following the graduation of the twenty-four members of the Class of 1864, Special Orders No. 125, published on June 27, 1864, announced the appointment of the following cadet officers and non-commissioned officers for the Session 1864-1865:

Atwill .... 3rd Sgt. C	Hayes, T. .... 1st Sgt. A	Ross, E. M. .... Captain A
Barney .... 2nd Sgt. C	Henry .... Sgt.-Major	Royster .... 1st Sgt. B
Barton .... 3rd Sgt. A	James, J. .... 3rd Sgt. B	Shaw .... 1st Lieut. A
Cocke, P. ...... 1st Corp. A	Jarratt .... 4th Sgt. B	Smith, F. .... 2nd Corp. B
Cocke, W. .... 1st Corp. B	Johnson, P. ... 4th Corp. D	Smith, W. .... 1st Corp. C
Crawford .... 2nd Corp. C	Kennedy ..... 3rd Corp. A	Stacker .... 1st Corp. D
Crichton .... Q. M. Sgt.	Lee, F. .... 3rd Sgt. D	Stuart, J. .... Captain B
Davenport .... 1st Lieut. &	Marks .... 2nd Corp. D	Taylor, C. .... 3rd Corp. C
Quartermaster		
Davis, A. .... 5th Sgt. A	Marshall, A. ... 1st Sgt. D	Taylor, W. .. 3rd Corp. B
Dillard .... 2nd Corp. A	Martin .... 2nd Lieut. C	Thomson, P. .. 5th Sgt. D
Dinwiddie ...... 2nd Sgt. D	McCorkle .... 3rd Corp. D	Triplett .... 4th Sgt. C
Douglass .... 2nd Lieut. B	Moorman .... 4th Corp. C	Tunstall, J. .... 4th Sgt. A
Duncan .... 2nd Lieut. A	Nelson .... 1st Lieut. D	Washington .. 4th Corp. B
Echols .... 1st Lieut. B	Patton .... 2nd Lieut. D	Wise, J. .... 5th Sgt. B
Evans .... Captain C	Penn .... 4th Sgt. D	Wise, L. C. .. 1st Lieut. C
Ezekiel .... 5th Sgt. C	Pizzini .... Captain D	Wood, J. .... 2nd Sgt. A
	Redwood ...... 4th Corp. A	Woodbridge .... 1st Lieut.
Glazebrook ...... 1st Sgt. C	Ridley, R. ...... 2nd Sgt. B	and Adjutant

The New Market Cross of Honor

In 1904, forty years after the Battle of New Market, the V. M. I. Alumni Association presented to each member of the New Market Corps a bronze "Cross of Honor." Suspended from a bar bearing the words "For Valor" is a cross on which appears, around the seal of the State of Virginia, "V. M. I. Cadet Battalion, New Market, May 15, 1864."

On each token is engraved the name of the recipient and in those cases where the cadet had passed away his "Cross of Honor" was presented to his nearest of kin.

Appendix

When the plans for erecting the New Market Battle Monument took definite form, a committee determined that the bronze tablets around the pedestal of the monument should bear the names of all cadets who were members of the corps on May 12, 1864. The names so inscribed, which include eight officers and three musicians, total two hundred ninety-five (295).

No contemporary records have been located which show the names of the cadets who were

 a. Left in Lexington to guard the Institute,
 b. In the hospital or on surgeon's certificate, or
 c. Detailed from the various companies to form the artillery
  detachment.

The loss of these records is probably due to the destruction of the Institute buildings four weeks after the battle and to the absence of the corps in the interim.

The table given below has been compiled from numerous reports made by officers and by members of the corps over a long period of time. Until the original list or some equivalent contemporary record is discovered, it is not likely that the figures in the following list can be materially improved on, although it is probable that they are not absolutely correct. The figures appear to be as follows:

	CADETS	TOTAL STRENGTH	IN THE BATTLE
Officers	...	8	6
Cadets in battle	257	257	257
Cadets left in Staunton	3[1]	3	...
Musicians	...	3	...
Total leaving Lexington	260	271	263
Cadets absent:			
Family affliction	1[2]		
Surgeon's Certificate	4[3]		
On guard at V. M. I.	19[4]	24	24
Total cadets in the corps	284		
Total strength of the New Market Corps Organization as shown on the Battle Monument		295	
Engaged in the battle			263

---

[1] The surgeon's report of July 1, 1864, says three, but gives no names; another report, made years later, names one (Sketch 253) and states there was only one.
[2] See Sketch No. 65.   [3] See Sketches Nos. 73, 118, 154, 217.
[4] The surgeon's report of July 1, 1864, says 27, but gives no names; it may

Age.

The average age of the cadets engaged in the battle was seven days less than eighteen years, or about two months less than the average age at entrance of the present day cadet. Incidentally, of every three cadets in the battle, two (the exact ratio is fractionally greater) of them were members of the Class of 1867, the fourth class.

On the day of the battle the extreme ages were:

Youngest:	Lewis S. Davis	15	years	0	months	28	days
	Robert F. Lee*	15	"	3	"	2	"
	John Roane	15	"	3	"	28	"
	Samuel B. Adams	15	"	4	"	7	"
Oldest:	James S. Larrick........	25	"	8	"	16	"
	Albert Boggess	24	"	9	"	22	"
	John W. Wyatt	24	"	8	"	6	"

Casualties

The casualties† have been noted on page 6, but it was not until several months after the battle that the returns were complete. The cases of Hartsfield and Haynes (Sketches Nos. 103 and 109) illustrate the difficulties encountered in obtaining complete records. The casualty list has not varied materially since the Civil War and may be considered complete. Contemporary reports of things seen are usually the best evidence but contemporary compilations made under the stress of battle are frequently inadequate as may be observed from the following reports, some of which have not heretofore been published:

Telegram.   Staunton, May 16, 1864.
General W. H. Richardson,
    Adjutant General.

The Corps of Cadets were with General Breckinridge in the fight with Sigel yesterday at New Market, and behaved splendidly. They lost 5 killed and 15 wounded, to wit: Cadets Cabell, Jones, Crockett, McDowell, and Stanard killed; and Cadets Garrett, Stuart, Hill, Randolph, Johnston, Dillard, Berkeley, Wise, Triplett, Marshall, Shriver, Watson, Read, Turner, and Whitson, wounded.

                                  H. M. BELL,
                         Major and Quartermaster.

(Official Records. Series I, Vol. LI, Part 2, page 938. This is the first official report of the battle. The list is inadequate and the name "Whitson" was probably intended for "Gibson.")

---

imply that this figure includes all absentees; it states that the number of cadets actually engaged in the battle was 245. For the nineteen listed above, see Sketches Nos. 20, 34, 59, 95, 106, 124, 127, 131, 134, 139, 155, 236, 237, 247, 248, 256, 285, 288, 295.

    *In the corps but not in the battle.

    †Men on the casualty list are subjects of the following sketches (an asterisk indicates, killed or mortally wounded): 9*, 18, 26, 30, 33*, 37, 43, 49, 57*, 60, 66, 67, 82, 85, 86, 89, 100, 101, 103*, 109*, 112, 115, 119, 123*, 125, 126*, 128, 147, 153, 160*, 163, 164, 169, 183, 184, 189, 190, 197, 199, 219, 220, 224, 225, 226, 229, 232*, 235, 249, 255, 258, 264, 271*, 274, 276, 282, 283, 292.

Written with a lead pencil and sent to Lexington by Cadet Ricketts.

New Market, Va.
May 16th, 1864.

Gen. F. H. Smith,
  Supt. V. M. I.

Sir, I have the honor to report that in the battle of yesterday, the cadets were all engaged, and bore a most important and conspicuous part. We have to mourn the loss of 5 cadets killed, and 37 cadets and one officer wounded. Their names are: Cabell, W. H., Crockett, C., Jones, J., McDowell, & Stanard killed; White, T., Dillard, Gibson, Randolph, Macon, Dickinson (slightly), Upshur, Darden, Woodlief, Smith, F., Smith, E., Waller, Haynes, Garnett, Goodwin (slightly), Peirce (slightly), Jefferson, Marshall, M., Atwill, Moorman, Merritt, Shriver, S., Garrow, Read, C. H., Pendleton, R., Wise, J. (slightly), Triplett, Wise, L. (slightly), Berkeley, Christian, Stuart, J. A., Wheelright, Meade (slightly), Bransford, Spiller, G., Johnson, P. (slightly) wounded. Lieut. Hill is, I regret to say, severely wounded in the head; Col. Ship was struck with a spent ball but is for duty this morning.

The wounded have received every attention possible under the circumstances; they are quartered in private houses in and around the town. Coffins will be made for the dead during the day and their bodies will be interred in the cemetery this afternoon.

So soon as arrangements can be made, the wounded will be taken to Staunton.

We need supplies of all kinds for the wounded; please have them sent as soon as possible. I will send for the articles now in Staunton. Dr. Madison is here, and he and Dr. Ross are giving their whole time to the wounded.

Cadet Ricketts can give you many particulars as to the great gallantry and splendid conduct of the cadets.

I am, Sir,
Very Respectfully
Yr. obdt. svt.
WILLIAM GILHAM,
Act. Supt.

Immediately on receipt of Colonel Madison's report on May 17, 1864, General Smith transmitted the information and lists therein contained to General Wm. H. Richardson, the Adjutant General in Richmond. He also added the following:

"Besides sending Col. Gilham and Col. Ross to aid in providing every comfort for the cadets; I ordered Surgeon Madison, Assistant Surgeon Ross, Hospital Steward Kahle, the Hospital Attendant, with four servants, an ambulance, and full medical supplies to accompany the command. On Saturday, in anticipation of a fight, I sent a wagon with supplies of coffee, sugar, tea, and other comforts. I have succeeded in getting a private conveyance and go down tomorrow, although still very unwell, and shall take clothing and other supplies to meet the necessities of the wounded."

In submitting his annual report, dated July 1, 1864, Col. Madison, the surgeon, said in speaking of the New Market Campaign:

"The battalion was immediately put under marching orders and made the entire distance of eighty-one miles in four days, and this too while exposed to incessant rains, and marching over roads heavy with mud. But notwithstanding the unaccustomed exposure, only three cadets were made sick by it, and left in Staunton. A guard of twenty-seven had been previously detailed to remain in barracks, while the remaining gallant band (two-hundred and forty-five strong) rushed into their first battle. . . . Of the cadets, five were killed on the field, one died on the following day (the 16th of May), and one on the 1st of June. Of the remaining thirty-nine, twenty-eight were slightly, and eleven severely wounded; but most fortunately, no limbs required removal, the only amputation performed being a partial one of the hand. Two days after the battle the battalion was ordered to Staunton, and thence to Richmond, accompanied by Assistant Surgeon Ross. They returned to Lexington on the 8th of June (leaving Captain Robinson and five cadets sick in Richmond)."

Lt. Col. Scott Shipp's official report was written on July 4, 1864, and makes no summary of the casualties other than to mention one or two and to say, "The cadets did their duty, as the long list of casualties will attest." (Official Records, Series 1, Vol. XXXVII, Part 1, pp. 90-91.)

The Cadet Artillery Section

The official orders of May 11, 1864, directed that a section of artillery would accompany the corps and

"First sergeants were ordered to detail eight artillerists from each of the four companies, to report for duty immediately, and man a section of artillery." (The End of an Era, p. 288.)

Difficulty in procuring horses delayed the departure of the artillery but it overtook the corps at the end of the first day's march at Midway. In the battle of New Market the cadet artillerists went into action before the cadet infantry and were engaged throughout the battle. They did not, of course, participate in the charge of the cadet battalion.

With the exception of Cadet Captain Minge, the names of the cadets in the artillery detail have not been mentioned in the official reports and so, as a matter of record, the names of twenty-four cadets who have been identified as being on this detail are listed below—their regular assignments were Company A, 7; Company B, 5; Company C, 7; and Company D, 5:

Captain C. H. Minge, in command; Lieutenants F. W. Claybrook and L. Welch, in charge of pieces;* Corporals O. A. Glazebrook and P. Henry, gunners; W. G. Bennett, J. A. Crichton, A. J. Davis,† L. S. Davis, W. C. Hayes, J. S. Larrick, F. T. Lee, J. W. McCorkle,† P. H. Morgan, A. W. Overton, D. S. Peirce,† G. A. Seaborn, W. T. Smith, C. B. Tate, W. C. Taylor, P. C. Temple, A. P. Thomson, J. S. Webb, and H. C. Whitehead.

---

*Lieutenants were assigned instead of sergeants because, as first classmen, they had studied gunnery.

†His sketch shows his regular company assignment only; in the battle of New Market he served with the cadet artillery section.

Index

Breinigsville, PA USA
02 December 2009
228532BV00004BA/61/A